2,000
GUITARS

THE ULTIMATE COLLECTION

WITH CONTRIBUTIONS FROM

Tony Bacon

Dave Burrluck

Walter Carter

Paul Day

Ben Elder

Teja Gerken

Dave Hunter

Mikael Jansson

Richard Johnston

John Morrish

Michael Simmons

Jerry Uwins

Michael Wright

2,000
GUITARS

THE ULTIMATE COLLECTION

CHARTWELL
BOOKS

2,000 GUITARS
THE ULTIMATE COLLECTION

This edition published in 2015 by

Chartwell Books

an imprint of Book Sales

a division of Quarto Publishing Group USA Inc.

142 West 36th Street, 4th Floor

New York, New York 10018

This edition published by arrangement with
Outline Press Limited, 3.1D Union Court,
20-22 Union Road, London SW4 6JP,
United Kingdom

ISBN: 978-0-7858-3354-3

Library of Congress Cataloging-in-Publication Data
available upon request.

CONCEPT Nigel Osborne

DESIGN Paul Cooper Design

EDITORS John Morrish, Thomas Jerome Seabrook,
Robert Webb

PRODUCTION Jessie French

Printed by Regent Publishing Services, China

CONTENTS

A

Acoustic 8
Aelita 8
Airline 8
AK 8
Alamo 8
Albanus 8
Alembic 8
Alvarez 8
Ampeg 10
Antoria 10

Aria 10
Arias 12
Armstrong 12
Art & Lutherie 12
Ashborn 12
Ayers 12

B

Baldwin 14
Banzer 14

Barbero 14
Barker 14
Bartolini 14
BC Rich 15
Benedetto 16
Bernabe 16
Bigsby 17
Bohmann 18
Bond 18
Bouchet 18
Bourgeois 18
Bozo 18
Breedlove 20
Brook 20
Brian Moore 20
Brune 20
Burns 20
Buscarino 22

C

Campellone 22
Carrington 22
Carvin 22
Casio 22
Chandler 22
Charvel 24
Clearsound 24
Collings 24
Contreras 26
Coral 26
Cort 26
Crafter 27
Custom Kraft 27

D

Danelectro 28
D'Angellico 30
D'Aquisto 32
Dean 34
Dean (Christopher) 34
DeArmond 34
Defil 34
Dias 34
Ditson 34

Dobro 36
Domino 36
Dwight 36
Dyer 38

E

Earthwood 38
Eastwood 38
Eggle 38
Egmond 38
Eko 40

Electar 40
Electra 40
Electro 40
Elite 40
Encore 40
Epiphone 42
ESP 48
Esteso 48
Estrada 48
Euphonon 48

F

Fender 50
   Telecaster 50
   Stratocaster 60
   Jazzmaster 74
   Jaguar 76
   Thinline 80
   Bass 82
Fenton-Weill 88
Fernandes 88
Fernández 88

Fischer 88
Fleta 88
Fodera 88
Framus 90
Franklin 90
Friederich 90
Froggy Bottom 90
Furch 90
Futurama 90
Fylde 92

G

G&L 92
Galanti 92
Gallotone 92
Garcia 92
Gemelli 92
Giannini 92
Gibson 94
   Les Paul Gold-top 94
   Les Paul Custom 98
   Les Paul Junior/
     Special 100
   Les Paul Standard 102
   Arch-top 124
   Thinline 132
   Acoustic 136
   Bass 144
Gilbert 146
Gittler 146
Godin 146
Godwin 146
Gordon-Smith 146

Goya 146
Gretsch 148
   Solid 148
   Semi-solid 154
   Acoustic 162
Grimes 164
Grimshaw 164
Guild 164
Guyatone 168

H

Hagström 168
Hallmark 168
Hamer 170
Hang Dong 170
Harmony 170
Harvey Thomas 173
Hauser 175
Hayman 174
Haynes 174
Heartfield 174

Heritage 174
Hernández 174
Hofner 176
Hohner 178
Hollenbeck 178
Hondo 178
Hopf 178
Hoyer 178
Humphrey 178
Hutl 178

I

Ibanez 180
   Electric 180
   Acoustic 186

J

Jackson 188
James Tyler 190
Jaydee 190
John Birch 190

K

Kalamazoo 190
Kapa 190
Karnak 190

Kawai 190
Kay 190
Kent 194
Klein 194
Klira 194
Knight 194
Knutson 194
Kohno 194
Koontz 194
Kramer 194
Krawczak 196
Krundaal 196
Kubicki 196
Kustom 196

L

La Flor de Cadiz 196

La Baye 198
Lacey 198
Lacôte 198
Lakewood 198

Lakland 198
Landola 198
Larrivée 198
Larson 198
Levin 198
Line 6 198
Lowden 200

M

Maccaferri 200
Magnatone 202
Majestic 202
Mancuso 202
Manson 202
Manzer 202
Marlin 202
Marshall 202

Martin 204
Mates 218
Maton 218
Maurer 218
Maya 218
McGlincy 218
Megas 218
Melobar 218
Melody 218
Messenger 218
Micro-Frets 218
Mighty Mite 220
Modulus 220
Monteleone 220
Mosrite 220
Music Man 222
Musima 224
Muzicka Naklada 224

N

National 224
Ned Callan 228
Nickerson 228
Nightingale 228
Norma 228
Norman 228
Nuñez 228

O

Oahu 228
Old Kraftsman 228
Onyx 230
Oribe 230
Orpheum 230
Ovation 230
Overwater 232

P

Páges 232
Pangborn 232
Panormo 232
Paramount 232

Parker 232
Paul Reed Smith (PRS) 234
    Electric 234
    Acoustic 258
    Bass 258
Peavey 260
Pedulla 260
Prairie State 260
Preston 260
Premier 260

R

Ramírez 262
Rebeth 264
Regal 264
Ribbecke 264
Rickenbacker 266
    Solid 266
    Semi-solid 270
    Bass 276

Rick Turner 278
Robin 278
Rockinger 278
Rodriguez 278
Roger 278
Roland 278
Romanillos 278
Royal 278
Rozas 278
Rubio 280
Ruck 280

S

Saloman 280

contents

Samick 280
Santa Cruz 280
San Jose 280

Scharpach 280
Schecter 280
Schmidt 282
SD Curlee 282
Seagull 282
Selmer 282
Serenader 282

Shergold 282
Silvertone 282
Simon & Patrick 282
Simplicio 282
Simpson 282

Slingerland 282
Smallman 284
Smith 284
Somogyi 284
Spector 284
Stahl 284
Standel 284
Starfield 284
Starforce 284
Status 284
Steinberger 286
Stella 286
Stepp 286
Stetson 286
Stewart & Bauer 286
Stonehenge 286
Stratosphere 286
Stromberg 288
Suhr 288
Sunn 288
Supro 288
Synthaxe 288

T

Tacoma 290
Takamine 290
Taylor 292
    Electric 292
    Acoustic 292
Teisco 298
Telesforo Julve 298
Teuffel 298
Thames 298
Thibout 298
Thomas 298

Thompson 298
Tobias 298
Tokai 298
Tom Anderson
    Guitarworks 300
Toms 300
Torres 300
Travis Bean 300
Triggs 300
Tune 300

V

Vaccaro 302
Valley Arts 302
Vanden 302
Van Eps 302
Vega 302
Veillette-Citron 302
Velázquez 304

Veleno 304
Vigier 304
Vivi-Tone 304
Vox 304

W

Wal 306
Walker 306
Wandre 306
Warwick 306
Washburn 306
    Electric 306
    Acoustic 308
Watkins 310
Weissenborn 310
Welson 310
Westone 310
Wikanowski 310
Wilson 310
Wolfram 310
Wornum 310
Wurlitzer 310

Y

Yamaha 312
    Solid 312
    Semi-solid 314
    Acoustic 314
Yamato 318

Z

Zeidler 318
Zemaitis 318
Zenith 318
Zon 318

1971 Acoustic Black Widow

1978 Aelita

1984 AK Admiral

1954 Albanus Seven-string

1962 Alamo Titan

1964 Airline Res-o-Glass

■ **ACOUSTIC** The Acoustic name is normally associated with instrument amplification, but 1972 saw this U.S. company move into the electric guitar market via the Black Widow six- and four-string solids. Most examples came from Aria in Japan, but a final batch was built in the United States by Mosrite, prior to Acoustic pulling the plug on the project in 1975.

■ **AELITA** This is actually a model name, rather than the brand of the maker, which was the Rostov-on-Don factory that formed part of Kavkaz musical production union in the USSR. Manufactured during the 1970s, this six-string combined unusual styling with surprisingly primitive construction and components for that period.

■ **AIRLINE** Airline was the house brand of Montgomery Ward, a major mail-order company in America. During the 1950s and 1960s it appeared on instruments sourced from guitar companies such as Kay and Valco, most being similar to these makers' own models.

■ **AK** This brand name is formed by the initials of Russian guitar maker Alexander Krasnoshchekov, located in Leningrad. The Admiral pictured was part of a project intended to produce better quality USSR electrics, but this failed and only five were built.

■ **ALAMO** Alamo was a strictly low budget American brand that targeted the entry-level end of the market during the 1950s and 1960s. Simple lap steels and amplifiers were partnered by basic, but colorful and oddly shaped solid electrics, later joined by equally cost-conscious semis.

■ **ALBANUS** Carl Albanus Johnson, maker of the Albanus guitar, was a Swedish immigrant to America who began as a violin maker. He is thought to have learned guitar-making with Elmer Stromberg and began building arch-tops in the 1950s. His instruments were built to order and he made only about a hundred in his lifetime.

■ **ALEMBIC** Founded in 1969, Alembic established a style of design and construction subsequently copied by countless makers worldwide, especially during the late 1970s and early 1980s. This comprised an innovative combination of laminated exotic woods, active electronics, and abundant brass hardware employed on through-neck, up-market instruments. Alembic is best known for basses, being the first to break new ground in this field, but guitars have also figured strongly over a forty-year production span.

■ **ALVAREZ** Alvarez is an importer of acoustic guitars based in St Louis, Missouri. In the 1970s its guitars were imported from Japan. Today it is owned by LOUD Technologies, owner of Mackie, Ampèg, Crate, and other music brands, and produces guitars in China and Korea.

■ **ALVAREZ-YAIRI** Alvarez-Yairi guitars are a range of flat-top and classical guitars handbuilt in the workshop of Kazuo Yairi in Kani, Japan, and imported to the United States by Alvarez.

Kazuo Yairi's guitars are labeled K. Yairi outside the United States. Sada Yairi was another member of the Yairi family, who built guitars in his own workshop in Nagoya, Japan.

1971 Alembic Bass Number 1
Owned by Jack Casady of Jefferson Airplane

acoustic solidbody

1981 Alvarez Artist Missouri Nine-string

1972 Alvarez-Yairi Model 5011

1989 Alvarez-Yairi Classical

1975 Sada-Yairi Model 726

1983 K.Yairi AR300

1992 Alvarez Dana E650 "Scoop Model"

■ Guitars featured here are by Acoustic, the U.S. amplification company; the Kavkaz instrument firm of the former USSR; American mail-order brand Airline; AK, another USSR company; the budget U.S. brand Alamo; American arch-top builder Albanus; the California-based Alembic company; and various Alvarez and Yairi-related brands.

1976 Alembic Bass Spider
Owned by The Who's John Entwistle

1976 Alembic Eight-string Bass
Owned by Greg Lake

1980 Alembic Tenor Bass
Owned by jazz bassist Stanley Clark

1978 Alembic Series 1

acousticalvarez

1960 Ampeg Dan Armstrong Lucite

1970 Dan Armstrong Bass

1966 Ampeg AEB-1 Bass

1966 Ampeg AUB-1 Fretless Bass

1967 Ampeg ASB-1 Bass

1969 Ampeg Dan Armstrong Lucite

■ **AMPEG** Although this U.S. brand is best known for bass amplification, the company has made a few forays into the instrument business. The first occurred during the early 1960s, via an agreement with British maker Burns to re-badge some of its existing instruments. This tie-up proved shortlived and was succeeded by a series of distinctively styled U.S.-made basses that stayed around until the end of the decade. The company was keen to try again, this time enlisting the services of U.S. designer Dan Armstrong, who came up with guitar and bass models made from clear Perspex, a material that provided their "See Through" nickname. These innovative instruments attracted more attention, including from Rolling Stone Keith Richards, but production ceased prematurely in 1972.

The next year saw the launch of the Japanese-manufactured Stud solids and Signet acoustic line. Reissues of the Dan Armstrong "See Throughs" have appeared in recent years, sourced from the Far East, along with less-expensive, all-wood equivalents.

■ **ANTORIA** Dating back to the 1950s, the Antoria brand was employed by UK importers J.T. Coppock, located in Leeds, England. The earliest Antoria electrics were made in Japan by Guyatone, and Hank Marvin of British instrumental group The Shadows used just such a six-string in his early days.

By the 1970s the range had become copy-orientated and this continued throughout the following decade. Many Antorias were virtually identical to their Ibanez equivalents, which isn't really surprising as they emanated from the same Japanese sources.

Production switched to the Korean Samick factory during the 1980s, but most models maintained the copy approach. The brand subsequently disappeared when it was decided to market models under Samick's own name, but the Antoria name has recently been revived by a new British distributor.

■ **ARIA** Aria, based in Nagoya, Japan, was founded in 1956 by Shiro Arai. The company's first instruments were classical guitars, but in the early 1960s it introduced a range of electric guitars. Back then these Guyatone-made models were pretty primitive, but build quality improved when Aria manufacture switched to the Matsumoku company, a major maker subsequently responsible for innumerable instruments under a worldwide variety of brand names.

In keeping with most Japanese companies, Aria design shifted from originality to impersonation during the late 1960s, and the 1970s catalog concentrated on copies carrying Aria, Aria Diamond, or eventually Aria Pro II logos. In contrast, the latter part of the decade saw a return to more individuality and further improvements in quality that would do much to change the playing public's perception of Japanese-made instruments as merely cheap imitations. The desire to be different continued through the 1980s, although the company was never slow to absorb influences or follow fashion.

Economics prompted a change to Korean production and Aria continued to keep abreast of changing market trends during the next decade, with rock-orientated guitars followed by instruments that were more retro-flavored. Cost-effective Chinese manufacture was added in the new millennium, along with Japanese-made reissues of certain original milestone Aria models. These upmarket instruments contrast with the range of ultra-affordable electrics offered under the recently revived Aria Diamond brand.

aria solids

1985 Aria Pro II ZZ series

1968 Aria ADSG 12T

1977 Aria Pro II PE-160

1979 Aria Pro II PE-1000

1983 Aria Thor-Sound TS-500

1982 Aria Urchin Deluxe

1999 Aria M-650T

■ The New York-based Ampeg firm made some interesting "See Through" plastic guitars but is better known for its basses, including the first production fretless bass. Shown here too are guitars by Far East brand Antoria, and by Aria, one of the leading Japanese makers, including early solidbody Pro II models.

1989 Antoria Rockstar EG1935

aria semis

1989 Aria Artist TA60

solidbodyaria

1969 Aria HF A588

1993 Aria SPE Sandpiper

1998 Aria NXG

1998 Aria AW-130

1999 Aria AMS-04

1993 Aria SP99 Sandpiper

■ **ARIAS** Vicente Arias began his career in Ciudad Real, Spain, some 125 miles south of Madrid, before moving to the capital early in the twentieth century. He became the most important guitar maker to come out of Madrid, with the exception of the Ramírez dynasty. He is the only near-contemporary of Antonio de Torres whose guitars represent any sort of challenge to the master. His guitars are lighter and smaller all around than those of Torres, and use a range of different body shapes. Internally, the guitars use four, six, seven, and even eleven struts on the soundboard.

Arias is a mysterious figure; there is no birth certificate or photograph, all such documentation supposedly having been destroyed in a fire in Ciudad Real. He died in Madrid in 1912, leaving no known heirs, successors, or apprentices.

■ **ARMSTRONG** Starting up in the early 1970s, British luthier Rob Armstrong is best known for acoustic guitars, favored by famous players such as Gordon Giltrap and Bert Jansch. However, this Coventry-based builder has also produced a variety of electrics, including the eye-catching Kellogg's Corn Flakes model built for Fairport Convention's Simon Nicol.

■ **ART & LUTHERIE** Part of Robert Godin's LaSiDo company in Quebec, Canada, Art & Lutherie was originally conceived as a good-value, entry-level line that would feature all-Canadian tonewoods (and optional electronics). Upon their debut in 1994, Art & Lutherie guitars shared LaSiDo design features, including laminated wild cherry bodies, bolt-on necks, and lacquer finishes. Initial Art & Lutheries were dreadnoughts with maple necks, walnut fingerboards and bridges (rosewood was used later), and either natural solid cedar or spruce tops, or colored finishes over laminated cherry tops. Cutaways appeared in the late 1990s. In around 1996 the Ami model debuted, a steel- or nylon-stringed parlor guitar with a full-scale fingerboard, now popular as both a travel and blues guitar.

■ **ASHBORN** Before the Civil War, one of the largest guitar factories in America was run by James Ashborn in Wolcottville, Connecticut. Born in England, Ashborn began to make guitars in the late 1840s, selling to the big New York music publishers Firth, Pond, and Company (later J. Firth Sons) and William Hall and Son, whose labels Ashborn's instruments usually carry. Featuring a robust tone for their size, most were small gut-string parlor guitars with fan-braced spruce tops in a variety of grades, with different woods (often laminated over spruce) and decoration. Many had special patented wooden spindle peg tuners. In 1864 Ashborn was elected state senator and ended his guitar-making.

■ **AYERS** Ayers had its international launch in 2002, representing an unusual tie-up involving three countries. Designer and production consultant (and coiner of the Oz-evocative name) is established Australian luthier Gerard Gilet; the company, Ayers Music, operates out of Taiwan, but production is sourced from Vietnam. The brand-dedicated Ho Chi Minh City factory achieves consistently high quality starting from near-budget prices. An important marketing plus is that the line-up—including dreadnought, auditorium, arch-top, classical, and slot-head grand concert designs—features all-solid timbers throughout.

1855 Ashborn

2000 Aria ASP-930

2002 Ayers ACSM-E

2002 Ayers DS

1870 Arias

1906 Arias

■ Further guitars here by Aria illustrate the modern brand's diversity and range. Also on these pages are instruments by Spanish classical maker Vicente Arias; UK builder Rob Armstrong; the Canadian brand Art & Lutherie; the old American maker Ashborn; and Australia-based Ayers.

2002 Art & Lutherie AA85

1980 Aria Pro II SB1000 Bass

1978 Armstrong Corn Flakes
Owned by Simon Nicol of Fairport Convention

1965 Baldwin Double Six

1965 Baldwin Baby Bison

1964 Bartolini

1985 Barker Seven-string Arch-top

1986 Barker Arch-top

1954 Barbero

1991 Banzer

■ **BALDWIN** In 1965 this Ohio-based specialist maker of pianos and organs bought the Burns company of England for $250,000. After Baldwin took control there were "transition" examples; a few guitars even carried both Burns and Baldwin brands. In 1966 the existing Nu-Sonic, GB65, and CB66 models were dropped and various changes made. Most significant was a new "flattened-scroll" headstock, replacing the original Burns type on most models. The Baby Bison and Vibraslim were redesigned with a new, short Rezo-tube vibrato. In 1967 Baldwin introduced the Gibson 335-like 700 series, with Italian-made bodies. In 1970 Baldwin discontinued Burns production, concentrating its efforts on Gretsch, which it had acquired in 1967.

■ **BANZER** Don Banzer was a guitar maker in Ashtabula, Ohio, who died in 1995. He built some 220 guitars in total. He was mainly known for his classical guitars, one of which was played by Jorge Morel.

■ **BARBERO** Marcelo Barbero (1904–1956) began his career in Madrid, Spain, in 1923 in the workshop of José Ramírez I, who died that year. He worked for José Ramírez II until 1930 when he began repairing and building instruments from his own premises. In 1936 he was called up to fight in the Spanish Civil War, before returning to Ramírez, while also moonlighting as a repairer. In 1944, he was hired by the widow of Santos Hernández to complete numerous guitars left unfinished when Santos died. During this time Barbero also made instruments in his own name, and when he started his own workshop some years later his guitars initially showed a marked influence from Santos Hernández. In time he moved away from the very light and bright-sounding flamenco pattern to a fuller sound intended for guitarists who wished to play solo rather than merely accompanying singers and dancers. He also made classical guitars, in rosewood rather than the cypress used for flamenco instruments.

■ **BARKER** William Barker of Bartonville, near Peoria, Illinois, built this seven-string arch-top in 1985. The seventh string is tuned to A below low E.

■ **BARTOLINI** The early 1960s guitar boom overtook many Italian accordion makers, who survived by catering for the new craze. Bartolini was one of numerous brand-names to appear on the flamboyant guitars that resulted. Styling varied, but multiple pushbutton selectors and an abundance of sparkle or pearloid plastic were shared by most, echoing the accordion ancestry.

■ **BC RICH** BC Rich founder Bernardo Chavez Rico (1941–1999) began as a flamenco and classical guitarist making acoustic guitars in his father's Los Angeles shop in the early 1960s. In 1969 he built his first electrics—Gibson copies—before moving on to through-neck, pointy-shaped solidbodies with onboard pre-amps and lots of switches. His guitars became popular among heavy guitarists like Tony Iommi, Rick Derringer, Nikki Sixx, Blackie Lawless, Kerry King, and Lita Ford.

Now owned by Hanser Music Group, BC Rich continues to produce guitars in radical shapes in the United States, China, and Korea. Its "Handcrafted Shop" recently recreated BC Rich's first four original guitar designs—the Seagull, Mockingbird, Bich, and Eagle—to mark the fortieth anniversary of the company's first electrics. The shop also handbuilds guitars to customers' own designs.

1979 BC Rich
Mockingbird Standard

1981 BC Rich
Eagle

1983 BC Bich NJ

On these pages, the guitars
are by the Burns-related
Baldwin brand; U.S. classical
maker Don Banzer; the Spanish
classical builder Marcelo
Barbero; the Italian brand
Bartolini; obscure U.S. maker
Barker; and B.C. Rich, the U.S.
maker noted for unusual body
shapes.

1985 BC Rich
Bitch Bass

1996 BC Rich Ignitor

1969 BC Rich B45
Dreadnought

1996 BC Rich EMI Model

solidbody bc rich

1992 Benedetto Pine Guitar

2003 Benedetto La Venezia

arch-tops

2003 Benedetto Anima e Corpo Seven-string

1996 Benedetto La Cremona Azzura

1992 Bernabe

■ **BENEDETTO** Robert Benedetto (born 1946) began making guitars in 1968 in New Jersey. He is known for pioneering a modern school of arch-top design that simplified the ornate, traditional style of D'Angelico and D'Aquisto. In 1999, he was hired by the Fender company to consult on its Guild line of arch-tops. When the agreement with Fender ended, in 2006, he opened Benedetto Guitars in Savannah, Georgia. A team of fourteen builders currently produces forty guitars a month. Benedetto himself continues to build one-off custom-order guitars. He was one of twenty-one luthiers commissioned by collector Scott Chinery to build a blue arch-top.

■ **BERNABE** Paulino Bernabe (1932–2007) became interested in guitar building while learning classical guitar. In 1954 he became an apprentice in the Ramírez workshop, in Madrid, Spain, rising to head artisan. In 1969 he began building guitars on his own account. While rooted in the Madrid school, he began to innovate, employing more complex strutting systems and using unusual woods, including flame maple, pear, and camphorwood. In 1977 Bernabe's son, also Paulino (born 1960), joined him as his apprentice. He continues to build fine guitars in a workshop in the north of Madrid.

■ **BIGSBY** Although perhaps better known for the ever-popular, add-on vibrato tailpiece that bears his name, Californian Paul Bigsby was one of the pioneers of the modern electric guitar. The innovative instrument he built in 1948 for country star Merle Travis predated Leo Fender's earliest efforts by a year, arguably influencing the latter and including many features that are now taken for granted.

Bigsby subsequently combined his skills as an engineer, inventor, woodworker, and guitarist to create custom-built instruments for many of the era's leading players. His guitars came in varying shapes and sizes, often with distinctive scrolled body styling, while pickups and much of the hardware were Bigsby's own. Custom needs were also catered for, so some Bigsbys boasted more than one neck, while fancy features were common.

The 1958 catalog included the Standard guitar, offered with one or two pickups and optional vibrato. This set specification implied a certain amount of mass-manufacture was involved, but instead Bigsby always worked on an individual order basis and apart from some templates few concessions were made to speed up the construction process. Bigsby never considered expanding his business or increasing production quantities, and the consequent delays could prove frustrating for some customers. However, most clients obviously thought the wait was worthwhile, because big names such as Grady Martin, Hank Garland, and Billy Byrd could be seen proudly putting their Bigsby guitars to good use during the 1950s.

Single- and multi-neck lap steels actually formed a bigger part of Bigsby's business and he produced the first example featuring pedals, starting a whole new instrument genre and playing style in the process.

It's estimated that, in addition to custom-order instruments, only around twenty-five standard electric six-strings were built, plus about three times as many steels. In the late 1950s, Bigsby focused more on manufacturing his increasingly successful vibrato unit. However, he still couldn't keep pace with its popularity and, overwhelmed with orders, decided that enough was enough, selling his company in 1966 to Ted McCarty, then president of Gibson. The latter resigned this post and took over Bigsby until Gretsch subsequently acquired it in 1999.

benedetto**solidbody**

1948 Bigsby T-8
Three-neck Steel

1948 Bigsby
"Merle Travis"

1948 Bigsby
Number II

■ Robert Benedetto is an American maker of high-end arch-top guitars. Paulino Bernabe made classical guitars in Spain, and his son continues the fine tradition. Paul Bigsby, based in California, was among the first to make a solidbody electric guitar. The double-cutaway Bigsby here has the original owner's name inlaid in the top pickguard, but we have blocked it out for privacy.

1951 Bigsby "Jack Parsons"

1952 Bigsby "Grady Martin" Double-neck

1955 Bigsby Double Cutaway

1954 Bigsby Whitaker

solidbodybigsby

1984 Bond Electraglide

1896 Bohmann Grand Concert

1910 Bohmann Harp Guitar

■ **BOHMANN** Joseph Bohmann was born in Neumarkt, Bohemia (now the Czech Republic), in 1848. He immigrated to Chicago and established American Musical Industry in 1878, becoming an early supplier to Sears. His labels styled him the "World's Greatest Instrument Maker," a boast backed up by wins in eight international competitions between 1888 and 1904. He offered twelve models of guitar, which were noted for playability and tone, as well as strength. Harp guitars were a specialty; he produced many designs, some featuring sympathetic strings mounted inside the body and tuned from the outside.

■ **BOND** Bond was established in Inverness, Scotland, by guitar maker Andrew Bond. Its Electraglide guitar was launched in 1984. Where a normal guitar fingerboard has a row of frets, the Electraglide had a one-piece aluminum "pitchboard," with a step and gentle incline between each "fret" position. Composite plastic materials were used for most of the instrument, and touch-switches, color-coded LEDs, and digital read-outs replaced control knobs. The instrument looked futuristic, but in many ways it merely underlined the strengths of traditional guitar design. Bond collapsed during 1985 having made around 1,400 guitars. Players had generally been unwilling to adapt to the guitar's idiosyncrasies, although enthusiasts included Mick Jones, The Edge, and Dave Stewart.

■ **BOUCHET** Robert Bouchet (1898–1986) was a painter, art teacher, and amateur guitarist who began making guitars in Paris, France, at age forty-eight. He had acquired an instrument from Julian Gomez Ramírez, but lost it, and decided to make a replacement, having observed Gomez Ramírez in his workshop. His first guitars imitated Torres, but later he developed his own plantilla (body shape) and strutting system. He only built some 150 guitars in his lifetime. Owners included Ida Presti and Alexandre Lagoya. Julian Bream had three built for him.

■ **BOURGEOIS** Dana Bourgeois (born 1953) is a maker of acoustic guitars prized by players including Ry Cooder, James Taylor, and Ricky Skaggs. He began working full-time as a luthier in 1978. In 1995, after working with Martin, Paul Reed Smith, and Gibson, he formed Bourgeois Guitars. He had built more than 1,000 instruments when, in 2000, he established a new company, Pantheon Guitars, in Lewiston, Maine. With his team of eight co-workers he currently builds about thirty Bourgeois guitars a month. His instruments are especially popular with country and bluegrass players, particularly his dreadnoughts and jumbo orchestra models.

■ **BOZO** Bozo Podunavac (born 1928) learned to build fretted instruments in the late 1940s in what was then Yugoslavia. In 1959 he moved to the United States and found a job in Chicago repairing instruments. In 1964 he started making guitars, at first based on the dreadnought body shape, under the name Bozo. In 1968 he developed an unusual variation, the "Bell Western," with a large lower bout and a smaller, squarer upper bout. Podunavac offered the guitar in six- and twelve-string versions, usually heavily ornamented. He also produced arch-tops and requinto guitars, which combined a three-quarter size body with a full-scale neck. Podunavac stopped building guitars in the early 1980s due to illness, but began again in the mid 1990s. In 1996 he was one of twenty-one luthiers commissioned to build a blue arch-top for collector Scott Chinery. He still builds a small number of instruments, mainly twelve-strings, at his home in East Englewood, Florida.

1954 Bouchet

1961 Bouchet
Classical

2002 Bourgeois
Vintage OM

1998 Bourgeois
Martin Simpson
Model

1998 Bourgeois OMC

1996 Bozo Chicagoan

■ Featured here are guitars by early
U.S. maker Bohmann; shortlived high-
tech UK builder Bond; French
classical maker Bouchet; U.S.
acoustic builder Dana Bourgeois; and
U.S. maker Bozo Podunavac.

1996 Bozo Requinto

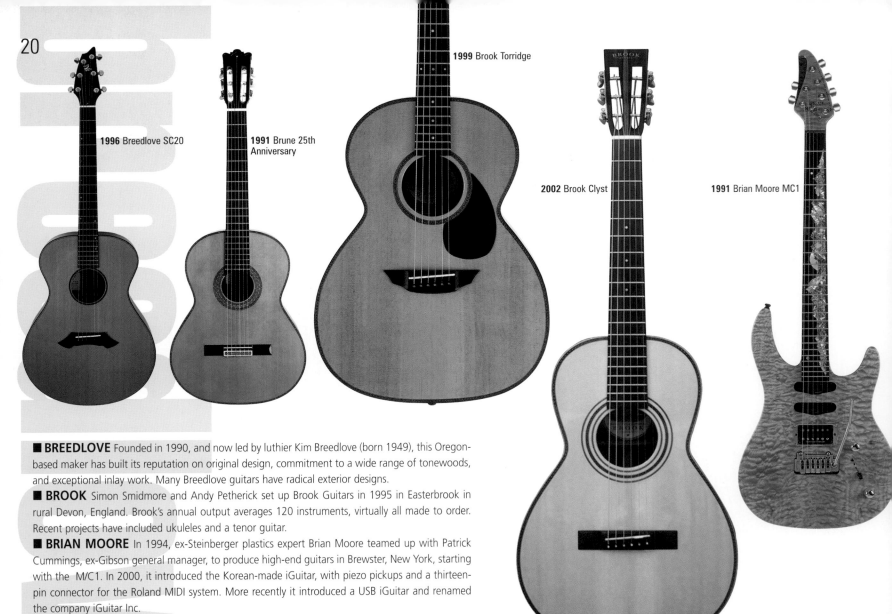

1996 Breedlove SC20

1991 Brune 25th Anniversary

1999 Brook Torridge

2002 Brook Clyst

1991 Brian Moore MC1

■ **BREEDLOVE** Founded in 1990, and now led by luthier Kim Breedlove (born 1949), this Oregon-based maker has built its reputation on original design, commitment to a wide range of tonewoods, and exceptional inlay work. Many Breedlove guitars have radical exterior designs.

■ **BROOK** Simon Smidmore and Andy Petherick set up Brook Guitars in 1995 in Easterbrook in rural Devon, England. Brook's annual output averages 120 instruments, virtually all made to order. Recent projects have included ukuleles and a tenor guitar.

■ **BRIAN MOORE** In 1994, ex-Steinberger plastics expert Brian Moore teamed up with Patrick Cummings, ex-Gibson general manager, to produce high-end guitars in Brewster, New York, starting with the M/C1. In 2000, it introduced the Korean-made iGuitar, with piezo pickups and a thirteen-pin connector for the Roland MIDI system. More recently it introduced a USB iGuitar and renamed the company iGuitar Inc.

■ **BRUNE** A former professional flamenco player, Richard Brune (born 1949) of Evanston, Illinois, began making guitars in 1966, specializing in flamenco and classical instruments. He is also a collector, restorer, instrument dealer, and prolific writer and lecturer on the guitar. In 1991 he created the Twenty-Fifth Anniversary edition of his own Artist model; only twenty-five were made.

■ **BURNS** James Ormston Burns (1925-1998) set up his own company in 1960. The earliest Burns electrics proved popular with many semi-pro players of the day, the Vibra Artist in particular incorporating advanced features such as a heelless neck and twenty-four-fret fingerboard.

Next came the Black Bison, an aptly titled combination of carved wood, complex circuitry, and over-engineering. It proved costly and time-consuming to construct, soon prompting a suitably rationalized replacement that was the first Burns with a bolt-on neck. This was subsequently joined by many simpler and less expensive guitars that became the mainstay for British beat groups unable to afford imported American alternatives.

Such economic considerations didn't concern The Shadows, but the UK's leading instrumental outfit still switched from Fender to Burns in 1964, as only the latter could offer the replacement required for their trademark Stratocasters. This was the Marvin; designed in conjunction with the group's lead guitarist Hank Marvin, it was destined to become the most desirable of all Burns six-strings.

However, the following year the Baldwin company of the United States took control of Burns. By now the range boasted various solids and semis in six-, four-, or twelve-string form and most continued to be manufactured until Baldwin pulled the plug on production in 1970.

After dabbling with occasional Ormston and Hayman designs, Jim Burns reemerged in 1973 with a range marketed under the Burns UK brand. Odd shapes were the order of the day, with the Concorde-inspired, angular Flyte being the best known, but players didn't find any example very appealing and the company collapsed in 1977.

After a two-year break, Burns was back under the Jim Burns banner. Although original designs such as the Scorpion took precedence over plundering the past, new versions of the Marvin and Bison eventually appeared, but erratic quality and bad management brought the curtain down in 1984.

The latest chapter in the Burns saga started in 1992, when guitar builder Barry Gibson acquired the Burns name and established the Burns London company, producing authentic re-creations and

1961 Burns Bison

1964 Burns Marvin

1977 Burns UK Flyte

1979 Burns Nu-Sonic

1979 Burns Scorpion

1960 Burns Vibra Artist

1999 Burns Club Marquee

1962 Burns Bison Bass

■ Over these pages you'll find guitars by Breedlove, a U.S. maker often using unusual designs; Brook, a British acoustic maker; Brian Moore, the U.S. maker of iGuitar instruments; Richard Brune, Illinois-based builder of classical guitars; and Burns, the innovative and sometimes stylish UK maker.

1999 Burns Drifter

solidbodyburns

1995 Campellone Special

1996 Buscarino Virtuoso

1996 Carrington

1996 Carrington

updated versions of original classics. Jim Burns subsequently came on board, acting as consultant until his death in 1998 at age seventy-three. The company is still going strong after sixteen years, with the earlier hand built UK-made models eventually giving way to high quality limited editions and cheaper equivalents all sourced from the Far East.

■ **BUSCARINO** John Buscarino (born 1950) of Franklin, North Carolina, was apprenticed to both classical maker Augustine LoPrinzi and arch-top builder Robert Benedetto. A maker for more than twenty years, he handbuilds a range of models that include arch-tops, a single-cutaway classical, and a solidbody. In 1996 he was one of twenty-one luthiers commissioned by collector Scott Chinery to build a blue arch-top.

■ **CAMPELLONE** Mark Campellone (born 1954) of Providence, Rhode Island, is representative of the new breed of American arch-top makers that has taken the heritage of D'Angelico and Stromberg into the twenty-first century. After having studied guitar and worked as a pro musician and guitar repairman, Campellone built his first arch-top guitar in 1988. Campellone's guitars are inspired by the huge eighteen-inch orchestra models of the 1930s and 1940s. All are made from the finest wood and have tailpieces of brass and ebony. In 1996 he was one of twenty-one arch-top makers commissioned by Scott Chinery to build a blue guitar.

■ **CARRINGTON** Chris Carrington (born 1952) of Rockwall, Texas, is a builder of classical and flamenco guitars. A classical guitarist by training, he specializes in guitars designed to accommodate amplification devices (pickups, mics, wireless transmitters, MIDI controllers, and so on) without compromising their acoustic qualities. Carrington owners include Benjamin Verdery and Al DiMeola.

■ **CARVIN** Carvin operates almost exclusively through mail-order sales. Founded in 1946 as Kiesel Electronics, it adopted its current name three years later. Originally it sold pickups and accessories before branching out to amplifiers, guitars, basses, and other gear. In 1954, its first mail-order catalog was introduced. The same year it introduced its first original, the SGB solidbody with a distinctive body point. Its designs came into their own in the 1980s, with the introduction of radical shapes and exotic woods. Carvin guitars are built to order, and a huge list of options means that each is effectively custom-made, although it does now offer a small number of instruments from stock. In 1988, it switched to through-neck designs, which continue to dominate. It builds more than 1,000 guitars and basses every year at its factory in San Diego, California.

■ **CASIO** This Japanese company took a tentative step into guitar synthesizers in 1987. The DG-20 (for Digital Guitar) had its own synthesizer, amp, and speaker built-in. The MG-500 and MG-510 MIDI six-strings were more conventional instruments for the serious player. Roland had paved the way in guitar synthesis, but in 1988 came Casio's superior PG-380, offering a more player-friendly, full-fledged alternative. This Fender-influenced, Floyd Rose-equipped solidbody had all the technical bits arranged in a very accessible manner. The less expensive PG-300 debuted in 1990, sporting a Strat-style pickup layout and vibrato unit. Casio's final guitar synth came three years later with the simplified and shortlived G-393.

■ **CHANDLER** Originally a supplier of guitar components, based in California, Chandler expanded operations in 1991 to include complete instruments. These included custom-built examples and a selection of standard production models initially offered in kit form. Additions to the fully-assembled line in the following year included the Rickenbacker-like 555 and the ultra-offset Austin Special. This single-cutaway solidbody equipped with lipstick pickup was based on a guitar originally made for Keith Richards by U.S. luthier Ted Newman-Jones. Current models include the 555, the Futurama, and the Metro Baritone, along with a twelve-string bass and several lap steels.

1959 Carvin SGB-3

1985 Carvin V220T

1997 Carvin Alan Holdsworth

1987 Casio MG500
Midi Guitar

1992 Chandler Austin Special

1987 Casio DG20
Digital Guitar

DG-20 CASIO DIGITAL GUITAR

■ Guitars featured here are by five
different American makers:
Buscarino (based in North
Carolina); Campellone (Rhode
Island); Carrington (Texas); Carvin
(California); and Chandler
(California). Also here are three
examples of Japanese maker
Casio's attempts during the 1980s
to make a successful liaison
between guitar and synthesizer.

1988 Casio PG-380
Guitar Synthesizer

1965 Carvin 2-MS Double-neck

1986 Charvel
Model 4

1986 Charvel
Model 5

1989 Charvel
Contemporary
Spectrum

1989 Charvel
Fusion Custom

1995 Charvel
San Dimas

1986 Charvel
Model 1 Bass

1991 Charvel Surfcaster

1978 Clearsound Strat

■ **CHARVEL** In 1974 Wayne Charvel set up a guitar repair business in Azusa, California, and began supplying hardware replacement parts, a line that expanded to include bodies, necks, pickups and, ultimately, complete guitar kits. In 1978, after moving to nearby San Dimas, Charvel sold his company to employee Grover Jackson.

In 1979, Jackson introduced the first Charvel-brand guitars. One of the early efforts was seen under the fast-moving fingers of a rising guitar star, Edward Van Halen. Then, at the start of the 1980s, Jackson launched a new line under his own name. The Charvel brand was reserved for bolt-on-neck guitars with essentially Fender-style bodies and necks—as well as Gibson- or Vox-inspired alternatives and an original four-point "star" shape. During the 1980s, Charvel became a leading builder of "superstrats," some featuring through-neck construction, slimmer-horned bodies, and pointy headstocks as well as humbucker pickups and vibratos. It began to manufacture in Japan and Korea, only restarting U.S. production in 1994.

The acquisition of Jackson/Charvel by the Japanese electronic musical instrument company Akai in 1997 temporarily marked the end of Charvel-brand instruments, but in 2001 the brand was bought by Fender, which restarted Charvel production in the United States. It now produces a range of Strat- and Tele-based models, called San Dimas and So-Cal, closely modeled on the instruments of Charvel's heyday.

■ **CLEARSOUND** The concept of constructing guitars from unconventional materials has been explored by various makers over the past fifty years. Clear plastic proves a popular choice, being employed on both upmarket instruments and less-expensive alternatives. A low-cost example is this late 1970s Stratocaster-style solid, bearing the very appropriate Clearsound brand banner.

■ **COLLINGS** Collings Guitars of Austin, Texas, is probably the most progressive of America's mid-size guitar companies when it comes to construction methods, yet the instruments it builds are highly traditional in appearance and always pay respectful homage to the originals they emulate. Whether it's a D2H, patterned after a 1930s Martin D-28, or a sixteen-inch arch-top design derived from a 1920s Gibson L-5, each model is distinctly a Collings from headstock to tailblock.

Recently the company has introduced a line of solidbody and semi-acoustic electrics. Rather than building copies, Collings uses classic instruments and designs from America's "Golden Era" of guitar-making as stylistic templates. Founder Bill Collings, who began building instruments in the 1970s, now employs some fifty people in a factory of 22,000 square feet, and uses computer-controlled milling machines to cut parts to high standards of accuracy and consistency.

Collings customers include Lyle Lovett, Keith Richards, Pete Townshend, Emmylou Harris, Andy Summers, David Crosby, Chris Hillman, Joni Mitchell, Don Felder, John Sebastian, Lou Reed, John Fogerty, Brian May, Joan Baez, John Prine, and many more. In 1996 Collings was one of twenty-one guitar makers commissioned to build a blue arch-top for collector Scott Chinery.

1996 Collings Custom

1994 Collings C10

1981 Collings D 2H

1990 Collings OM2-H

1990 Collings D3

■ Charvel is a U.S. brand, best known for its links with Eddie Van Halen. Later the brand was sold and is now owned by Fender, who continue to produce Charvel-brand guitars. Also shown here is an unusual plastic Japanese-made Clearsound guitar, and a good selection of instruments made by the respected high-end flat-top maker Collings, based in Texas.

1994 Collings 000-2H

1998 Collings OM2-H

1999 Collings CJSB Lyle Lovett

2000 Collings C10C

2001 Collings Baby

2001 Collings ASB (feature guitar)

acousticcollings

1967 Coral Sitar

■ **CONTRERAS** Manuel Contreras (1928–1994) joined the Ramírez workshop in Madrid, Spain, in 1959, leaving in 1962 to start building instruments under his own name. They were large, traditionally fan-strutted classical models in the Ramírez mould, which he continued to build throughout his career. But Contreras was also an experimenter. A conversation with a customer, Celedonio Romero, led him to build, in 1974, the first of his "double-top" guitars. The second top, which resonates in sympathy with the first, is placed just in front of the instrument's back. Then in 1983 a discussion with the Uruguayan player Abel Carlevaro led to a more visually arresting experiment. The Carlevaro model had a one-sided waist, a slot around the edge of the top instead of a soundhole, and double sides and back. Contreras's son Pablo (Manuel Contreras II), born in 1957, continues to balance tradition and innovation.

■ **CORAL** In 1966 the entertainment conglomerate MCA bought Danelectro. A year later it introduced a new line of Danelectro-made guitars, branded Coral. Coral produced solid and hollowbodied guitars, but its most famous product was the Coral Sitar. Introduced in 1967, it was co-designed by session-man Vinnie Bell, who had spotted a demand in New York studios for sitar sounds. The secret was the flat plastic "bridge" that gave a buzzy sound—and made intonation almost impossible. There was also a bank of thirteen extra "drone" strings tuned in half-steps. Coral died along with Danelectro in 1969.

■ **CORT** Based in Korea, Cort is one of the largest guitar manufacturers in the world, producing instruments for many other companies. It was founded in 1973 when American instrument wholesaler Jack Westheimer joined forces with Yung H. Park. Westheimer had previously imported guitars from Japan under the Teisco, Kingston, Cortez, and Emperador brands. The new company produced its first guitars using the Cort name (shortened from Cortez) in 1977. In acoustic guitars it made a breakthrough in 1994 with the Earth series, in OM, dreadnought, and classical styles, later expanded into twelve-string and parlor models. A second line of dreadnoughts, the NTL series, appeared in 1999. It began building electrics under the Cort name from 1984, starting with beginner-grade copies and progressing to its own designs. The Cort line today ranges from acoustics to solid, semi-hollow, and hollowbody electric guitars, as well as acoustic and electric basses.

■ **CRAFTER** The company that became Crafter was begun by HyunKwon Park in 1972 in the basement of his home in Seoul, Korea. It produced classical guitars for the home market, later adopting the Crafter name for its exports, which now cover a range of acoustic and electro-acoustic styles. By 2001 it had a workforce of 140, producing some 60,000 instruments a year. Former Ultravox frontman Midge Ure, Status Quo, and Katie Melua are among Crafter's user roster.

■ **CUSTOM KRAFT** This was a brand for entry-level guitars and amps made for St. Louis Music, a Missouri distributor. The first Custom Krafts were Kay-made arch-tops in the mid 1950s. From 1961 until about 1965 many Custom Krafts were variants of Kay hollowbodies (including Kay's Thinlines), with at first a few Japanese solids. In 1963 the Valco-made Ambassador solidbodies debuted. Valco purchased Kay in 1967, but both companies collapsed in 1968. Custom Krafts continued into 1970, increasingly using non-U.S. parts.

contrerassolidbody

1967 Coral Firefly

1970 Cort Kingston V-4
Mockingbird

1976 Cort Cortez J6000

2002 Cort Earth 1200

1999 Cort Larry Coryell

1983 Contreras Carlevaro

2000 Crafter CTS-155C

■ On these pages, the guitars are by
the Spanish classical builder Contreras;
the Danelectro-related brand Coral,
including its famous electric sitar;
Korean manufacturers Cort and Crafter;
and Custom Kraft, a Kay and Valco-
related U.S. brand.

1966 Custom Craft
Ambassador

solidbody**custom kraft**

1956 Danelectro U2

1966 Danelectro
Guitarlin 4123

1958 Danelectro Short
Horn Double-neck 3923

1956 Danelectro
Silvertone G01301L

■ **DANELECTRO** New Yorker Nathan Daniel started his Danelectro company in 1946, initially supplying amplifiers to mail-order companies. One, Sears, Roebuck, then asked Daniel to supply an ultra-affordable electric guitar and in 1954 Danelectro's low-budget ethos was born. That six-string carried Sears's Silvertone logo, but Danelectro's own-brand equivalents appeared the following year. The earliest examples were solidbodied, but construction soon evolved into the company's classic no-frills formula for keeping down production costs. This included a shaped wooden body frame, faced front and back with Masonite (hardboard), while vinyl tape hid the unfinished sides. Hardware was equally basic and pickups were encased in tubular covers obtained from a lipstick manufacturer.

In 1956 the original U-series expanded to include a six-string bass—an all-new Danelectro idea that proved quite popular with session players, as well as a certain Duane Eddy. Single-cutaway styling was updated in the later 1950s to an all-new shape with twin shallow cutaways, employed on a revised range that soon included a double-neck bass/guitar model. The same period produced the radical Guitarlin, with extra-long, lyre-like horns forming the extended cutaways required to reach no fewer than thirty-one frets. Together with the matching Longhorn bass, this six-string opened the door to new design ideas and very few subsequent Danos could be described as derivative. The late 1950s also brought a move to a bigger facility in Neptune, New Jersey, and production increased considerably over the next five years, as did the Danelectro catalog, with new additions including the novel-looking Bellzouki twelve-string.

Helped by the ongoing Sears contract, the company enjoyed a successful share of the mid-1960s booming market for electric guitars, with Danelectro and Silvertone production peaking at around 200 instruments per day. However, in 1966 Nat Daniel sold Danelectro to the MCA entertainment conglomerate. The new owners soon instigated some changes, including various fresh models and a new partner brand, Coral. The latter logo adorned another "first": the electric sitar, designed by Vinnie Bell and introduced in 1967. A Danelectro-branded "Baby Sitar" appeared at the same time and, although much simpler, it actually sounded similar.

Despite this activity and innovation, sales declined and the Sears contract was cancelled in 1968. The following year, MCA finally called it a day and shut down all Danelectro production. This was effectively the end of the story for the next twenty-five years, but in 1995 the Evets Corporation acquired the rights to the Danelectro name. The brand officially reappeared in 1997, at first adorning a series of effects pedals, but instrument production resumed the next year, although now sourced from Korea.

The new range rapidly expanded to include revivals of U.S. oldie originals, plus some updated interpretations and all-new designs. Production stopped five years later, when Danelectro decided to concentrate solely on their very successful stompboxes. However, 2005 saw the launch of a revised and leaner line of guitars and basses.

danelectro solidbody

1998 Danelectro
U2 '56 Reissue

1999 Danelectro
U3 '56 Reissue

1999 Danelectro Hodad

1961 Danelectro
Twelve-string
Bellzouki

1969 Danelectro
Electric Sitar

danelectro basses

1958 Danelectro Long Horn Bass 4423

1958 Danelectro Long Horn 4623
Owned by Duane Eddy

1958 Danelectro UB-2

1958 Danelectro Shorthorn
Bass Model 3412

■ Danelectro was a brand
begun by Nat Daniel in New
York in the mid-1940s. Its
electric guitars were basic,
cheap—and surprisingly
effective. Many have now
become collectable workhorses,
and more recently the brand
was revived to offer modern
players the idiosyncrasies and
benefits of models such as the
six-string bass and the
distinctive Long Horn.

1955 D'Angelico Electric
(left-handed)

1955 D'Angelico
Electric Arch-top

2002 D'Angelico NY2

1960 D'Angelico
Electric Arch-top

■ **D'ANGELICO** John D'Angelico, born in New York in 1905, started off copying the original f-hole arch-top, the Gibson L-5, designed by Gibson's Lloyd Loar in 1922. D'Angelico developed his own pickguard shape, with a small "stair-step" on the outer edge, and he engraved his name in a large piece of mother-of-pearl in the headstock, but otherwise his guitars looked very much like the Gibson, right down to the dip in the center of the headstock. Following Gibson's lead, by 1936 D'Angelico had introduced the seventeen- and eighteen-inch models.

The same year he began using model names. His least expensive model was the Style A (which lasted until 1945), with a seventeen-inch wide body. Style B (until 1948) was the same size and like Style A had block inlay and parallel bracing, but with the ornamental headstock that would become an instant identifier of a D'Angelico guitar.

Many Italian-style "bowlback" mandolins of the nineteenth century had an ornamental cutout near the top of the headstock. D'Angelico adapted the idea so that the cutout opened at the top of the headstock in a "broken scroll pediment" design. Within the cutout, D'Angelico placed a small button or "ornamental cupola." Just below the cutout, he inlaid his name in a flowing script style, and on a small banner underlining his name he engraved "New York." Both models were superseded by the seventeen-inch Excel and the eighteen-inch New Yorker, which first appeared during 1936. Both had X-braced tops.

Many D'Angelico guitars were made to the personal preferences of individual customers and hence varied in specifications. The typical New Yorker is easily recognizable by its large deco-style peghead inlay that suggests the stair-step design of a New York skyscraper building. The motif is repeated across the guitar. The Excel is only slightly less ornate. The peghead inlay looks something like a military medal, and the pearl blocks in the fingerboard usually do not have a diagonal slash, but it still has the appearance of a formidable instrument.

D'Angelico made two guitars for jazz great Oscar Moore: an Excel in 1946 and an Excel cutaway in 1948. Country legend Chet Atkins ordered an Excel cutaway in 1950, which he played until 1954. Another jazz legend, Johnny Smith, was well-known for playing a D'Angelico until he received his own Guild signature model in 1956.

D'Angelico had two assistants, one of whom, Vincent "Jimmy" DiSerio, is virtually unknown now in guitar circles. He worked in the D'Angelico shop between 1932 and 1960 and then left for a job with the Favilla guitar company. The other assistant, James L. D'Aquisto, joined D'Angelico in 1952 and would go on to become a legendary arch-top maker in his own right, as well as a design innovator.

D'Angelico died in 1964 at age fifty-nine. He made a total of 1,164 numbered guitars, the last ten of which were finished by D'Aquisto. His Excel and New Yorker models, particularly the examples with a cutaway body, are still held in the highest esteem, not only as the ultimate "players" but also as the epitome of the classic era of the arch-top guitar. Today, a new operation, D'Angelico Guitars Of America, based in New Jersey, offers re-creations of many of the original models.

d'angelicosemi-solidbody

1933 D'Angelico
L-5 Style

1939 D'Angelico
New Yorker

■ John D'Angelico built guitars
at his New York City workshop,
defining the look and sound of
the arch-top acoustic style with
his powerful, stylish instruments.
He worked from the early 1930s
into the 1960s, and his guitars
now have the added distinction
of being valued as top-flight
collectors' items.

1941 D'Angelico Special

1950 D'Angelico
New Yorker

1949 D'Angelico Special

1955 D'Angelico Excel Cutaway

1957 D'Angelico New Yorker Cutaway Special ("The Teardrop")

1960 D'Angelico
New Yorker

1961 D'Angelico Excel Cutaway

acoustic d'angelico

1965 D'Aquisto Electric

1973 D'Aquisto New Yorker, Seven-string

1978 D'Aquisto New Yorker Special

1991 D'Aquisto Centura Electric

1987 D'Aquisto Jazz Master

1992 D'Aquisto Solo

■ **D'AQUISTO** James L. D'Aquisto, born in 1935 in Brooklyn, New York, was a seventeen-year-old aspiring jazz guitarist when he accepted an invitation to work at John D'Angelico's shop. When D'Angelico died in 1964, D'Aquisto bought the business. He finished ten guitars that D'Angelico had started, and as those instruments were seen and heard by musicians, he became accepted as D'Angelico's successor, moving from Brooklyn to Long Island, east of New York City, in 1966.

Although D'Aquisto kept D'Angelico's model names—Excel for seventeen-inch guitars, New Yorker for eighteen-inch—he quickly incorporated his own designs. The headstock inlay on his New Yorker was a large scroll instead of the skyscraper figure of a D'Angelico. By 1967 he had modified the f-holes to elongated S-holes and changed the cutout at the top of the headstock from a flattened "broken scroll" to a circular shape.

As a player—which D'Angelico was not—D'Aquisto was not only able to fine-tune the tone and feel of his instruments to suit his customers, he was also able to assess accurately the results of his experimentation with various aspects of guitar construction and design, particularly the bridge, tailpiece, and soundholes.

By 1969 he had done away with the ornamental inlay on the bridge. By 1973 the metal tailpiece had been replaced with an ebony unit. He also changed the pickguard material from celluloid to ebony and gave it a sleek, elongated shape. The modernistic look began to carry over to other features as well, as he removed layers of plastic binding and the large pearl fingerboard inlays that had been standard fare on high-quality arch-tops since the early 1930s. His New Yorker Classic of 1985 represented the fulfilment of his all-wood quest, with wood binding, wood headstock veneer, and no pearl inlay.

By the mid-1980s D'Aquisto was firmly established as the leading independent guitar maker, and also as one of the most versatile, with oval-hole arch-tops, seven-strings, twelve-strings, steel-string flat-tops, nylon-string classicals, and even hollow and solidbody electrics to his name.

In 1987, with his Avant Garde arch-top model, he began focusing on soundholes. The Avant Garde featured two oversized holes with an elongated triangular shape. His next model, the Solo, had similar soundholes, except that they were in two segments (for a total of four holes), and it featured an enlarged headstock cutout. His Centura model also had the large headstock cutout, with beveled veneers to simulate binding—a forgotten traditional technique that was popular on "jazz" banjos of the 1920s.

At the beginning of 1995 D'Aquisto took his soundhole experimentation to a new level with his Advance model, which featured large elliptical holes, plus a set of inserts that the player could put into the soundholes in various combinations to achieve as many as eighteen different tonal shadings.

Whether D'Aquisto's vision for the future of arch-top guitar design was still developing or fully realized will never be known, for he died in 1995, just a few months after finishing the Advance. In recent years, Aria of Japan have offered re-creations of some D'Aquisto models.

d'aquisto semi-solidbody

1968 D'Aquisto New Yorker

1977 D'Aquisto Flat-Top Deluxe

1982 D'Aquisto Classical

1973 D'Aquisto New Yorker Oval Hole

1985 D'Aquisto New Yorker Classic

1992 D'Aquisto Solo

1991 D'Aquisto Centura

1988 D'Aquisto Avant-Garde

1993 D'Aquisto Solo "Teardrop"

■ Jimmy D'Aquisto worked with John D'Angelico in New York City for thirteen years before D'Angelico's death in 1964. D'Aquisto gradually began work on his own line of high-end handmade guitars, and before his own untimely death in 1995 came to define the art of the modern arch-top guitar.

1994 D'Aquisto Advance

1975 Defil Jola 2

■ **DEAN** U.S. guitar maker Dean Zelinsky (born 1957) started the Dean company in 1976. The first instruments to appear were upmarket interpretations of familiar Gibson designs, all featuring a distinctive large V-shaped headstock. During the next decade the range became more rock-orientated, increasingly including examples imported from the Far East, and by the end of the 1980s the catalog was completely Korean.

Zelinsky subsequently sold the Dean name, and the 1990s saw two changes of ownership. In 1993, Korean-sourced Deans were joined by relaunched American-made models and this manufacturing combination has continued ever since.

Dean Zelinsky had maintained contact during all these various upheavals, acting in a consultancy capacity. However, in 2008 he decided to finally sever all ties with the company that still bears his first name, setting up a completely independent operation called DBZ Guitars.

■ **DEAN (CHRISTOPHER)** Christopher Dean (born 1958) built his first guitar at age seventeen. In 1985, after working alongside leading British maker Paul Fischer, he established his own workshop in Kingham, Oxfordshire, England, where he handbuilds fine classical instruments to order. Customers include leading British players Mark Ashford, Gilbert Biberian, and the Eden Stell Guitar Duo.

■ **DE ARMOND** During the 1950s and 1960s, the De Armond name was mainly associated with pickups and foot pedals made by parent company Rowe Industries. Fender bought the brand in 1997 and chose it to adorn a new range of guitars and basses built by Cort in Korea.

Launched the following year, the line comprised solids, semis, and arch-top electrics, all designs being derived from instruments originally produced by Guild, another company now owned by Fender. These less-expensive equivalents offered exceptional quality. Perhaps their popularity threatened sales of the real thing, because Fender subsequently replaced the obvious Guild-style features and components, before finally phasing out the Korean-made models completely and replacing them with inferior Indonesian-origin alternatives.

■ **DEFIL** Defil was Poland's major guitar manufacturer, producing a wide range of acoustics and electrics that included solids and semis sold throughout Eastern Europe during the 1960s and 1970s. This company certainly survived for a further two decades, still offering all types of guitars and other stringed instruments.

■ **DIAS** Belchior Dias was a maker of guitars in late sixteenth-century Lisbon, Portugal. An earlier guitar by him is in the collection of the Royal College of Music in London. This five-course instrument, tentatively attributed to Dias or his workshop, and built around 1590, is one of the earliest guitars known to have survived. It was extensively rebuilt in twentieth century, but the parchment rose in place of the soundhole is said to be original. It has a flat back and ten tied-on frets.

■ **DITSON** Oliver Ditson was a music publisher in Boston before expanding into musical instrument sales. His company had its own instrument manufacturing arm from the 1860s to the early part of the twentieth century. Between 1916 and 1930 its guitars were built by Martin. Ditson is credited with offering the first dreadnought, long before Martin introduced such a guitar under its own name.

1999 DeArmond M-75T Bluesbird

1980 Dean Golden Elite

1985 Dean Hollywood Z

deansolidbody

1906 Ditson Model 261

1590 Dias Five
Course Guitar

1920 Ditson Style 1-45

1987 Dean (Christopher)

1916 Ditson Dreadnought

■ Featured here are guitars by the U.S. brand Dean; the
British classical maker Christopher Dean; DeArmond,
formerly a pickup brand but adapted by Fender for a line
of guitars in the 1990s; the Polish brand Defil; the old
Portuguese maker Belchior Dias; and U.S. brand Ditson,
best known for its pioneering collaboration with Martin
on the Dreadnought design of flat-top acoustics.

acousticditson

1929 Dobro Model 55

1930 Dobro Model 35

1935 Dobro Model 62

resonator guitars

1934 Dobro Artist M-16

■ **DOBRO** John Dopyera (1893-1988) was the inventor of the resonator guitar and founder of the National String Instrument Company which built and marketed it. In 1928 he left the company and set up the Dobro Manufacturing Company to produce a cheaper and louder resonator design. Unlike the National guitar, the Dobro used a single cone that fit into the guitar body like a bowl, with an eight-armed aluminum "spider" transmitting vibrations from the bridge into the cone.

The range expanded from three at launch to eight by 1930, distinguished by choice of woods and level of ornamentation. In 1933, Dobro merged with National to form the National-Dobro Corporation. The same year, it licensed Regal to produce Dobros alongside its own. By the late 1930s, however, the Hawaiian guitar players for whom the resonators had been invented had moved on to electric instruments, and the Dobro was in danger of dying out. Production stopped on the United States' entry into World War II and did not restart afterward, although National-Dobro, now renamed as Valco, retained the name.

However, in response to the Dobro's emergence in bluegrass, Ed and Rudy Dopyera, John's brothers, began making the instruments in 1962 under the DB Original brand. They regained the right to use the Dobro name in 1964 and made instruments under the Dobro brand for two years, at which time they sold the Dobro name to Semie Moseley, a noted electric guitar maker who sold Dobros under his Mosrite brand name. In 1970, Dopyera family members reacquired the Dobro brand name and formed the Original Musical Instrument Company to make the instruments. Gibson acquired the company in 1993, moving Dobro production to Nashville, Tennessee, where the instruments are made in public view at Gibson's Bluegrass Showcase, located in the Opry Mills retail mall.

Although John Dopyera's single-cone creation of 1928 almost died out in the 1930s and 1940s, it is firmly established now, as proven on the high end by a growing number of individuals making custom resonator guitars and, on the low-end, by the availability of cheap Asian-made models. Although Dobro is widely used as a generic name for any resonator guitar, Gibson these days restricts the use of the trademark name to its own instruments.

■ **DOMINO** Located in New York, Maurice Lipsky and Co. were prominent instrument importers. During the late 1960s their Domino brand appeared on electric guitars boasting evocatively impressive names like the Baron and Californian Rebel. Aimed at the affordable end of the market, Domino models were mainly derivative designs sourced from several Japanese makers, including Kawai and Matsumoku.

■ **DWIGHT** Dwight was a house brand belonging to Sonny Shields Music in East St. Louis, Illinois, a sizeable music store owned by Charles Dwight Shields. Dwight guitars targeted the beginner, but rather than being cheap imports, they were rebadged versions of existing U.S.-manufactured guitars. Some were Valco-made Supros, while others originated from Epiphone, being built at Gibson's Kalamazoo factory. Sold between 1963 and 1968, these Dwight examples were identical to their Epiphone equivalents, apart from the different headstock logo and an appropriate "D" on the pickguard.

1935 Dobro No. 100

1964 Dobro Wood Body Hawaiian

dobro**resonator**

1985 Dobro F60

1986 Dobro F-60 "F" Hole Classic

1973 Dobro Model 33 H

■ Following a split from National, John Dopyera founded Dobro in the late 1920s, making a new line of resonator instruments. The brandname has now become synonymous with this type of guitar. Also here are a couple of guitars by a U.S. importer's brand, Domino, and an in-house U.S. retailer's brand, Dwight.

1964 Dobro Metal Body Spanish

1962 Dwight Coronet

1967 Domino California Rebel

1967 Domino Baron

solidbodydwight

1973 Earthwood Acoustic Bass

1920 Dyer Symphony Harp Guitar Style 7

1920 Dyer Symphony Harp Guitar Style 8

■ **DYER** William John Dyer was an instrument dealer in St. Paul, Minnesota, at the turn of the twentieth century. His range of harp guitars was built by Carl and August Larson, following a design by Chris Knutsen that featured a hollow arm extending from the upper bass-side bout of the guitar. The W.J. Dyer and Bro. company survived until the 1940s.

■ **EARTHWOOD** Earthwood guitars were created in the early 1970s by Ernie Ball, the string maker, of San Luis Obispo, California. All were flat-top jumbos with solid spruce tops and maple bolt-on necks. The Earthwood acoustic bass, introduced in 1972, was the first of its kind, intended to cater for electric bass players who wanted to play acoustic music and who could not play the string bass. It had a large flat-top body and a full thirty-four-inch bass neck.

■ **EASTWOOD** Rochdale-based Brian Eastwood has to be Britain's foremost maker of wacky axes, although one of his best known six-strings doesn't bear his name. The Bender Distortorcaster is a Dali-esque, melted and twisted mutation of Fender's finest and Eastwood has since added equally warped reworkings of other familiar electric friends. Early Eastwood oddballs include three-dimensional cartoon-like creations, often built for use as eye-catching stage props, such as the Blue Moon model seen here.

■ **EGGLE** In 1990 British maker Patrick Eggle was building instruments under his own Climaxe brand, but the following year he was part of a new company, the Patrick Eggle Music Company, established in Coventry. Its initial catalogue comprised variations of the Berlin, a PRS-influenced six-string derived from the earlier Climaxe model. The range grew gradually over the next two years, but financing problems prompted a merger in late 1993 with Gary Levinson's Blade guitar company, based in Switzerland. A revised line continued under the new Blade-Eggle regime, but in 1994 Patrick Eggle left the company bearing his name and the brand logo changed to just Eggle.

More economic upheavals occurred the following year, as well as the end of the Levinson liaison. A restructured Eggle company traded until 1996, when it was sold to a UK music retailer, but all instrument production ceased by 2000. Another change of ownership two years later brought about a revival of the brand and the current Patrick Eggle Guitars catalog combines some established Eggle designs with all-new models. Patrick Eggle himself now builds acoustics under the Patrick James Eggle brand.

■ **EGMOND** Founded by Uilke Egmond, this Dutch company started making instruments in 1934, but hit the big time during the guitar boom of the late 1950s and early 1960s, supplying mainly low-cost and equally low-quality acoustics and electrics to literally thousands of aspiring axe-heroes. George Harrison and Brian May began on the Toledo acoustic, while Paul McCartney aimed a little higher via the Solid 7 electric. The Lucky 7 was another hugely popular start-up six-string and as with many imported Egmonds, this usually carried the logo of UK distributors Rosetti. Production continued until the early 1970s when, like so many makers worldwide, Egmond succumbed to the Japanese guitar invasion.

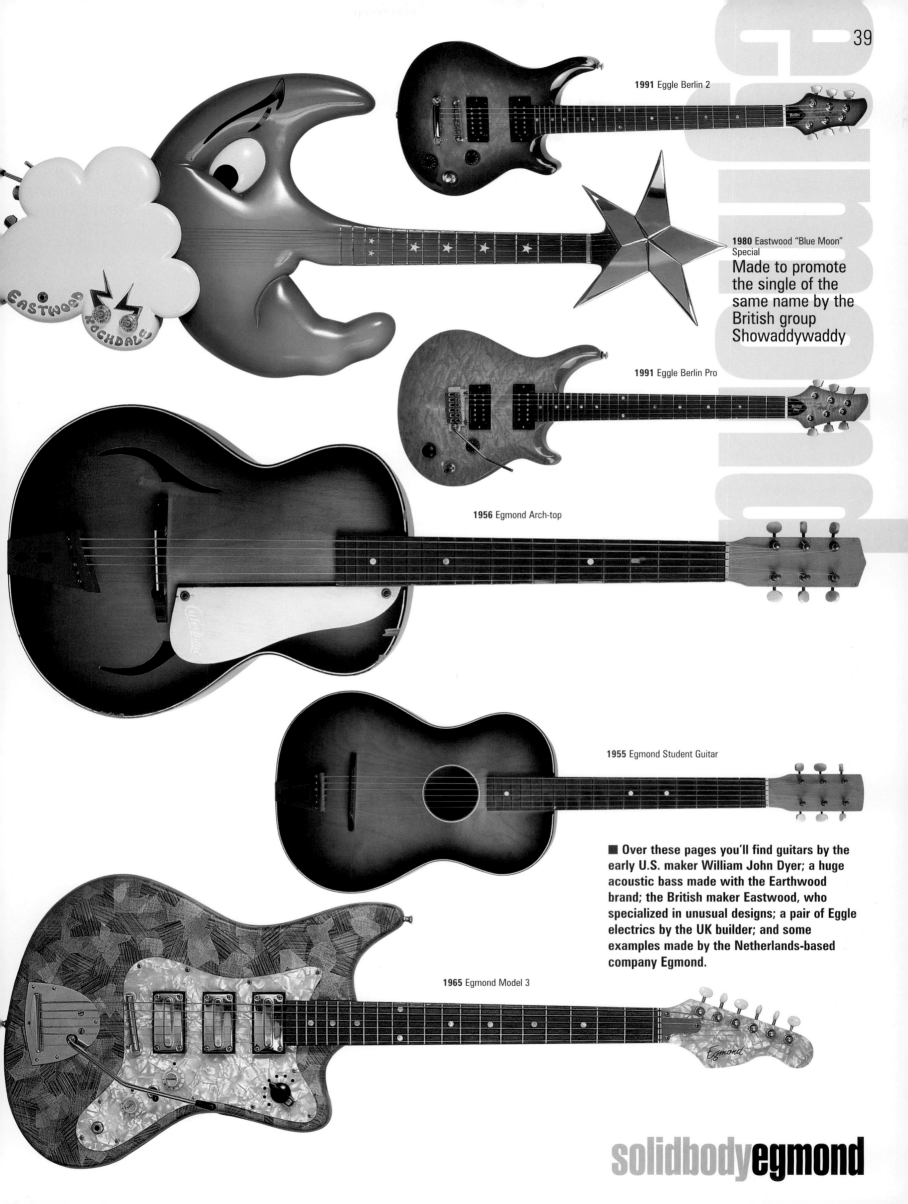

1991 Eggle Berlin 2

1980 Eastwood "Blue Moon" Special
Made to promote the single of the same name by the British group Showaddywaddy

1991 Eggle Berlin Pro

1956 Egmond Arch-top

1955 Egmond Student Guitar

■ Over these pages you'll find guitars by the early U.S. maker William John Dyer; a huge acoustic bass made with the Earthwood brand; the British maker Eastwood, who specialized in unusual designs; a pair of Eggle electrics by the UK builder; and some examples made by the Netherlands-based company Egmond.

1965 Egmond Model 3

solidbodyegmond

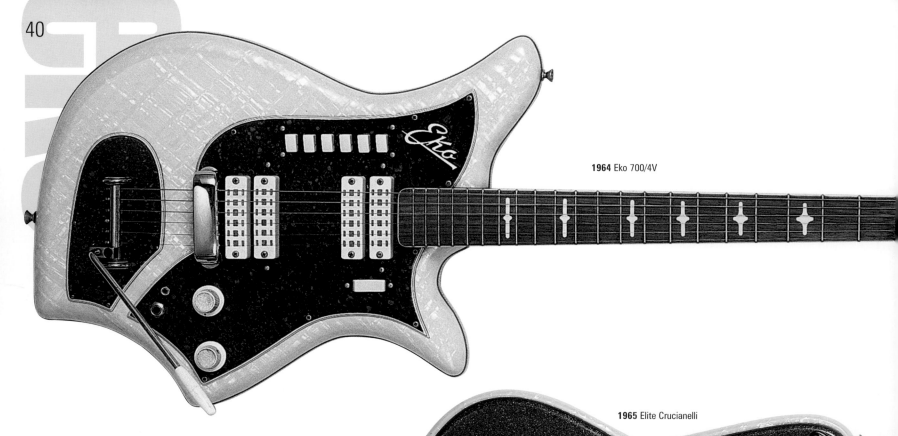

1964 Eko 700/4V

1965 Elite Crucianelli

■ **EKO** Oliviero Pigini started out in the Italian accordion-making industry, but set up his own guitar company in 1959, choosing Eko as the brand name.

Acoustics came first and electrics followed in 1960, some sporting accordion-style sparkle plastic finishes, a feature common to the many makers worldwide who switched from squeezers to strummers. Models of all types were added to a rapidly expanding catalog and Eko moved to a much larger factory in Recanati.

Product quality improved but Eko's fortunes took a downward turn during the next decade. Pigini had been killed in a car crash in 1967 and increasing Japanese competition was adversely affecting sales. Even so, Eko kept trying, launching new models that matched changing market trends.

All production ceased in the mid 1980s, but the company continued and the name soon resurfaced on a range of Far Eastern imports. More recent years have seen Eko explore its past via similarly sourced re-creations of earlier electrics.

■ **ELECTAR** Epiphone introduced the Electar range of electric guitars in 1935. This model dates from around 1937.

■ **ELETCTRA** Owned by U.S. importers St. Louis Music, the Electra logo first appeared in the early 1970s on Japanese-made copies. More originality occurred at the end of the decade in the form of the higher-priced MPC series, equipped with interchangeable effects modules.

The 1980s range came in a wide variety of shapes, from traditional to pointy. Unsurprisingly, many models were similar to those from Westone, both brands being manufactured by the Japanese Matsumoku company. The connection was completed in 1985, when the Electra name was replaced by Westone.

■ **ELECTRO** This was a brandname originally employed by the company that would become Rickenbacker on various electric guitars, starting with its ground-breaking "Frying Pan" lap steel, launched in 1932. About two years later the company, known then as the Electro String Instrument Corporation, added the Rickenbacker name to its instruments. In the 1950s, the Electro was dropped and Rickenbacker became the only brand banner, but the company chose to revive the Electro logo in 1964 for use on two six-string solids.

■ **ELITE** This name appeared on guitars made by the Italian accordion company Crucianelli during the 1960s. Some were solids covered in contrasting color sparkle or pearl plastics, which was common among the many Italian accordion makers who turned their hand to electric guitar production at this time. Other models were more conventional, including slimline semi-acoustics also marketed bearing the Vox brand.

■ **ENCORE** Belonging to long-established UK distributor John Hornby Skewes, this brand has adorned its instruments for well over three decades. It has always been associated with the entry-level end and very affordable equivalents of famous name models. Quality has continued to improve in recent years.

■ Guitars featured here include two Italian brands: Eko and Elite, both known for some eye-catching 1960s models. Encore is a UK importer's brand. Last on these pages, three confusingly similar brands: Electar is an Epiphone-related name from the 1930s; Electra is a U.S. importer's brand; and Electro is a Rickenbacker-related name used until the 1950s.

1937 Electar Century

1983 Electra Lady XV11RD

1989 Encore SE1

1964 Electro ES-17

1963 Eko P2 Angela

1978 Eko BA4NPE Fretless
Acoustic Bass

1962 Eko P12 Betty

1958 Epiphone Crestwood

1958 Epiphone Crestwood

1961 Epiphone
Crestwood Custom

1962 Epiphone
Crestwood Custom

1963 Epiphone Crestwood Deluxe

■ **EPIPHONE** Anastasios Stathopoulo began making his own-label fiddles, lutes, and Greek lioutos in Turkey in the late nineteenth century. His family emigrated to the United States in 1903 and Anastasios continued to make instruments, including mandolins, under the A. Stathopoulo label, in Long Island City, Queens, New York. By 1911 or so, he was also making some parlor guitars.

Anastasios died in 1915 and his son Epaminondas (known as Epi) took over. Two years later the company became known as the House Of Stathopoulo and, following World War I, began making banjos as well. In 1924 Epiphone Recording Series banjos were introduced and four years later the official name was changed to the Epiphone Banjo Company.

Epiphone began producing guitars around 1927, introducing its first line of production guitars, the Recording series. The Recordings had unusual asymmetrical bodies, with a humped upper shoulder and a dramatically swept, pointed treble cutaway. These had engraved celluloid banjo-style heads and tuners and came as either flat-tops or arch-tops. Accompanying these, Epiphone had a line of more conventional flat-top instruments that had rounded figure-eight bodies and regular heads and tuners.

In the early 1930s the company's famous Masterbilt line of f-hole arch-tops debuted. The first Masterbilts were excellent-quality guitars, with fourteen-fret necks, carved spruce tops, and solid sides and backs made of materials ranging from curly maple on the fancy grand auditorium De Luxe to walnut and mahogany on the humbler concert-sized Olympic model. The Masterbilts came in shaded (sunburst) finishes.

Some of the new flat-tops introduced at the same time also had f-holes. These quickly changed to round holes and came in fourteen-fret Spanish and twelve-fret Hawaiian versions. The better Madrid and Navarre models featured a large auditorium body with round shoulders and thick waist, not unlike a later Harmony Sovereign, often referred to as a "round-shouldered" dreadnought. As early as 1932 better Epis featured neck reinforcement.

In 1934 the auditorium flat-tops were joined by a new FT (flat-top) series of folk style guitars. The FT and arch-top lines continued to expand as the 1930s progressed. The Masterbilts were a hit, and Epiphone had become a guitar company.

The Epiphone operation was renamed Epiphone Inc. in 1935 and introduced a line of electric arch-tops and amplifiers, initially called Electraphone but quickly changed to Electar, making it a major competitor to Gibson. Many of the early Electar amps were made by Nat Daniel, who would later found Danelectro. Early Electar guitars were non-cutaway arch-tops (and lap-steels) that had pickups with large handrests over the strings.

In 1938 Epiphone debuted its first classical guitars, the Concert, Alhambra, and Seville. By 1939 Epiphone-brand electric arch-tops included the Century, Coronet, and Zephyr (fitted with a large distinctively shaped oval pickup). In 1939 Epiphone's Herb Sunshine was one of the first to conceive of adjustable polepieces on pickups to achieve a better balance of sound, and these soon began to appear on Epiphones.

Epiphone introduced its first cutaway, the Soloist Emperor, in 1941. Also debuting in 1941 were the FT 110 and 79 (numbers stood for prices) with a new square-shouldered dreadnought shape, recognizable today as the typical dreadnought body style.

Epi Stathopoulo died in 1943 and control of Epiphone went to his brothers, Orphie and Frixo. In 1948 Epiphone introduced its first single-cutaway arch-top acoustics, versions of the earlier Emperor and DeLuxe,

epiphone**solidbody**

1977 Epiphone Scroll 250

1960 Epiphone Coronet

1970 Epiphone ET-270

1990 Epiphone Coronet USA

1989 Epiphone Les Paul Custom

2009 Epiphone "Emily the Strange"

■ The first guitars with the Epiphone brand appeared around 1928, at the same time as the formation in New York City of the Epiphone Banjo Company. Since then, the name has appeared on a huge variety of guitars; shown here are some of Epiphone's more interesting solidbody electric guitars.

1989 Epiphone Flying V

2008 Epiphone Les Paul Ultra II

2008 Epiphone "1958" Explorer

solidbodyepiphone

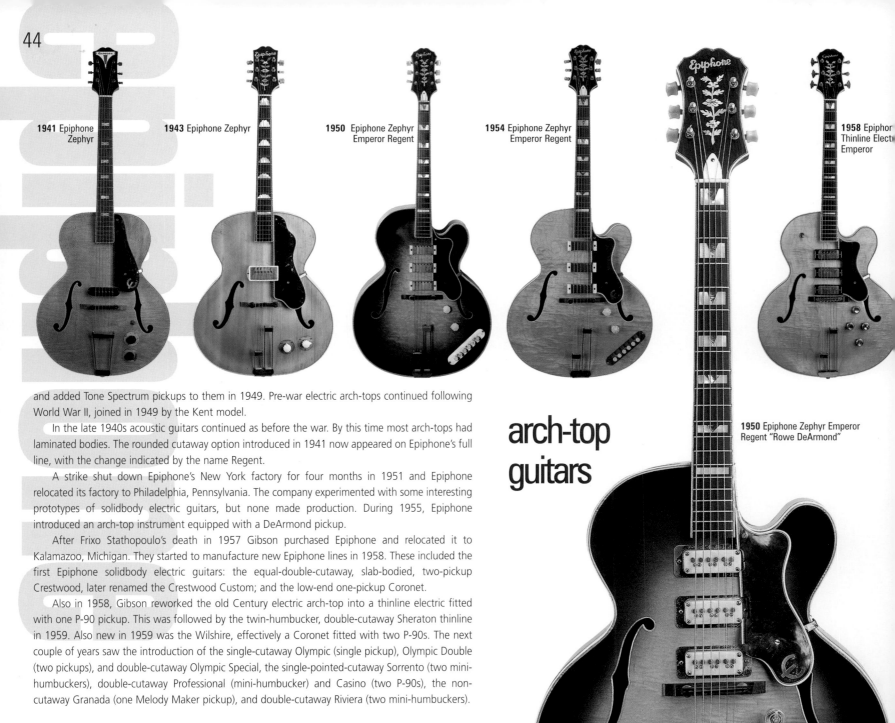

1941 Epiphone
Zephyr

1943 Epiphone Zephyr

1950 Epiphone Zephyr
Emperor Regent

1954 Epiphone Zephyr
Emperor Regent

1958 Epiphon
Thinline Elect
Emperor

arch-top
guitars

1950 Epiphone Zephyr Emperor
Regent "Rowe DeArmond"

and added Tone Spectrum pickups to them in 1949. Pre-war electric arch-tops continued following World War II, joined in 1949 by the Kent model.

In the late 1940s acoustic guitars continued as before the war. By this time most arch-tops had laminated bodies. The rounded cutaway option introduced in 1941 now appeared on Epiphone's full line, with the change indicated by the name Regent.

A strike shut down Epiphone's New York factory for four months in 1951 and Epiphone relocated its factory to Philadelphia, Pennsylvania. The company experimented with some interesting prototypes of solidbody electric guitars, but none made production. During 1955, Epiphone introduced an arch-top instrument equipped with a DeArmond pickup.

After Frixo Stathopoulo's death in 1957 Gibson purchased Epiphone and relocated it to Kalamazoo, Michigan. They started to manufacture new Epiphone lines in 1958. These included the first Epiphone solidbody electric guitars: the equal-double-cutaway, slab-bodied, two-pickup Crestwood, later renamed the Crestwood Custom; and the low-end one-pickup Coronet.

Also in 1958, Gibson reworked the old Century electric arch-top into a thinline electric fitted with one P-90 pickup. This was followed by the twin-humbucker, double-cutaway Sheraton thinline in 1959. Also new in 1959 was the Wilshire, effectively a Coronet fitted with two P-90s. The next couple of years saw the introduction of the single-cutaway Olympic (single pickup), Olympic Double (two pickups), and double-cutaway Olympic Special, the single-pointed-cutaway Sorrento (two mini-humbuckers), double-cutaway Professional (mini-humbucker) and Casino (two P-90s), the non-cutaway Granada (one Melody Maker pickup), and double-cutaway Riviera (two mini-humbuckers).

By 1966 the line had expanded to include the double-cutaway Al Caiola Custom (two mini-humbuckers), the Howard Roberts Standard (one sharp cutaway, oval soundhole and a mini-humbucker), the Caiola Standard (two P-90s), three-pickup Crestwood Deluxe, and a Wilshire twelve-string. The popularity of the thinlines increased that year when John Lennon and George Harrison used new Casinos on-stage in the final Beatles concerts. The group's Epis were also all over the band's latest album, *Revolver*.

Gibson kept the principal Epiphone acoustic cutaway models, including the Emperor, Deluxe, Triumph, and Zenith, but dropped the rest. Epiphone flat-tops were consolidated into the older round-shouldered (Texan) and square-shouldered (Frontier) dreadnoughts, and folk models (Cortez, Caballero).

With the folk revival in progress, more dreadnoughts joined the line in 1963 (Excellente, El Dorado, Troubadour), as well as the first twelve-strings (Bard, Serenader). A Folkster appeared in 1966. All of these Kalamazoo-made Epiphones lasted until the end of the 1960s, the last few shipping in 1970.

The first Japanese-made Epiphones also appeared around 1970, including the 1802 Stratocaster-style solidbody, later renamed the ET-270, and the 5102T ES-335-style thinline, renamed the EA-250. The company also added two "copies" of its venerable Crestwoods, the ET-278 and ET-275. This Epiphone line-up remained unchanged into the early 1970s. By the mid 1970s they were joined by another Crestwood, the ET-290N in natural maple with a maple fingerboard, and a high-end, walnut-topped EA-255 thinline, these last two both with gold hardware.

By 1974 most models in the acoustic 100 series continued to have bolt-on necks, but some fancier 300 and 500-series set-neck models were offered, including the FT-550 and FT-565 twelve-string with three-piece jacaranda and maple backs. Also available was a nice blonde Super Jumbo model. >

1964 Epiphone Casino
Right-handed model strung left-handed by its owner, Paul McCartney

epiphonesemi-solidbody

1958 Epiphone Thinline
Electric Emperor

1961 Epiphone Emperor

1958 Epiphone Sheraton E212TN

1958 Epiphone Sheraton E212T

1965 Epiphone
Sheraton E212T

1964 Epiphone Casino
Owned by
John Lennon

■ Epiphone was bought by Gibson in the late
1950s, and all production moved to the new
owner's base in Kalamazoo, Michigan. Since then,
Gibson has made Epiphone guitars in the U.S. as
well as in various Far Eastern factories. Shown
here are pre and post-Gibson hollowbody electric
models from the 1940s until recent years.

1960 Epiphone Sorrento

1997 Epiphone Supernova
Noel Gallagher Model

semis

1995 Epiphone Casino

2009 Epiphone
Dot Studio

2009 Epiphone Dot

semi-solidbody epiphone

1962 Epiphone Professional

semi-acoustics

1999 Epiphone Les Paul ES Limited Edition

In 1976 Epiphone added the distinctive new Scroll models to its catalog, fitted with two humbuckers and pre-Gibson-style Epiphone headstock, differing in finishes and trim. They were available through 1979.

As the end of the decade approached, Gibson marketed the Epiphone "Rock 'n' Roll Star Solidbody Line Up" in Japan, guitars similar to the Scrolls but with equal cutaways and no scrolls, bearing the old Epi names Olympic Custom, Olympic, and Wilshire. The shortlived Genesis series was added to the Epiphone line in 1981.

Epiphone acoustics continued to be made in Japan probably through the early 1980s. PR-series flat-tops included six- and twelve-string dreadnoughts and folk-style guitars. Two classicals were offered, with solid or laminated cedar tops. By this time the Epiphone line included a pair of folk-style models with single cutaways, one with a pickup system.

Gibson slowly transferred production to a new factory in Nashville, Tennessee, where labor costs were lower than in Kalamazoo and began making Epiphones in America again. In 1982 they unveiled the Epiphone Spirit version of the same-name Gibson model. This featured an Explorer-style headstock, whereas the Epi had a typical Gibson-style "open-book" head. One final Epiphone solidbody was made at Kalamazoo, which featured a Gibson-style neck glued into a body cut out in the shape of the continental United States.

Gibson's revived the Epiphone brand in 1984, primarily as a vehicle for Korean-made low-end instruments. The new Epiphone By Gibson line included versions of both Gibson and Fender stalwarts. These early Korean-made Epiphones were replaced by a considerably expanded line, including the Les Paul 3, Les Paul 2, and Les Paul 1. Also offered were two Epiphone Firebirds. The late-1980s acoustic line was all Korean and consisted of a number of natural and black dreadnoughts and classicals, all but the top models made with laminated tops.

Six Strat-style guitars were offered in late 1986, from the top-of-the-line X-1000, to the S-310. Most of this line-up continued to be available into 1989. Epiphone tapped a host of celebrities to endorse its new lines, including Les Paul and Chet Atkins.

In 1988 Gibson hit on the formula that would bring success to the Epiphone brand in the 1990s and beyond. Two new proper set-neck Les Paul copies were introduced, the Custom and the Standard. In 1989 Epiphone revamped the whole line. During the makeover Gibson returned to making a few special Epiphones in Nashville.

One American-made Epiphone, introduced in 1990, was the U.S.A. Coronet. This presented a clever combination of old and new, reviving the defunct 1960s Epiphone shape and set-neck design, and adding a new reverse-Explorer headstock plus a five-way pickup selector switch, as well as a circuit board that provided humbucker, single-coil, out-of-phase and series/parallel sounds. In 1991 Epiphone briefly added to the bottom of its line an inexpensive bolt-on-neck Les Paul, the LP-300, and the Stratocaster-style S-300, which would last only a year. By 1995 American Epiphone production had ended.

By the late 1990s there was an almost bewildering array of Korean-made Epiphone acoustics. Dreadnoughts included both traditional square-shouldered and round-shouldered (Advanced Jumbo) dreadnoughts, increasingly with solid tops (including mahogany), some with cutaways. There were copies of the Gibson Dove and a Don Everly signature model; Venetian cutaway thin-body acoustic-electrics, including a Jeff "Skunk" Baxter model; classicals, including cutaway models; and even spider and biscuit-bridge resonator guitars.

The most striking aspect of Epiphones produced in the late 1990s and beyond was the veritable explosion of Les Paul variants: from exotic, transparent, and sparkle finishes to good looking flamed-maple and birdseye-maple caps. There were seven-string versions, one with f-holes, and even a Metal Edition, as well as a signature model for Slash of Guns N' Roses that came with the correct Duncan pickups, just like the more expensive Gibson version. >

1959 Epiphone Rivoli Bass

1965 Epiphone Riviera Twelve-string

1966 Epiphone Caiola Custom

epiphonesemi-solidbody

1928 Epiphone Recording D

1929 Epiphone Recording E

■ Epiphone has proved to be a useful brand name for the Gibson company, who started making Epiphones in 1958. Not only does it continue to appear on the hollowbody guitars that made the brand's name back in pre-Gibson New York days, but also it appears now on a variety of new models. Shown here is a selection dating from the 1920s to the 1990s.

1934 Epiphone De Luxe (with added pickup)

1935 Epiphone Emperor (with added pickup)

1937 Epiphone Emperor

1954 Epiphone Emperor Cutaway

1941 Epiphone Emperor

acousticepiphone

1936 Epiphone Madrid

1941 Epiphone FT-79

1958 Epiphone Frontier FT-110

1958 Epiphone Texan

1963 Epiphone C-24 Classical

1999 Epiphone AJ-15 Dreadnought

1998 ESP M-250

1929 Esteso Classical

1934 Esteso Flamenco

The Les Paul Ultra II, launched in 2008, mixed a regular magnetic pickup and a special pickup to create acoustic-like sounds as well as the regular electric tones from the instrument. In the thinline series, a swathe of old names still managed to conjure up the heritage of 1950s and 1960s designs. They provided a vintage-style alternative to parent-company Gibson's thinlines, always more fashionable in this area. As Epiphone moved into the twenty-first century, the emphasis on copying Gibson acoustic models began to recede, although the basic direction remained the same.

■ **ESP** Established in 1975, ESP (Electric Sound Products) started off making guitar parts, but soon progressed to actual instruments. Like so many other Japanese makers of the time, this Tokyo-based company initially concentrated mainly on copies, although these were contrasted by exotic custom creations.

From the 1980s onward, ESP embraced the rock guitar market and original designs dominated, although many were still quite derivative, catering for changing trends. ESP is still going strong, now boasting a worldwide roster of endorsees.

■ **ESTESO** The guitars built by Domingo Esteso (1882–1937) date from the most romantic era of Spanish guitar-making and are sought after by both classical and flamenco enthusiasts. Esteso was born in San Clemente de Cuenca, east of Madrid, and joined the great Manuel Ramírez as a teenage apprentice.

After Ramírez's death in 1916, Esteso set up on his own account, initially producing guitars for Manuel's widow, who sold many of them on to a company in Buenos Aires, Argentina. The instruments are in the small, light style of the era, use standard fan-bracing, and produce a slightly soft, mellow tone. Some are quite ornate. When he died, Esteso left his workshop in the hands of his widow and his three nephews, the brothers Faustino, Mariano, and Julio Conde, who would become celebrated makers in their own right.

■ **EUPHONON** Euphonon guitars are among the least remembered yet most successful creations of Carl and August Larson and their Maurer and Co. of Chicago. Euphonon replaced the Maurer brand around 1935 when the Larsons jumped on the increasingly popular fourteen-fret bandwagon.

The guitars featured a new square-shouldered shape and a solid headstock, but otherwise had signature Larson construction. Bodies were mahogany, rosewood, or figured maple. Student-grade models were built in the 13¾-inch size with ladder-braced tops, but better models had laminated, X-braced "stressed" tops and larger sizes of fifteen-inch to sixteen-inch, even nineteen-inch. Many had typical Larson inlays, some fancy trim, but others sported more modern pearl blocks. Toward the end of the 1930s Euphonon gained a dreadnought, with a body like a cross between a Martin and Gibson of that style. The Euphonon line ended in the early 1940s when Maurer and Co. closed down.

1999 Epiphone
AJ-30CE

2000 Epiphone EJ-160E
John Lennon Model

■ Guitars featured here include our final
selection of Epiphone instruments; a modern
example from the Japanese brand ESP; a brace
of old Spanish Esteso classical guitars; and
some unusual guitars from Euphonon, one of
the brands used in the 1930s and early 1940s
by the talented Larson Brothers of Chicago.

2002 Epiphone EL-00

1935 Euphonon Dreadnought

1973 Estrada

1936 Euphonon

1940 Euphonon

1941 Euphonon Dreadnough

classical
guitars

acousticeuphonon

1952 Fender Student Steel Model

1952 Fender Esquire

1953 Fender Esquire

1955 Fender Esquire

1955 Fender Champ Steel

esquires

1959 Fender Esquire

■ **FENDER** No other company has contributed more to the look and sound of the solidbody electric guitar than Fender. Clarence Leo Fender's original firm changed the course of popular music by revolutionizing the design and manufacture of electric guitars.

So successful did Fender become that in 1965 the business was sold to the giant CBS conglomerate for $13 million, an unprecedentedly large figure. Yet the whole affair had started around twenty years earlier when Leo made some electric steel guitars with a few thousand dollars that he'd earned from a record-player design. From these humble beginnings grew one of the largest and most splendidly original musical instrument manufacturers in the world.

During its early years the southern California company came perilously close to failing. It was Leo Fender's sheer determination, combined with his luck in surrounding himself with clever, dedicated people, that helped pull the Fender company through difficult times.

Leo was born in 1909, in a barn near the Anaheim/Fullerton border in the Los Angeles area. His parents ran a "truck farm," growing vegetables and fruit for the market, and had put up the barn first before they could afford to build a house. A friend once recalled that when Leo was small his father had told him that the only thing worthwhile in the world was what you accomplished at work—and that if you weren't working you were lazy, which was a sin. It seems that Leo would judge everyone around him by that measure . . . and himself hardest of all.

Although he went on to study accountancy and began his working life in the accounts sections of the state highway department and a tire distribution company, Leo's hobby was always electronics, and in his twenties he built amplifiers and PA systems for use at public events such as sports and religious gatherings, and dances. In about 1939 Leo opened the Fender Radio Service, a store at Fullerton in the Los Angeles area. Leo had lost his accounting job earlier in that decade of Depression. His new shop brought instant introductions to many local musicians including professional violinist and lap-steel guitarist "Doc" Kauffman. Doc had worked on electric guitar designs for another local company, Rickenbacker.

Lap-steel, or Hawaiian, guitar playing, had been fashionable in the United States since the 1920s and was still tremendously popular at the time Leo opened his store. A lap-steel guitar sits horizontally on the player's lap, and its strings are stopped not by the frets, but with a sliding steel bar held in the player's nonpicking hand. As the most prevalent type of guitar in America at the time, lap-steels were the first guitars to "go electric" in the 1930s. Several innovative companies had started to experiment with electro-magnetic pickups, attaching them to guitars and connecting them to small amplifiers. During the 1930s and later, the term "Spanish" was used to identify the other (less popular) hold-against-the-body type of guitar.

Leo had already begun to look into the potential for electric guitars and to play around with pickup designs. Leo and Doc built a solidbody guitar in 1943 to test these early pickups. Some of the revenue went into starting their shortlived company, K&F (Kauffman & Fender), and the two men began proper production of electric lap-steel guitars and small amplifiers in November 1945. **>**

fendersolidbody

1953 Fender Telecaster

1951 Fender Nocaster

1952 Fender Telecaster

telecasters

1956 Fender Telecaster

1957 Fender Telecaster

■ Fender began business in the mid 1940s as a small firm making steel guitars and small amplifiers. In 1950, it launched the first commercial solidbody electric guitar, at first named Esquire, then Broadcaster, and from 1951 renamed Telecaster. The Esquire survived as a one-pickup version of the Telecaster; the Tele is still in production.

nocaster & broadcaster

1950 Fender Broadcaster

solidbodyfender

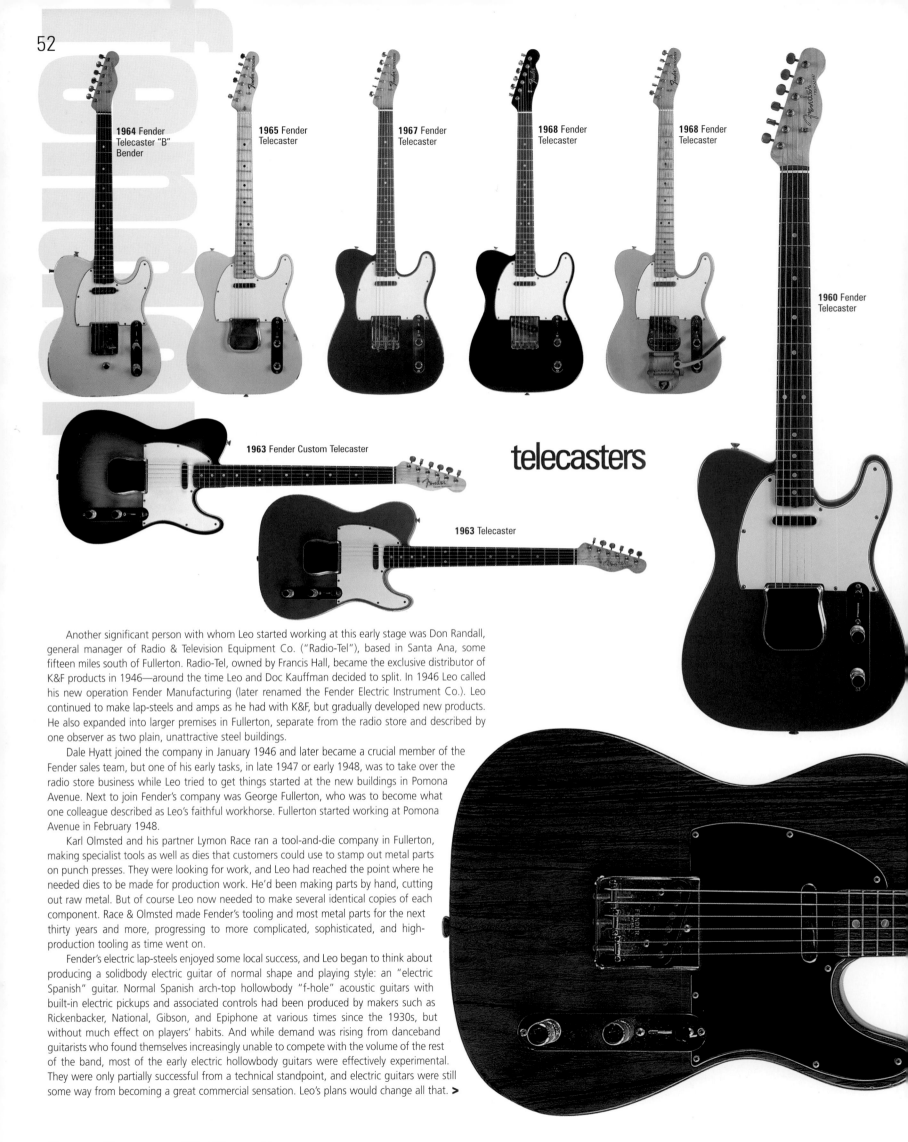

1964 Fender Telecaster "B" Bender

1965 Fender Telecaster

1967 Fender Telecaster

1968 Fender Telecaster

1968 Fender Telecaster

1960 Fender Telecaster

1963 Fender Custom Telecaster

telecasters

1963 Telecaster

Another significant person with whom Leo started working at this early stage was Don Randall, general manager of Radio & Television Equipment Co. ("Radio-Tel"), based in Santa Ana, some fifteen miles south of Fullerton. Radio-Tel, owned by Francis Hall, became the exclusive distributor of K&F products in 1946—around the time Leo and Doc Kauffman decided to split. In 1946 Leo called his new operation Fender Manufacturing (later renamed the Fender Electric Instrument Co.). Leo continued to make lap-steels and amps as he had with K&F, but gradually developed new products. He also expanded into larger premises in Fullerton, separate from the radio store and described by one observer as two plain, unattractive steel buildings.

Dale Hyatt joined the company in January 1946 and later became a crucial member of the Fender sales team, but one of his early tasks, in late 1947 or early 1948, was to take over the radio store business while Leo tried to get things started at the new buildings in Pomona Avenue. Next to join Fender's company was George Fullerton, who was to become what one colleague described as Leo's faithful workhorse. Fullerton started working at Pomona Avenue in February 1948.

Karl Olmsted and his partner Lymon Race ran a tool-and-die company in Fullerton, making specialist tools as well as dies that customers could use to stamp out metal parts on punch presses. They were looking for work, and Leo had reached the point where he needed dies to be made for production work. He'd been making parts by hand, cutting out raw metal. But of course Leo now needed to make several identical copies of each component. Race & Olmsted made Fender's tooling and most metal parts for the next thirty years and more, progressing to more complicated, sophisticated, and high-production tooling as time went on.

Fender's electric lap-steels enjoyed some local success, and Leo began to think about producing a solidbody electric guitar of normal shape and playing style: an "electric Spanish" guitar. Normal Spanish arch-top hollowbody "f-hole" acoustic guitars with built-in electric pickups and associated controls had been produced by makers such as Rickenbacker, National, Gibson, and Epiphone at various times since the 1930s, but without much effect on players' habits. And while demand was rising from danceband guitarists who found themselves increasingly unable to compete with the volume of the rest of the band, most of the early electric hollowbody guitars were effectively experimental. They were only partially successful from a technical standpoint, and electric guitars were still some way from becoming a great commercial sensation. Leo's plans would change all that. >

fendersolidbody

1970 Fender
Telecaster

1970 Fender
Telecaster

1972 Fender
Telecaster

1968 Fender
Telecaster

1969 Fender Telecaster

1968 Fender
Telecaster

1969 Fender Telecaster

1969 Fender Telecaster

1969 Rosewood Telecaster

■ In the 1960s and 70s, Fender's Telecaster
continued to attract guitarists with its simple,
direct playability. Unusual Teles included
some with a stringbending B-bender, for
steel-like effects; a garish paisley red finish
achieved with patterned wallpaper; and a
model with a heavy body of solid rosewood,
played by George Harrison at The Beatles'
famous "rooftop" concert.

1974 Fender Telecaster

1972 Fender
Telecaster

1984 Fender Telecaster
Standard Bowling Ball

1984 Fender Telecaster
Standard Bowling Ball

1984 Fender Telecaster
Standard Bowling Ball

A number of guitar makers, musicians, and engineers in America were wondering about the possibility of a solidbody instrument. Such a design would curtail the annoying feedback often produced by amplified hollowbody guitars, at the same time reducing the guitar body's interference with its overall tone and thus more accurately reproducing and sustaining the sound of the strings.

Rickenbacker had launched a relatively solid Bakelite-body electric guitar in the mid-1930s—the type that Leo's friend Doc Kauffman had played—while around 1940 guitarist Les Paul built a personal test-bed electric guitar in New York that used parts from a variety of instruments mounted on a solid central block of pine. In Downey, California, about fifteen miles to the west of Fender's operation in Fullerton, Paul Bigsby had a small workshop where he spent a good deal of time fixing motorcycles and, later, making fine pedal-steel guitars and vibrato units. He also ventured into the solidbody electric guitar and mandolin field, hand-building a limited number of distinctive instruments. He'd started this in 1948 with the historic Merle Travis guitar, an instrument with through-neck construction and hollowbody "wings." Fender seems to have been influenced by the earlier instruments of Bigsby's—George Fullerton says that he and Leo knew Paul Bigsby and had seen Merle Travis playing his Bigsby guitar.

Leo started work in the summer of 1949 on the instrument that we now know as the Fender Telecaster, effectively the world's first commercially marketed solidbody electric guitar, and still very much alive today. The guitar, originally named the Fender Esquire and then the Fender Broadcaster, first went into production in 1950. Early prototypes borrowed their headstock design from Fender's lap-steels, with three tuners each side, but the production version had a smart new headstock with all six tuners along one side, allowing strings to meet tuners in a straight line and obviating the traditional "angled back" headstock. Fender's new solidbody electric guitar was unadorned, straightforward, potent, and—perhaps most significantly—ahead of its time. As such it did not prove immediately easy for the salesmen at Fender to sell, as Don Randall of Radio-Tel found when he took some prototypes to a musical instrument trade show in Chicago during the summer of 1950. In fact, Randall was aghast to find that competitors generally laughed at the new instrument, calling the prototypes canoe paddles, snow shovels, and worse. **>**

telecasters

1977 Fender Telecaster

1984 Fender '52 Telecaster

1983 Fender Gold Elite Telecaster

1983 Fender Gold Elite Telecaster

1987 Fender Contemporary Telecaster

■ During the 1980s Fender noted the historical value of its Telecaster, the world's first commercial solidbody electric. The '52 Telecaster was its first proper reissue, designed to look as it had done thirty years earlier. Meanwhile, the Elite Telecasters brought the Tele up to date with modern pickups, revised controls, and plain colors.

telecaster
variants

1989 Fender Telecaster 40th Anniversary

1990 Fender "Knebworth" Telecaster Custom Shop

solidbodyfender

1990 Fender Jerry Donahue Telecaster

1990 Fender James Burton Telecaster

1991 Fender Danny Gatton Telecaster

1993 Fender Clarence White Telecaster

1998 Fender Will Ray Signature Telecaster

signature models

1997 Fender Hellecaster Will Ray Jazz-a-Caster

A small number of pre-production one-pickup Esquire models without truss rods were made in April 1950, with another tiny production run of two-pickup Esquires two months later. General production of the better-known single-pickup Esquire with truss rod did not begin until January 1951. But in November 1950, a truss rod was added to the two-pickup model, its name was changed to Broadcaster, and the retail price was fixed at $170. The Broadcaster name was shortlived, halted in early 1951 when Gretsch, a large New York–based instrument manufacturer, indicated its prior use of "Broadkaster" on various drum products.

At first, Fender simply used up its "Fender Broadcaster" decals on the guitar's headstock by cutting off the "Broadcaster" and leaving just the "Fender" logo; these no-name guitars are known among collectors today as Nocasters. The new name decided upon for the Fender solid electric was Telecaster, coined by Don Randall. The Telecaster name was on headstocks by April 1951, and at last Fender's new $189.50 solidbody electric had a permanent name.

At Fender, practicality and function ruled. There was none of the hand-carving of selected timbers one would find in the workshops of established arch-top guitar makers. With the Telecaster, Fender made the electric guitar into a factory product, stripped down to its essential elements, built up from easily assembled parts, and produced at a relatively affordable price. Fender's methods made for easier, more consistent production—and a different sound. Not for Fender the fat, Gibson-style jazz tone, but a clearer, spikier sound, something like a cross between a clean acoustic guitar and a cutting electric lap-steel.

One of the earliest players to appreciate this new sound was Jimmy Bryant, best known for his staggering guitar instrumental duets with pedal-steel virtuoso Speedy West. Bryant soon took to playing the new Fender solidbody. He was respected by professionals in the music business for his session work, including recordings made with Tennessee Ernie Ford and Ella Mae Morse among others. Bryant also made television appearances on country showcases, and would highlight Fender's exciting new solidbody for the growing television audience.

It was western swing, a lively dance music that grew up in Texas dancehalls during the 1930s and 1940s, that popularized the electric guitar in the United States, at first with steel guitars. Many of its steel players used Fender electrics, notably Noel Boggs and Leon McAuliffe, but there were also some electric-Spanish guitarists in the bands, like Tele-wielding Bill Carson. **>**

fendersolidbody

1991 Fender American Standard Telecaster

1992 Fender Set Neck Telecaster Country Artist

1994 Fender Egyptian Telecaster

1995 Fender American Classic Telecaster

1995 Fender Telecaster Junior

2001 Fender Muddy Waters Tribute Telecaster

2002 Fender "Go Cat Go" Telecaster

■ A signature model is a guitar with a personal set of features, as endorsed by a famous player. This set of mainly 90s Telecasters illustrates the trend, with models for Jerry Donahue and Will Ray, who even named their band The Hellecasters; James Burton, who played with everyone from Elvis Presley to Emmylou Harris; and Muddy Waters, who took the Tele to the blues.

signature reissue models

2000 Fender Leo Fender Broadcaster

2001 Fender '63 Telecaster Relic

1997 Fender 50s Telecaster

solidbodyfender

2006 Fender '51
Nocaster Relic

2006 Fender '59
Esquire Relic

2007 Fender Vintage
Hot Rod '52 Tele

2008 Telecaster
Custom

reissues & relics

2003 Fender Standard
Telecaster (left-handed)

2004 Fender American
Deluxe Telecaster QMT

Business began to pick up for the Fender company as news of the Telecaster spread, and as Radio-Tel's five salesmen began to persuade instrument store owners to stock the instrument. Early in 1953 Fender's existing sales setup with Radio-Tel was reorganized into a new Fender sales distribution company, which was operational by June. Based like Radio-Tel in Santa Ana, Fender Sales had four business partners: Leo, Don Randall, Radio-Tel owner Francis Hall, and salesman Charlie Hayes. Hayes was killed in a road accident and in late 1953 Hall bought the Rickenbacker company, so in 1955 Fender Sales became a partnership owned by Leo and Don Randall. It was Randall who actually ran this pivotal part of the Fender business.

The sales side of Fender was, therefore, in capable hands. Another important addition to the team occurred in 1953 when steel guitarist Freddie Tavares, best known for his swooping steel intro over the titles of the *Looney Tunes* cartoons, joined the California guitar maker, helping Leo design new products. Also in 1953 three new buildings at South Raymond Avenue and Valencia Drive were added to the company's manufacturing premises. As well as just two electric guitars, the Telecaster and Esquire, Fender had at this time a line of seven amplifiers (Bandmaster, Bassman, Champ, Deluxe, Princeton, Super, Twin Amp), five electric steel guitars (Custom, Deluxe, Dual, Stringmaster, Student) and its revolutionary electric bass guitar, the Precision, that had been introduced two years earlier.

Another newcomer, Forrest White, joined the company after Leo asked if he'd be interested in helping sort out some "management problems" at Fender. White was shocked by the disorganized mess he found at the workshops and agreed, beginning work at Fender in May 1954. He soon began to put the manufacturing operations into order.

Now Leo had able men—Forrest White and Don Randall—poised at the head of production and sales. He had a new factory and a small but growing reputation. All he needed now was more new products. And along came the stylish Fender Stratocaster, the epitome of tailfin-flash American design of the 1950s.

Leo was listening hard to players' comments about the "plain vanilla" Tele and Esquire, and during the early 1950s he and Tavares began to formulate the guitar that would become the Stratocaster. Some musicians were complaining that the sharp edge on the Telecaster was uncomfortable, so the team began to fool around with smoothed contouring on the body. The Stratocaster was eventually launched during 1954—samples around May and June were followed by the first proper production run in October. It was priced at $249.50 (or $229.50 without vibrato) plus $39.50 for a case. The new Fender was the first solidbody electric with three pickups, and also featured a new-design built-in vibrato unit (or "tremolo" as Fender called it) to provide pitch-bending and shimmering chordal effects for the player. It was the first self-contained vibrato unit: an adjustable bridge, tailpiece, and vibrato system all in one. Not a simple mechanism for the time, but a reasonably effective one. It

fendersolidbody

1976 Fender
Telecaster Deluxe

1977 Fender
Telecaster Custom

2005 Fender '72 Telecaster
Deluxe

■ Recent Telecasters have reflected the
full range of modern playing, from made-
to-look-old Relics that conjure up the
beauty of a vintage classic, through
reissues of the 1970s humbucker'd Teles
like the Custom and the Deluxe, to state-
of-the-art new versions of the oldest
solidbody electric on the block.

1977 Fender Telecaster Custom

customs & deluxes

2006 Fender Classic '72 Telecaster Custom

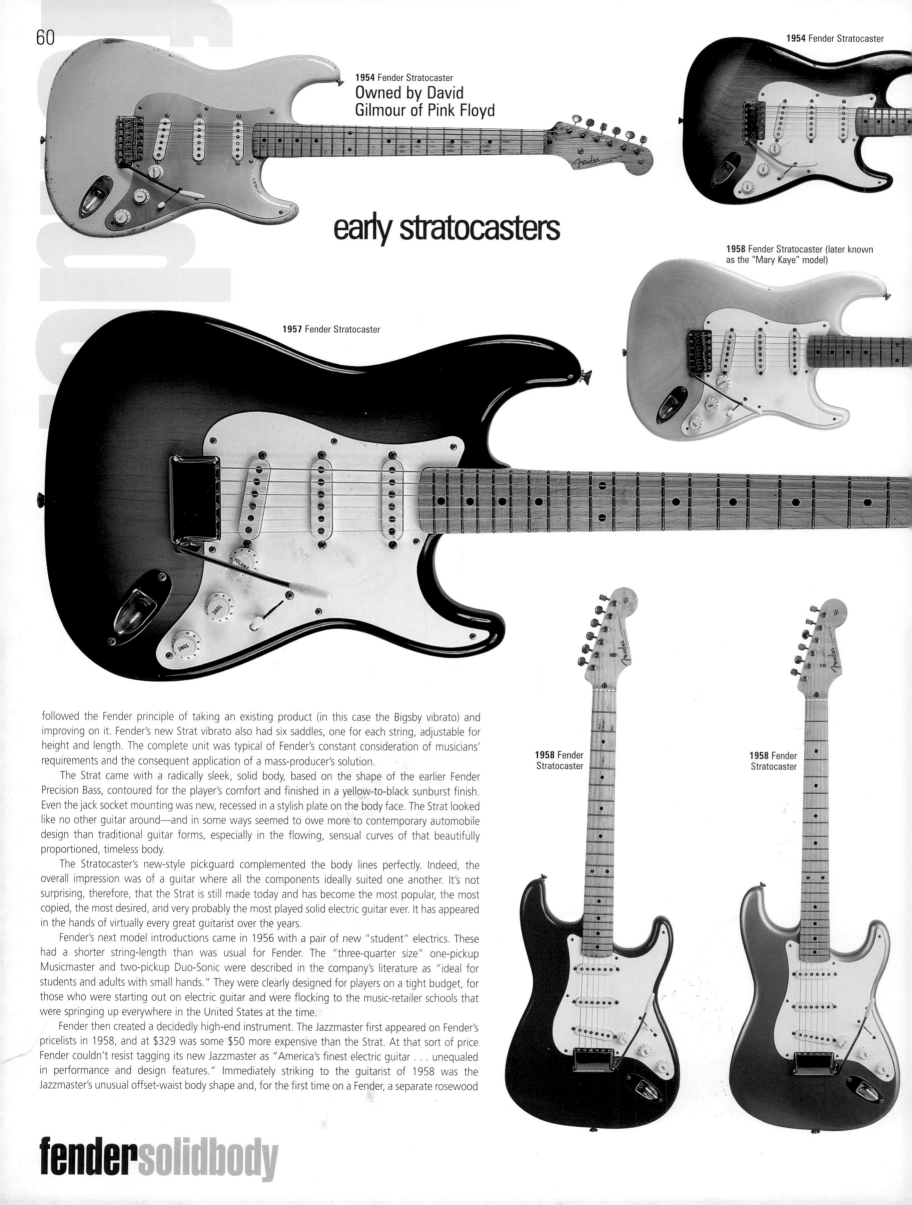

1954 Fender Stratocaster
Owned by David Gilmour of Pink Floyd

1954 Fender Stratocaster

early stratocasters

1958 Fender Stratocaster (later known as the "Mary Kaye" model)

1957 Fender Stratocaster

1958 Fender Stratocaster

1958 Fender Stratocaster

followed the Fender principle of taking an existing product (in this case the Bigsby vibrato) and improving on it. Fender's new Strat vibrato also had six saddles, one for each string, adjustable for height and length. The complete unit was typical of Fender's constant consideration of musicians' requirements and the consequent application of a mass-producer's solution.

The Strat came with a radically sleek, solid body, based on the shape of the earlier Fender Precision Bass, contoured for the player's comfort and finished in a yellow-to-black sunburst finish. Even the jack socket mounting was new, recessed in a stylish plate on the body face. The Strat looked like no other guitar around—and in some ways seemed to owe more to contemporary automobile design than traditional guitar forms, especially in the flowing, sensual curves of that beautifully proportioned, timeless body.

The Stratocaster's new-style pickguard complemented the body lines perfectly. Indeed, the overall impression was of a guitar where all the components ideally suited one another. It's not surprising, therefore, that the Strat is still made today and has become the most popular, the most copied, the most desired, and very probably the most played solid electric guitar ever. It has appeared in the hands of virtually every great guitarist over the years.

Fender's next model introductions came in 1956 with a pair of new "student" electrics. These had a shorter string-length than was usual for Fender. The "three-quarter size" one-pickup Musicmaster and two-pickup Duo-Sonic were described in the company's literature as "ideal for students and adults with small hands." They were clearly designed for players on a tight budget, for those who were starting out on electric guitar and were flocking to the music-retailer schools that were springing up everywhere in the United States at the time.

Fender then created a decidedly high-end instrument. The Jazzmaster first appeared on Fender's pricelists in 1958, and at $329 was some $50 more expensive than the Strat. At that sort of price Fender couldn't resist tagging its new Jazzmaster as "America's finest electric guitar . . . unequaled in performance and design features." Immediately striking to the guitarist of 1958 was the Jazzmaster's unusual offset-waist body shape and, for the first time on a Fender, a separate rosewood

■ The Stratocaster began life in 1954 as Fender's flashier follow-up to the three-year-old Telecaster. It had three pickups, a contoured body for player comfort, and a Synchronized Tremolo, or vibrato, that was "Leo Fender's pride and joy." At first the guitar's regular look was a two-tone sunburst, but custom finishes soon began to appear in beautiful solid colors.

1958 Fender Stratocaster

1959 Fender Stratocaster
Owned by
Hank Marvin

1959 Fender Stratocaster

1959 Fender Stratocaster

'50s models with rosewood fingerboards

1959 Fender Stratocaster

solidbodyfender

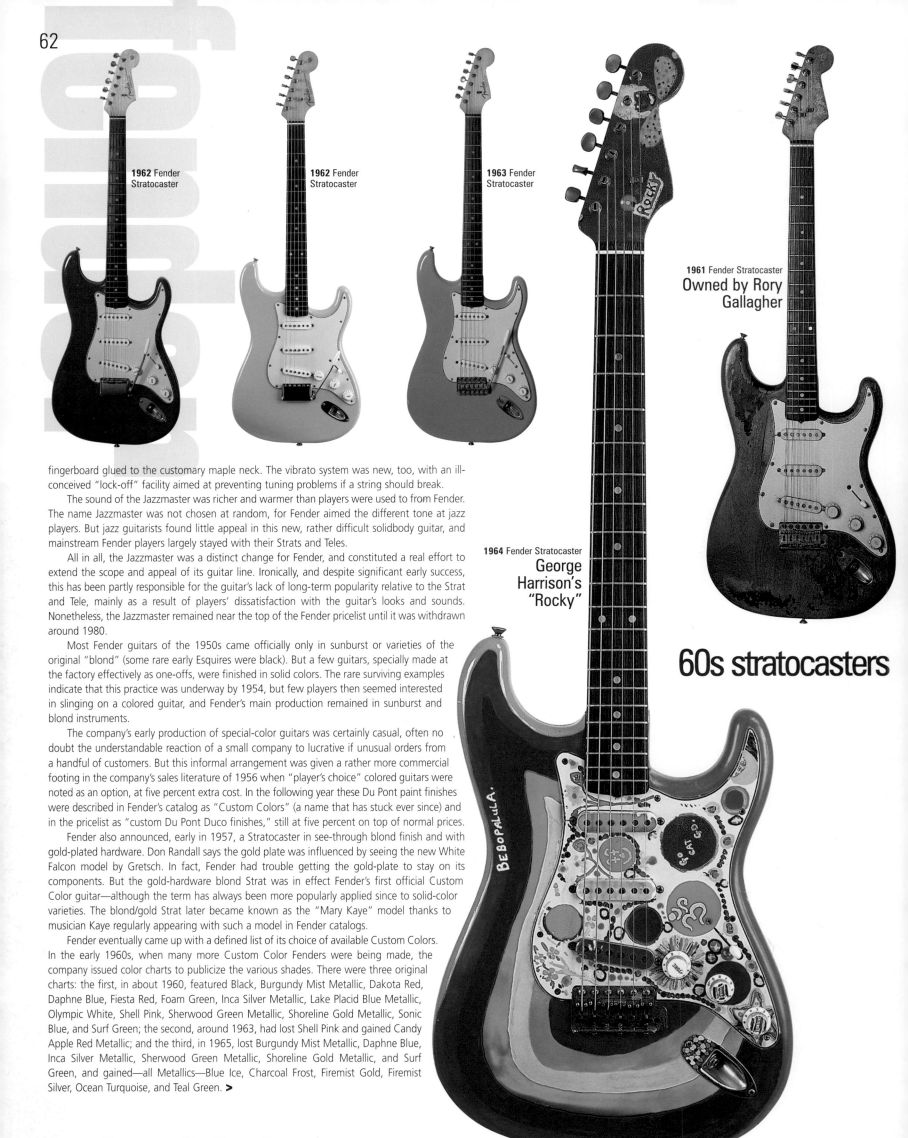

1962 Fender
Stratocaster

1962 Fender
Stratocaster

1963 Fender
Stratocaster

1961 Fender Stratocaster
Owned by Rory
Gallagher

1964 Fender Stratocaster
George
Harrison's
"Rocky"

60s stratocasters

fingerboard glued to the customary maple neck. The vibrato system was new, too, with an ill-conceived "lock-off" facility aimed at preventing tuning problems if a string should break.

The sound of the Jazzmaster was richer and warmer than players were used to from Fender. The name Jazzmaster was not chosen at random, for Fender aimed the different tone at jazz players. But jazz guitarists found little appeal in this new, rather difficult solidbody guitar, and mainstream Fender players largely stayed with their Strats and Teles.

All in all, the Jazzmaster was a distinct change for Fender, and constituted a real effort to extend the scope and appeal of its guitar line. Ironically, and despite significant early success, this has been partly responsible for the guitar's lack of long-term popularity relative to the Strat and Tele, mainly as a result of players' dissatisfaction with the guitar's looks and sounds. Nonetheless, the Jazzmaster remained near the top of the Fender pricelist until it was withdrawn around 1980.

Most Fender guitars of the 1950s came officially only in sunburst or varieties of the original "blond" (some rare early Esquires were black). But a few guitars, specially made at the factory effectively as one-offs, were finished in solid colors. The rare surviving examples indicate that this practice was underway by 1954, but few players then seemed interested in slinging on a colored guitar, and Fender's main production remained in sunburst and blond instruments.

The company's early production of special-color guitars was certainly casual, often no doubt the understandable reaction of a small company to lucrative if unusual orders from a handful of customers. But this informal arrangement was given a rather more commercial footing in the company's sales literature of 1956 when "player's choice" colored guitars were noted as an option, at five percent extra cost. In the following year these Du Pont paint finishes were described in Fender's catalog as "Custom Colors" (a name that has stuck ever since) and in the pricelist as "custom Du Pont Duco finishes," still at five percent on top of normal prices.

Fender also announced, early in 1957, a Stratocaster in see-through blond finish and with gold-plated hardware. Don Randall says the gold plate was influenced by seeing the new White Falcon model by Gretsch. In fact, Fender had trouble getting the gold-plate to stay on its components. But the gold-hardware blond Strat was in effect Fender's first official Custom Color guitar—although the term has always been more popularly applied since to solid-color varieties. The blond/gold Strat later became known as the "Mary Kaye" model thanks to musician Kaye regularly appearing with such a model in Fender catalogs.

Fender eventually came up with a defined list of its choice of available Custom Colors. In the early 1960s, when many more Custom Color Fenders were being made, the company issued color charts to publicize the various shades. There were three original charts: the first, in about 1960, featured Black, Burgundy Mist Metallic, Dakota Red, Daphne Blue, Fiesta Red, Foam Green, Inca Silver Metallic, Lake Placid Blue Metallic, Olympic White, Shell Pink, Sherwood Green Metallic, Shoreline Gold Metallic, Sonic Blue, and Surf Green; the second, around 1963, had lost Shell Pink and gained Candy Apple Red Metallic; and the third, in 1965, lost Burgundy Mist Metallic, Daphne Blue, Inca Silver Metallic, Sherwood Green Metallic, Shoreline Gold Metallic, and Surf Green, and gained—all Metallics—Blue Ice, Charcoal Frost, Firemist Gold, Firemist Silver, Ocean Turquoise, and Teal Green. **>**

fender**solidbody**

1964 Fender Stratocaster

1965 Fender Stratocaster

■ Strats from the early 1960s can be great guitars, but none are so collectable as the "custom color" models that were painted with exotic finishes such as lake placid blue and fiesta red. Jimi Hendrix made good use of a white Strat. George Harrison went so far as to decorate his Strat with psychedelic dayglo paints and nail-varnish. CBS bought Fender in 1965.

1965 Fender Stratocaster

1965 Fender Stratocaster

1968 Fender Stratocaster
One of many Strats played by Jimi Hendrix

1965 Fender Stratocaster

CBS models

1966 Fender Stratocaster

solidbodyfender

CBS period stratocasters

1979 Fender 25th
Anniversary Stratocaster

■ **Fender was on a roll in the 1970s, certainly in terms of the sheer number of instruments the company produced during that decade. The year 1979 marked the 25th anniversary of the Strat, and Fender celebrated with a curious silver-finish model that had very little to do with the original.**

1979 Fender 25th Anniversary Stratocaster

1973 Fender Stratocaste

1973 Fender Stratocaste

The automobile industry was clearly having a profound effect upon U.S. guitar manufacturers in the 1950s, not least in this ability to enhance the look of an already stylish object with a rich, sparkling paint job. Fender used paints from Du Pont's Duco nitro-cellulose lines, such as Dakota Red or Foam Green, as well as the more color-retentive Lucite acrylics like Lake Placid Blue Metallic or Burgundy Mist Metallic. Decades later the guitars bearing these original Fiesta Reds, Sonic Blues, Shoreline Golds, and the like have proved very desirable among collectors, many of whom rate a Custom Color Fender, especially an early one, as a prime catch. This is despite the prevalence of recent "refinishes" which have become so accurate that even alleged experts can occasionally be fooled into declaring fake finishes as original. Some players find it difficult to understand why collectors can pay a very high premium simply for the promise that a particular layer of paint is "original."

At Fender in the late 1950s a few cosmetic and production adjustments were made to the company's electric guitars. The Jazzmaster had been the first Fender with a rosewood fingerboard, and this material was adopted for other models around 1959. The company also altered the look of its sunburst finish at the time, adding red to give a three-tone yellow-to-red-to-black effect. By 1959 Fender employed a hundred workers in nine buildings.

The last "new" Fender electrics of the 1950s were the bound-body Custom versions of the Esquire and Telecaster, new for 1959. Forrest White got advice on the process of binding from Fred Martin, head of the leading American flat-top acoustic guitar manufacturer Martin. The Customs each listed at just $30 more than the regular unbound versions, but far fewer of these were sold.

As Fender entered the 1960s, the company boasted an extended list of products in addition to its electric guitars. The company's July 1961 pricelist, for example, noted thirteen amplifiers, five steel guitars, two pedal-steel guitars, and two bass guitars.

The next electric six-string design to leave Fender's production line was the Jaguar, which first showed up in sales material during 1962. It used a similar offset-waist body shape to the Jazzmaster, and also shared that guitar's separate bridge and vibrato unit, although the Jaguar had the addition of a spring-loaded string mute at the bridge. Fender rather optimistically believed that players of the time were so obsessed with gadgets that they would prefer a mechanical string mute to the natural edge-of-the-hand method. He was wrong. There are many elements of playing technique that simply cannot be replaced by hardware. **>**

1975 Fender Rhinstone Stratocaster

fendersolidbody

stratocaster internationals

1980 Fender The Strat

1980 Fender International Color Stratocaster

1980 Fender International Color Stratocaster

1980 Fender International Color Stratocaster

1980 Fender International Color Stratocaster

1978 Fender Stratocaster, Antigua Finish

solidbodyfender

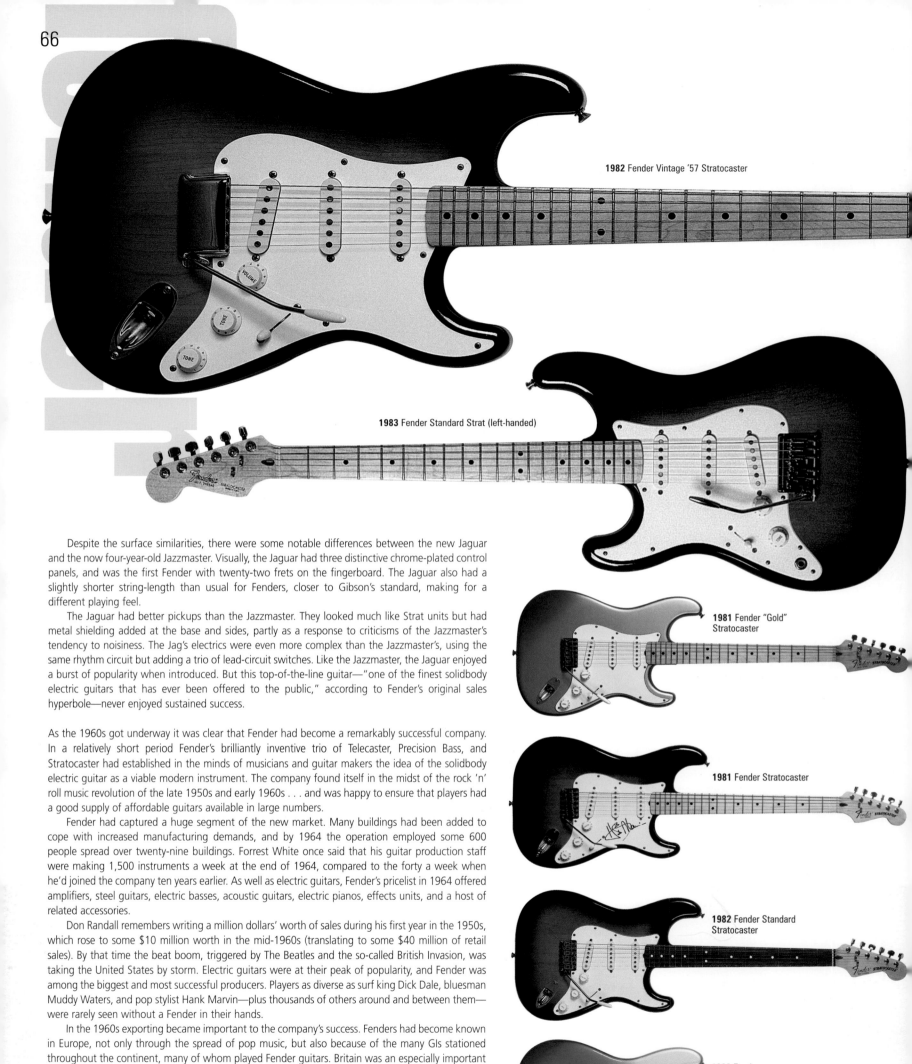

1982 Fender Vintage '57 Stratocaster

1983 Fender Standard Strat (left-handed)

1981 Fender "Gold" Stratocaster

1981 Fender Stratocaster

1982 Fender Standard Stratocaster

1983 Fender Stratocaster Elite

Despite the surface similarities, there were some notable differences between the new Jaguar and the now four-year-old Jazzmaster. Visually, the Jaguar had three distinctive chrome-plated control panels, and was the first Fender with twenty-two frets on the fingerboard. The Jaguar also had a slightly shorter string-length than usual for Fenders, closer to Gibson's standard, making for a different playing feel.

The Jaguar had better pickups than the Jazzmaster. They looked much like Strat units but had metal shielding added at the base and sides, partly as a response to criticisms of the Jazzmaster's tendency to noisiness. The Jag's electrics were even more complex than the Jazzmaster's, using the same rhythm circuit but adding a trio of lead-circuit switches. Like the Jazzmaster, the Jaguar enjoyed a burst of popularity when introduced. But this top-of-the-line guitar—"one of the finest solidbody electric guitars that has ever been offered to the public," according to Fender's original sales hyperbole—never enjoyed sustained success.

As the 1960s got underway it was clear that Fender had become a remarkably successful company. In a relatively short period Fender's brilliantly inventive trio of Telecaster, Precision Bass, and Stratocaster had established in the minds of musicians and guitar makers the idea of the solidbody electric guitar as a viable modern instrument. The company found itself in the midst of the rock 'n' roll music revolution of the late 1950s and early 1960s . . . and was happy to ensure that players had a good supply of affordable guitars available in large numbers.

Fender had captured a huge segment of the new market. Many buildings had been added to cope with increased manufacturing demands, and by 1964 the operation employed some 600 people spread over twenty-nine buildings. Forrest White once said that his guitar production staff were making 1,500 instruments a week at the end of 1964, compared to the forty a week when he'd joined the company ten years earlier. As well as electric guitars, Fender's pricelist in 1964 offered amplifiers, steel guitars, electric basses, acoustic guitars, electric pianos, effects units, and a host of related accessories.

Don Randall remembers writing a million dollars' worth of sales during his first year in the 1950s, which rose to some $10 million worth in the mid-1960s (translating to some $40 million of retail sales). By that time the beat boom, triggered by The Beatles and the so-called British Invasion, was taking the United States by storm. Electric guitars were at their peak of popularity, and Fender was among the biggest and most successful producers. Players as diverse as surf king Dick Dale, bluesman Muddy Waters, and pop stylist Hank Marvin—plus thousands of others around and between them—were rarely seen without a Fender in their hands.

In the 1960s exporting became important to the company's success. Fenders had become known in Europe, not only through the spread of pop music, but also because of the many GIs stationed throughout the continent, many of whom played Fender guitars. Britain was an especially important market in the 1960s because of the worldwide success of its pop groups. Up to the start of the 1960s it had been virtually impossible for British musicians to buy Fenders, because of a government ban

fendersolidbody

1983 Fender Standard Stratocaster

1987 Fender American Standard Stratocaster

1988 Fender '57 Stratocaster

1988 Fender Eric Clapton Stratocaster, First Version

1988 Mary Kaye Stratocaster

1988 Fender Strat XII

1988 Fender Yngwie Malmsteen Stratocaster

80s stratocasters

1989 Fender Blue Flower Stratocaster

■ Here's a selection of Strats from the 1980s, including the revised form of the regular model, named the American Standard; a couple of unusual 12-string and double-neck versions; the vintage-flavored '57 model; the Elite, with its modern appointments; and some signature models named for Eric Clapton and Yngwie Malmsteen.

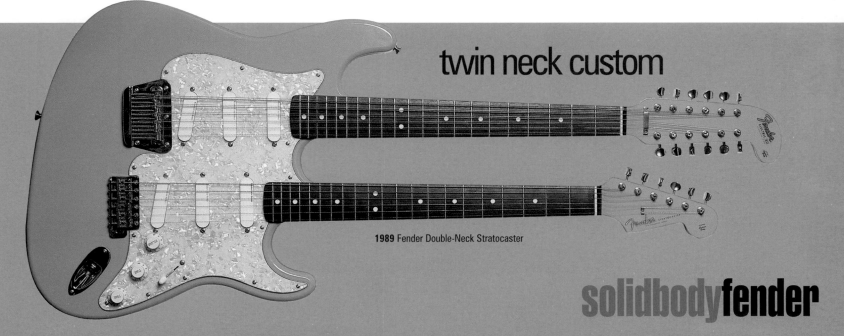

twin neck custom

1989 Fender Double-Neck Stratocaster

solidbodyfender

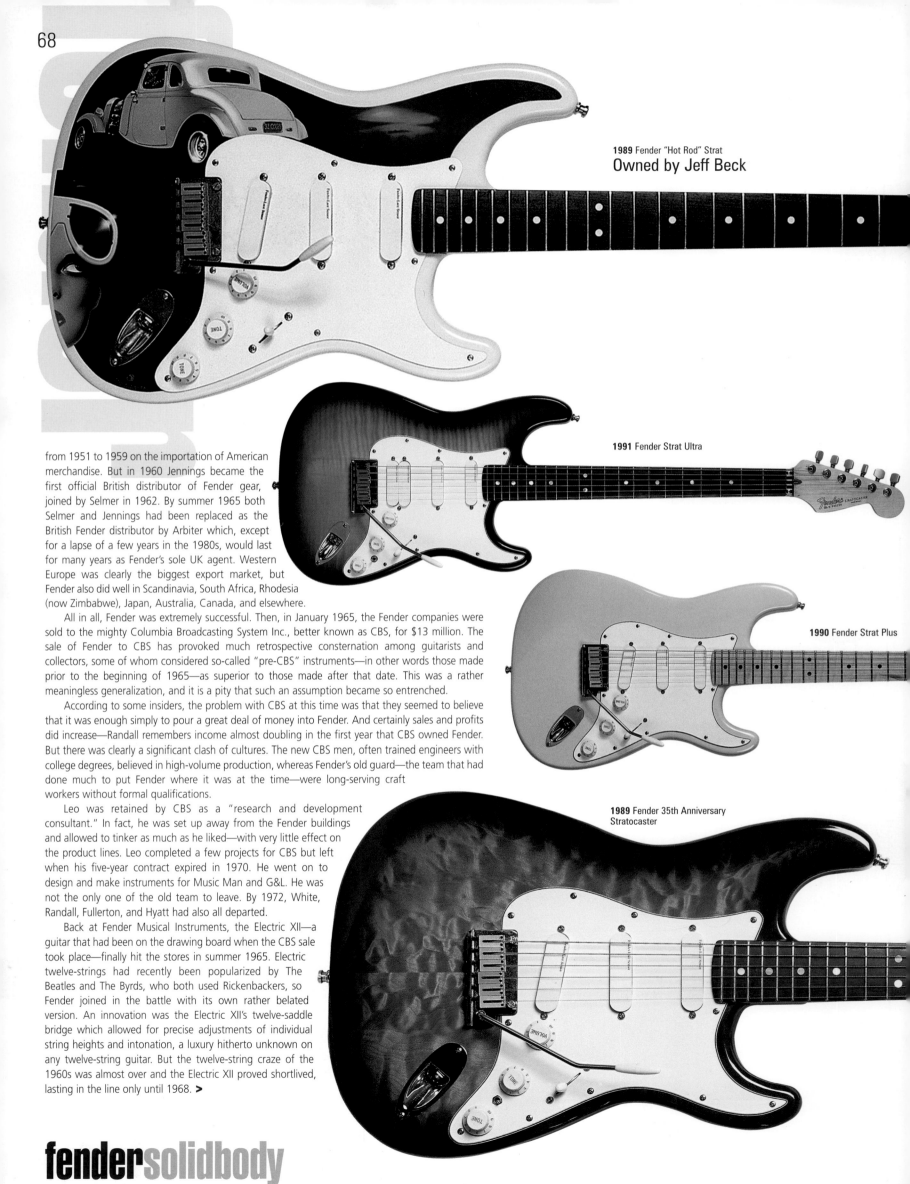

1989 Fender "Hot Rod" Strat
Owned by Jeff Beck

1991 Fender Strat Ultra

1990 Fender Strat Plus

1989 Fender 35th Anniversary
Stratocaster

from 1951 to 1959 on the importation of American merchandise. But in 1960 Jennings became the first official British distributor of Fender gear, joined by Selmer in 1962. By summer 1965 both Selmer and Jennings had been replaced as the British Fender distributor by Arbiter which, except for a lapse of a few years in the 1980s, would last for many years as Fender's sole UK agent. Western Europe was clearly the biggest export market, but Fender also did well in Scandinavia, South Africa, Rhodesia (now Zimbabwe), Japan, Australia, Canada, and elsewhere.

All in all, Fender was extremely successful. Then, in January 1965, the Fender companies were sold to the mighty Columbia Broadcasting System Inc., better known as CBS, for $13 million. The sale of Fender to CBS has provoked much retrospective consternation among guitarists and collectors, some of whom considered so-called "pre-CBS" instruments—in other words those made prior to the beginning of 1965—as superior to those made after that date. This was a rather meaningless generalization, and it is a pity that such an assumption became so entrenched.

According to some insiders, the problem with CBS at this time was that they seemed to believe that it was enough simply to pour a great deal of money into Fender. And certainly sales and profits did increase—Randall remembers income almost doubling in the first year that CBS owned Fender. But there was clearly a significant clash of cultures. The new CBS men, often trained engineers with college degrees, believed in high-volume production, whereas Fender's old guard—the team that had done much to put Fender where it was at the time—were long-serving craft workers without formal qualifications.

Leo was retained by CBS as a "research and development consultant." In fact, he was set up away from the Fender buildings and allowed to tinker as much as he liked—with very little effect on the product lines. Leo completed a few projects for CBS but left when his five-year contract expired in 1970. He went on to design and make instruments for Music Man and G&L. He was not the only one of the old team to leave. By 1972, White, Randall, Fullerton, and Hyatt had also all departed.

Back at Fender Musical Instruments, the Electric XII—a guitar that had been on the drawing board when the CBS sale took place—finally hit the stores in summer 1965. Electric twelve-strings had recently been popularized by The Beatles and The Byrds, who both used Rickenbackers, so Fender joined in the battle with its own rather belated version. An innovation was the Electric XII's twelve-saddle bridge which allowed for precise adjustments of individual string heights and intonation, a luxury hitherto unknown on any twelve-string guitar. But the twelve-string craze of the 1960s was almost over and the Electric XII proved shortlived, lasting in the line only until 1968. **>**

fendersolidbody

1990 Fender Hank Marvin Stratocaster

1991 Fender Jeff Beck Signature Strat

1992 Fender Stevie Ray Vaughan Strat

signature models

1992 Fender Seven String "Alex Gregory" Signature Strat

■ Fender made efforts in the 1990s to attract modern players to the venerable Stratocaster, adding modern hardware and pickup combinations that contemporary guitarists would expect. Not all of these efforts were successful, but Fender could always rely on signature models that publicized the Strat's popularity with players like Jeff Beck and Stevie Ray Vaughan.

1991 Fender American Standard Stratocaster

1989 Fender HLE Stratocaster

1995 Fender 40th Anniversary 1954 Stratocaster

1995 Fender Bonnie Raitt Stratocaster

1995 Fender The Moto Stratocaster

1995 Fender Foto-flame Stratocaster

1996 Fender Lone Star Strat

special edition stratocasters

1996 Fender '54 Stratocaster FMT

1998 Fender Big Apple Strat

1995 Fender Custom Shop "Art Guitar"

One of Fender's first CBS-era pricelists, dated April 1965, reveals a burgeoning line of products in addition to the company's eleven electric guitar models. The other lines included three bass guitars, six flat-top acoustic guitars, and fifteen amplifiers.

During 1966 CBS completed the construction of a new Fender factory, situated next to Fender's buildings on the South Raymond site in Fullerton, at a cost of $1.3 million. Meanwhile, some cosmetic changes were being made to various Fender models. In 1965 the Stratocaster gained a broader headstock, effectively matching that of the Jazzmaster and Jaguar. Also during 1965 the fingerboards of the Electric XII, Jaguar, and Jazzmaster were bound, while the following year the same trio was given block-shaped fingerboard inlays rather than the previous dot markers. Generally, CBS seemed to be fiddling for fiddling's sake.

A firm innovation—at least for Fender—came in the shape of a new line of hollowbody electrics. These were the first such electrics from Fender, which until this point was clearly identified in the player's mind as a solidbody producer. Evidently the strong success of Gibson's ES line of semi-solidbodies and to a lesser extent models by Gretsch and others must have tempted CBS and its search for wider markets.

German maker Roger Rossmeisl, brought into the company by Leo Fender in 1962 to design acoustic guitars, became responsible for the new electric hollowbodies. Launched in 1966, the Coronado thinline guitars were Fender's first Rossmeisl electric designs to appear and, despite their conventional, equal-double-cutaway, bound bodies with large, stylized f-holes, they employed the standard Fender bolt-on neck and headstock design. Options included a

fendersolidbody

1993 Fender Harley-Davidson 90th Anniversary Commemorative Strat

1996 Fender 50th Anniversary Stratocaster

1996 Fender '60 Stratocaster

1996 Fender '62 Stratocaster

1997 Fender Jimi Hendrix Monterey Strat

■ The Stratocaster has been an outstandingly successful guitar since its birth in the mid-1950s. Many solidbody electric instruments have been made by competing companies. Yet still the Strat appears as appealing as ever to modern guitarists, and still the legacy of Jimi Hendrix lives on, apparently as much through his use of a Fender Strat as through his remarkable music.

1998 Fender Strat Big Apple

1997 Fender Jimi Hendrix Strat (left-handed)

solidbodyfender

1997 Fender
Relic Stratocaster

1998 Fender Relic
'60s Stratocaster

2001 Fender Highway
One Stratocaster HSS

2007 Fender Rory Gallagher
Tribute Stratocaster

new vibrato tailpiece, and there was also a twelve-string version that borrowed the Electric XII's "hockey-stick" headstock. Rossmeisl was also on the team that came up with a lightweight version of the Tele in 1968. The Thinline Telecaster had three hollowed-out cavities inside the body and a modified pickguard shaped to accommodate the single, token f-hole. It was also around this time—and quite apart from Fender—that Byrds guitarist Clarence White and drummer Gene Parsons came up with their "shoulder strap control" B-string-pull device that fitted into a Telecaster. It was designed to offer string-bends within chords to emulate pedal-steel-type sounds.

Rossmeisl was let loose with a couple of guitar designs that were even less like the normal run of Fenders than the Coronado models had been. Rossmeisl's specialty was the so-called "German carve" taught to him by his guitar-making father. This applies a distinctive "dished" dip around the top edge of the body, following its outline. Rossmeisl adopted this feature for the new hollowbody arch-top electric Montego and LTD models, all eminently traditional but still obstinately using Fender's customary bolt-on neck. From all reports there were very few of these made, and the models are rarely seen today.

Toward the end of the 1960s came firm evidence that CBS was trying to wring every last drop of potential income from unused Fender factory stock that would otherwise have been written off. Two shortlived guitars, the Custom and the Swinger, were assembled from these leftovers.

As the close of the 1960s loomed, Fender took a boost when an inspired guitarist by the name of Jimi Hendrix applied the Stratocaster's sensuous curves and glorious tone to his live cavorting and studio experiments. Salesman Dale Hyatt once said—only half-jokingly, one suspects—that Hendrix caused more Stratocasters to be sold than all the Fender salesmen put together.

Although George Harrison and John Lennon had each acquired a Stratocaster in 1965 for studio use, and Paul McCartney bought an Esquire a year or two later, the public face of

1997 Fender John
Jorgensen Hellecaster

fender**solidbody**

1956 Fender Musicmaster

1960 Fender Perspex Duo-sonic

1956 Fender Duo-sonic

2007 Fender American VG Stratocaster

■ The Stratocaster may still be a valid choice for the guitarist of today, and yet back in the 1950s Fender had to produce new models to offer a full range for its dealers to sell to players of all levels of ability and affluence. The Musicmaster and Duo-Sonic were originally aimed at students starting their affair with the electric guitar.

1997 Fender Carved Top Stratocaster

solidbodyfender

1960 Fender Jazzmaster

1960 Fender Jazzmaster

1960 Fender Jazzmaster

1961 Fender Jazzmaster

1961 Fender Jazzmaster

1961 Fender Jazzmaster

The Beatles remained distinctly Fenderless, which led Don Randall to try to persuade manager Brian Epstein to get his boys into Fender. Probably during 1969, Randall managed to secure a meeting with Lennon and McCartney in London. The results were the band's Fender-Rhodes pianos, a Jazz Bass, and a VI six-string bass, as well as Harrison's Rosewood Telecaster—all visible at various times during the *Let It Be* movie.

The 1970s are believed by many to be the poorest years of Fender's production history, and there can be little doubt that quality control slipped as more low-standard Fenders were made. But some fine Fenders were made in the 1970s as well. During the decade, however, CBS cut back on the Fender product lines and offered hardly any new models. The last Esquire of the period was made in 1970, the year in which the Duo-Sonic also died. The Jaguar disappeared around 1975, and by 1980 the Bronco, Jazzmaster, Musicmaster, and Thinline Tele had all been taken out of production.

So it was that by the start of the 1980s the guitarist who wanted to buy a new Fender electric had little choice beyond the company's ever-reliable Strats and Teles. And apart from a few shortlived exceptions, these came mostly in sunburst, blond, black, or natural. It was hard to resist the feeling that the newly-important calculations of the balance sheet had become firmly established at Fender and had taken precedence over the company's former creativity. A few new electric models were introduced in the 1970s, but mostly these were variations on familiar themes. Part of Fender's distinction had come from using bright-sounding single-coil pickups; the warmer, fatter-sounding humbucking types were always considered then as a Gibson mainstay. Nonetheless, in keeping with changing market trends, the Telecaster was given a humbucking pickup at the neck position to create the Telecaster Custom in 1972, and similar dabbling led to a sort of Tele-meets-Strat-meets-Gibson: the two-humbucker, Strat-necked Telecaster Deluxe of 1973.

The company made another attempt at thinline hollowbody electrics in 1976 with the ill-fated, shortlived Starcaster, again aimed at competing with Gibson's ever-popular ES line.

By 1976 Fender had a five-acre facility under one roof in Fullerton and employed over 750 workers. Some new "student" models appeared at this time to replace the Musicmaster, Bronco, Duo-Sonic, and Mustang. The Lead I and Lead II guitars of 1979 were simple double-cutaway solids, but not especially cheap at $399. They were followed by the single-cutaway Bullet series which began production in 1981. Fender did briefly attempt to have these models produced in Korea, to eliminate tooling costs, but after a number of problems manufacturing resumed at home.

In the early 1980s the CBS management appears to have decided that Fender needed some new blood to help reverse the decline in the company's fortunes. During 1981 key personnel were recruited from the American musical instrument operation of

1958 Fender Jazzmaster Prototype

1959 Fender Jazzmaster

1959 Fender Jazzmaster

fendersolidbody

1962 Fender Jazzmaster

1962 Fender Jazzmaster

1962 Fender Jazzmaster

1962 Fender Jazzmaster

1963 Fender Jazzmaster

1963 Fender Jazzmaster

jazzmasters

1963 Fender Jazzmaster

1966 Fender Jazzmaster

2008 Fender Jazzmaster

■ With the Telecaster and Stratocaster in place, Fender wanted a new top-of the-line model, and in 1958 launched the Jazzmaster. It had a new offset-waist body, a control layout with a separate rhythm circuit, a floating vibrato system, and the first appearance of a rosewood fingerboard on a Fender guitar.

solidbodyfender

1959 Fender Jaguar

1964 Fender Jaguar

1966 Fender Jaguar

1966 Fender Jaguar

1960 Fender Jaguar

jaguars

the giant Japanese company Yamaha, including John McLaren, Bill Schultz, and Dan Smith. It appeared that they were brought in to turn around the reputation of Fender and make a profit once again. One of the new team's recommendations was to start alternative production of Fenders in Japan, to combat orientally produced copies. A joint venture was officially established in March 1982.

In the United States the new management team was working on a strategy to return Fender to its former glory. The plan was for Fender in effect to copy itself, by recreating the 1950s and 1960s guitars that many players and collectors were spending large sums of money to acquire. The result was the Vintage reissue series, consisting of a maple-neck "57" and rosewood-fingerboard "62" Strat, as well as a "52" Telecaster. These Vintage reproductions were not exact enough for some die-hard Fender collectors, but generally the guitars were praised and welcomed. Production of the Vintage reissues was planned to start in 1982 at Fender U.S. (Fullerton) and at Fender Japan (Fujigen). But changes being instituted at the American factory meant that the U.S. versions did not come on-stream until early 1983. Fender Japan's guitars at this stage were being made only for the internal Japanese market, but Fender's European agents were putting pressure on the Fullerton management for a low-end Fender to compete with the multitude of exported models being sold in Europe and elsewhere by other Japanese manufacturers.

So Fender Japan made some less costly versions of the Vintage reissues for European distribution in 1982, with the Squier brand. At the end of 1983, with the U.S. factory still not up to the scale of production the team wanted, Fender Japan also built a Squier Stratocaster for the American market. This instrument, together with the earlier Squier Stratocasters and Telecasters, saw the start of the sale of Fender Japan products around the world, and a move by Fender to become an international guitar manufacturer.

A shortlived pair from the U.S. factory at this time were the Elite Stratocaster and Elite Telecaster, intended as radical new high-end versions of the old faithfuls. Unfortunately the vibrato-equipped Elite Strat came saddled with a terrible bridge. In-fighting at Fender had led to last-minute modifications of the vibrato design, and the result was an unwieldy, unworkable piece of hardware. The Elite Strat also featured three pushbuttons for pickup selection, which were not to the taste of players brought up on the classic Fender pickup switch. There were good points—the new pickups, the effective active circuitry, and an improved truss-rod design—but they tended to be overlooked and the Elites were dropped by the end of 1984.

Three new-design Fender lines were introduced in 1984, made by Fender Japan and intended to compete with some of Gibson's popular models. The overall name for the new instruments was the Master Series, encompassing electric arch-top D'Aquisto models, with design input from American luthier Jimmy D'Aquisto, and semi-solid Esprit and Flame guitars. Significantly, they were the first Fender Japan products with the Fender rather than Squier headstock logo to be sold officially outside Japan, and the first Fenders with set-necks. Their overtly Gibson image was to be their undoing. Most players wanted recognizable Fenders from Fender.

In the mid-1980s CBS decided that it had finally had enough of this part of the music business, and wished to sell Fender Musical Instruments. It invited offers and at the end of January 1985, almost exactly twenty years since acquiring it, CBS confirmed that it would sell Fender to an investor group led by Bill Schultz, then president of Fender Musical Instruments. The contract was completed in March 1985 for $12.5 million. It's interesting to compare this with the $13 million that CBS

1961 Fender VI

1964 Fender Mustang

1965 Fender Marauder

■ The Jaguar was Fender's next attempt at a model above the Stratocaster in features and price. It was based on the Jazzmaster but had more complex controls, and its twenty-two frets on a shorter neck made for easier playing. Oddities at the time included a six-string bass, the VI, and an electric twelve-string, the XII.

1966 Fender Electric XII

1966 Fender Electric XII

twelve-strings

1965 Fender Electric XII

solidbodyfender

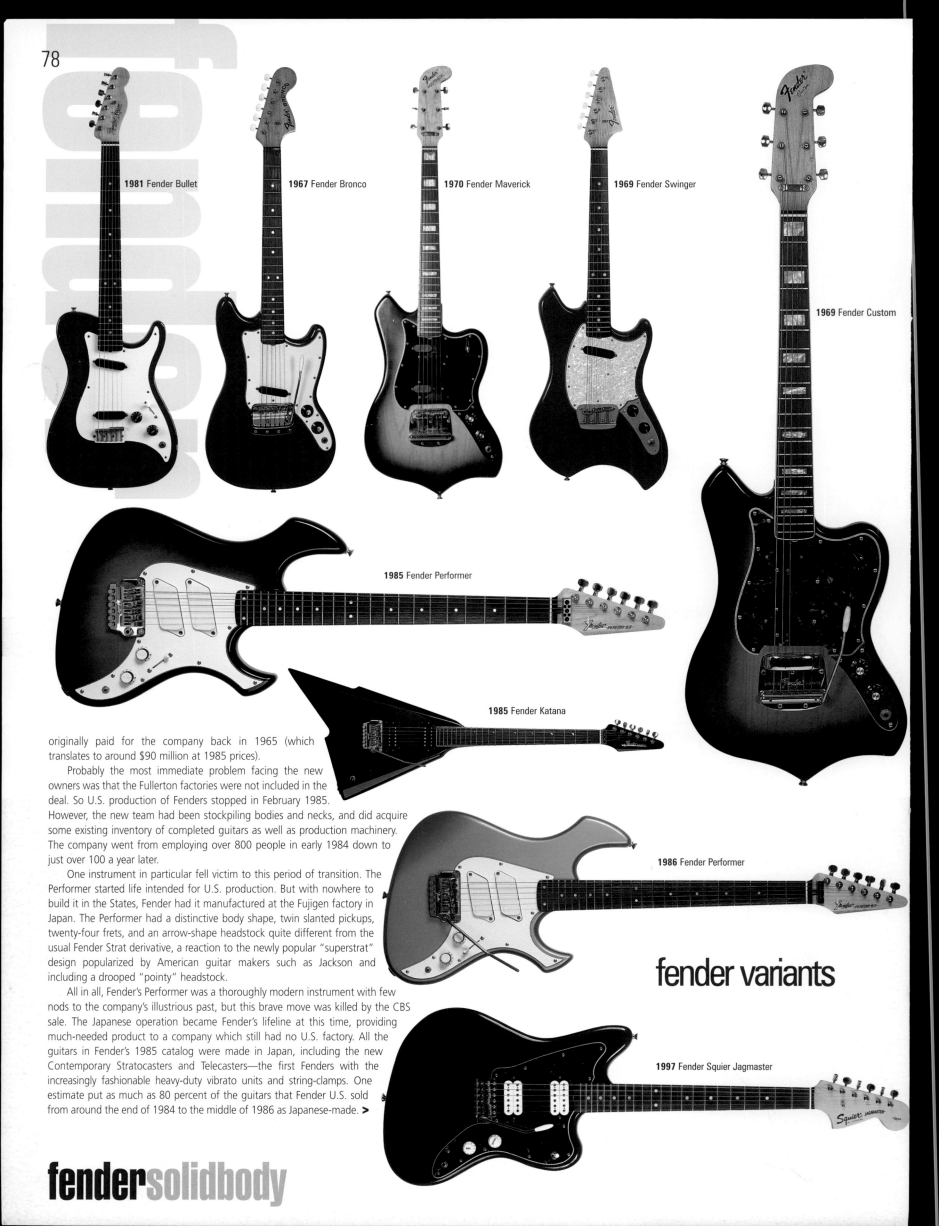

1981 Fender Bullet

1967 Fender Bronco

1970 Fender Maverick

1969 Fender Swinger

1969 Fender Custom

1985 Fender Performer

1985 Fender Katana

originally paid for the company back in 1965 (which translates to around $90 million at 1985 prices).

Probably the most immediate problem facing the new owners was that the Fullerton factories were not included in the deal. So U.S. production of Fenders stopped in February 1985. However, the new team had been stockpiling bodies and necks, and did acquire some existing inventory of completed guitars as well as production machinery. The company went from employing over 800 people in early 1984 down to just over 100 a year later.

One instrument in particular fell victim to this period of transition. The Performer started life intended for U.S. production. But with nowhere to build it in the States, Fender had it manufactured at the Fujigen factory in Japan. The Performer had a distinctive body shape, twin slanted pickups, twenty-four frets, and an arrow-shape headstock quite different from the usual Fender Strat derivative, a reaction to the newly popular "superstrat" design popularized by American guitar makers such as Jackson and including a drooped "pointy" headstock.

All in all, Fender's Performer was a thoroughly modern instrument with few nods to the company's illustrious past, but this brave move was killed by the CBS sale. The Japanese operation became Fender's lifeline at this time, providing much-needed product to a company which still had no U.S. factory. All the guitars in Fender's 1985 catalog were made in Japan, including the new Contemporary Stratocasters and Telecasters—the first Fenders with the increasingly fashionable heavy-duty vibrato units and string-clamps. One estimate put as much as 80 percent of the guitars that Fender U.S. sold from around the end of 1984 to the middle of 1986 as Japanese-made. **>**

1986 Fender Performer

fender variants

1997 Fender Squier Jagmaster

fender**solidbody**

1991 Fender Prodigy II

1997 Fender Champ

1998 Fender Cyclone

1998 Fender Tornado

2004 Fender Tornado

■ Beyond the well-known Telecasters and Stratocasters, Fender has made many other models over the years: a few were successful but many soon left the catalogue. Around 1970, the Custom, Maverick, and Swinger simply used up leftover parts from other models. Fender's budget Squier brand first appeared in the early 1980s.

2005 Fender Showmaster Elite

1997 Fender Squier Supersonic

hybrids

1996 Fender Jagstang (left-handed)

1997 Fender Venus

solidbodyfender

1968 Fender Thinline
Telecaster

1969 Fender Thinline
Telecaster

1971 Fender Thinline
Telecaster

telecaster thinlines

1991 Fender HMT Acoustic Electric

1976 Fender Starcaster

1966 Fender Wildwood
Coronado II

semi-solid models

1966 Fender Coronado XII

1968 Fender Wildwood
Coronado XII

Fender finally established its new factory at Corona, about twenty miles east of the defunct Fullerton site. Production started on a very limited scale toward the end of 1985. But Dan Smith and his colleagues wanted to reestablish the U.S. side of Fender's production with some good, basic Strats and Teles that would be seen as a continuation of the best of Fender's American traditions. That plan translated into the American Standard models: the Strat version was launched in 1986; the Tele followed two years later.

The American Standard was an efficacious piece of reinterpretation. It drew from the best of the original Stratocaster but was updated with a flatter-camber twenty-two-fret neck and a revised vibrato unit based on twin stud pivot points. Once the Corona plant's production lines reached full speed, the American Standard Stratocaster proved extremely successful for the revitalized Fender operation. By the early 1990s, the instrument was a best seller, notching up some 25,000 sales annually. In many markets today, including the United States, the American Standard Stratocasters and Telecasters remain the best-selling U.S.-made Fender models.

In 1987 the Fender Custom Shop was established at the Corona plant, enabling Fender to fulfill special orders for players who had the money and the inclination. The Shop's activities effectively divide into the one-offs, or Master Built guitars—instruments made by one person with acute attention to detail and a price to match—the limited, numbered-run editions; and a general line of "catalog" models which it calls Stock Team.

Signature instruments now form an important part of the Fender line. Some are made in the Custom Shop, others at the Corona factory or further afield, and each one is generally endowed with features favored by the named artist, from Jeff Beck, Eric Clapton, and Stevie Ray Vaughan, to Jimi Hendrix, Dick Dale, and Waylon Jennings.

In 1988 the Custom Shop produced the 40th Anniversary Telecaster, its first limited-edition production run. At that time most players and collectors (and Fender itself) believed that the first Broadcaster/Telecaster had been produced in 1948, hence the timing of the anniversary model. John Page, head of Fender's Custom Shop, says that it took some eighteen months to build the full edition of 300 guitars—and then many Fender dealers were upset because the company only made 300. So the Shop's next limited run, the HLE Stratocaster (Haynes Limited Edition), was upped to 500 units.

fender semi-solidbody

1971 Fender Thinline Telecaster

1972 Fender Thinline Telecaster

1996 Fender D'Aquisto
Custom Ultra

1997 Fender D'Aquisto
Deluxe

1968 Fender
Montego II

1968 Fender LTD

■ While best known for solidbody electric guitars and basses,
Fender has dabbled with hollowbody electrics over the years.
Some, like the Thinline Telecaster, simply had hollow chambers
within a regular solid body, while others, such as the rare
Montego and the models made in collaboration with luthier
Jimmy D'Aquisto, were fully hollow "jazz boxes."

2000 Fender D'Aquisto
Classic Rocker

1963 Fender Palomino

semi-solidbodyfender

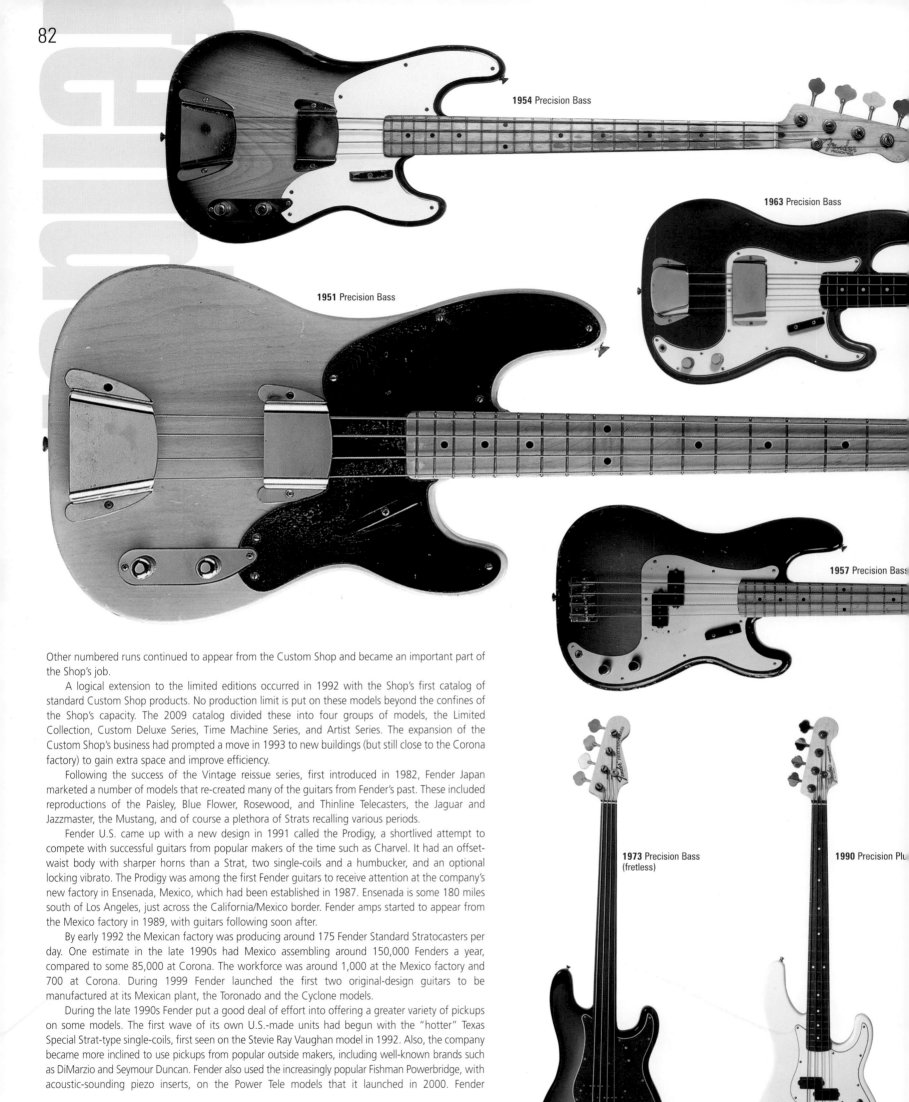

1954 Precision Bass

1963 Precision Bass

1951 Precision Bass

1957 Precision Bass

1973 Precision Bass (fretless)

1990 Precision Plus

Other numbered runs continued to appear from the Custom Shop and became an important part of the Shop's job.

A logical extension to the limited editions occurred in 1992 with the Shop's first catalog of standard Custom Shop products. No production limit is put on these models beyond the confines of the Shop's capacity. The 2009 catalog divided these into four groups of models, the Limited Collection, Custom Deluxe Series, Time Machine Series, and Artist Series. The expansion of the Custom Shop's business had prompted a move in 1993 to new buildings (but still close to the Corona factory) to gain extra space and improve efficiency.

Following the success of the Vintage reissue series, first introduced in 1982, Fender Japan marketed a number of models that re-created many of the guitars from Fender's past. These included reproductions of the Paisley, Blue Flower, Rosewood, and Thinline Telecasters, the Jaguar and Jazzmaster, the Mustang, and of course a plethora of Strats recalling various periods.

Fender U.S. came up with a new design in 1991 called the Prodigy, a shortlived attempt to compete with successful guitars from popular makers of the time such as Charvel. It had an offset-waist body with sharper horns than a Strat, two single-coils and a humbucker, and an optional locking vibrato. The Prodigy was among the first Fender guitars to receive attention at the company's new factory in Ensenada, Mexico, which had been established in 1987. Ensenada is some 180 miles south of Los Angeles, just across the California/Mexico border. Fender amps started to appear from the Mexico factory in 1989, with guitars following soon after.

By early 1992 the Mexican factory was producing around 175 Fender Standard Stratocasters per day. One estimate in the late 1990s had Mexico assembling around 150,000 Fenders a year, compared to some 85,000 at Corona. The workforce was around 1,000 at the Mexico factory and 700 at Corona. During 1999 Fender launched the first two original-design guitars to be manufactured at its Mexican plant, the Toronado and the Cyclone models.

During the late 1990s Fender put a good deal of effort into offering a greater variety of pickups on some models. The first wave of its own U.S.-made units had begun with the "hotter" Texas Special Strat-type single-coils, first seen on the Stevie Ray Vaughan model in 1992. Also, the company became more inclined to use pickups from popular outside makers, including well-known brands such as DiMarzio and Seymour Duncan. Fender also used the increasingly popular Fishman Powerbridge, with acoustic-sounding piezo inserts, on the Power Tele models that it launched in 2000. Fender

fenderbass

■ The 1951 Fender Precision Bass, or "P Bass," was the first commercial solidbody electric bass guitar. Six years later, Fender settled on the style we now recognize as the modern Precision. Various revised versions ensued, but there remains a strong appeal in the "retro" style of an original or reissue Precision.

1992 Jamerson Tribute Precision Bass

1966 Precision Bass

precision basses

1998 American Vintage '62 Precision Bass

1997 Precision Bass

2006 Classic Series '50s Precision Bass

2008 Time Machine '59 Precision Bass

jazz basses

1960 Fender Jazz Bass

1961 Fender Jazz Bass

1990 Fender Jazz Plus V

manufactures some of its own pickups at the Fender Mexico plant for use on guitars assembled there. This includes not just single-coil units, but also humbuckers—and so it seemed to Fender an obvious move to develop and make humbuckers at Corona. The first guitars with Fender's new U.S.-made humbuckers were the California "Fat" models of 1997: the Fat Strat had a bridge humbucker while the Fat Tele came with a neck humbucker.

In the mid-1990s Fender began again to revisit one of its favorite locations: the past. A common request from some artists was for the Custom Shop to make them a replica of a favorite old guitar, usually because the original was too valuable to risk taking on the road. After Keith Richards told the Shop that some replicas made for him for a Stones tour looked too new ("bash 'em up a bit and I'll play 'em") the Shop began to include wear-and-tear distress marks to replicate the overall look of a battered old original. Then Master Builder J.W. Black came up with the idea of offering these aged replicas as standard Custom Shop catalog items, called Relics.

The Shop made two aged 1950s-era samples: a Nocaster (the in-between Broadcaster/Telecaster with no model name) and a "Mary Kaye" Strat (blond body, gold-plated parts). Soon the Custom Shop was reacting to the demand generated from these samples by offering a line of three Relic Strats and a Relic Nocaster. The Relics have proved remarkably successful and the line has expanded.

The Custom Shop has since reorganized the line and offered three types of "re-creations" in a renamed Time Machine series. First, the N.O.S.—"New Old Stock"—guitars were pristine replicas produced as close as possible to original brand-new instruments that would have come off the Fender production line during the particular period concerned. Next, the Closet Classics are meant to be like guitars bought new years ago, played a bit, and shoved under the bed or in a closet. Third is the Relic style, with "aged" knocks and wear added by the Shop.

The Time Machine guitars, and particularly the Relics, are the nearest that Fender has got in new instruments to the almost indefinable appeal of vintage guitars, something that most modern manufacturers—and certainly most collectors—had thought was firmly locked away in the past.

Meanwhile there were truly new guitars. Well . . . almost new guitars. In Nirvana, Kurt Cobain played his favored left-hand Fender Jaguar (a modified '65 sunburst) as well as a Mustang. Around 1993, he cut up some photos of the two guitars, sticking them together and trying out different combinations. Larry Brooks in Fender's Custom Shop was given the paste-ups and asked to create a design for a new instrument, which Cobain played. Following his untimely death in 1994, Cobain's family collaborated with Fender to release a production version, by that time named the Fender Jag-Stang. The model hit the market in 1996 but has been on pricelists only intermittently since then.

In November 1998 Fender opened a new factory, still in Corona, California. The

1999 Fender Jaco Pastorius Jazz Bass

1999 Fender Jaco Pastorius Tribute Jazz Bass

fenderbass

1960 Fender Jazz Bass

■ Fender's dynamic bass duo was completed in 1960 with the launch of the Jazz Bass, with a different playing feel than the Precision and a fuller tone available from the new pickups and control system. Fender followed trends with a modern five-string Jazz, and the best known player of the instrument, Jaco Pastorius, has been honored with signature models.

1964 Fender Jazz Bass

1977 Fender Jazz
Owned—and modified—by Marcus Miller

1977 Fender Jazz Bass

1964 Fender Jazz Bass

1966 Fender Jazz Bass

bassfender

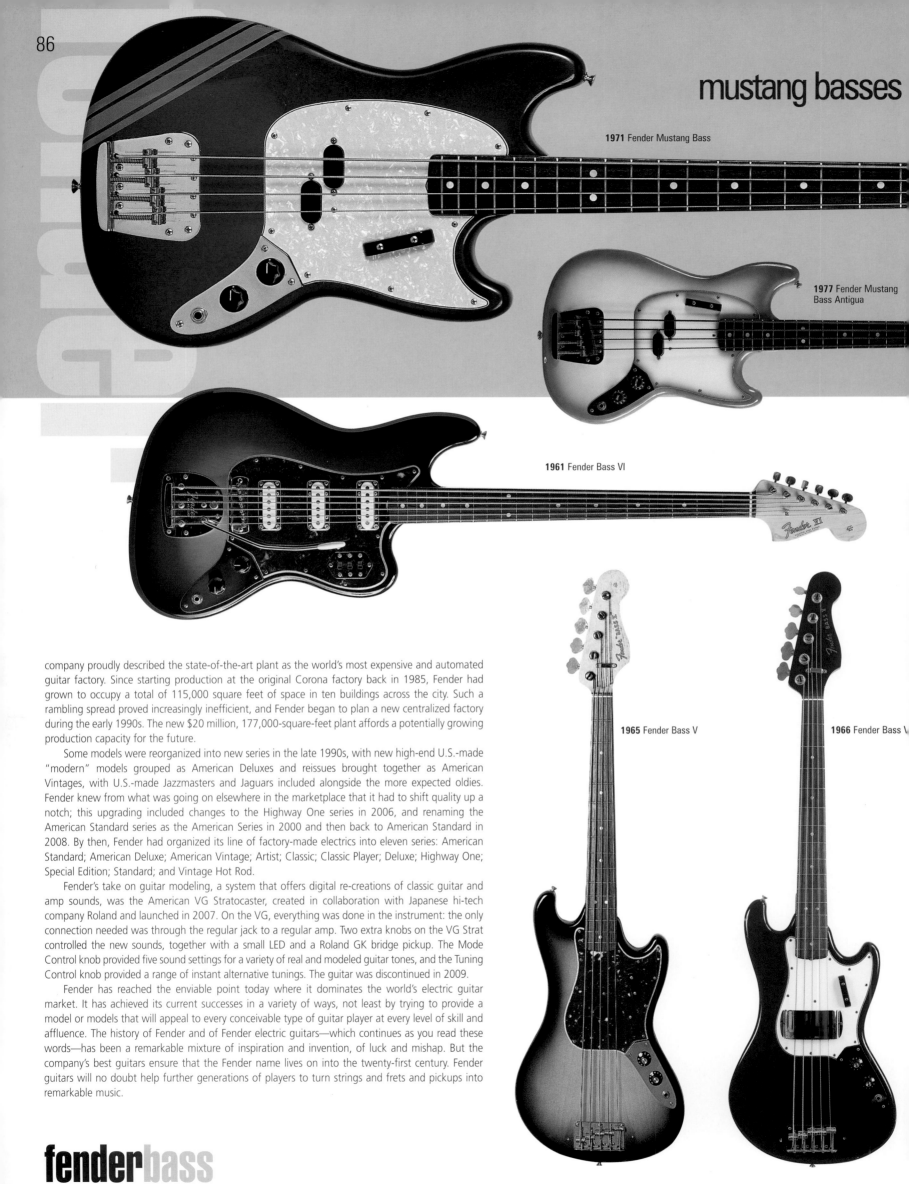

mustang basses

1971 Fender Mustang Bass

1977 Fender Mustang Bass Antigua

1961 Fender Bass VI

1965 Fender Bass V

1966 Fender Bass V

company proudly described the state-of-the-art plant as the world's most expensive and automated guitar factory. Since starting production at the original Corona factory back in 1985, Fender had grown to occupy a total of 115,000 square feet of space in ten buildings across the city. Such a rambling spread proved increasingly inefficient, and Fender began to plan a new centralized factory during the early 1990s. The new $20 million, 177,000-square-feet plant affords a potentially growing production capacity for the future.

Some models were reorganized into new series in the late 1990s, with new high-end U.S.-made "modern" models grouped as American Deluxes and reissues brought together as American Vintages, with U.S.-made Jazzmasters and Jaguars included alongside the more expected oldies. Fender knew from what was going on elsewhere in the marketplace that it had to shift quality up a notch; this upgrading included changes to the Highway One series in 2006, and renaming the American Standard series as the American Series in 2000 and then back to American Standard in 2008. By then, Fender had organized its line of factory-made electrics into eleven series: American Standard; American Deluxe; American Vintage; Artist; Classic; Classic Player; Deluxe; Highway One; Special Edition; Standard; and Vintage Hot Rod.

Fender's take on guitar modeling, a system that offers digital re-creations of classic guitar and amp sounds, was the American VG Stratocaster, created in collaboration with Japanese hi-tech company Roland and launched in 2007. On the VG, everything was done in the instrument: the only connection needed was through the regular jack to a regular amp. Two extra knobs on the VG Strat controlled the new sounds, together with a small LED and a Roland GK bridge pickup. The Mode Control knob provided five sound settings for a variety of real and modeled guitar tones, and the Tuning Control knob provided a range of instant alternative tunings. The guitar was discontinued in 2009.

Fender has reached the enviable point today where it dominates the world's electric guitar market. It has achieved its current successes in a variety of ways, not least by trying to provide a model or models that will appeal to every conceivable type of guitar player at every level of skill and affluence. The history of Fender and of Fender electric guitars—which continues as you read these words—has been a remarkable mixture of inspiration and invention, of luck and mishap. But the company's best guitars ensure that the Fender name lives on into the twenty-first century. Fender guitars will no doubt help further generations of players to turn strings and frets and pickups into remarkable music.

fenderbass

1973 Fender
Mustang Bass

1966 Fender
Mustang Bass

1969 Fender
Mustang Bass

1968 Fender Telecaster Bass

1972 Fender
Telecaster Bass

1968 Fender
Telecaster Bass

telecaster basses

■ Not many players venture further than a
Precision or Jazz Bass from Fender, but the
company has produced a number of other
models, including a strange and shortlived five-
string, the V, and the Telecaster Bass, originally
a reissue of the early-style Precision.

1995 Fender Stu Hamm Urge Signature

1982 Fender Squier Vintage
Series '62 Jazz Bass

bassfender

1956 Fernandez

1983 Paul Fischer

1973 Fernandez

■ **FENTON-WEILL** Previously known as Burns-Weill, this British brand began in 1960, when Jim Burns left Henry Weill to set up his own company. Henry decided to continue and compete with his former partner via a range of solids and semis produced until 1966. Weill also supplied instruments to various UK distributors, including Dallas, Hohner, and Rose-Morris.

■ **FERNANDES** Dating from 1969, Fernandes is now Japan's major guitar manufacturer. Over the next three decades, imitation gave way to more original design ideas, including the Sustainer solids introduced during the 1990s, which incorporate an electro-magnetic system to supply indefinite sustain at any volume. These and more conventional alternatives appear alongside models bearing partner brand Burny.

■ **FERNANDEZ** Arcángel Fernández (born 1931) was apprenticed to Marcelo Barbero in Madrid, Spain, in 1954. Following Barbero's death, in 1956, his widow asked Fernández to finish some guitars, including this one, under the label "Viuda [widow] de Marcelo Barbero, constructor Arcángel Fernández." Fernández later produced guitars under his own name.

■ **FISCHER** Paul Fischer (born 1951), of Chipping Norton, Oxfordshire, England, is one of Britain's most esteemed luthiers. He began his career as an instrument maker in 1956, building harpsichords and clavichords. Later he joined the guitar maker David Rubio, building a wide range of instruments, before leaving to establish his own studio in 1975. Here he has concentrated on classical guitars, many using his own "taut" system, which replaces the traditional fan-strutting of the top with a grid design for greater projection. But he has also built replicas of baroque and nineteenth-century instruments, as well as contemporary guitars with up to ten strings. An exemplary craftsman, he is very interested in unconventional woods, and has traveled to the Brazilian rain forest to pursue his researches.

■ **FLETA** Ignacio Fleta (1897–1977) was one of the greatest classical guitar makers of the twentieth century. Trained as a maker of violins, cellos, and other stringed instruments, he dedicated himself to classical guitar in 1955 after hearing Segovia, who was to become his most celebrated customer. Later Fleta enthusiasts would include Alexandre Lagoya, John Williams, Jorge Morel, Ichiro Suzuki, and Carlos Bonell. Working from his tiny apartment in Barcelona, Spain, for many years, he built no more than twenty guitars a year. They are notable for their unusual method of construction—he built the body first before attaching the neck with a kind of dovetail joint—their distinctive strutting pattern, and their slightly plump look, due to broader dimensions in the waist and upper bout. In the 1960s Fleta began using soundboards in western red cedar, as introduced by Ramírez in Madrid. He was joined by his sons Francisco and Gabriel in the 1960s, and the firm became known as Ignacio Fleta y Hijos (sons). They continued the tradition after their father's death.

■ **FODERA** Having previously worked for Ken Smith, Vinnie Fodera and Joey Lauricella set up their own bass-making company in 1983, located in Brooklyn, New York. Fodera instruments, such as this six-string Anthony Jackson signature model, target the non-traditional bass player.

fenton-weill solidbody

1962 Fenton-Weill Triplemaster

1993 Fernandes FR5S

1989 Fodera Jackson Contrabass

■ The guitars featured here are by the small 1960s British brand Fenton-Weill; three classical makers, Fernandez, Fischer, and Fleta; the big Japanese manufacturer Fernandes; and Fodera, a bass specialist located in New York City.

1945 Fleta Jazz Guitar

1954 Fleta Classical

1975 Fleta Classical

solidbodyfodera

1959 Framus
Holywood 5/132

1965 Framus Strato
Deluxe 5/168

1975 Framus
Nashville

1974 Framus
Super Yob

1965 Framus
Melodie

1963 Framus 5/98 King

1965 Framus Smallbody

■ **FRAMUS** Derived from the company name, Frankische Musikindustrie, Framus has been a prominent German brand since Fred Wilfer set up shop in 1946. The Framus factory was initially located in the Erlangen area, but a move to Bubenreuth in 1954 coincided with the introduction of the first Framus electric guitars.

The catalogue continued to grow and the Star bass was added in 1956. The Hollywood semi-solid six-strings arrived two years later, but in 1963 this line was replaced by the fully solid, Fender-flavored Strato series. The latter's styling ideas also extended to various Framus semis and basses of the time.

Framus's popularity peaked during the 1960s and the catalogue expanded, as did production. At one point it had the largest guitar factory in Europe. The next decade brought increasing Far Eastern competition and Framus fought back via its own copy range, updated designs, and a few all-new instruments.

Despite these efforts, sales declined and the company officially went under in the late 1970s. However, Framus instruments continued to appear until 1983, when the Warwick brand name replaced the famous logo. Set-up by Wilfer's son Hans-Peter, Warwick has concentrated very successfully on basses, but re-launched the Framus name in 1995 on a range of upmarket six-strings that has since reestablished Framus as a major German brand.

■ **FRANKLIN** Luthier Nick Kukich (born 1954) established his company (a one-man operation for most of its existence) in Franklin, Michigan, in 1976, before moving to Sandpoint, Idaho. Primarily known for OM-style guitars, Franklin is often credited with helping to revive interest in these instruments. Now based in Rocheport, Missouri, Kukich took a break from guitar-making between 1996 and 2004, but is once again producing OM, "Prairie State," and dreadnought instruments.

■ **FRIEDERICH** Daniel Friederich (born 1932) built his first guitar as a guitar student, establishing himself as a professional maker in Paris, France, in 1959. He has always taken a keen interest in scientific investigations into classical guitar design and has successfully tailored his instruments to the tastes of different players. His guitars have a distinctive raised "spearhead" on the headstock.

■ **FROGGY BOTTOM** Froggy Bottom was founded in 1970 by luthier Michael Millard (born 1947). Its workshop in Newfane, Vermont, now produces about 100 guitars annually. Froggy Bottom offers flat-top steel-strings ranging from a small twelve-fret parlor guitar to the baritone Model B. Although the company has a fixed line of models, its emphasis remains on custom orders.

■ **FURCH** This Czech maker, headed by Frantisek Furch (born 1958), began producing guitars clandestinely in 1981, since private enterprise was illegal during the Communist era. Since the "Velvet Revolution" of 1989, however, the company has flourished. Its range includes traditional dreadnought, jumbo, grand auditorium, OM, and arch-top styles. In the United States and Canada, Furch's instruments are marketed under the Stonebridge brand.

■ **FUTURAMA** Coined by UK importers Selmer, the Futurama logo adorned a varying selection of guitars and basses in the 1950s and 1960s. The earliest electrics emanated from Czechoslovakia in the late 1950s. The first of these was the Fender-influenced Resonet Grazioso, although Selmer soon came up with the much more commercial Futurama brand name. This surrogate Strat proved very popular with cash-strapped UK players and further variations followed, but in 1963 Selmer switched almost all sourcing to Swedish makers Hagstrom. Lasting until 1965, the revised line included six- and four-string solids, most being merely rebranded equivalents of existing Hagstrom models. One exception was the Coronado Automatic—the most upmarket Futurama—which was built specially for Selmer. The name also adorned a few Japanese electrics and acoustics.

framussolidbody

1960 Futurama 3

1960 Futurama Resonet

1997 Froggy Bottom D Standard

2002 Froggy Bottom H12 Deluxe

■ On these pages, the guitars are by the major German brand Framus; the OM-style specialist Franklin; steel-string flat-top maker Froggy Bottom; classical builder Friedrich; Czech-based acoustic maker Furch; and the British import brand Futurama.

2000 Furch D25-SR

2001 Furch F26

1983 Franklin SC270

1981 Friedrich Classical

acousticfuturama

2001 Fylde Single Malt

1970 Giannini CraViola

2000 Fylde Alchemist

FYLDE Fylde Guitars was started in 1973 by Roger Bucknall (born 1950) on the Fylde coast of Lancashire, England. It moved to Penrith, Cumbria, in 1996, where Bucknall and his small team produce about 100 guitars a year as well as some 250 mandolins, mandolas, bouzoukis, and so on. Fylde owners include Ritchie Blackmore, Martin Carthy, Sting, Cliff Richard, Keith Richards, Eric Bibb, Graham Coxon, Andy Summers, and Pete Townshend.

G & L The first G & L instruments appeared in 1980, bearing a brand name derived from the initials of business partners George Fullerton and Leo Fender. Early designs from the company, based in Fullerton, California, were in the established Fender mould, although humbuckers held sway over single coils and the three-bolt neck showed how Leo's former company should have done it. Additional upmarket guitars and basses were soon joined by models smaller in size and price. Apart from the occasional odd-looking exception, styling stayed Fender-ish, with strong hints of Strat, Tele, Mustang, and Precision. G & L later catered for the growing rock-machine market via various suitably equipped solids, but traditional themes still tended to dominate design.

Leo Fender died in early 1991, and later that year G & L was acquired by another California-based company, BBE Sound. The range has since continued successfully, with mainstay models being joined by new additions that include various signature instruments, commemorative editions, revivals, and custom creations.

G & L's Tribute series initially appeared in 1998, originally combining Japanese construction with American components. Production moved to Korea in the new millennium and the catalogue now offers fifteen more-affordable alternatives to their all-American inspirations.

GALANTI Galanti was another Italian accordion company that moved into guitar production during the boom times of the 1960s, although it was also known for electronic organs. Production continued into the 1970s and the range spanned solids and semis, the former including the Grand Prix series. Similar to models marketed under the Goya name, these six-strings employed push-button selectors that hinted at their accordion heritage.

GALLOTONE Gallotone manufactured cheap guitars in South Africa in the 1950s and 60s. The most famous Gallotone player was John Lennon, whose Gallotone Champion sold for £155,500 ($250,000) at auction in 1999.

GARCIA Enrique Garcia (1868–1922) was trained in Madrid, Spain, by either José Ramírez I or, more likely, Manuel Ramírez, but moved to Barcelona in the early 1890s. Barcelona had its own guitar-making practices, but Garcia was firmly in the tradition of Torres, though using a modified, asymmetrical form of his fan-strutting. Garcia built some 300 guitars in his lifetime and was celebrated throughout Europe and South America. Today his guitars are prized by collectors for their excellent and often ornate workmanship. The instrument on this page, however, was modified beyond recognition by Dionisio Gracia in Buenos Aires, Argentina, who fitted a new top with an elongated soundhole.

GEMELLI Gemelli was yet another Italian accordion maker-turned-guitar builder seeking success during the 1960s. The brand belonged to Benito and Umberto Cingolani, based in Recanati. Some models were similar to those from Bartolini, with colorful plastics and a pearl finish fingerboard, while multiple push-switches were equally standard.

GIANNINI Giannini was founded in 1900 by Tranquillo Giannini in Sao Paulo, Brazil, and is still flourishing today. Its distinctive Craviola guitar came in six-string, twelve-string, and classical versions.

1960 Galanti Grand Prix

1962 Gallotone Champion

1912 Garcia

fyldeacoustic

■ Featured here are acoustic guitars by Fylde (England) and Gallotone (South Africa); a modified classical by Garcia (Spain); some oddities by Giannini, Galanti, and Gemelli (all Italy); and some electrics by G&L (USA), one of the firms that Leo Fender set up following his departure from the Fender company.

1964 Gemelli 195/4/V

1977 Giannini Acoustic Electric

1984 G&L Cavalier

1989 G&L Asat

1989 G&L Comanche

1987 G&L L2000 Bass

1991 G&L Six-string Bass

acousticgiannani

electric pioneer

1940 Gibson Les Paul Log

les paul gold-tops

1952 Gibson Les Paul Gold-top

1952 Gibson Les Paul Gold-top
(left-handed)

1952 Gibson Les
Paul Gold-top

■ **GIBSON** Orville H. Gibson began manufacturing musical instruments in Kalamazoo, Michigan, around 1894. He had a refreshingly unconventional mixture of ideas about how to construct his mandolin-family instruments and oval-soundhole guitars. He would hand-carve the tops and backs, but would cut sides from solid wood rather than using the usual heating-and-bending method. Also unusual was the lack of internal bracing, which he thought degraded volume and tone. Gibson would often have his instrument's bodies decorated with beautiful inlaid pickguards and a distinctive crescent-and-star logo on the headstock. The only patent that Orville ever received—in 1898—was for his mandolin design that featured the distinctive one-piece carved sides and a one-piece neck.

In 1902 a group of businessmen joined Orville Gibson to form the Gibson Mandolin-Guitar Manufacturing company. The instruments that the new operation produced illustrated the diverse range of fretted stringed instruments available in the United States during the early decades of the twentieth century. The mandolin was clearly the most popular, and Gibson would soon find itself among the most celebrated of mandolin makers, thanks in no small part to the enormously influential F-5 model that would appear in 1922. Gibson also instigated a successful teacher-agent system to sell its mandolins. This was in contrast to the normal distribution operated by most instrument companies that would be based on a network of retailers.

Orville left the Gibson company in 1903, receiving a regular royalty from the company for the following five years and then a monthly income until his death in 1918. A year earlier the company had moved to new premises on Parsons Street, Kalamazoo (which it occupied until 1984).

Once Orville left Gibson, changes began to be made to his original construction methods, apparently for reasons of efficiency, for ease of production and, indeed, for improvement. Orville's sawed solid-wood sides were replaced with conventional heated-and-bent parts, and his inlaid, integral pickguard was replaced around 1908 with a unit elevated from the instrument's surface: the "floating pickguard." It was devised by Gibson man Lewis Williams, and the general design is still used today by many producers of arch-top guitars.

The guitar began to grow in importance during the late 1920s and into the 1930s, largely replacing the previously prominent tenor banjo. It became essential that any company demanding attention among guitarists should be seen as inventive and forward-thinking in this vital new area. Gibson obliged with many six-string innovations, including Ted McHugh's adjustable truss-rod, which did an excellent job of strengthening the instrument's neck. Truss-rods are virtually obligatory on today's guitars.

Thanks to the creativity of gifted employees such as Lloyd Loar, Gibson also established individual landmarks like the L-5 guitar of the early 1920s. With its novel f-holes and

gibsonsolidbody

1954 Gibson Les Paul Gold-top

1954 Gibson Les Paul "All" Gold-top

1953 Gibson Les Paul Gold-top

1955 Gibson Les Paul Gold-top

1956 Gibson Les Paul Gold-top

■ Although Gibson guitars were first made by Orville Gibson in the 1890s, the current firm's origins are in the Gibson Mandolin-Guitar Manufacturing company, set up in 1902. The earliest Gibson solidbody electrics were steel guitars, but the Les Paul Model of 1952 began its modern line of solidbody "Spanish" instruments.

solidbodygibson

1958 Gibson Les Paul Gold-top

refined gold-tops

1957 Gibson Les Paul Gold-top

"floating" pickguard, this model virtually defined the look and sound of the early arch-top acoustic guitar. It soon established itself and was played in a variety of musical styles, none more appealing than the "parlor jazz" epitomized by the incomparable Eddie Lang.

Lloyd Loar was an experienced musician who had started to work at Gibson in 1919 as a designer. His best-known achievements were the Master Models series that included that ground-breaking L-5 guitar. Loar left Gibson in 1924 and around 1933 formed a company with ex-Gibson man Lewis Williams, primarily to manufacture electric instruments, which they called Vivi Tone or Acousti-Lectric. The potential of electric instruments fascinated Loar, who had devised an early experimental electric pickup while at Gibson in the 1920s. But Loar and Williams's offerings appear to have been too radical to make any commercial impact, and within a few years of its inception their company closed. Loar died in the early 1940s at the age of fifty-seven.

As players demanded more volume from their guitars, Gibson dutifully increased the size of its acoustic instruments, introducing the superb, huge arch-top Super 400 model in 1934. Later in the decade came Gibson's "jumbo" J-series flat-tops. It was around then that Gibson introduced its first electric guitars: the Electric Hawaiian E-150 cast aluminum steel guitar in 1935, and the following year's EH-150 steel, plus an f-hole hollowbody, the ES-150—Gibson's first arch-top electric.

The non-cutaway ES-150 electric guitar was a very significant addition to the catalog for Gibson. It effectively marked the start of the company's long-running ES series—the initial letters standing for "Electric Spanish." It's worth noting that, in this context, the term "Spanish" of course had nothing at all to do with nylon-string round-soundhole guitars. Instead, it was being used to distinguish this type of guitar from its Hawaiian-style cousin, the one generally played on the lap.

The ES-150 was famously taken up by Charlie Christian, the genius who showed jazz players what an electric guitar was for. Playing clear, single-note runs as if he were a horn player, Christian virtually invented the idea of the electric guitar solo. The "bar" pickup of the earliest ES-150 models, which was designed by Walt Fuller at Gibson, has subsequently become known as the "Charlie Christian" pickup as the guitarist was by far its best-known user, even though Christian's career was cut tragically short by his early death in 1942 at the age of just twenty-five. Gibson tentatively built on these low-key electric experiments, adding the budget ES-100 arch-top in 1938, and following this with its most expensive pre-war electric model, the ES-300, in 1940. When America entered the war two years later Gibson effectively put a halt to its guitar production. As instrument manufacturing gradually recommenced afterward, Gibson rightly concluded that the electric guitar was set to become an important part of its reactivated business.

Around this time Gibson also manufactured instruments with a number of brand names in addition to the most famous one. A good deal of the instruments bearing these names were acoustics, but electrics did appear with the following brands: Capital, Cromwell, Old Kraftsman, Recording King (all made for a mail-order companies), and Kalamazoo (a low-end in-house brand). **>**

gibson**solidbody**

1957 Gibson Les Paul Gold-top

1982 Gibson Les Paul Gold-top 30th Anniversary

■ Gibson's Les Paul line had begun with the Gold-top model of 1952, but by 1957 the guitar had several improvements and was fitted with the new humbucking pickups, designed to reduce the hum that could interfere with regular single-coil pickups. The various Gold-top models have continued in production since Gibson's reissues of 1968.

1968 Gibson Les Paul Gold-top Reissue

1957 Gibson Les Paul Gold-top (left-handed)

1994 Gibson Les Paul Gold-top Classic Centennial

1954 Gibson Les Paul
Custom Prototype

1954 Gibson Les Paul
Custom

1957 Gibson Les Paul
Custom, Alnico Pickups

1957 Gibson Les Paul Custom
Owned by Keith Richards

1957 Gibson Les Paul Custom

1960 Gibson Les Paul Custom

1989 Gibson Les Paul Custom
35th Anniversary

In 1944 the Chicago Instrument Company (CMI) purchased a controlling interest in Gibson. Gibson's manufacturing base remained at its original factory, purpose-built in 1917 at Kalamazoo, which was roughly equidistant between Detroit and Chicago—the location for Gibson's new sales and administration headquarters at CMI. It was at this time that Gibson began to pioneer electric guitars with cutaways. A cutaway offered easier access to the now audible and musically useful area of the upper fingerboard, previously of little use to quiet acoustic players who tended to limit their fret-based ramblings primarily to the headstock end of the neck. Talented and imaginative guitarists openly welcomed the artistic potential of the cutaway . . . and began to investigate the dusty end of the fingerboard.

Gibson debuted several significant new arch-top electric guitars in the late 1940s. The ES-350 of 1947 and two years later the ES-5 and sharp-cutaway ES-175 were all aimed at players who were prepared to commit themselves to fully integrated electric instruments.
The ES-350 was the first of the company's new-style cutaway electrics, and at first bore the "Premier" tag of the pre-war cutaway acoustics. The 350 was followed in 1949 by the new single-pickup ES-175, Gibson's first electric with a "pointed" cutaway style and a pressed, laminated top. This construction contributed a distinctively bright, cutting tone color to the 175. A two-pickup version, the ES-175D, was added in 1953.

The ES-175 became a popular instrument and was Gibson's first really successful electric guitar. It has made a particular impact among electric jazz musicians, including such luminaries as Joe Pass, while also attracting eclectic modern players like Steve Howe and Pat Metheny.

The ES-5 also debuted in 1949 and was the first electric guitar with three pickups—it was effectively a three-pickup ES-350. However, before long, players found that it was less controllable than they wanted. As with all Gibson's immediate post-war electric guitars, the ES-5 had no pickup switching. Instead, each pickup had a separate volume control, which meant the only way to achieve a balance between the pickups was to set the three volume knobs at relative positions.

So it was that in 1956 Gibson issued the ES-5 model with redesigned electronics, this time with a new name: the ES-5 Switchmaster. Three individual tone knobs were added alongside the three volume controls, and near the cutaway a four-way pickup selector switch was added, hence the new model name. The switch, explained a Gibson catalog of the time, "activates each of the three pickups separately, a combination of any two, or all three simultaneously." **>**

1974 Gibson Les Paul Custom
20th Anniversary

1997 Gibson Les Paul Custom

■ The Les Paul Custom, first issued in 1954, was Gibson's high-end companion to the Gold-top. Changes were made to the type and number of pickups during its early years, but like the Gold-top, the various Custom models have continued in production since Gibson's reissues of 1968.

1990 Gibson Les Paul Custom

1968 Gibson Les Paul Custom

les paul customs

1992 Gibson Les Paul
Custom Plus

1994 Gibson Les Paul Custom
Black Beauty '57 Centennial

2000 Gibson Les Paul
Custom Peter Frampton

solidbodygibson

1956 Gibson Les Paul TV

■ Three new guitars in the Les Paul line during the mid-1950s were "student models" aimed at beginners. The single-pickup Junior and TV and two-pickup Special shared the body shape and general style of the more expensive Les Pauls but had a flat-top body and simpler electrics.

1957 Gibson Les Paul TV

1958 Gibson Les Paul TV

les paul juniors

At a time when Fender had just launched its stylish three-pickup Stratocaster, and Epiphone was offering models with a six-button "color tone" switching system, Gibson probably felt the ES-5 Switchmaster was a potential market leader. But it never caught on. And anyway, by now Gibson had produced proper electric versions of its great arch-top acoustics, the L-5 and the Super 400.

In 1951 Gibson became serious about the electric guitar, launching the Super 400CES and the L-5CES (the initials stand for Cutaway, Electric, Spanish). For the 400CES, Gibson built on its existing Super 400C acoustic model, and for the L-5CES combined elements of its acoustic L-5C and electric ES-5 guitars. The new electric models had modified and stronger internal "bracing" to make them less prone to feedback when amplified.

The generally large proportions of the eighteen-inch-wide acoustic bodies of the earlier models were retained for these impressive new electrics in the Gibson line. For the 400CES model, the acoustic 400's high-end appointments remained—such as split-block-shape fingerboard inlays, a "marbleized" tortoiseshell pickguard, and a fancy "split-diamond" headstock inlay.

At first the electric 400 and L-5 came with a pair of Gibson's standard single-coil P-90 pickups, but in 1954 changed to more powerful "Alnico" types with distinctive rectangular pole pieces. The Alnico nickname comes from the magnet type used in these pickups. A "rounded"-cutaway body style lasted from the launch of the two electrics in 1951 until 1960, when a new "pointed" cutaway was introduced. Gibson reverted to the original rounded design in 1969.

An immense variety of players has at different times been drawn to the power and versatility of Gibson's two leading arch-top electrics. The Super 400CES has attracted bluesman Robben Ford, country players like Hank Thompson and Merle Travis (whose custom 400 was described in 1952 as Gibson's "most expensive guitar ever"), rock 'n' roller Scotty Moore, and a number of fine jazz guitarists including George Benson and Kenny Burrell. The L-5CES has also had its fans and adherents over the years, including jazzmen such as Wes Montgomery and John Collins, as well as the fine country-jazzer Hank Garland.

Ted McCarty had joined Gibson back in March 1948, having worked at the Wurlitzer organ company for the previous twelve years. In 1950 he was made president of Gibson. Gibson was finding it hard in the post-war years to get back into full-scale guitar production, and McCarty's first managerial tasks were to increase the effectiveness of supervision, to bolster efficiency, and to improve internal communication.

Gibson began to work on a solidbody design soon after Fender's original Telecaster-style model had appeared in 1950. McCarty had a good team working on the project, including production head John Huis, as well as employees Julius Bellson and Wilbur Marker, while the sales people were

gibsonsolidbody

1964 Gibson Les Paul Melody Maker

1955 Gibson Les Paul Special TV

les paul specials

1959 Gibson Les Paul Special (three-quarter scale)

1959 Gibson Les Paul Special

1954 Gibson Les Paul Junior

1960 Gibson Les Paul Junior

'58 les paul standards

1958 Gibson Les Paul Standard

1958 Gibson Les Paul Standard

1958 Gibson Les Paul Standard

1958 Gibson Les Paul Standard
Jimmy Page's "Number One"

1958 Gibson Les Paul Standard

regularly consulted through manager Clarence Havenga. It took them all about a year to come up with satisfactory prototypes for a new Gibson solidbody—at which point McCarty began to think about guitarist Les Paul, who was just about the most famous guitar player in America.

In the 1940s Les Paul had been a member of the supergroup Jazz At The Philharmonic, and had played prominent guitar on Bing Crosby's hit "It's Been a Long, Long Time" (a Billboard Number One in 1945). Crosby encouraged Paul to build a studio into the garage of the guitarist's home in Hollywood, California, and it was here that he hit upon his effective "multiple" recording techniques. These early overdubbing routines allowed Paul to create huge, magical orchestras of massed guitars, arranged by the guitarist to play catchy instrumental tunes. Les Paul and his New Sound signed to Capitol Records, with the first release, "Lover," a hit in 1948.

Paul found even greater popularity when he added vocalist Mary Ford to the act. They had married in 1949, and the following year the duo released their first joint record. Guitars and now voices too were given the multiple recording treatment, and big hits followed for Les Paul & Mary Ford including "The Tennessee Waltz" (1950) and "How High the Moon" (1951). The duo performed hundreds of personal appearances and concerts, and were heard on NBC Radio's *Les Paul Show* every week for six months during 1949 and 1950. Their networked television series *The Les Paul & Mary Ford Show* began in 1953, beamed from their extravagant new home in Mahwah, New Jersey. As the 1950s got underway, Les Paul & Mary Ford—"America's Musical Sweethearts"—were huge stars.

Les Paul's obsessive tinkering with gadgetry was not restricted to the recording studio. The teenage Lester, drawn to the guitar, had soon become interested in the idea of amplification. In the late 1930s his new jazz-based trio was broadcasting out of New York on the Fred Waring radio show, with Paul playing a number of Gibson models. The guitarist exercised his curiosity for electric instruments and his flair for technical experimentation by adapting and modifying an Epiphone guitar.

Around 1940, Les Paul used to go at weekends into the empty Epiphone factory in New York in order to fiddle with what he would call his "log" guitar. The nickname was derived from the 4x4-inch solid block of pine which the guitarist had inserted between the sawed halves of the body that he'd just dismembered. He then carefully rejoined the neck to the pine log, using some metal brackets, and mounted on the top a couple of crude pickups he'd made for himself.

He later modified a second and third Epiphone, which he called his "clunkers," this time chopping up the bodies to add metal strengthening braces, and again topped off with Paul's own pickups. Despite their makeshift origins, the modified "clunker" Epiphones often accompanied Paul and Ford on stage and in recording studios throughout the 1940s and into the early 1950s.

Paul was not alone in his investigations. Several unconnected explorations into the possibility of a solidbody electric guitar were being undertaken elsewhere in America at this time, not least at the California workshops of Rickenbacker, National, Bigsby, and Fender. A solidbody electric was appealing because it would dispose of the complicated construction of an acoustic guitar, and instead use solid wood (or some other rigid material) to support the

gibsonsolidbody

1959 Gibson Les Paul Standard

1959 Gibson Les Paul Standard

1959 Gibson Les Paul Standard Cherry
Owned by
George
Harrison

1959 Gibson Les Paul Standard
Owned by
Paul
Kossof

'59 les paul standards

■ The sunburst-finish Les Paul Standard, originally made from 1958 to 1960, is one of the most revered electric guitars of all time, as this roster of famous and gorgeous instruments from the first two years of production reveals. The 1959 models are particularly well regarded.

1959 Gibson Les Paul Standard
Owned by Peter Green

1959 Gibson Les Paul Standard

1959 Gibson Les Paul Standard
Owned by Jeff Beck

1959 Gibson Les Paul Standard
Jimmy Page's "Number Two"

solidbodygibson

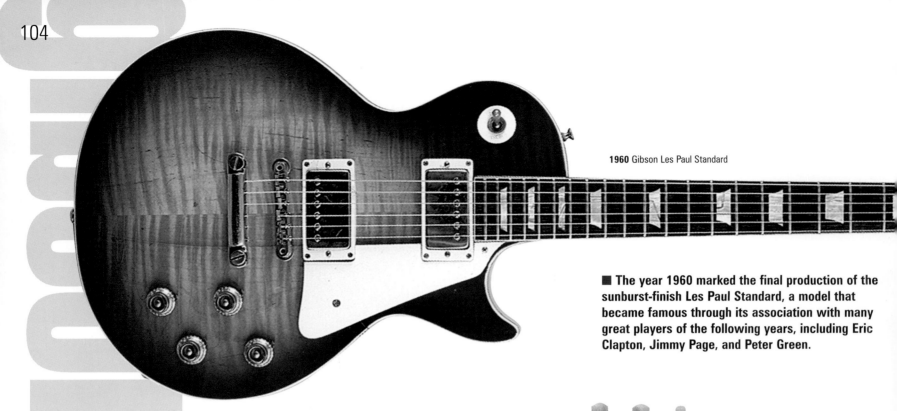

1960 Gibson Les Paul Standard

■ **The year 1960 marked the final production of the sunburst-finish Les Paul Standard, a model that became famous through its association with many great players of the following years, including Eric Clapton, Jimmy Page, and Peter Green.**

strings and pickups. It would also curtail the annoying feedback sometimes produced by amplified acoustic guitars, and reduce the body's interference with the guitar's overall tone, thus more accurately reproducing and sustaining the sound of the strings.

During the 1940s, Paul had decided that he would take his "log" idea to a major guitar manufacturing company in order to try to generate some real interest in its commercial potential. He decided—accurately, as it turned out—that Epiphone would not continue in its present form as a strong force in the guitar world. So around 1946 Paul took his crude log guitar to Gibson's parent company, CMI in Chicago, with the intention of convincing them to market such a semi-solid guitar. No doubt with all the courtesy that a pressurized city businessman could muster, the boss of CMI showed Les Paul the door. A startled Paul recalls that they laughed at his guitar, dismissing him as "the guy with the broomstick."

But some years later, as we've seen, Gibson was developing ideas for a solidbody electric guitar in the wake of Fender's new instrument, and Gibson president Ted McCarty decided to contact the now hugely popular Les Paul. A meeting took place, probably in 1951. McCarty's intention was to interest Paul in publicly playing Gibson's newly designed guitar in return for a royalty on sales—an arrangement generally referred to now as an "endorsement" deal. It was certainly not a new arrangement for Gibson: the company's Nick Lucas flat-top acoustic model of 1928 had exploited the popularity of Lucas, known as "the crooning troubadour," to produce the contemporary guitar industry's first "signature" instrument.

Gibson's meeting with Les Paul around 1951 was the first opportunity the guitarist had to see the prototype of what would soon become the Gibson Les Paul solidbody electric. A deal was struck: Paul's royalty on Les Paul models would be 5 percent, and the term of the contract was set at five years. Paul's respected playing and commercial success added to Gibson's weighty experience in manufacturing and marketing guitars made for a strong and impressive combination.

The new Les Paul guitar was launched by Gibson in 1952, probably in the spring of that year, and was priced at $210 ($20 more than Fender's Telecaster). Today, this first style of Les Paul model is nearly always called the "Gold-top" because of its distinctive gold-finished body face. The Gold-top's solid body cleverly combined a carved maple top bonded to a mahogany "back," uniting the darker tonality of mahogany with the brighter sound of maple.

Gibson had made a one-off all-gold hollowbody guitar in 1951 for Paul to present to a terminally ill patient whom he had met when making a special hospital appearance. This presentation guitar presumably prompted the all-gold arch-top electric ES-295 model of 1952 (effectively a gold-finished ES-175) and was probably the inspiration for the color of the first Les Paul model. Almost all the other design elements of the first Gibson Les Paul have precedents in earlier Gibson models—for example, the instrument's layout of two P-90 single-coil pickups and four controls (which comprised a volume and tone pair for each pickup) was already a feature of Gibson's CES electric arch-tops that had been launched the previous year. The general body outline and glued-in mahogany neck also followed established Gibson traditions, while the "crown"-shape inlays on the rosewood fingerboard had first appeared on the 1950 incarnation of the ES-150 model. Several Gibson acoustics had already appeared with the same scale-length as the new Les Paul.

The new Les Paul came with a new height-adjustable combined bridge/tailpiece which was bar-shaped and joined to long metal rods that anchored it to the bottom edge of the guitar. This was designed by Les Paul and intended for use on arch-top guitars. (Gibson also sold it as a separate replacement accessory.) It proved unsuitable for the new solidbody, and was quickly replaced by a new purpose-built "stud" bar-shaped bridge/tailpiece, phased in around 1953. This was mounted to the top of the body with twin height-adjustable studs, hence the nickname. **>**

1960 Gibson Les Paul Standard

1960 Gibson Les Paul Standard

gibson**solidbody**

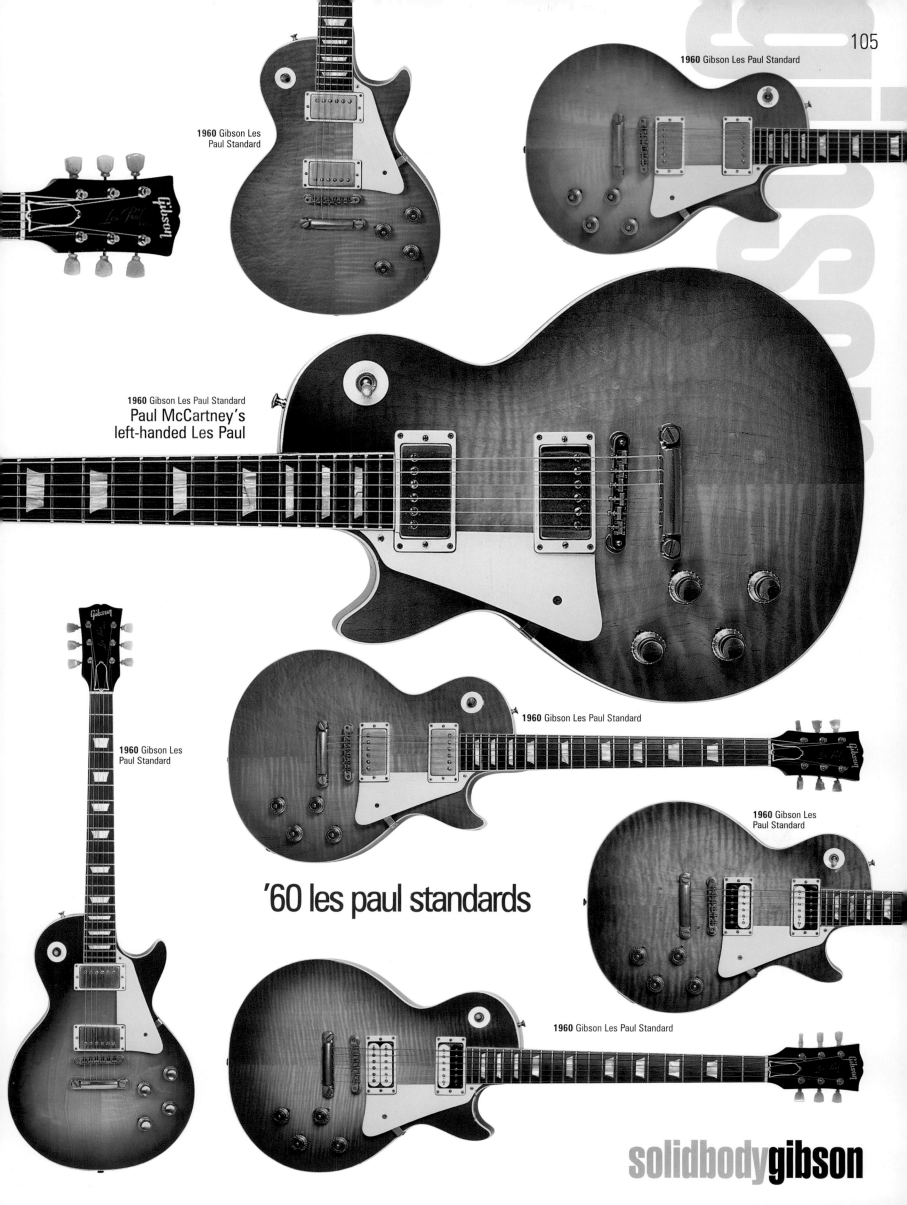

1960 Gibson Les Paul Standard

1960 Gibson Les Paul Standard

1960 Gibson Les Paul Standard
Paul McCartney's
left-handed Les Paul

1960 Gibson Les Paul Standard

1960 Gibson Les Paul Standard

1960 Gibson Les Paul Standard

1960 Gibson Les Paul Standard

'60 les paul standards

1960 Gibson Les Paul Standard

solidbodygibson

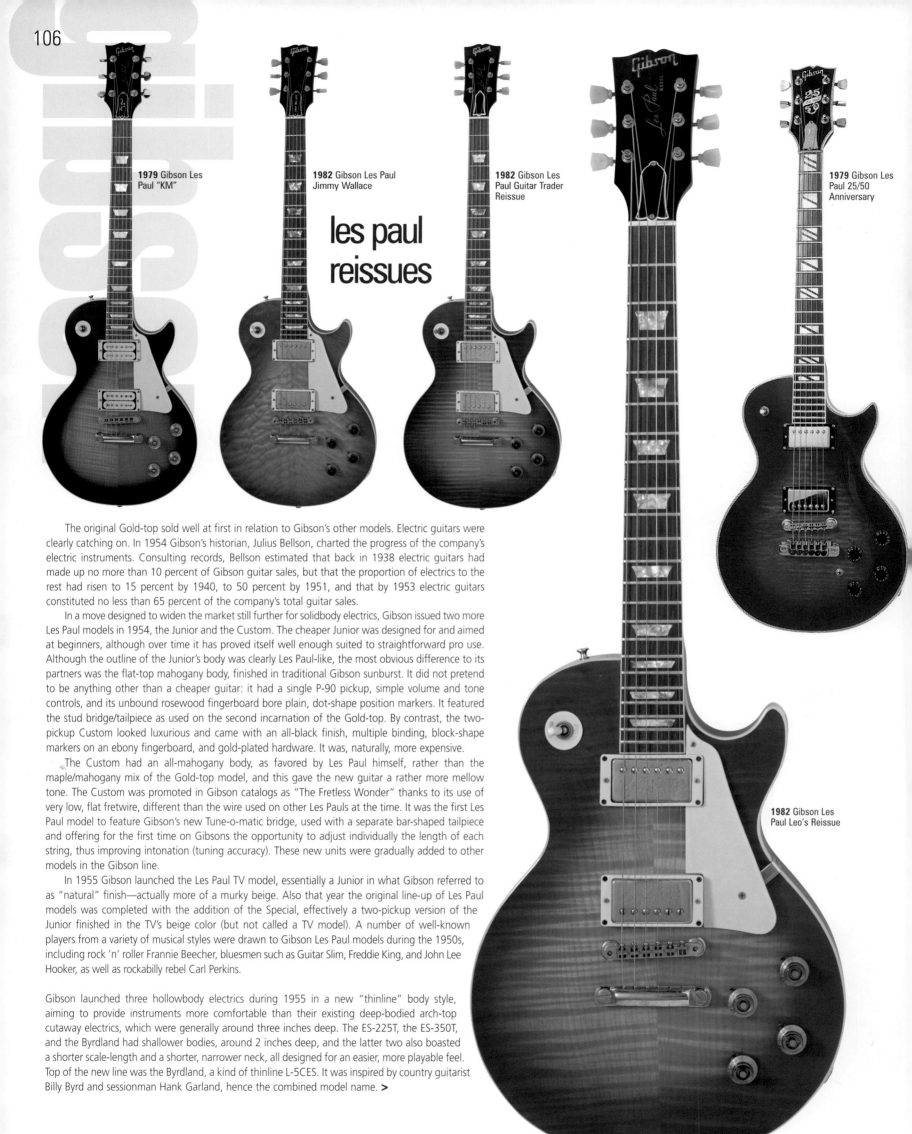

1979 Gibson Les Paul "KM"

1982 Gibson Les Paul Jimmy Wallace

1982 Gibson Les Paul Guitar Trader Reissue

les paul reissues

1979 Gibson Les Paul 25/50 Anniversary

1982 Gibson Les Paul Leo's Reissue

The original Gold-top sold well at first in relation to Gibson's other models. Electric guitars were clearly catching on. In 1954 Gibson's historian, Julius Bellson, charted the progress of the company's electric instruments. Consulting records, Bellson estimated that back in 1938 electric guitars had made up no more than 10 percent of Gibson guitar sales, but that the proportion of electrics to the rest had risen to 15 percent by 1940, to 50 percent by 1951, and that by 1953 electric guitars constituted no less than 65 percent of the company's total guitar sales.

In a move designed to widen the market still further for solidbody electrics, Gibson issued two more Les Paul models in 1954, the Junior and the Custom. The cheaper Junior was designed for and aimed at beginners, although over time it has proved itself well enough suited to straightforward pro use. Although the outline of the Junior's body was clearly Les Paul-like, the most obvious difference to its partners was the flat-top mahogany body, finished in traditional Gibson sunburst. It did not pretend to be anything other than a cheaper guitar: it had a single P-90 pickup, simple volume and tone controls, and its unbound rosewood fingerboard bore plain, dot-shape position markers. It featured the stud bridge/tailpiece as used on the second incarnation of the Gold-top. By contrast, the two-pickup Custom looked luxurious and came with an all-black finish, multiple binding, block-shape markers on an ebony fingerboard, and gold-plated hardware. It was, naturally, more expensive.

The Custom had an all-mahogany body, as favored by Les Paul himself, rather than the maple/mahogany mix of the Gold-top model, and this gave the new guitar a rather more mellow tone. The Custom was promoted in Gibson catalogs as "The Fretless Wonder" thanks to its use of very low, flat fretwire, different than the wire used on other Les Pauls at the time. It was the first Les Paul model to feature Gibson's new Tune-o-matic bridge, used with a separate bar-shaped tailpiece and offering for the first time on Gibsons the opportunity to adjust individually the length of each string, thus improving intonation (tuning accuracy). These new units were gradually added to other models in the Gibson line.

In 1955 Gibson launched the Les Paul TV model, essentially a Junior in what Gibson referred to as "natural" finish—actually more of a murky beige. Also that year the original line-up of Les Paul models was completed with the addition of the Special, effectively a two-pickup version of the Junior finished in the TV's beige color (but not called a TV model). A number of well-known players from a variety of musical styles were drawn to Gibson Les Paul models during the 1950s, including rock 'n' roller Frannie Beecher, bluesmen such as Guitar Slim, Freddie King, and John Lee Hooker, as well as rockabilly rebel Carl Perkins.

Gibson launched three hollowbody electrics during 1955 in a new "thinline" body style, aiming to provide instruments more comfortable than their existing deep-bodied arch-top cutaway electrics, which were generally around three inches deep. The ES-225T, the ES-350T, and the Byrdland had shallower bodies, around 2 inches deep, and the latter two also boasted a shorter scale-length and a shorter, narrower neck, all designed for an easier, more playable feel. Top of the new line was the Byrdland, a kind of thinline L-5CES. It was inspired by country guitarist Billy Byrd and sessionman Hank Garland, hence the combined model name. **>**

gibsonsolidbody

custom models

1983 Gibson Les Paul Standard Custom

2001 Gibson Les Paul Standard Custom

1980 Gibson Les Paul
Heritage Standard 80

1982 Gibson Les
Paul Standard '82

1982 Gibson Les Paul
Heritage Standard 80 Award

1982 Gibson Les Paul
Heritage Standard 80 Elite

1980 Gibson Les Paul
Heritage Standard 80

1984 Gibson Les Paul
Guitar Trader Reissue

■ As more players were drawn to the quality and tone of the original 1958–60 Les Paul Standard models, Gibson and some dealers, such as Guitar Trader and Jimmy Wallace, tried to re-create the original, with mixed results. Gibson's Custom Shop began in the 1980s making one-offs and special runs.

1983 Gibson Les Paul Standard Reissue

1984 Gibson Les Paul Standard Reissue

1993 Gibson Les Paul '59 Flametop Reissue

1985 Gibson Standard Resissue

An important player who grasped the possibilities of these new friendlier electrics from Gibson was Chuck Berry, the most influential rock 'n' roll guitarist of the 1950s. Berry chose a brand-new, natural-finish ES-350T to fuel his startlingly fresh hybrid of boogie, country, and blues. In hindsight, it's remarkable that this great player did not appear in any Gibson advertising at the time—but then nor did any other black guitarist of the period.

Jazz players still kept Gibson's name prominent in the arch-top electric field. Of the guitarists in the poll for the prestigious U.S. jazz magazine *Down Beat* in 1956, Gibson could count six of the top ten as being loyal to the company: Barney Kessel (most often seen with an ES-350); Tal Farlow (also principally a 350 man); Les Paul (no prizes for guessing his six-string of choice); Herb Ellis; Jimmy Raney; and Jim Hall (the last three all favoring Gibson ES-175s).

New humbucking pickups were developed by Seth Lover in the Gibson workshops. The idea was to cut down the hum and electrical interference that plagued standard single-coil pickups, Gibson's ubiquitous P-90 unit included. Lover contemplated the humbucking "choke coil" found in some Gibson amplifiers, installed to eliminate the hum dispensed by their power transformers.

From those beginnings, Lover extrapolated a pickup design that employed two coils wired together electrically "out of phase" and with opposite magnetic polarities. The result was less prone to picking up extraneous noise, in the process giving a powerful, clear tone.

During 1957 Gibson started to fit its electric guitars with the new humbuckers. The Les Paul Custom was promoted to a three-pickup guitar in its new humbucker-equipped guise. Today many guitarists and collectors make a point of seeking out the earliest type of Gibson humbucking pickup, which is now known as a "PAF" because of the small "patent applied for" label attached to the underside. The PAF labels appear on pickups on Gibson guitars dated up to 1962 (even though the patent had been granted in 1959). Some who prefer the sound of PAF-label humbuckers say that later humbuckers sound different because of small changes made to coil-winding, magnet grades, and wire-sheathing.

Gibson purchased the old Epiphone brand of New York in 1957, relocating the operation to its Kalamazoo base. The following year Gibson released the first of its new Epiphones, effectively creating for itself a second-tier line. Some of these "new" guitars continued existing Epiphone models, but others were new Epiphone equivalents of Gibson models—for example the Casino, very similar to a Gibson ES330 (but with an Epiphone logo, of course).

In fact, 1958 proved to be one of the most significant years in Gibson's entire history. During that heady twelve months the company issued the radical new Explorer and Flying V solidbodies, changed the finish of its Les Paul model to a gorgeous sunburst, introduced the brand new semi-solid ES-335 and ES-355 guitars, changed the body outlines of the Les Paul Junior and Les Paul Special to a useful double-cutaway shape, and brought out its first double-neck electric guitars. Each of these designs would, to a greater or lesser extent, become classics over the coming years, and today some of them qualify as the most revered electric guitars ever made.

The Gibson Modernistic series of guitars was first seen in public during 1958. Fender's flamboyant designs such as the Stratocaster and the Jazzmaster had been leaving Gibson's rather staid electric models behind as rock 'n' roll burst forth. Guitar makers became increasingly aware that, beyond the usual considerations of quality and playability, there was an immense and largely untapped value in sheer visual appeal. So the designers at Gibson temporarily set aside their customary preoccupation with curvaceously elegant forms to come up with the boldly adventurous Flying V and Explorer—a pair of stark, linear creations. The body of the Flying V had an angular, pointed, arrow-head shape, while that of the Explorer was an uncompromising study in offset rectangles. Most Explorers have a long, drooping headstock with the tuners in a line on one side. But a small number (sometimes referred to as Futura models) had an unusual V-shaped head.

Both Flying V and Explorer were made from Korina (a timber tradename for an African relative of mahogany, sometimes known as limba). Gibson used a different

gibson**solidbody**

1987 Gibson Les Paul Standard Reissue

■ Finally, in the 1980s, Gibson began to make proper reissues of its most celebrated Les Paul models, with the sunburst Standard the leading contender. From 2008, the company issued several 50th anniversary instruments to mark the birth of the famed original guitars.

1999 Gibson Standard '58 Figuretop Reissue

les paul reissues

1999 Gibson Les Paul Historic 1959
Reissue 40th Anniversary

2008 Gibson Les Paul 1958 Reissue
Aged 50th Anniversary

aged reissues

2001 Gibson Les Paul Standard
'58 Figuretop Reissue

solidbodygibson

2008 Gibson Les Paul Historic Standard 60

2006 Gibson Les Paul Historic 1959 Reissue Vos

2003 Gibson Les Paul Historic 1959 Reissue

2001 Gibson Les Paul Historic 1958 Reissue

2001 Gibson Les Paul Historic 1959 Reissue

2003 Gibson Les Paul Historic 1959 Reissue

historic reissues

control layout on the V and Explorer than the one they generally employed on two-humbucker electrics: on the Modernistics, the player was offered a volume knob per pickup but just one overall tone control. The small numbers produced would turn the Modernistics into future collectables of the rarest kind. In fact, only ninety-eight of the original Flying V were made, with a further twenty or so assembled in the early 1960s from existing parts.

Gibson's factory records for the original Explorer are not so clear, but the best estimates among collectors and other experts put production at just twenty-two instruments, with a further sixteen assembled later. A good number of reissues and redesigns of both the Flying V and Explorer has followed, especially during their bouts of popularity with metal guitarists and others in subsequent decades.

Among players drawn to the Flying V in its various guises were Albert King in the 1950s, Jimi Hendrix in the 1960s, Marc Bolan and Andy Powell in the 1970s, Mick Mars and Michael Schenker in the 1980s, and Jim Martin and Tim Wheeler in more recent years. Perhaps more importantly (or disgracefully, depending on your viewpoint) this late-flowering popularity of Gibson's Modernistic duo of Flying V and Explorer would be the trigger for any number of outlandishly shaped solidbody guitars, especially during the late 1970s and 1980s.

A third guitar in the original 1958 Modernistic series, the Moderne, was planned but never actually reached general production or distribution, even though a patent for the design was filed in summer 1957. No prototype or other incarnation of the original Moderne has ever turned up, despite much searching by desperate collectors.

Also in 1958, Gibson made a radical design-change to three of the Les Paul models, as well as a cosmetic alteration to another that would later take on enormous importance. The single-pickup Les Paul Junior and TV models were revamped with a completely new double-cutaway body shape, apparently as a reaction to players' requests for more access to the top frets than the previous single-cutaway design allowed. The new cutaways did the trick. The Junior's fresh look was enhanced with a new cherry red finish. The TV adopted the new double-cutaway design as well, along with a rather more yellow-tinged finish.

When the double-cutaway design was applied to the two-pickup Les Paul Special during the following year, the construction was not an immediate success. Gibson had overlooked the fact that

gibson**solidbody**

1990 Gibson Les Paul Classic "1960"

classic reissues

1995 Gibson Les Paul Classic Plus

1996 Gibson Les Paul Classic
Premium Plus Limited Edition

1997 Gibson Les Paul Classic
Premium Plus Custom Shop

1996 Gibson Les Paul
Classic Premium Plus
Limited Edition

1996 Gibson Les Paul
Classic Premium Plus
Limited Edition

1996 Gibson Les Paul
Classic Premium Plus
Custom Shop

1996 Gibson Les Paul
Classic Premium Plus
Limited Edition

1997 Gibson Les Paul
Classic Premium Plus
Custom Shop

■ The Les Paul Classic was a re-creation
of the feel and vibe of a 1960-era Les Paul.
It was launched on the 30th anniversary in
1990 and remained in the catalogue until
2008. "Historic" is one of the many names
used by Gibson for its increasingly more
detailed and successful reissues of earlier
glories.

solidbodygibson

1995 Gibson Jimmy Page Les Paul

1996 Gibson Joe Perry Les Paul

1997 Gibson Gibson Ace Frehley Les Paul

1999 Gibson Zak Wylde "Bullseye" Les Paul

2000 Gibson Gary Moore Les Paul

1989 Gibson Orville Yamano Les Paul

1995 Gibson Les Paul '60 Corvette

les paul signature models

2003 Gibson Les Paul Duane Allman

the cavity for the neck pickup in the Special's new body severely weakened the neck-to-body joint. In fact, the neck could potentially snap off at this point. The error was soon corrected when Gibson's designers moved the neck pickup further down the body, resulting in a stronger joint. The new double-cutaway Special was offered in cherry or the new TV yellow.

Sales of Gibson's Les Paul Gold-top had gradually declined during the late 1950s, and in a bid to improve sales in 1958 Gibson changed the look by applying its more traditional cherry sunburst finish. This sunburst Les Paul is generally known as the Les Paul Standard, although Gibson did not refer to it as such in their literature until 1960, and the guitar itself never bore the name.

Gibson must have deduced that the unusual gold finish of the original Les Paul model was considered too unconventional, and to some extent they were proved right. Sales of the Gold-top had declined from a high of 920 in 1956 to just 434 in 1958, the year of the new Standard. After the sunburst model appeared, sales then climbed to 643 in 1959. But when they dipped again in 1960, Gibson decided that this change of finish had not been enough, and that the only way to attract new customers was to completely redesign the Les Paul.

So the sunburst Standard was dropped, having existed for a little short of three years. Here again was one of Gibson's sleeping giants: almost ignored at the time, this instrument would become an ultra-collectable object in later years. Players and collectors came to realize that the guitar's inherent musicality, as well as its short production run (some 1,700 examples were made between 1958 and 1960), added up to a modern classic. This reevaluation was prompted originally in the middle and late 1960s when a number of guitarists discovered that the Gibson Les Paul had enormous potential for high-volume blues-based rock. It turned out that the Les Paul's inherent tonality coupled with its humbucking pickups— played through a loud tube amp—made a wonderful noise.

Of course, this newly discovered sonic potential of the Les Paul was

gibson**solidbody**

1980 Gibson Les Paul Pro Deluxe

1969 Gibson Les Paul Deluxe

1971 Gibson Les Paul Recording (First Version)

1978 Gibson Les Paul Recording (Second Version)

1969 Gibson Les Paul Professional

1969 Gibson Les Paul Personel

1969 Gibson Les Paul Deluxe

■ Gibson has issued many signature Les Pauls to mark the association with some of the famous names who have played the instrument. But Les Pauls have not been limited to the best-known models: included here are the low-impedance Professional, and the Deluxe with its mini-humbucking pickups.

1978 Gibson Les Paul Artisan

1976 Gibson Les Paul Artisan

1976 Gibson The Les Paul 2

the les paul

1978 Gibson The Les Paul

1978 Gibson The Les Paul

1978 Gibson Les Paul 25/50 Anniversary

something that neither Gibson nor Paul himself could possibly have planned. Leading early members of the Loud Les Appreciation Society were Mike Bloomfield in America and Eric Clapton in Britain. Demand for the old instruments rocketed. The original sunburst Gibson Les Paul Standard—the "burst" in guitar-speak—has since achieved almost mythological status, and genuine originals now regularly fetch six-figure sums on the collectors' market.

Gold-top Les Pauls mostly had maple tops made from two or more pieces of wood, safely hidden under the gold paint. Now that this maple top was on show through the transparent sunburst finish of the Standard, Gibson's woodworkers were more careful in selecting wood of good appearance.

A further innovation of 1958, and one that proved to be more successful at the time, was Gibson's new ES-335 guitar. This was a development of the company's "thinline" design that had begun with the Byrdland and the ES-350T three years earlier. When it came to the new 335, however, Gibson deployed a radical double-cutaway design, as well as the use of a novel solid block within the otherwise hollow body to create a new "semi-solid" structure.

Gibson's idea was effectively to combine a hollowbody guitar with a solidbody, not only in terms of construction but also in sonic effect. A problem for hollowbody electric guitar designers had been the screeching feedback that often occurred when the guitar was played with its amplifier set at high volume. The 335's solid maple block inside what Gibson described as its "wonder-thin" body tamed the feedback and combined pure solidbody sustain with the woody warmth of a hollowbody. This quality would endear the 335-style Gibson to a wide range of players, from B.B. King to jazz stylist Larry Carlton and Britpop pioneer Bernard Butler.

The "dot neck" 335—made between 1958 and 1962—has become a prime collectable guitar. In 1962 Gibson replaced the dots with block-shape markers. This might not make the guitar sound less good, but collectors feel the dot-neck feature marks a better period of quality and manufacturing standards, and therefore denotes a more desirable instrument. Players tend to be less selective and will generally tend to choose a 335 from any period—one that plays well, feels good, and is affordable.

The earliest 335 models were officially named ES-335T, the "T" at the end standing for "thinline" to emphasize and underline one of its most important features. Soon, however, a "D" was added by Gibson, meaning double pickups, as well as an extra "N" for natural-finish examples, resulting in the rather overwhelming model description of ES-335TDN. The sunburst 335 was originally made in greater numbers than the natural version, which was dropped in 1960. From that year the 335 was also available in a cherry red finish, known as the ES-335TDC.

The following year brought Gibson's first stereo guitar, the ES-345, along with optional stereo wiring for the ES-355. "Stereophonic" and its more common diminutive "stereo" had become buzzwords in the late 1950s, as first stereo pre-recorded tapes and then stereo records hit the market. The idea of a stereo guitar had originally been investigated by Jimmie Webster at Gretsch in New

1980 Gibson Les Paul Artist

1983 Gibson Les Paul
Spotlight Special ANT

1983 Gibson Les Paul
Spotlight Special

1983 Gibson Les Paul
Spotlight Special ASB

1979 Gibson Les Paul 25/50 Anniversary

1987 Gibson Les Paul Studio Lite

1979 Gibson Les Paul Artist

■ **More Les Paul peculiarities:**
The Les Paul (with definite
article), a high-end limited edition;
Artist, with complex electronics;
Spotlight Special, using leftover
woods; 25/50 Anniversary, for Les
Paul's 25-year association with
Gibson and 50th year in music;
and Studio Lite, with weight-
reduced body.

1993 Gibson Les Paul
Studio Lite

1997 Gibson Les Paul DC Pro

1997 Gibson Les Paul DC Satndard

1998 Gibson Les Paul DC Satndard

1996 Gibson Les Paul Smartwood Standard

1997 Gibson Les Paul Elegant

1996 Gibson Les Paul Ultima

les paul variants

1992 Gibson Les Paul 40th Anniversary

1994 Gibson Les Paul Standard Centennial

York City. Gretsch's pioneering system had worked by effectively splitting each pickup on a two-pickup guitar into two, so that one pickup could feed the output from the instrument's lower three strings to one amplifier, while the other pickup sent the higher three strings out to another amp.

Gibson would certainly have known about and examined the Gretsch system, and when it came to their own stereo guitars adopted a rather more straightforward system in 1959. Gibson's two-pickup circuitry simply directed the output of each complete pickup to a separate amplifier. In contemporary advertising, Gibson assured the guitarist of the day that it would soon be customary to plug in to a pair of amps and produce "a symphony of warm, full stereophonic sound."

Another new Gibson feature in the search for fresh electric tonalities was the Varitone control, offered on the ES-345 and some ES-355s. This switch selected one of six preset tone options, in combination with the pickup selector expanding to eighteen possible tonal shades. However, Gibson's Varitone and stereo capabilities were never especially popular among guitarists. Often, players would simply disconnect the confusing Varitone and, despite the stereo option, would just get on with playing what was undoubtedly a very good guitar in conventional "mono" mode.

Gibson's doubtless exhausted development team added one more innovation to the line during 1958: the company's first double-neck guitars. Always something of a compromise between convenience and comfort, the double-neck electric guitar was a relatively new idea, the first one having been custom-made by Paul Bigsby in California in 1952. The concept would have been obvious to Bigsby because he also made pedal-steel guitars, on which multiple necks are common.

A double-neck instrument is designed so that it can offer the player two different guitars in one instrument. An instant changeover from one neck to another saves the guitarist having to swap

gibson**solidbody**

2000 Gibson Les Paul
Standard Raw Power

2001 Gibson Les Paul
Junior Special Plus

2001 Gibson Les Paul
Class 5

2004 Gibson Les Paul
Voodoo

2003 Gibson Les Paul
Supreme

les paul variants

2006 Gibson Les Paul Digital HD 6X-Pro

2007 Gibson Les
Paul BFG

■ Gibson has built on its Les Paul line to create one of the world's best-known and most famous electric guitars. The Standard, Custom, and Gold-top models form the core of that line, but variations still abound, including double-cutaways, "digital" guitars, and all manner of alternatives at every price-point.

2007 Gibson Les Paul Robot

1958 Gibson Flying V

1967 Gibson Flying V
Owned by Jimi Hendrix

1979 Gibson Flying V Heritage

1981 Gibson Flying V-II

flying vs

1999 Gibson Flying V Gothic

between separate instruments. Clearly, this is especially useful for the stage musician. The most obvious drawback to the double-neck electric is the increased weight of the resulting instrument, as well as the general awkwardness involved in reaching beyond a neck in an ideal playing position to the other that is invariably too high or too low for comfort.

Gibson launched two double-necks in 1958. The EDS-1275 Double 12 had what became the most common combination for electric double-necks, mixing a six-string and a twelve-string neck. It looked something like an extended ES-175 with its twin pointed cutaways. The more unusual EMS-1235 Double Mandolin had one standard six-string neck, plus a short-scale neck with six strings tuned an octave higher than a guitar, supposedly to mimic the sound of a mandolin.

These first Gibson double-necks were produced only to special order, their hollow bodies made with carved spruce tops and maple backs and sides. The instruments are rare today. Around 1962 Gibson changed the double-necks to a solidbody style, which made them look more like extended SG models. They remained custom-order-only instruments. The most famous player to opt for a Gibson double-neck was Jimmy Page who regularly used one on stage.

Gibson's first low-end solidbody—aside from earlier Les Paul Juniors—was the Melody Maker, launched in 1959. At first it had a simple "slab" single-cutaway body, though this was modified to a double-cutaway body two years later. An option was a short scale-length, another feature aimed at the smaller fingers of beginners. The last change to the Melody Maker came in 1965 when it adopted the style of Gibson's SG solidbody. This type of body design would last until the Melody Maker was dropped from the Gibson line during the early 1970s, although it was reissued in 2007.

Sales of Les Pauls declined in 1960, after a peak in 1959, and by 1961 Gibson had decided on a complete redesign of the line in an effort to try to reactivate this faltering model. The company had started an expansion of the Kalamazoo factory during 1960 which more than doubled the size of the plant.

One of the first series of new models to benefit from the company's newly

gibsonsolidbody

1957 Gibson Flying V Prototype

1980 Gibson Moderne

■ The "Modernistic" solidbodies were a group of electric models that Gibson first sold in the late 1950s. The Flying V and Explorer each had a strangely shaped body—quite remarkably so for the period. A third model, the Moderne, didn't even make it to production at the time.

1963 Gibson Explorer

1980 Gibson Explorer Heritage Reissue Prototype

2006 Gibson X-Plorer New Century black

explorers

moderne

1958 Gibson Explorer Early Model Uncovered

1961 Gibson SG
Les Paul Junior

1963 Gibson SG
Les Paul Special

1961 Gibson SG
Les Paul Special

1961 Gibson SG Les
Paul Standard

■ When Gibson noticed the original Les Paul design was not selling, the company devised the new and distinctly modern SG style, with its almost sculpted look and angular, pointed body. Double-neck guitars meant live performers could use two different types of guitar, often six and twelve-string, without changing instruments.

1963 Gibson SG Les Paul Standard
Owned by Eric Clapton

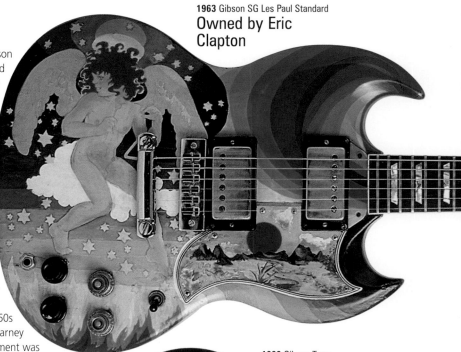

1998 Gibson Tony
Iommi Les Paul SG 2

expanded production facilities was the completely revised line of Les Paul models. Gibson redesigned the Junior, Standard, and Custom models, adopting a distinctly modern, sculpted double-cutaway design. The "Les Paul" name was still used at first, but during 1963 Gibson began to call these new models the SG Junior, the SG Standard, and the SG Custom. (Confusingly, the SG name was used earlier on old-style Les Pauls, with the old-design TV and Special renamed as the SG TV and the SG Special in 1959.) The transition models—those produced between 1961 and 1963—had the new SG design but the old Les Paul names, and are now known to collectors and players as SG/Les Paul models.

Les Paul's name was dropped for a number of reasons. Partly it was because the connection with the guitarist was less of a commercial bonus for Gibson than it had been. His popularity as a recording artist had declined: he'd had no more hits after 1955. Crucially, Les Paul and Mary Ford had separated in May 1963 and were officially divorced by the end of 1964, and Paul did not want to sign any fresh contract with Gibson that would bring in new money while the divorce proceedings were underway. So his contract with Gibson was terminated in 1962, and the following year Les Paul models became SG models ("Solid Guitar"). SG-style solidbodies have attracted a number of players over the years, including John Cipollina, Eric Clapton, Tony Iommi, Robbie Krieger, Tony McPhee, Pete Townshend, Angus Young, and Frank Zappa.

Gibson produced a number of new electric arch-top signature models in the 1960s named for jazz guitarists such as Barney Kessel and Tal Farlow. The body of the Gibson Barney Kessel (1961) featured an unusual double "sharp" cutaway. More successful as an instrument was the Tal Farlow model (1962), visually distinguished by an ornate swirl of extra binding at the cutaway. Back in the solidbody department, Gibson was determined to take on its chief rival, Fender, and came up with the Firebird guitars (and matching Thunderbird bass). Launched in 1963, the Firebirds clearly recognized the solidbody style of the West Coast firm while retaining the style and workmanship for which Gibson was known. Gibson called upon car designer Ray Dietrich to out-Fender Fender.

Dietrich devised the new Firebird line with sleek, asymmetrical bodies that looked a little as if Gibson's old Explorer design had been modernized with some additional curves. The new elongated body shape featured a "horn-less" upper portion that had the effect of making the lower cutaway appear to protrude further. This unbalanced "lop-sided" effect has since gained the original Firebirds the nickname "reverse body" among collectors and players.

There were four models in the 1963 Firebird line. The Firebird I had a single pickup and was the only model without a vibrato unit. The Firebird III had two pickups and a "stud"-style bridge, while the Firebird V had two pickups and a Tune-o-matic bridge. The glorious top-of-the-line Firebird VII had three pickups. >

1964 Gibson EDS-1275 Double Neck
Owned by Steve Howe

1961 Gibson SG
Les Paul Custom

1961 Gibson SG
Les Paul Custom

1990 Gibson SG
Les Paul Custom

1962 Gibson SG Les Paul Standard

1988 Gibson SG-90D

1964 Gibson EDS-1275 Double Neck

gibson SG series

solidbodygibson

1976 Gibson S-I

1979 RD Artist

1979 RD Artist

1981 Gibson
Victory MV-X

1991 Gibson
M-III Standard

reverse-body firbirds

They were the first Gibson electrics to employ through-neck construction. They were also unusual in that they featured a "flipped Fender" headstock which was fitted with banjo-style tuners. This meant that players had to adjust tuning in an unfamiliar way, reaching around to the back of the headstock. But at least the design of the headstock showed a clean outline to the audience. The Firebirds were all fitted with special smaller-than-normal humbucking pickups which were without adjustable pole pieces. Standard finish for the Firebirds was sunburst.

However, Gibson went further than adopting just a Fender vibe for the new line. The company also borrowed Fender's custom color idea, applying to the new line of guitars a range of paints more often employed to brighten up the look of the latest automobiles. One of Gibson's ten new Firebird colors was in fact identical to a Fender color. However, Gibson used the Oldsmobile name for it—Golden Mist—while Fender had opted for the Pontiac term, Shoreline Gold.

Despite the striking appearance of the Firebirds, and their prominent use in the 1960s and later by players such as Brian Jones and Johnny Winter, the ploy didn't work. Gibson's sales of electric guitars during the 1960s had to rely on classic 1950s designs such as the great semi-solid ES-335. Fender understandably complained about similarities to its patented "offset waist" design feature, pointing primarily to the Jazzmaster and Jaguar in its line, and so Gibson tried to fix things by reworking the Firebirds in 1965.

Gibson came up with a new Firebird shape that flipped the old one into a slightly more conventional if still quite Fender-like outline, known now as the "non-reverse" body. Gibson also dropped the through-neck construction in favor of its customary set-neck. The new Firebird I had two single-coil pickups, the Firebird III three single-coil pickups, the Firebird V two mini-humbuckers, and the Firebird VII three mini-humbuckers. Still unsuccessful, the Firebirds were grounded by 1969. Since then, the non-reverse Firebirds have been used even less by well-known players than the marginally more favored reverse versions.

British musicians had virtually been starved of any American-made guitars between 1951 and 1959, thanks to a government ban on importation during that period. Distribution of Gibson in Britain was patchy until Selmer, a London-based wholesale company, started officially to import Gibson guitars into the UK during 1960. Selmer was in the right place when the ban was lifted. The company's famed store in London's Charing Cross Road was at the heart of an area alive with music publishers, small studios, and instrument retailers, a mecca for both the budding and successful musician. Jeff Beck bought his first Les Paul Standard from the Selmer store; Steve Howe purchased his favorite ES-175D there; and Robert Fripp acquired his prized Les Paul Custom at the store in 1968.

In 1965 Gibson's Kalamazoo brand was revived as the company decided to feed a strong demand for bargain electric guitars. At first the entry-level Kalamazoo electrics had Fender-style offset cutaways, although later in the 1960s a shape more like Gibson's own SG was adopted. A handful of different models appeared in this KG series, but they were all dropped by the turn of the decade. The company launched a newly revised version of the Flying V during the second half of the 1960s. The reworked model had more conventional hardware than the original late-1950s V, without the through-body stringing. Gibson also redesigned the control layout for these models first issued during 1967, with the three knobs now forming a triangular group rather than the three-in-a-line style of the original. These new-style Vs would stay in the Gibson catalog until the late 1970s.

Les Paul's musical activities had been very low-key since the mid-1960s, but in 1967 he began a new association with Gibson that resulted in a reissue program for Les Paul models. By the time Stan Rendell became president of Gibson in early 1968 the decision to recommence manufacturing Les

1965 Gibson Firebird
III Non-Reverse

1993 Gibson Nighthawk Special

1982 Gibson Corvus II

1985 Gibson Spirit II XPL

1985 Gibson Q-300 Alpha Series

1988 Gibson US-1

1963 Gibson Firebird VII Reverse Body
Owned by Phil Manzanera

1963 Gibson Firebird V Reverse Body

1961 Gibson Firebird I Reverse Body

■ Created by an automobile designer, the new Firebird series of 1963 was a further attempt by Gibson at a new, modern style. Later versions adopted a "non-reverse" body. Gibson has continued to offer new and often unusual solidbody models, but none with much success.

1999 Gibson Firebird VII Historic Collection Reverse Body

1965 Gibson I No-Reverse Firebird

1964 Firebird V Reverse

non-reverse firebirds

solidbodygibson

1936 Gibson ES-150

1945 Gibson ES-140

early ES models

Paul guitars had been made by the CMI management in Chicago and a new contract was negotiated with Paul. In 1968 Gibson reintroduced the relatively rare two-humbucker Les Paul Custom, and the Gold-top Les Paul with P-90 pickups and Tune-o-matic bridge. They sold well, and Gibson clearly had a success in the making. The only mystery so far as many guitarists were concerned was why they'd waited so long.

An important change to Gibson's ownership occurred in 1969. The new owner, Norlin Industries, was formed that year with the merger of Gibson's parent company, CMI, with ECL, an Ecuadorian brewery. There was a shift in emphasis at Gibson toward the rationalization of production, which meant that changes were made to some of the company's instruments built during the 1970s (and, to some extent, to those made into the 1980s). Generally, such alterations were made for one of three reasons. The first and apparently most pressing requirement was to save money. Second, Gibson wished to limit the number of guitars returned for work under warranty. Lastly, there was a distinct desire to speed up production of Gibson guitars at the Kalamazoo factory.

The guitar design department at Gibson gave a change of style and name to the recently re-introduced Les Paul Gold-top model in 1969, when the Les Paul Deluxe took its place. The Deluxe was the first "new" Les Paul model for fourteen years, and was prompted by calls for a Gold-top with humbucking pickups rather than the single-coil P-90s of the existing reissue model.

In 1969 came the first wave of Gibson Les Paul guitars with low-impedance pickups: the Les Paul Professional and the Les Paul Personal. The Personal was, as the name implied, in keeping with one of Paul's own modified Les Paul guitars, even copying his odd feature of a microphone socket on the top edge of the body. Both guitars had a complex array of controls, seemingly aimed at recording engineers rather than guitarists, and required connection with the special cord supplied, which had an integral transformer to boost the output from the low-impedance stacked-coil humbucking pickups to a level suitable for use with normal high-impedance amplifiers. Predictably, the guitars were not a great success and did not last long in the Gibson line.

The company had another go at low-impedance instruments during 1971 with the Les Paul Recording, which would remain in the line until 1980, and in 1972 the L-5S. The name of this single-cutaway solidbody alluded to Gibson's great old electric hollowbody model, the L-5CES. A few years into its life the new L-5S was changed from low-impedance pickups to regular humbuckers—but that still made no difference to its popularity.

Gibson's final fling with low-impedance pickups was reserved for the company's thinline style and was launched during 1973 as the two-pickup gold-colored Les Paul Signature. The Signature models never really fired players' imaginations, and by the end of the 1970s they were out of production.

Demand for guitars had increased during the early 1970s, and so the company built a second Gibson factory at Nashville, Tennessee, some 500 miles south of Kalamazoo. The factory eventually

1956 Gibson ES-140T

1938 Gibson EH-150 Lap Steel

1938 Gibson EH-150 Lap Steel Double-neck

lap steels

gibson**hollowbody**

1945 Gibson ES300

1938 Gibson ES300

1949 Gibson ES-350 Special Prototype

■ The ES-150 was Gibson's first hollowbody electric guitar, launched in 1936. Since then, the company has produced many more ES models—the name means Electric Spanish—adding to a successful line that runs alongside the company's solidbody models.

1947 Gibson ES350

1957 Gibson ES 350T

1955 Gibson ES-350T

thinline models

hollowbody gibson

1949 Gibson ES-5

1950 Gibson ES-5

1956 Gibson ES-5
Switchmaster
**Owned by
Jimmy Pruett**

1957 Gibson ES-5
Switchmaster

ES-5s

1955 Gibson ES-5
Switchmaster

opened in June 1975. Gibson's original intention was to keep both Kalamazoo and Nashville running. Nashville was designed to produce very large quantities of a handful of models, while Kalamazoo was more flexible and had the potential to specialize in small runs. Nashville was thus the obvious choice to produce the models in Gibson's solidbody line required in the greatest volume at the time—the Les Paul Custom and Deluxe models—along with various other solidbody models.

As if to highlight the contrast between the capabilities of the two plants, Gibson introduced two new Les Paul models in 1976. First was the Les Paul Pro Deluxe, effectively a Deluxe with P-90 pickups and an ebony fingerboard. It was produced in large quantities at Nashville. The other new model was the Les Paul, a spectacular limited-edition model that was notable for Gibson's employment of various fine woods for virtually the entire instrument. Many parts that on a normal electric guitar would be made from plastic were hand-carved from rosewood, including the pickguard, backplates, control knobs, and truss-rod cover. Very few (probably well under a hundred) were produced from 1976 to 1979. As the limited stocks of handmade wooden parts ran out, so normal plastic items were substituted, along with less ornate binding.

Each example had a numbered oval plate on the back of the headstock. Number twenty-five was presented to Les Paul just prior to the 1977 Grammy Awards ceremony. The $3,000 price tag on the Les Paul made it four times the cost of the next most expensive Les Paul model on the 1976 pricelist. During the previous year, Gibson had in fact introduced a number of other new models and a reissue. These included a revitalized Explorer, plus two new solidbodys: the all-maple single-cutaway L-6S, as endorsed by Carlos Santana, and the Les Paul-shape bolt-on-neck Marauder with humbucker and angled single-coil pickups. The S-1 was a sort of three-pickup Marauder that also sported that model's V-shape headstock, and it joined the line in 1976. None of these lasted long.

The 25/50 Les Paul was intended to celebrate Les Paul's twenty-fifth year with Gibson (presumably it had been planned for 1977) and his fiftieth year in the music business. The silver and gold themes generally associated with these anniversaries were reflected in the guitar's chrome- and gold-plated hardware. Once again Les Paul himself was presented with a special example: this time he received guitar number one at a party given in his honor by Gibson, who launched the Les Paul 25/50 Anniversary model during 1978. Despite its relatively high price, the 25/50 sold well.

Gibson's new RD models first appeared in 1978, and incorporated a package of complex "active" electronics. This kind of circuit had been popularized by Alembic at the start of the 1970s and was designed to boost the signal and widen the tonal range of a guitar. The circuit was powered by an on-board battery. The body of the RD series was an even curvier version of the previous decade's Firebird "reverse body" design.

This kind of "hi-fi" guitar was prompted by the apparent competition from synthesizers, which had become big business during the late 1970s. Gibson's parent company Norlin figured that a hook-up with Moog, one of the synthesizer field's most famous names of the time, might re-capture some of the ground that guitars seemed to be losing

ES-175s

1949 Gibson ES-175N

1949 Gibson ES-175

1956 Gibson ES-225TDN

1957 Gibson ES-175

Owned by Steve Howe

1991 Gibson ES-135

■ Gibson's first three-pickup guitar was the ES-5, later modified as the Switchmaster with the aim of providing better control. The ES-175 model, first available in 1949, has proved a particular favorite with jazz players; the ES-295 has the appearance of a hollowbody Les Paul Gold-top.

1952 Gibson ES-295

1958 Gibson ES-5 Switchmaster

hollowbodygibson

1940 Gibson Super 400
Premiere N

1934 Gibson Super 400
**Owned by Muzzy
Marcellino**

1951 Gibson Super
400 CESN

to the new keyboards. In fact, one of the RD models—the Standard—was a regular electric, without the active circuit, which was reserved for the Custom and Artist models. Gibson's RD line did not, however, prove popular and was soon gone from the catalog. Many guitarists disliked what they considered the "unnatural" sounds of active circuitry, and this was a major factor in the downfall of the RD series.

In 1979 Gibson expanded the RD concept into two of its more mainstream electric series, the ES thinlines and the Les Pauls. Gibson had to adapt the large RD circuit board to fit into these more confined body designs. Each of the new Artist models had three knobs, for volume, bass, and treble, and three switches, for brightness, expansion, and compression. However, these models also failed to grab many guitarists, and the Artists did not last long: the Les Paul Artist hobbled on to 1981, while the ES Artist survived until 1985.

A happier project was the Les Paul Heritage Series, one of the first conscious attempts by Gibson to try to make Les Pauls in a way that many players thought was no longer possible. A reasonably healthy market had been building since the late 1960s in so-called "vintage" guitars. This trend was fueled by the general feeling that Gibson "didn't make them like they used to," combined with the prominent use of older instruments by many of the most popular guitarists of the day. While to some extent this was flattering in general to the Gibson name (and to others such as Fender and Gretsch whose guitars were also associated with the vintage trend), it did not help a manufacturer whose main priority was to continue to sell new guitars (especially its new models).

Some U.S. dealers who specialized in older instruments—such as Strings & Things and Music Trader—had already begun to order selected new models with vintage-style appointments from Gibson's Kalamazoo plant, which since the onset of the Nashville factory was beginning to lean more heavily toward shorter, specialized runs of guitars. For the Heritage Series Les Pauls, Gibson's team used a 1954 pattern sample for the carving of the body top, changed the then-regular neck construction to three-piece mahogany, disposed of then-current production oddities such as the "volute" carving below the back of the headstock, and moved a little closer to older pickup specifications. Especially attractive maple was selected for the tops of these new Les Paul models, which were touted as limited editions and were not included on the company's general pricelist.

Launched in 1980, the two Heritage Series models were the Heritage Standard 80 and the Heritage Standard 80 Elite, the latter with an ebony fingerboard and an even more desirable "quilt" figured maple top. Whether as a result of the influence of the Heritage models or a general awareness of market demands, Gibson began at this time to rectify some of the general production quirks instituted in the 1970s, removing from its standard models the volute, for example, and gradually reverting to one-piece mahogany necks.

An oddity issued in 1980 was the Les Paul-shape Sonex 180 which had what Gibson called a Multi-Phonic body. This was in fact a wooden core with a plastic outer skin, following a relatively shortlived 1980s trend for experimental non-wood guitars. The Sonex lasted less than four years in the Gibson line. That same year Gibson issued one of its first signature guitars for a black player, the double-cutaway thinline B.B. King model, in Standard and Custom versions. Both had stereo wiring and were without f-holes, the Custom adding a

gibsonhollowbody

1958 Gibson Super 400 CES

1960 Gibson Super 400 CES

1964 Gibson Super 400 CES 50th Anniversary

1969 Gibson Super 400 CES

1984 Gibson Super 400 CES

1976 Gibson Super 400 CES-WR

super 400 arch-top family

1951 Gibson Super 400 CES

■ The Super 400 was Gibson's biggest acoustic arch-top guitar, and soon players began to fit pickups for louder work. Gibson noticed—and in 1951 launched the Super 400CES, an integrated electric arch-top model that was one of its most prestigious instruments, available in a number of variations over the years.

1962 Gibson Super 400 CES Special

1962 Gibson Super 400 CESN

1962 Gibson Super 400 CESN

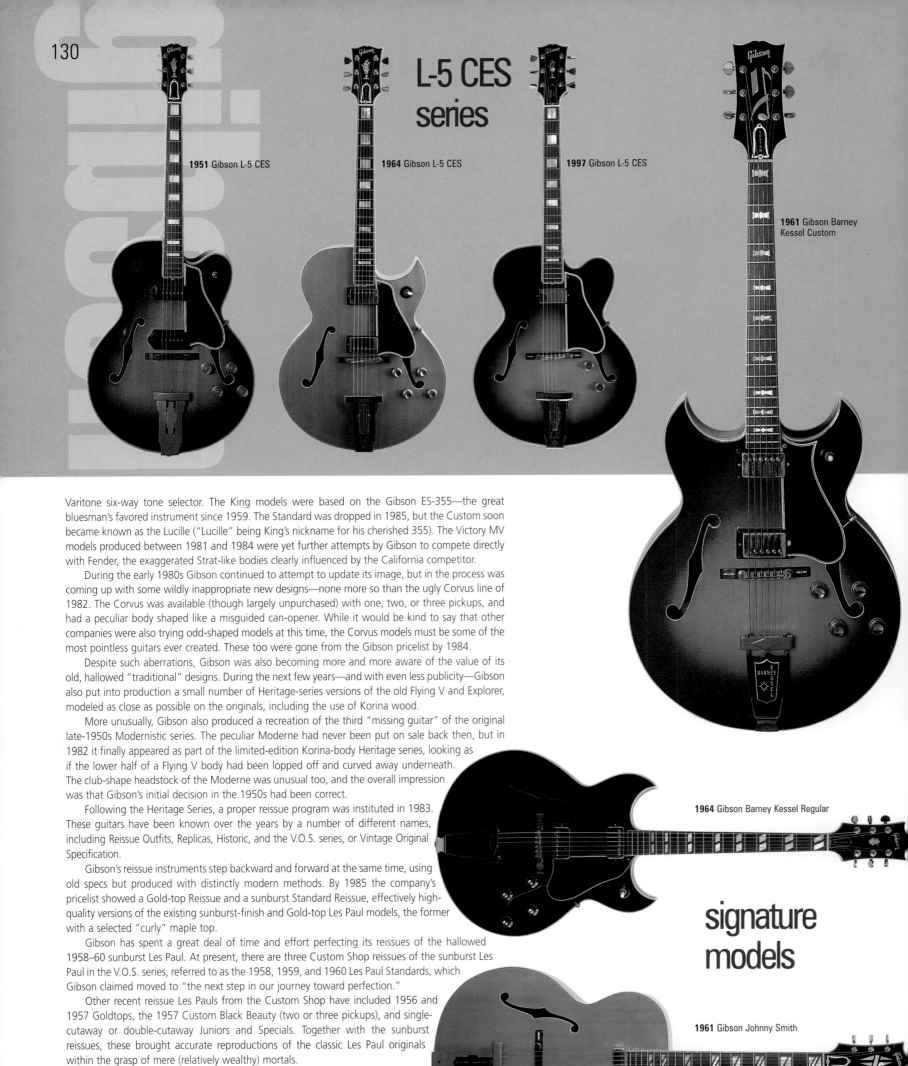

1951 Gibson L-5 CES

L-5 CES series

1964 Gibson L-5 CES

1997 Gibson L-5 CES

1961 Gibson Barney Kessel Custom

Varitone six-way tone selector. The King models were based on the Gibson ES-355—the great bluesman's favored instrument since 1959. The Standard was dropped in 1985, but the Custom soon became known as the Lucille ("Lucille" being King's nickname for his cherished 355). The Victory MV models produced between 1981 and 1984 were yet further attempts by Gibson to compete directly with Fender, the exaggerated Strat-like bodies clearly influenced by the California competitor.

During the early 1980s Gibson continued to attempt to update its image, but in the process was coming up with some wildly inappropriate new designs—none more so than the ugly Corvus line of 1982. The Corvus was available (though largely unpurchased) with one, two, or three pickups, and had a peculiar body shaped like a misguided can-opener. While it would be kind to say that other companies were also trying odd-shaped models at this time, the Corvus models must be some of the most pointless guitars ever created. These too were gone from the Gibson pricelist by 1984.

Despite such aberrations, Gibson was also becoming more and more aware of the value of its old, hallowed "traditional" designs. During the next few years—and with even less publicity—Gibson also put into production a small number of Heritage-series versions of the old Flying V and Explorer, modeled as close as possible on the originals, including the use of Korina wood.

More unusually, Gibson also produced a recreation of the third "missing guitar" of the original late-1950s Modernistic series. The peculiar Moderne had never been put on sale back then, but in 1982 it finally appeared as part of the limited-edition Korina-body Heritage series, looking as if the lower half of a Flying V body had been lopped off and curved away underneath. The club-shape headstock of the Moderne was unusual too, and the overall impression was that Gibson's initial decision in the 1950s had been correct.

Following the Heritage Series, a proper reissue program was instituted in 1983. These guitars have been known over the years by a number of different names, including Reissue Outfits, Replicas, Historic, and the V.O.S. series, or Vintage Original Specification.

Gibson's reissue instruments step backward and forward at the same time, using old specs but produced with distinctly modern methods. By 1985 the company's pricelist showed a Gold-top Reissue and a sunburst Standard Reissue, effectively high-quality versions of the existing sunburst-finish and Gold-top Les Paul models, the former with a selected "curly" maple top.

Gibson has spent a great deal of time and effort perfecting its reissues of the hallowed 1958–60 sunburst Les Paul. At present, there are three Custom Shop reissues of the sunburst Les Paul in the V.O.S. series, referred to as the 1958, 1959, and 1960 Les Paul Standards, which Gibson claimed moved to "the next step in our journey toward perfection."

Other recent reissue Les Pauls from the Custom Shop have included 1956 and 1957 Goldtops, the 1957 Custom Black Beauty (two or three pickups), and single-cutaway or double-cutaway Juniors and Specials. Together with the sunburst reissues, these brought accurate reproductions of the classic Les Paul originals within the grasp of mere (relatively wealthy) mortals.

A hostile takeover of Norlin by Rooney Pace occurred in 1984. All the main Gibson production was now handled at the Nashville plant. Kalamazoo had become

1964 Gibson Barney Kessel Regular

signature models

1961 Gibson Johnny Smith

gibson**hollowbody**

1955 Gibson Byrdland

1969 Gibson Byrdland

byrdland series

1967 Gibson Byrdland Special

1964 Gibson Tal Farlow Signature

1964 Gibson Trini Lopez Standard Signature

■ The L-5CES has appeared with various styles of pickups and cutaways. Meanwhile, Gibson's electric hollowbody guitars attract top players, some of whom have been honored by the company with special models. The Byrdland mixed ideas from Billy Byrd and Hank Garland, while jazzmen Barney Kessel, Johnny Smith, and Tal Farlow each had a Gibson signature guitar.

2004 Gibson Johnny A Signature

hollowbodygibson

1958 Gibson ES-335

1958 Gibson
ES-335TD

1958 Gibson
ES-335T

1960 Gibson
ES-335T

a specialist factory making custom orders, banjos and mandolins, and as far as Norlin was concerned the closure of this factory became inevitable. The last production at Kalamazoo was in June 1984, and the plant closed three months later, after more than 65 years' worthy service since the original building had been erected by Gibson. It was of course an emotional time for managers and workers, many of whom had worked in the plant for a considerable time. Three of them—Jim Deurloo, Marv Lamb, and J.P. Moats—rented part of the Kalamazoo plant and started their new Heritage guitar company in April 1985. Over at the Nashville plant, the emphasis had been on large runs of a small number of models, but this had to change when it became Gibson's sole factory.

In January 1986 three businessmen—Henry Juskiewicz, David Berryman, and Gary Zebrowski, who had met while classmates at Harvard business school—completed their purchase of the Gibson operation for $5 million. The inevitable "restructuring" of the Gibson business occurred, and as seems so often to be the case in such undertakings, many employees lost their jobs. However, today the company appears to be relatively healthy again. As well as tailoring the reissue program to sensibly defined areas, the new owner—with guitar-fan Juskiewicz at the helm—also continued to innovate and try new models. But such new designs still apparently have little effect on players who know that Gibson means classics.

A number of signature electric hollowbodies appeared from 1986, not dissimilar to some of the well-known Gretsch Chet Atkins models, but now with Gibson touches. The Country Gentleman and the Tennessean were in production until 2005, when, following Chet's death in 2001, his estate ended the association with Gibson.

The superstratlike US-1 model debuted during 1986 and introduced musicians to a new idea from Gibson in the construction of solidbody guitars. For the new guitar, the company decided to employ a core of "chromite" (balsa wood) at its heart. Chromite had the effect of reducing the weight of the maple-top US-1, and Gibson also applied the new material to the Les Paul Studio Lite model in 1991.

New in that same year of 1991 was the solidbody M-III line, a series of radically styled double-cutaway guitars fitted with flexible circuitry. Unfortunately, Gibson's customers again felt the design and the electronics of the new M-III guitars too "un-Gibson," and the various M-IIIs, including the Les Paul-shape Classic/M-III and the Studio Lite/M-III, did not last long in the line.

The Custom Shop idea was revived in the 1980s at Nashville and the present Custom Shop at Gibson continues the traditional role of making oddities for wealthy players but also provides more mainstream inspiration for the current Custom Shop lines. The 2009 catalog included everything from a Zakk Wylde "Bullseye" Les Paul to a Wes Montgomery L-5CES.

An interesting addition to the burgeoning line of the Custom Shop's "new/old" Les Pauls was the Aged 40th Anniversary model of 1999. Essentially, this was yet another move toward a more accurate reproduction of those hallowed 1959-period flame-top Les Paul Standards. The major difference with the 40th Anniversary recreation was, however, the aged finish. **>**

1964 Gibson ES-335TDC
Owned by Eric Clapton

gibson semi-solidbody

1959 Gibson ES-335TDN

■ Gibson's ES-335, first available in 1958, was a masterful mix of two different styles of electric guitar: a solidbody and a hollowbody. The thinline hollow body has a solid block running down the center, producing a unique blend of tones that has attracted many fine guitarists, especially blues players.

1960 Gibson ES-335TDN

1961 Gibson ES-335TDC

ES-335 thinlines

1965 Gibson ES-335 12 String

1998 Gibson ES-335 Lucille

2005 Gibson Eric Clapton ES-335

semi-solidbody gibson

1959 Gibson ES-330

hollowbody 330s

1960 Gibson ES-330TDN

1958 Gibson ES-355

1959 Gibson ES-355TDSV Custom

1960 Gibson ES-355TDSV Stereo

Gibson set about giving the 40th Anniversary model a look that suggested it had actually been used for forty years. The paint colors were made to appear faded, the nickel parts on the instrument—such as the pickup covers—were realistically tarnished, the lacquer "skin" was cracked and effectively dulled, and all manner of dings and knocks were added to the guitar. Like Fender and its Relics, Gibson aimed to recreate the almost indefinable allure of a vintage guitar with this model—at a stiff price, of course.

Gibson expanded its electric production in 1999 into a building on the famous Beale Street in Memphis, about 200 miles from the Nashville HQ. The new location, called the Gibson Beale Street Showcase, also features a live performance venue. In 2002, the manufacturing section became part of Gibson's Custom Division and today it produces the ES semi-hollowbody model electrics.

Gibson USA's 2009 catalog was based on retro, and included a slew of Les Paul variants, half a dozen SGs, a Firebird V, a few Explorers and Flying Vs, and a Melody Maker, while Gibson's Custom, Art & Historic division added yet more Les Pauls, SGs, all the company's current ES series and arch-top electric offerings, and a brace of Flying Vs.

In 2006, Gibson began shipping its long-promised digital guitar, the HD.6X-Pro. This was a regular Les Paul with an extra hex pickup between bridge pickup and bridge, which directs signals via an ethernet cable to an analog-to-digital converter box. That box in turn allowed the player to feed various combinations of strings to a computer for use with recording software or similar programs. That did not last long, however, and Gibson's tech direction was enhanced in 2007 with a series of Robot guitars. Regular designs—mainly Les Pauls and SGs— are offered with a clever self-tuning system that works with powered tuning pegs. The system offers standard tuning and six programmable tunings. A further development in 2009 was the Dark Fire Les Paul, which matched an improved Robot system with some of the digital guitar's features and potential.

Many more signature models have appeared from Gibson in recent years, including an L-5CES named for Wes Montgomery (1993), an ES-175 for Steve Howe (2001), ES-335s for Andy Summers (2001), Larry Carlton (2002), Eric Clapton (2005), and Alvin Lee (2005), an Explorer for Allen Collins (2003), a Flying V for Lenny Kravitz (2001), an EDS-1275 double-neck for Jimmy Page (2007), SGs for Tony Iommi (1998, 2001) and Angus Young (2000), as well as Les Pauls for Jimmy Page (1995, 2004, 2009), Joe Perry (1996, 2003), Slash (1997, 2004, 2008), Ace Frehley (1997), Zakk Wylde (1999, 2004), Peter Frampton (2000), Gary Moore (2000, 2009), Dickey Betts (2001), Gary Rossington (2002), Duane Allman (2003), Neal Schon (2005), Warren Haynes (2006), Joe Bonamassa (2008), Steve Jones (2008), and Michael Bloomfield (2009). There is no doubt that classic Gibsons will continue to be seen in the hands of succeeding generations of inspired musicians and in the care of their industrious creator.

Orville Gibson invented the arch-top guitar in the 1890s, and the company that bore his name went on to lead the development and refinement of the arch-top as it is known today. When Gibson began making flat-top guitars in the late 1920s, the company quickly became one of the leading makers. **>**

355s

gibson**semi-solidbody**

1970 Gibson Les Paul Jumbo

1971 Gibson Gold Crest brown

1973 Gibson Les Paul Signature

1978 Gibson Super V Ces

1978 Gibson Kalamazoo Award

1979 Gibson ES Artist

1958 Gibson EDS-1275 Double Twelve

1959 Gibson ES-345

1960 Gibson ES-345TDSV Special

345s

1963 Gibson ES-345TDSV Custom Stereo

■ Variations on the thinline ES-335 soon began to appear from Gibson. The ES-355 and ES-345 had better appointments and electronic additions, while the ES-330 disposed of the 335's solid center body block, continuing life as a thinline hollowbody electric. Meanwhile, the solidbody line spawned Les Paul variants and other new models.

1960 Gibson ES-345TD

semi-solidbodygibson

1912 Gibson Style U Harp

1905 Gibson Style O

1903 Gibson Style O

Orville's earliest surviving instrument is an unusual ten-string guitar-mandolin creation dated 1894. He also made a highly ornamented harp guitar, a large zither, and one guitar with an elaborate pearl butterfly inlaid into the top below the bridge, but most of the other guitars and mandolins that survive are relatively plain instruments. The back and sides of the guitars were made of walnut, at a time when the vast majority of guitars (and mandolins, too) were made of rosewood. The tops were carved out of spruce and were not as highly arched as contemporary arch-tops. The headstocks had a rounded upper edge and were so wide that they are known today as "paddle heads." After the arched top, the most radical new feature of Orville's guitars was their size, which was noticeably larger than those of his contemporaries.

After Orville left Gibson, in 1903, the new company immediately published a catalog that included two lines of arch-top guitars: the Style O series, with an oval soundhole, and the Style L with a conventional round hole. Style O was available in several degrees of ornamentation, ranging from the plain O and O-1 to the fancy O-3, which was bound in alternating pieces of white and green pearl. In addition, each level of ornamentation was offered in three sizes. The Style L offering was organized in similar fashion.

In the grand Gibson vision, the guitar was a member of the mandolin family, and this association was nowhere so obvious as in the redesigned Style O model of 1908, which would be called the Style O Artist guitar within a few years. Still one of the most striking guitar designs ever conceived, the new Style O featured a scrolled upper bass bout, inspired by the scroll on Gibson's F-style mandolins (one of Orville's designs), and had the body "cut away" on the treble side, providing free access to the fifteenth fret at a time when most guitars had only twelve frets clear of the body.

The first catalog also included two versions of what would become one of the dinosaurs of the guitar world—the harp guitar, an instrument with a standard guitar neck and an additional set of sub-bass strings. Gibson wasn't the only maker of harp guitars, but it promoted them more heavily than any other maker. After the company's first catalog, subsequent catalogs always devoted the center spread to the Style U harp guitar. The instrument was large, unwieldy, and expensive, and it never caught on.

In 1912, Gibson introduced a sixteen-inch guitar with a standard, symmetrical body shape, calling it the L-4. The L-4 became the standard-bearer of Gibson's guitar line through the mandolin craze, through the tenor banjos of the Jazz Age, and into the early years of the guitar era.

In 1919 Gibson hired Lloyd A. Loar, a mandolin virtuoso who also had some new ideas for instrument design. The plan was for Loar to develop a whole family of mandolin instruments that would rekindle interest in mandolins and revive the company. Loar's new Style 5 line included a

gibsonacoustic

1898 Gibson O.H. Style

1906 Gibson Style O

■ Gibson's earliest acoustic guitars were unusual hand-made instruments, built around the start of the 20th century in Orville Gibson's original workshop in Kalamazoo, Michigan. A shortlived oddity was the large harp guitar. Gradually, modern styles evolved as the guitar became more popular into the 1920s.

1906 Gibson Style U

early acoustics

1906 Gibson L Artist

1924 Gibson L-4

acoustic**gibson**

1928 Gibson Nick Lucas "Florentine"

1929 Gibson HG-24

early flat-tops and arch-tops

1929 Gibson L-5

1932 Gibson L-75

1933 Gibson L-12

guitar: the L-5. It replaced the traditional round or oval soundhole with a pair of violin-style f-holes and sported two recent improvements that set Gibson apart from other makers: the adjustable truss-rod in the neck and the height-adjustable bridge. Both inventions became industry standards.

In 1926 Gibson offered its first flat-top. The L-1, one of the company's original arch-top models, had been discontinued in 1925, and the name was appropriated for the new flat-top. Like the arch-top, it was only 13 inches wide and not very impressive, but it would become famous a half-century later as the guitar that blues legend Robert Johnson held in a studio photograph from the mid 1930s. It has the circular lower body shape typical of Gibson's arch-tops—a shape that would later be copied for Gibson's most famous flat-top, the J-200.

The guitar was making deep inroads into mainstream popular music, too, by the late 1920s, thanks in part to Nick Lucas. The man who had committed the first hot guitar solo to wax in 1922—"Pickin' The Guitar"—had become one of the leading pop singers—or "crooners"—and he accompanied himself on guitar. Gibson enlisted the endorsement of Lucas, first making a custom guitar for him and then, in 1928, introducing an official Nick Lucas model. The next year Gibson introduced the L-2 flat-top, which fell between the Lucas and L-1 in ornamentation.

Also in 1929, Gibson introduced a trio of HG models (HG for Hawaiian Guitar). All three had a new body shape, with a thicker waist than any other style of Gibson. The 16-inch model served as the prototype for Gibson's classic "round-shouldered dreadnought" design. The same year, the L-10 arrived, followed in 1930 by another f-hole model, the L-12, and the L-7. All of the new Gibsons had maple back and sides, and all were 16 inches wide.

The company added two smaller, 14 arch-tops to the line in 1932: the f-hole L-75 and the roundhole L-50. Both had stubby bodies, shorter than any of the 14-inch flat-tops that had recently appeared. In 1934 Gibson "advanced" the body sizes of all of the 16-inch arch-tops to seventeen inches. The smaller models would be advanced to 16 inches a year later.

To establish Gibson once and for all as the leading maker of arch-tops, the company introduced a new model called the Super 400, costing almost twice as much as the L-5. Also in 1934, Gibson appropriated the shape of its largest HG (Hawaiian) model of 1929 and introduced it as the Jumbo. Perhaps the most enduring effect of the Jumbo, which was only produced for two years, was the confusion it started in the area of flat-top body nomenclature. Gibson would continue to use "jumbo" for all its sixteen-inch flat-tops, regardless of body shape, while the rest of the guitar world came to describe the shape of Gibson's Jumbo and all subsequent similar models as "round-shouldered dreadnoughts" (to distinguish them from Martin's "square-shouldered" shape), reserving the "jumbo" term for later flat-tops with a large circular lower bout. The Jumbo was succeeded in late 1936 by a pair of dreadnoughts, the J-35 and the Advanced Jumbo. The J-35 is often cited as Gibson's finest pre-war large-body flat-top.

In 1939 Gibson introduced a rounded cutaway on the L-5 and Super 400, designating them Premier models. By that point, the electric guitar had gained a foothold, and the acoustic arch-top had reached the end of its evolution. Only four Gibson models would survive World War II: the Super 400, L-5, L-7, and L-50. The L-7C (C for cutaway body) and the L-50 last appeared in 1970, and Gibson offered the last acoustic L-5C and Super 400C in 1981. However, the decline of the acoustic arch-top by no means meant a similar decline of interest in acoustic guitars. It only indicated a shift in player preference to flat-top models.

Gibson's attempt to beat the arch-top competition with the Super 400 had been successful, and in late 1937 the company made a similar move in the flat-top arena, starting with a seventeen-inch flat-top made for singing-cowboy movie star Ray Whitley. Although it was labeled as an L-5 Special,

1934 Gibson L-C Century

1934 Gibson Martelle Deluxe

gibson acoustic

1942 Gibson Super 400

1935 Gibson Super 400

1939 Gibson Super 400 Premier N

1939 Gibson Super 400C

1968 Gibson Super 400 CN-Wal

1996 Gibson Super 400 Custom

super 400s

1977 Gibson Super 400C-WR

■ The L-5 was Gibson's first arch-top acoustic, designed by Lloyd Loar and first sold in 1922. The arch-top style reached its zenith at Gibson with the mighty Super 400 models, and both the L-5 and Super 400 were treated to a body cutaway in 1939. A true rarity was the one-off L-10 double-neck guitar and banjo.

1936 Gibson L-10 Double-neck

1958 Gibson L-5 CT

L series

1939 Gibson L-5 Premier

acoustic gibson

1952 Gibson Super 300

1935 Gibson Jumbo Custom

1939 Gibson Advanced Jumbo

1957 Gibson Super 300C

1939 Gibson SJ-200

1937 Gibson SJ-200 "Ray Whitley" jumbo

the style officially appeared a year later as the Super Jumbo—a larged-bodied, highly ornamented flat-top that was initially available only as a custom order. Then came the SJ-200, which quickly became a badge of identification for country singers; it remains the flagship model of an acoustic line that now consists almost exclusively of flat-tops.

After the war, Gibson abandoned rosewood, traditionally considered to be the best wood for flat-tops. All of the LG and dreadnought models had mahogany back and sides, and the SJ-200 (soon to be just J-200) went back into production with maple back and sides. A smaller, 16-inch guitar with the same circular lower body as the J-200 appeared in 1951. Called the J-185, it had the maple back and sides of the J-200. Through the 1950s, while the LGs and dreadnoughts accounted for the bulk of Gibson's acoustic sales, the J-200 kept the Gibson image in front of music audiences.

Early in the 1950s, Gibson appropriated two features from its arch-top and electric lines to the flat-top line, but with limited success. The CF-100, a small body flat-top, debuted in 1951 sporting a cutaway with pointed bout. It was available with or without an electric pickup. Three years later a dreadnought body was fitted with a pickup and introduced as the J-160.

In the early 1960s, as folk music began to spur the demand for acoustic guitars, Gibson expanded the line with a pair of eye-catching new models. The Dove offered the square-shouldered dreadnought with a maple body, a pickguard inlaid with a pearl dove image, and an oversized bridge with abstract dove images inlaid in the bridge ends. The Everly Brothers model was similar to the J-180 "jumbo" (non-dreadnought) body with a black finish, double oversized pickguards, and a pinless bridge designed by the Everlys' father, Ike Everly.

The combination of higher production, unwise changes in specifications and increasing competition from cheap Japanese imports resulted in a slow deterioration of quality through the 1960s that picked up speed in the 1970s. One catalyst to Gibson's fall was the acquisition of CMI by Norlin. Norlin hired designers Michael Kasha and Richard Schneider to re-create the flat-top using modern technology and scientific testing methods. The result of their research and development, the Mark series, appeared in 1975. On paper, the Marks held great promise, but they failed the "playing" test miserably, leading Norlin to all but abandoned the acoustic line. Besides new Chet Atkins electric nylon-string guitars, nothing of note happened in the early 1980s except mounting losses and decreasing quality.

Back on its feet under new ownership in 1987, Gibson attempted to reassert its reputation for innovation with new models that took advantage of improvements in acoustic guitar amplification. These included the Star, three Starburst models, and a pair of EAS (Electric-Acoustic Starburst) models, which debuted in 1992. The acoustic properties

gibson acoustic

1938 Gibson SJ-100

super jumbos

2001 Gibson SJ-200
"Western Classic"

1954 Gibson J-200

■ Gibson reacted to calls from players for bigger guitars and to Martin's introduction of Dreadnought guitars by issuing its biggest flat-tops in the 1930s, the suitably named Jumbo and Super Jumbo. The style lives on in the popular flat-tops in the J series, including the J-45 that has attracted players from flatpicker Doc Watson to rock 'n' roller Buddy Holly.

1952 Gibson J-200

jumbos

1942 Gibson J-45 Jumbo

1966 Gibson J-45 Jumbo

2002 Gibson J-45 Jumbo

acousticgibson

■ Gibson flat-top acoustics have come in many styles, including signature models for famous players. Attempts to offer a practical and sonically acceptable amplified acoustic have absorbed Gibson many other makers; shown here are two successful Chet Atkins models, in nylon-string and steel-string versions.

1960 Gibson Hummingbird

of the EAS models were of secondary importance, as indicated by a shallower body and an arched back of laminated maple. In the dreadnought line, Gibson successfully introduced a rosewood square-shouldered model, the J-60, in 1992. In 1997 a new style of "thin-shouldered" dreadnought appeared and evolved into several established cutaway models. A line of no-frills models, dubbed the Working Man series, also gained acceptance due to their "more affordable" prices.

The company was equally successful in its efforts to recapture the magic of vintage Gibsons with reissue versions of classic models. Gibson brought the basic J-200, J-45, Dove, and Hummingbird back to the specifications of their respective golden years. The legendary pre-war rosewood dreadnought, the Advanced Jumbo, was reintroduced with a series of limited runs, beginning in 1990. The smallbody L-00 came back in 1991.

Gibson began promoting the J-200 as "The King of the Flat-Tops," and the J-200 line became a veritable kingdom, with over thirty different models offered in the 1990s. Additional offshoots included the trimmed-down J-150 and J-100 Xtra, the fancier J-250, J-1000, J-1500, and J-2000. Today more than fifty acoustic guitars are available under the Gibson name, including a long line of artist models in the names of Elvis Presley, Elvis Costello, John Lennon, Pete Townshend, Sheryl Crow, Emmylou Harris, Robert Johnson, and others.

With the success of Fender's Precision Bass, other guitar makers began to produce bass models. Gibson put out its Electric Bass toward the end of 1953. It had a solid mahogany violin-shaped body, evidently designed to appeal to double-bass players. This short-scale bass had an optional "spike" that fitted to the bottom of the body and allowed the bassist to play the instrument upright, like a double-bass. It was rarely used, but still remained a feature well into the 1960s. Gibson's "violin" design was copied a few years later, albeit with a hollow body, by the German company Hofner. This probably would have failed to make the history books had it not been adopted in 1961 by a young British musician named Paul McCartney.

Gibson added a few more short-scale bass guitars to its catalogue later in the 1950s, including in 1958 the EB-2, which was a bass version of the company's new ES-335 guitar. At the same time, Gibson renamed the violin-shaped Electric Bass the EB-1, but dropped it the following year, replacing it with the solidbody EB-0 (effectively a bass

1963 Gibson Everly Brothers

1968 Gibson C-0 Classical

gibson acoustic

J-160Es

1962 Gibson J-160E
Owned by George Harrison

1964 Gibson J-160E
Owned by John Lennon

1978 Gibson MK-53

1982 Gibson Chet Atkins CEC

1987 Gibson Chet Atkins SST

1999 Gibson J-50

2000 Gibson Sheryl Crow

2000 Gibson '60s Dove Reissue

acousticgibson

1912 Gibson
Mando Bass

1953 Gibson
Electric Bass

1958 Gibson EB-2

1958 Gibson EB-2

version of Gibson's double-cutaway Les Paul Junior guitar). Gibson seemed to view its bass models merely as four-string versions of the more important guitar models, and the company indulged guitarists who wanted to play bass by offering bass guitars only with short 30-inch scale-lengths.

In 1959, Gibson added a six-string bass, the hollowbody EB-6, to its line. It was essentially a regular six-string guitar down an octave, aimed principally at guitar players (and quite different from our modern idea of a six-string bass). In 1961 Gibson introduced the new EB-3 solidbody bass. This was in effect a bass version of the new SG guitar line, introduced the same year. A number of players were drawn to it, not least the talented British pair of Jack Bruce of Cream and Andy Fraser of Free.

A double-neck combining an EB-3 and an SG six-string appeared in 1962, the EBSF-1250. In 1963, Gibson issued a pair of new models, the single-pickup Thunderbird II and two-pickup Thunderbird IV. They were the company's first long-scale bass guitars and looked like four-string counterparts to Gibson's Firebird guitar models. As well as the long scale, the Thunderbird basses marked a departure for the company with through-neck construction and fully adjustable bridges. Original sales were poor. A revised "non-reverse" Thunderbird design with Gibson's regular glued-in neck appeared in 1966 after Fender complained of infringements to its patented offset-waist "reverse" body design.

In 1969, Gibson in the United States issued a Les Paul Bass (renamed Les Paul Triumph Bass in 1971) with low-impedance pickups. Bass players generally ignored these complicated Gibson basses, as well as the company's later Moog-influenced RD instruments. In 1973 it introduced the two-pickup Ripper and the sliding-pickup Grabber, long-scale basses sharing the same body. They were discontinued early in the 1980s.

Over the years, Gibson has remained relatively unsuccessful with bass guitars, although a number of players, mainly from the heavier end of rock, have toyed with the growling Gibson Thunderbird. Most notable was John Entwistle, who started using IVs around 1971 (there's one on *Quadrophenia*), but later Martin Turner (with his melodic lines in Wishbone Ash), Nikki Sixx (Mötley Crüe), and Jared Followill (Kings of Leon) also strapped on a T-Bird.

Gibson's current catalog includes Thunderbird and SG basses, plus the Tobias Growler and the Grabber II, a limited edition update of the Grabber.

gibsonbass

1961 Gibson EB-3

1966 Gibson EB-6 Bass

1965 Gibson EB-3

Bass guitars have never proved particularly successful for Gibson, although players such as Jack Bruce have found a place for them. The first one was the Electric Bass or EB-1, issued soon after Fender's innovative Precision of 1951, and a number of other models have followed since then.

1963 Gibson Thunderbird IV Bass

1962 Gibson EBSF-1250 Double Bass

1969 Gibson Les Paul Bass

1974 Gibson Grabber Bass G-1

bassgibson

1990 Gilbert Classical

gilbert classical guitars

1994 Gilbert Classical

1986 Gitler Bar Rashi

1968 Goya Rangemaster

1986 Gitler Skelleton

■ **GILBERT** John Gilbert (born 1922) was a toolmaker with Hewlett Packard in Palo Alto, California, when a friend gave him A.P. Sharpe's famous book, *Make Your Own Spanish Guitar*. He built and repaired instruments as a hobby until, in 1974, making them his career. His method was based on careful measurement, record-keeping, and experimentation, leading to guitars of great consistency and accuracy. In 1997, John Gilbert handed over his workshop to his son William, choosing to concentrate on his line of machine heads.

■ **GITTLER** Born in Cleveland, Ohio, guitarist/artist/inventor Allan Gittler (1928–2003) adopted a very individual approach to instrument design, eliminating every unnecessary component. First appearing in the mid-1970s, his electric guitars were appropriately ultra-minimalist and mostly made of steel tubing. In 1982 Gittler became Avraham Bar Rashi and emigrated to Israel, where less radical versions of his original creation were manufactured under the Gittler name by the Astron company during the latter 1980s.

■ **GODIN** This major Canadian brand started in 1987, a subsidiary of Robert Godin's LaSiDo company in Quebec. Initially Godin made replacement electric guitar necks and bodies. Fully-fledged instruments soon followed, many built for various well-known guitar brands, but Godin also developed his own acoustics and electrics. The former have since appeared under various LaSiDo logos, including Simon & Patrick, Art & Lutherie, La Patrie, Seagull, and Norman. Until recently, electrics always employed the Godin name, but now LaSiDo also produces a retro-flavored range bearing the Richmond brand.

■ **GODWIN** Godwin organs were made by Sisme and during the 1970s this Italian company offered guitarists the chance to enjoy similar sounds via an amalgam of both instruments. The impressive-looking end result came in two versions, Professional and Super Professional, differing only in number of knobs and switches. Both were weighty and unwieldy, while performance was unpredictable and high prices didn't help sales. Godwin played it safer and cheaper with a conventional Les Paul copy and matching bass launched at the same time, but both these and the Guitar Organ proved equally shortlived.

■ **GORDON-SMITH** Consistently keeping a low profile, Gordon-Smith is the UK's longest established electric guitar brand, having survived thirty-five years. Gordon Whittam and John Smith started the company in 1974, but Whittam departed six years later, subsequently producing Gordy guitars. Smith has soldiered on solo ever since, manufacturing mainly Gibson-influenced designs that offer no-nonsense quality, dependable performance, and value for money—an appealing combination that usually incorporates Gordon-Smith's own pickups and hardware.

■ **GOYA** This brand-name appeared on a wide variety of instruments over four decades, imported into America and Canada from numerous manufacturing sources by assorted distributors. The first Goyas were early-1950s acoustics made by Levin in Sweden, while Hagstrom in the same country later provided electrics covered in sparkle and pearl plastic. The next decade brought Italian-origin solids and semi-acoustics, manufactured by companies such as Galanti and Zero Sette. Goyas of the 1970s came from Japan, with electrics including original designs as well as the inevitable Fender and Gibson look-alikes. Martin imported Japanese-made Goya models in the early 1980s, and many were imitations of the real thing, even some electrics. The brand eventually ended up on a Korean-sourced series that survived until the mid-1990s.

1996 Godin G-1000

1998 Godin LG-XT

1999 Godin Radiator

■ Guitars featured here are by classical maker John Gilbert (USA); the entirely individual Gittler, based in the United States and later Israel; the major Canadian brand Godin; the Italian organ builder Godwin; British electric-guitar maker Gordon-Smith; and the extensively used Goya brandname.

1989 Godin LP Baggs Electro Acoustic

1979 Gordon Smith Gypsy "60" SS

1976 Goodwin Guitar Organ

1958 Goya Bass

1949 Gretsch Electromatic Lap Steel

1953 Gretsch Duo Jet

1969 Gretsch Duo Jet

1995 Gretsch Duo Jet 6128

■ **GRETSCH** Friedrich Gretsch emigrated to the United States from Germany in 1872 at age sixteen. After working for a manufacturer of drums and banjos in New York City, he set up his own company there in 1883 to make drums, banjos, tambourines, and toy instruments. His eldest son, Fred, took over at age fifteen on Friedrich's death in 1895.

In 1916 construction was completed of a large ten-story building at 60 Broadway, Brooklyn, just by the Williamsburg Bridge. This imposing building housed the factory and offices of the Gretsch company for many years. In the early 1930s the guitar began to replace the banjo in general popularity, and in about 1933 the first Gretsch-brand guitars appeared, a line of arch-top and flat-top acoustics. They were offered alongside Gretsch's burgeoning wholesale list of other makers' instruments, including guitars from the "big two" Chicago manufacturers, Kay and Harmony. The first Gretsch-brand arch-top electric was introduced around 1939—the shortlived Electromatic Spanish model, which was made for Gretsch by Kay.

In 1942 Fred was replaced as company president by his third son, William Walter (Bill) Gretsch, who headed Gretsch until his premature death six years later. Bill's brother Fred Gretsch Jr., already the company's treasurer, then took over as president. It was Fred Jr. who would steer the company through its glory years during the 1950s and 1960s.

After World War II ended, Gretsch placed a new emphasis on supplying guitars for professional musicians. The first new Gretsch electric guitar of the post-war era revived the Electromatic Spanish model name, this arch-top debuting in 1949 alongside a number of Synchromatic acoustic guitars. The single-coil pickup of the Electromatic Spanish was the first of many made for Gretsch by Rowe Industries of Toledo, Ohio, a company run by Harry DeArmond. A few years later the DeArmond pickup would receive its official Gretsch name, the Dynasonic.

Cutaway-body electrics followed in 1951. The Electromatic and Electro II in effect proved that Gretsch now took seriously the expanding electric guitar business. Helping to launch the models was a new Gretsch man, Jimmie Webster, a qualified piano-tuner and inspired guitarist. Webster used an unusual "touch" playing system, similar to the one popularized much later by Eddie Van Halen. Webster became an important ambassador for Gretsch, and probably did more than anyone else in the coming years to spread the word about Gretsch guitars, while in the process doing much to promote electric guitars and guitar-playing in general.

Gretsch certainly noticed the new solidbody electric guitar that Fender began marketing during 1950, mainly because the upstart California company chose to call it the Broadcaster. This was a model name that Gretsch still used—although Gretsch spelled it "Broadkaster"—for a number of its drum products. At Gretsch's request, Fender changed the name to Telecaster. When Fred Jr. saw that Fender and Gibson were actually beginning to sell these new-style solidbody guitars, he acted swiftly. In 1953 Gretsch launched its first solidbody, the single-cutaway Duo Jet. In fact, the guitar was a semi-solid with routed channels and pockets inside, but the visual effect was certainly of a solidbody instrument. In its early years the new Duo Jet had, unusually, a body front covered in a black plastic material, as used on some Gretsch drums. It also had Gretsch's unique two-piece strap buttons (an early take on the idea of locking strap buttons) and the Melita Synchro-Sonic bridge.

The Melita was the first bridge to offer independent intonation adjustment for each string, beating Gibson's Tune-o-matic version by at least a year. Three more solidbodies in the style of the Duo Jet were added to the Gretsch line in 1954 and 1955: the country-flavored Round Up, the Silver Jet, and the red Jet Fire Bird. The Silver Jet came with a silver sparkle finish on the front of its body, and this was another product of Gretsch's helpful drum department. **>**

1956 Gretsch Duo Jet
Owned by
Jeff Beck

1957 Gretsch Duo Jet
Owned by
George Harrison

1958 Gretsch Duo Jet

1955 Gretsch
Silver Jet

1962 Gretsch Silver Jet

1955 Gretsch Jet
Fire Bird

1995 Gretsch Silver Jet 6128

1995 Gretsch Sparkle
Jet 6129T

■ Gretsch dates back to a firm set up
in New York City in 1883 by German
immigrant Friedrich Gretsch. The
company's first "solidbody" electric
appeared in 1953, the Duo Jet,
modeled on Gibson's Les Paul of the
previous year but with routed
chambers in the otherwise solid body.
More Jet models followed.

1998 Gretsch Sparkle Jet 6129T

solidbodygretsch

1955 Gretsch White Penguin

1958 Gretsch White Penguin

2003 Gretsch White Penguin

1955 Gretsch Chet Atkins Solidbody 6121

That same year in the hollowbody lines the noncutaway Electromatic Spanish became the Corvette, the cutaway Electro II became the Country Club, and the Electromatic became the Streamliner. The Country Club would go on to be the most enduring model name in Gretsch's history.

Another significant addition to the Gretsch line in 1954 was the option of colored finishes beyond the normal sunburst or natural varieties. Automobile marketing was having a growing influence on guitar manufacturers in the early 1950s, and the theme was especially evident in Gretsch's colorful campaign of 1954, with a Cadillac Green option for the Country Club and a Jaguar Tan (a sort of dark gold) for the Streamliner. The paints came from DuPont, a company that also supplied most of the car companies at that time (and later Fender too). Gretsch drew yet again on its experience in finishing and lacquering drum products in different colors, artfully applying know-how that already existed within the operation to help make its guitars stand out in the market.

There had been isolated precedents for colored-finish guitars—including Gibson's all-gold ES-295 and gold-top Les Paul of 1952, as well as Fender's infrequent and as-yet unofficial custom colors—but for a few years Gretsch made the use of color into a marketing bonus almost entirely its own. Through the mid 1950s Gretsch added a number of pleasant two-tone options—yellows, coppers, ivories—contrasting a darker body back and sides against a lighter-colored body front on arch-top electrics such as the Streamliner (launched 1954), Convertible (1955), and Clipper (1956). This two-tone style was yet further evidence of inspiration from long-standing techniques used in the drum department.

The success of Gibson's new Les Paul guitar—well over 2,000 were sold in 1953 alone—alerted other manufacturers, including Gretsch, to the value of a "signature" model endorsed by a famous player. Today the practice is very familiar, but back in the 1950s it was a new, exciting, and potentially profitable area of musical-instrument marketing. Around 1954 Jimmie Webster succeeded in securing talented Nashville-based country guitarist Chet Atkins for this role, a move that in time would completely turn around Gretsch's fortunes.

After various discussions and meetings between the company and the guitarist, the Gretsch Chet Atkins Hollowbody 6120 model appeared in 1955. Atkins wasn't keen on the Western paraphernalia that Gretsch insisted on applying to the guitar—including cactus and cattle inlays, and a branded "G" on the body—but relented because he was so keen to get a signature guitar on to the market.

In fact, the decorations on the Hollowbody model were gradually removed over the following years. Gretsch had also added a Bigsby vibrato to the production model at Atkins's request. There was a Chet Atkins Solidbody, too—essentially a Round Up with a Bigsby vibrato, although, despite the name, the Solidbody still had Gretsch's customary semi-solid construction. Atkins had little to do with the Solidbody model, and it was dropped after a few years. >

gretschsolidbody

1962 Gretsch Princess

1962 Gretsch Corvette "Silver Duke"

1966 Gretsch Corvette "Gold Duke"

■ More solidbody electrics continued to appear from the New York–based Gretsch company, including the ultra-rare White Penguin and a signature model for Chet Atkins. The Princess was apparently aimed at female players, while the Astro Jet possessed one of the weirdest body shapes from any guitar maker.

1961 Gretsch Corvette

1963 Gretsch Twist

1966 Gretsch Astro Jet

solidbodygretsch

1977 Gretsch Super Axe 2

1975 Gretsch TK300

1969 Gretsch Roc Jet silver

1975 Gretsch Hi Roller

The Hollowbody, however, became Atkins's exclusive instrument for his increasingly popular work. It remained one of the most famous Gretsch models for many years, and Gretsch did good business from the new endorsement deal. Its 1955 catalog trumpeted: "Every Chet Atkins appearance, whether in person or on TV . . . and every new album he cuts for RCA Victor, wins new admirers to swell the vast army of Chet Atkins fans." The new Chet Atkins model effectively put Gretsch on the map.

Not content with the coup of attracting Chet Atkins to the company, Jimmie Webster also devised Gretsch's brand new high-end sensation, the White Falcon. First marketed by Gretsch in 1955, it was an overwhelmingly impressive instrument. The guitar's single-cutaway hollow body was finished in a gleaming white paint finish, as was the new "winged" headstock, and both bore gold sparkle decorations once again borrowed from the Gretsch drum department. All of the White Falcon's metalwork was finished in gold plate, including the deluxe Grover Imperial tuners with "stepped" buttons and the stylish new tailpiece—since nicknamed the "Cadillac" because its V shape is similar to the auto company's logo. The fingerboard markers of the White Falcon had suitably ornithoid engravings, and the gold plastic pickguard featured a flying falcon about to land on the nearby Gretsch logo. It was, simply, a stunner.

Some of Gretsch's more ostentatious banjos used gold trim, fancy fingerboard markers and rhinestone inlays, so it's fair to deduce that features of the White Falcon such as the distinctive jeweled knobs and feathery fingerboard inlays may well have been inspired by that part of the company's work. An early White Falcon prototype had been displayed at one of Gretsch's own local promotional events in March 1954, but the guitar's first big showing was at the major NAMM instrument trade show in Chicago four months later. Gretsch enticed dealers by billing the still experimental Falcon as one of their "Guitars Of The Future" along with the green Country Club and tan Streamliner.

Gretsch also produced a partner to the White Falcon in the company's standard-shape semi-solid style. This was the White Penguin, complete with all the Falcon features and released in 1956. It even had a little penguin waddling across the pickguard. Very few White Penguins were sold, and the model has since become regarded as one of the most collectable of all Gretsch guitars.

Gretsch benefited from the success stories of two early rock 'n' roll guitarists, both of whom used Chet Atkins Hollowbody guitars to power their sound. Eddie Cochran was an accomplished guitarist who landed a cameo spot in the 1956 movie *The Girl Can't Help It* and then made some blasting rock 'n' roll with his Hollowbody at the center of a churning mix of rockabilly, country, and blues; Duane Eddy turned out a string of hit records from the late 1950s, based on his deceptively simple instrumental style that will forever be known by the word that was attached to so many of the

gretsch**solidbody**

1975 Gretsch Committttee

Gretsch has never been afraid to visit the more unusual corners of guitar design, and the guitars pictured on these pages show just how strange some of those designs could be. Mixed in are a few sensible instruments, including the baritone Spectra Sonic, useful for its deep-tuned rich and lowly sound.

1979 Gretsch Beast Bst-1000

1961 Gretsch Bikini Double Neck

1989 Gretsch Travelling Wilbury's

2002 Gretsch Spectra Sonic C Melody Baritone

2004 Gretsch Electromatic Junior Jet II

solidbodygretsch

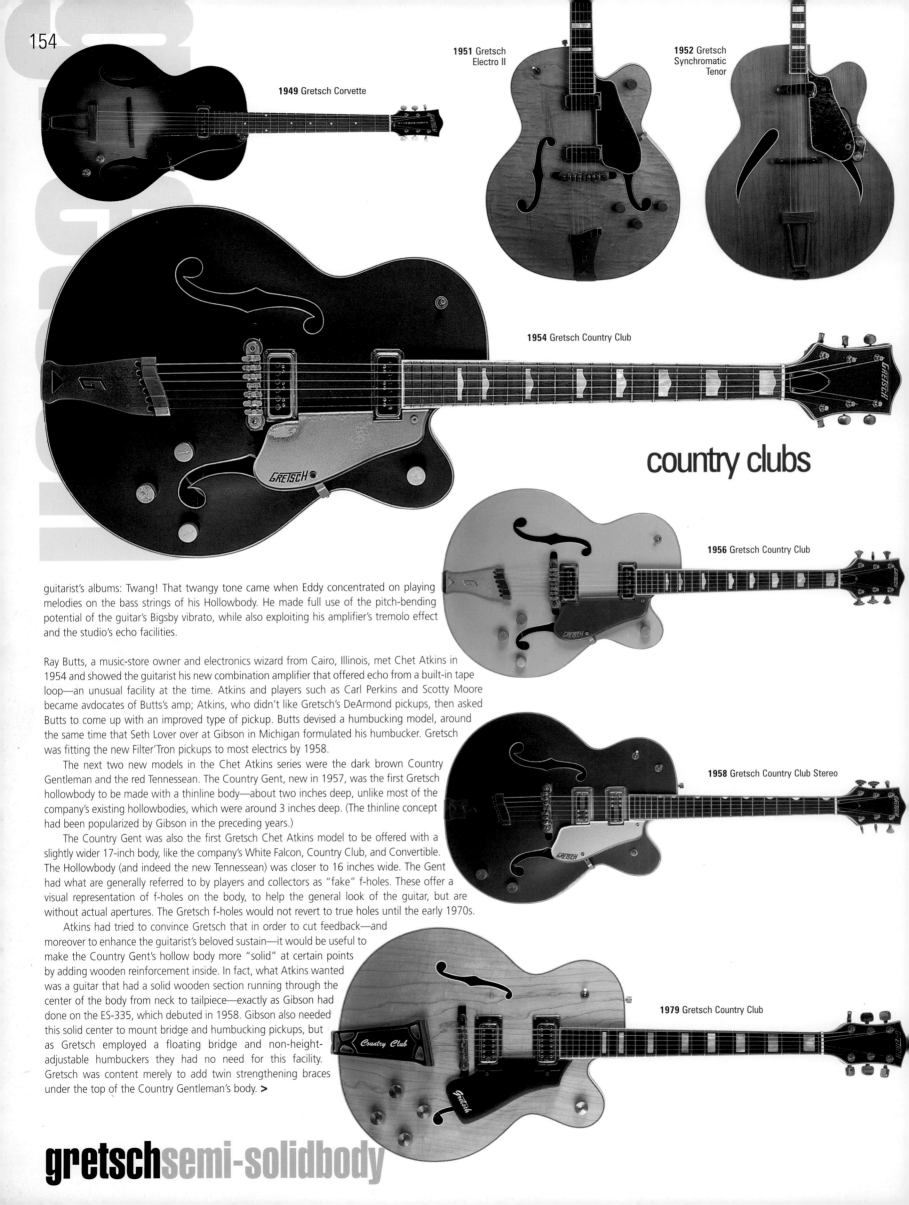

1949 Gretsch Corvette

1951 Gretsch Electro II

1952 Gretsch Synchromatic Tenor

1954 Gretsch Country Club

country clubs

1956 Gretsch Country Club

guitarist's albums: Twang! That twangy tone came when Eddy concentrated on playing melodies on the bass strings of his Hollowbody. He made full use of the pitch-bending potential of the guitar's Bigsby vibrato, while also exploiting his amplifier's tremolo effect and the studio's echo facilities.

Ray Butts, a music-store owner and electronics wizard from Cairo, Illinois, met Chet Atkins in 1954 and showed the guitarist his new combination amplifier that offered echo from a built-in tape loop—an unusual facility at the time. Atkins and players such as Carl Perkins and Scotty Moore became avdocates of Butts's amp; Atkins, who didn't like Gretsch's DeArmond pickups, then asked Butts to come up with an improved type of pickup. Butts devised a humbucking model, around the same time that Seth Lover over at Gibson in Michigan formulated his humbucker. Gretsch was fitting the new Filter'Tron pickups to most electrics by 1958.

The next two new models in the Chet Atkins series were the dark brown Country Gentleman and the red Tennessean. The Country Gent, new in 1957, was the first Gretsch hollowbody to be made with a thinline body—about two inches deep, unlike most of the company's existing hollowbodies, which were around 3 inches deep. (The thinline concept had been popularized by Gibson in the preceding years.)

The Country Gent was also the first Gretsch Chet Atkins model to be offered with a slightly wider 17-inch body, like the company's White Falcon, Country Club, and Convertible. The Hollowbody (and indeed the new Tennessean) was closer to 16 inches wide. The Gent had what are generally referred to by players and collectors as "fake" f-holes. These offer a visual representation of f-holes on the body, to help the general look of the guitar, but are without actual apertures. The Gretsch f-holes would not revert to true holes until the early 1970s.

Atkins had tried to convince Gretsch that in order to cut feedback—and moreover to enhance the guitarist's beloved sustain—it would be useful to make the Country Gent's hollow body more "solid" at certain points by adding wooden reinforcement inside. In fact, what Atkins wanted was a guitar that had a solid wooden section running through the center of the body from neck to tailpiece—exactly as Gibson had done on the ES-335, which debuted in 1958. Gibson also needed this solid center to mount bridge and humbucking pickups, but as Gretsch employed a floating bridge and non-height-adjustable humbuckers they had no need for this facility. Gretsch was content merely to add twin strengthening braces under the top of the Country Gentleman's body. >

1958 Gretsch Country Club Stereo

1979 Gretsch Country Club

gretsch semi-solidbody

1955 Gretsch Chet Atkins Prototype

1955 Gretsch Chet Atkins 6120 (early model)

■ The hollowbody electrics are the best-known Gretsch guitars, and a wonderfully idiosyncratic bunch they are. The company was among the first to use bright colored finishes to help its instruments stand out from the crowd, while the association with Chet Atkins proved to be a long and valuable one.

1957 Gretsch Chet Atkins 6120
Owned by Duane Eddy

1956 Gretsch Chet Atkins 6120

chet atkins models

1959 Gretsch Chet Atkins Hollowbody

1960 Gretsch Chet Atkins Hollowbody Custom

1962 Gretsch Chet Atkins Hollowbody

1967 Gretsch Chet Atkins Nashville (renamed Hollowbody)

semi-solidbodygretsch

1955 Gretsch Convertible Sal Salvador

1957 Gretsch Streamliner

1954 Gretsch Streamliner

convertibles & streamliners

1957 Gretsch Convertible

Another Jimmie Webster design, the new Space Control bridge, appeared around the same time. It was simpler than the Melita, and lacked intonation adjustment. Also new were "Neo-Classic" half-moon-shape markers at the edge of the fingerboard, which appeared around 1957.

In 1958 Gretsch marked the 75th anniversary of the company's founding with a pair of special Anniversary model guitars. These were offered in one- and two-pickup versions that have since been nicknamed as the Single Anniversary and Double Anniversary models. Remarkably, they lasted in the Gretsch catalog until as late as 1977. Meanwhile, the tireless Jimmie Webster collaborated with Ray Butts to come up with the first stereo guitar system, "Project-O-Sonic." At first they achieved a stereo effect by splitting the output of the pickups, sending the sound of the top three strings to one amplifier and the bottom three to another.

This stereo circuitry was first launched as an option on the Country Club and White Falcon models during 1958. Various modifications appeared over subsequent years, but stereo seemed too complex to capture many players' imaginations. Another questionable piece of Webster weirdness was "T-Zone Tempered Treble," which translates to the more simple description "slanted frets." Webster claimed that they improved intonation. The White Falcon and the new high-end Viking model bore the skewed frets from 1964, the fingerboard helpfully marked with offset dot markers in the slanted zone to warn innocent players.

The Country Gent, Hollowbody, and White Falcon changed to a double-cutaway style during 1961–62. Gibson was as ever the primary inspiration for this decision: since 1958 the Kalamazoo guitar-maker had increasingly employed double cutaways to successful effect. With such a body design, players could more easily reach the higher frets of the fingerboard and make fuller use of this upper register when soloing.

Gretsch's solidbody line moved to a double-cutaway style too, from 1961. Also that year, Gretsch decided that it needed a cheaper solidbody that could compete with Gibson's Les Paul Junior, and so came up with the low-end Corvette (a name borrowed from an early arch-top model). This was the company's first true solidbody guitar, and came complete with HiLo'Tron single-coil pickup.

The Gretsch Corvette started life with a "slab" body like the Junior, but later gained beveled-edge contours, aping Gibson's new SG. Another opportunist solidbody based on the Corvette was the Twist of 1962, which exploited the contemporary dance craze with its twisting red-and-white "peppermint" pickguard design.

During the guitar boom of the middle 1960s Gretsch moved its drum department out of the Brooklyn factory to another location a few blocks away, while a good deal of the company's wholesaling operations either ceased or were moved to the Chicago office. All this was to allow the whole of the seventh floor in Brooklyn to be turned over to guitar making, not least because of the popularity afforded Gretsch by George Harrison's prominent use of a Country Gentleman. No Harrison signature model ever appeared, but Gretsch did produce a shortlived Monkees model to cash in on

white falcons

1955 Gretsch White Falcon

gretsch semi-solidbody

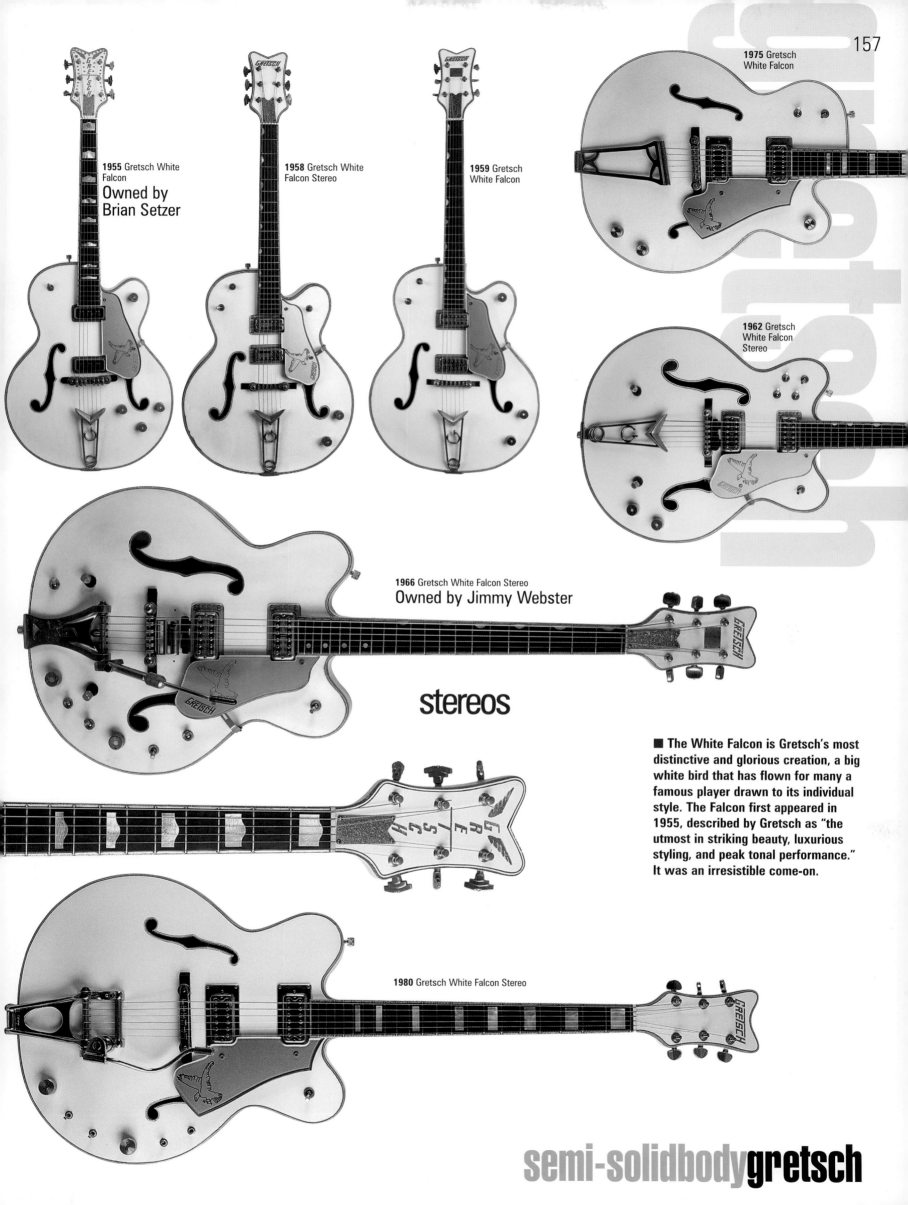

1955 Gretsch White Falcon
Owned by Brian Setzer

1958 Gretsch White Falcon Stereo

1959 Gretsch White Falcon

1975 Gretsch White Falcon

1962 Gretsch White Falcon Stereo

1966 Gretsch White Falcon Stereo
Owned by Jimmy Webster

stereos

1980 Gretsch White Falcon Stereo

■ The White Falcon is Gretsch's most distinctive and glorious creation, a big white bird that has flown for many a famous player drawn to its individual style. The Falcon first appeared in 1955, described by Gretsch as "the utmost in striking beauty, luxurious styling, and peak tonal performance." It was an irresistible come-on.

semi-solidbodygretsch

1957 Gretsch Clipper 1

1963 Gretsch Chet Atkins Tennessean

1958 Gretsch Tennessean 6119

tennesseans

1960 Gretsch Chet Atkins Tennessean

the television pop group of the 1960s. Through a marketing deal the group featured Gretsch instruments including drums and the company's twelve-string thinline electric introduced in 1966. The six-string Monkees model that Gretsch issued that same year had the group's distinctive guitar-shape logo on the pickguard and truss-rod cover.

By the mid 1960s models such as the high-end White Falcon came fitted with a gamut of guitar gadgets created by the ever-fertile mind of Jimmie Webster. Additionally there was a "standby" on/off switch, which on a stereo-equipped model meant a total of two control knobs and six switches, as well as a couple of levers behind the back pickup to operate padded string-dampers. Also, the vibrato tailpiece would sport a telescopic adjustable arm, while a Floating Sound frame-like device sat on a "fork" passing through the body and contacting the back. It was positioned in front of the bridge with the strings passing through it and was supposed to enhance tone and increase sustain. Webster's inspiration came from the tuning forks he used regularly as a piano tuner. Thus the top-of-the-line Gretsch models of the day were probably the most gadget-laden instruments on the market, assaulting players' imaginations with a plethora of possibilities. But some musicians were simply scared off.

In 1967 Gretsch was bought by D.H. Baldwin, an Ohio-based musical instrument company specializing in the manufacture of pianos and organs. In September 1970 Baldwin moved Gretsch production out of Brooklyn to a site in Booneville, Arkansas, well over 1,000 miles away. Very few personnel made the move southwest. Before the move, Gretsch made a number of limited-run instruments for various retailers, players, and teachers. Small-order batches in the 1960s included specially modified models for Gretsch dealers such as Sam Ash (Anniversary-style with cat's-eye shape soundholes), Sam Goody (twin-cutaway arch-top with "G-shaped" soundholes), and Sherman Clay (gold- and silver-finish Corvettes, later nicknamed the Silver Duke and the Gold Duke).

Special small-run "signature" guitars were also made, including a limited number for New York-based player/teacher/store-owner Ronny Lee, as well as some six- and seven-string models named for guitarist George Van Eps (the seven-string version of which remained in the catalog for ten years).

Gretsch produced the Van Eps single-cutaway arch-top models from 1968, in six-string as well as the seven-string versions. This underlined once again the company's compliant approach, enabling the manufacture of small numbers of limited-appeal instruments—even if it did mean tooling-up for the unique fourteen-pole humbuckers necessary for Van Eps's seven-string.

The first new Gretsch model of the Baldwin era was the undistinguished twin-cutaway thinline Rally, although it did have an unusual built-in active treble-boost circuit. More interesting, if hardly devastating, was a new line of Chet Atkins models. In 1972 the Deluxe Chet and the Super Chet

1959 Gretsch Chet Atkins Country Gentleman

1963 Gretsch Chet Atkins Country Gentleman

1962 Gretsch Chet Atkins Country Gentleman

1957 Gretsch Chet Atkins Country Gentleman

■ Gretsch's Country Gentleman and Tennessean models, designed in collaboration with Chet Atkins, appeared in the late 1950s, fitted with one (Tennessean) or two (Country Gent) of Gretsch's new Filter'Tron humbucking pickups. The original style was replaced in 1961 with a double-cutaway version, as used a few years later by George Harrison.

country gentlemen

1967 Gretsch Country Gentleman Custom (three-quarter size)

1973 Gretsch Chet Atkins Country Gentleman

semi-solidbody**gretsch**

1966 Gretsch Monkees Bigsby

1962 Gretsch Ronny Lee

1967 Gretsch 7585 Viking

1967 Gretsch Chet Atkins Nashville

1964 Gretsch 7585 Viking

were launched. The big, deep-body, single-cutaway arch-top style was the result of a collaboration between Atkins and Gretsch men Dean Porter and Clyde Edwards. The highly-decorated Super Chet sported an unusual row of control "wheels" built into the pickguard's edge, while the plainer Deluxe Chet had conventional controls. The Deluxe did not last long, but the Super stayed in the line for some seven years.

Two new low-end guitars came along in 1975: the Broadkaster solidbody and semi-hollow electrics. As usual Gretsch was to some extent following Gibson's lead—and on this occasion the path was an unpopular one. Gibson had launched the Marauder, its first solidbody guitar with a Fender-style bolt-on neck, in 1974; likewise, the Broadkaster solidbody was the first Gretsch with a bolt-on neck, while also displaying strong Strat-style influences. Neither of these new guitars drew much praise.

More new Chet Atkins signature models appeared in 1977. These were the effects-laden Super Axe, plus the gadget-less Atkins Axe. Both were gone from the line by 1980. Also in 1977 the company added a couple more solidbody electrics to the line, the TK 300 and the Committee. The TK 300 was another cheap bolt-on-neck solidbody, this time with a strange, asymmetric body, while the Committee followed a trend of the period for using through-neck construction. But these were uninspiring guitars by any standards, and appeared to be almost totally lacking in the character which had once been at the heart of Gretsch design. The last new Gretsch guitars to appear under Baldwin ownership were the unappealing Beast solidbodys, launched in 1979. While nobody realized it at the time, they marked the end of an era with a depressingly low note.

Although sales picked up a little in the early 1970s, Baldwin was disturbed to find that the business was still not returning a profit, despite various cost-cutting exercises. In early 1979, Baldwin bought the Kustom amplifier company, and by the end of the year had merged Gretsch with Kustom, moving the sales and administration office for the new combined operation to Chanute, Kansas.

Baldwin eventually decided to stop production of Gretsch guitars; very few instruments were manufactured beyond the start of 1981. Then, in 1985, Baldwin sold Gretsch . . . to Gretsch. Fred III was the grandson of the company's founder. He bought the company that bore his name and Gretsch guitar manufacturing was started again.

Fred III introduced updated versions of the classic Gretsch models of the past, no doubt having noticed the increasing prices that certain Gretsch instruments had been fetching for some time on the "vintage" guitar market. The unique character of Gretsch—in sound, looks, and playability—was appealing to yet another new generation of players. Negotiations for domestic production were unsuccessful, and so Gretsch decided to go "offshore", contracting a manufacturer in Japan.

However, in 1989 Gretsch offered an unusual forerunner to its forthcoming guitars with a series of Korean-made electrics intended to capitalize on the popularity of the fictional-family supergroup The Traveling Wilburys. The cheap and somewhat primitive guitars were loosely based on the group's old Danelectro instruments, and various models were issued, all boldly finished in what Gretsch called "original graphics" with a travel theme appropriate to the band's name.

Gretsch could no longer use Chet Atkins's name, now a Gibson property after the agreement with the player had come to an end. But in 1989 nine new models were launched. There were five hollowbodies: the Tennessee Rose, recalling a Tennessean; the Nashville; Nashville Western with

gretsch semi-solidbody

1966 Gretsch Twelve-string

1967 Gretsch Rally

1972 Gretsch Super Chet

1968 Gretsch Van Eps Seven-String

1974 Gretsch Country Roc

■ Gretsch was the first guitar maker to use the promotional push of an anniversary model, in this case to mark in 1958 the company's 75th year. The Chet Atkins connection continued as a major focus for Gretsch guitars, while a dalliance with The Monkees proved to be more shortlived.

anniversary models

1961 Gretsch Double Anniversary

1958 Gretsch Anniversary

1968 Gretsch Double Anniversary

semi-solidbody**gretsch**

1993 Gretsch Nashville
Brian Setzer 6120 SSUGR

1999 Gretsch Nashville Brian Setzer
Hot Rod 6120 SH

nashville models

1993 Gretsch Country
Classic II 6122-1962

1997 Gretsch Nashville
6120-6/12

G-brand and Western appointments; Country Classic, recalling a Country Club; and Country Classic double-cutaway. There were four solidbodies: the Duo Jet; Silver Jet; Jet Firebird; and Round Up. This initial selection was soon joined by a pair of White Falcons offered in single- or double-cutaway styles.

The biggest shake-up in Gretsch's recent history came with an alliance with Fender in 2003, with Fender developing, producing, marketing, and distributing Gretsch. Since then, virtually every model has been improved and new ones added to the catalog.

By 2008, with the Atkins model names back with Gretsch, the pricelist showed fifteen electric models. There were seven arch-tops: Anniversary; Chet Atkins Country Gentleman; Chet Atkins Hollowbody/Nashville (including U.S. Custom Shop version); Chet Atkins Tennessee Rose (Tennessean); Country Club; White Falcon (including Black Falcon and U.S. Custom Shop version). There were eight solids: Chet Atkins Solidbody; Duo Jet (including Custom Shop Relic version); Jet Firebird; Penguin; Power Jet; Power Jet Firebird; Silver Jet; Sparkle Jet. There is also a less expensive offshore series that revived the old Electromatic name. The company has also offered a number of signature models that honor well-known Gretsch players, including Brian Setzer (whose signature models began in 1993), Malcolm Young (1996), Duane Eddy (1997), Keith Scott (1999), Stephen Stills (2000), Bo Diddley (2000), Elliot Easton (2002), Billy F. Gibbons/Bo Diddley (2005), Reverend Horton Heat (2005), Bono (2005), Jimmie Vaughan (2007), David Lee (2008), and Billy Zoom (2008).

Fender have done good things for the brand, with the guitars evidently better than they've ever been and many guitarists still crazy for the keen sound and cool look of a Gretsch electric.

Gretsch's reputation as an acoustic guitar brand, meanwhile, rests mainly on its eye-catching 1940s Synchromatic arch-tops and the Texas-look, Brooklyn-made Rancher jumbo from a decade later. In the 1930s, Gretsch made student and professional arch-tops, as well as a few flat-tops, but the upper end of the arch-top line received a dramatic boost in 1939 with the introduction of the Synchromatic. Top of the line was the Synchromatic 400, a streamlined Deco vision with catseye soundholes and thirteen-layer binding with a line of gold accent sandwiched in the middle, designed to compete with Gibson's Super 400 and Epiphone's Emperor. In 1949 the company introduced a range of triangle-hole flat-tops. This design would reach its aesthetic extreme in 1954 with the introduction of the model 6022 Rancher, with its G-brand burned into the top and the other cowboy motifs that also adorned the Round-Up and Chet Atkins models in Gretsch's electric line.

The Chet Atkins era shifted the company's fortunes squarely to electric guitars, and Gretsch's acoustic guitars made little impact on the marketplace or public consciousness for many years. The Gretsch name revived in the early 1990a with an Asian line of mostly electric instruments that faithfully replicated classic Gretsches of the 1950s and 60s. The line expanded into a number of inexpensive instruments, many of which trumpeted the Synchromatic name more as a buzzword than for any resemblance or features connected to the namesake models. The Gretsch catalog today includes a range of Synchromatic and Rancher models, some with cutaways, as well as triangle-hole dreadnoughts.

gretsch semi-solidbody

2001 Gretsch Nashville Western 6120W-1957

2003 Gretsch Nashville Classic 6122-1959

■ Gretsch's Nashville line appeared in 1989. Gretsch could not use the old Chet Atkins model names because Atkins had become a Gibson endorser. More recently, the names have returned, and the classic Hollowbody and Country Gentleman are back at the heart of the Gretsch catalog.

2004 Gretsch Nashville Western 6120 WCST

1940 Gretsch Synchromatic 400

1953 Gretsch Synchromatic Custom

1955 Gretsch Custom

1954 Gretsch Rancher

1995 Gretsch Rancher

acoustics

1995 Gretsch White Falcon Rancher

1963 Gretsch 6070 Bass

bass

acousticgretsch

1996 Grimes Jazz Laureate

1954 Grimshaw Electric Deluxe

1970 Guild M-75
BCG Blues Bird

1970 Guild S-100

1963 Guild
Thunderbird S200

■ **GRIMES** Stephen Grimes (born 1948) began making arch-top mandolins in Seattle, Washington, in 1972. Two years later he turned to guitars, producing first arch-tops and then flat-tops. He now operates from Kula, Hawaii, building some twenty guitars a year. The Jazz Laureate is his flagship model. In 1996 he was one of twenty-one luthiers commissioned to build a blue guitar for the Scott Chinery collection.

■ **GRIMSHAW** Founded in 1934, Emile Grimshaw's company, based in London, England, initially produced banjos and acoustic guitars. Arch-top electrics debuted during the 1950s, including the popular SS Deluxe, which appealed to younger players thanks to a modern image created by unusual offset cutaway styling and teardrop soundholes.

Solids didn't feature strongly until the late 1960s, when the GS30 was launched as one of the first Les Paul look-alikes. This proved to be a Grimshaw best seller and was soon joined by other, less derivative designs, although imitations later returned in the form of Telecaster and Gibson SG copies. But the company faced increasing imported competition and had shut up shop by the early 1980s.

■ **GUILD** Guild shares the worldwide recognition afforded other illustrious U.S. makers such as Epiphone, Fender, Gibson, Gretsch, Martin, and Rickenbacker, but is the youngest member of this elite fraternity, having been started in 1952 by New York guitarist/music teacher Alfred Dronge.

Using equipment purchased from Epiphone, after its acquisition by Gibson, Dronge set up a small workshop staffed by a handful of craftsmen, including ex-Epiphone employees, while the Guild brand name was apparently borrowed from an amplifier company in San Diego. High quality soon earned recognition for the fledgling company and growing demand necessitated a move from New York to the first factory in Hoboken, New Jersey.

During the early years the catalog included hollowbodied electrics that unsurprisingly displayed distinct Epiphone overtones, such as the Stratford X-350. Flat-top acoustics also featured, like the Navarre, Valencia, and the more compact Troubador, while arch-top versions mostly mirrored their electric equivalents.

Appearing in 1954, the small size, hollow-bodied Aristocrat electric was Guild's lightweight answer to the Gibson Les Paul, but like many traditional-style U.S. makers, the company didn't really target the fast-growing "modern" guitar market until the next decade. Based on the earlier Slim Jim thinline semi, the single-cutaway Starfires were introduced in 1960 and became popular tools of the burgeoning beat group scene that soon followed. A twin-cutaway version debuted in 1963 as Guild finally acknowledged the influence of Gibson's successful ES-335.

The Johnny Smith Award, introduced in 1956, was the company's first artist-endorsed guitar, but the 1960s brought more converts to the Guild cause. Jazz ace George Barnes joined via his Acoustilectric model, while Duane Eddy defected from Gretsch in return for two signature six-strings. Even Britain's Bert Weedon got in on the act, courtesy of a suitably autographed Starfire.

It was ten years before Guild bothered with solidbody electrics, but the first examples launched in 1963 were surprisingly unconventional, with the flagship Thunderbird model featuring odd-looking mutated Fender styling, unconventional circuitry and a built-in stand. These partnered the semi-acoustic Starfire series that subsequently grew to include twelve-string and bass versions.

The company was acquired by the Avnet corporation in 1966 and increasing orders led to the establishment of a new factory in Westerly, Rhode Island, with all production transferred there from Hoboken by 1972. **>**

grimessemi-solidbody

1981 Guild X-79 Skyhawk

■ Two guitars here are by the Hawaii-based Grimes and the old English maker Grimshaw. The rest of the guitars on these pages are by Guild, with a mix of the solidbody and hollowbody electric models that the company has produced since its first factory began production in New Jersey in the 1950s.

1979 Guild S70D

2000 Guild Blues 90

1984 Guild Brian May BHM-1

arch-tops

1953 Guild Stuart X-550

1953 Guild Stuart X500

1954 Guild Stratford X-350

semi-solidbodyguild

arch-tops & solids

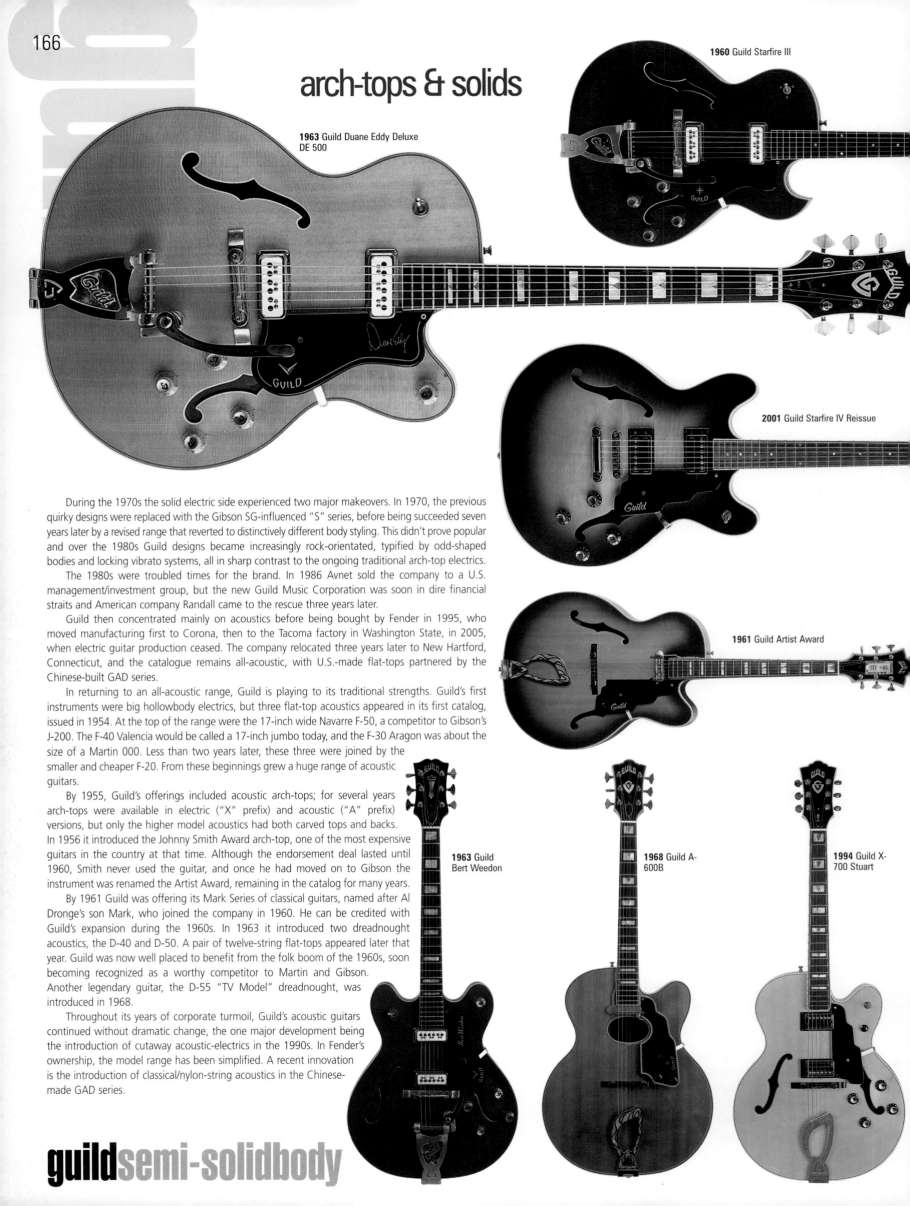

1963 Guild Duane Eddy Deluxe DE 500

1960 Guild Starfire III

2001 Guild Starfire IV Reissue

1961 Guild Artist Award

1963 Guild Bert Weedon

1968 Guild A-600B

1994 Guild X-700 Stuart

During the 1970s the solid electric side experienced two major makeovers. In 1970, the previous quirky designs were replaced with the Gibson SG-influenced "S" series, before being succeeded seven years later by a revised range that reverted to distinctively different body styling. This didn't prove popular and over the 1980s Guild designs became increasingly rock-orientated, typified by odd-shaped bodies and locking vibrato systems, all in sharp contrast to the ongoing traditional arch-top electrics.

The 1980s were troubled times for the brand. In 1986 Avnet sold the company to a U.S. management/investment group, but the new Guild Music Corporation was soon in dire financial straits and American company Randall came to the rescue three years later.

Guild then concentrated mainly on acoustics before being bought by Fender in 1995, who moved manufacturing first to Corona, then to the Tacoma factory in Washington State, in 2005, when electric guitar production ceased. The company relocated three years later to New Hartford, Connecticut, and the catalogue remains all-acoustic, with U.S.-made flat-tops partnered by the Chinese-built GAD series.

In returning to an all-acoustic range, Guild is playing to its traditional strengths. Guild's first instruments were big hollowbody electrics, but three flat-top acoustics appeared in its first catalog, issued in 1954. At the top of the range were the 17-inch wide Navarre F-50, a competitor to Gibson's J-200. The F-40 Valencia would be called a 17-inch jumbo today, and the F-30 Aragon was about the size of a Martin 000. Less than two years later, these three were joined by the smaller and cheaper F-20. From these beginnings grew a huge range of acoustic guitars.

By 1955, Guild's offerings included acoustic arch-tops; for several years arch-tops were available in electric ("X" prefix) and acoustic ("A" prefix) versions, but only the higher model acoustics had both carved tops and backs. In 1956 it introduced the Johnny Smith Award arch-top, one of the most expensive guitars in the country at that time. Although the endorsement deal lasted until 1960, Smith never used the guitar, and once he had moved on to Gibson the instrument was renamed the Artist Award, remaining in the catalog for many years.

By 1961 Guild was offering its Mark Series of classical guitars, named after Al Dronge's son Mark, who joined the company in 1960. He can be credited with Guild's expansion during the 1960s. In 1963 it introduced two dreadnought acoustics, the D-40 and D-50. A pair of twelve-string flat-tops appeared later that year. Guild was now well placed to benefit from the folk boom of the 1960s, soon becoming recognized as a worthy competitor to Martin and Gibson. Another legendary guitar, the D-55 "TV Model" dreadnought, was introduced in 1968.

Throughout its years of corporate turmoil, Guild's acoustic guitars continued without dramatic change, the one major development being the introduction of cutaway acoustic-electrics in the 1990s. In Fender's ownership, the model range has been simplified. A recent innovation is the introduction of classical/nylon-string acoustics in the Chinese-made GAD series.

guildsemi-solidbody

1976 Guild F-212CR-NT

1965 Guild F-50R-NT

1967 Guild Starfire Bass I

1963 Guild D-50

1961 Guild Mk I

■ More Guild guitars are featured here, including the acoustic flat-tops for which the brand is best known among many musicians. Its first such guitars were the F series, introduced in 1954, followed by the D series, and since then the brand has continued to produce top-quality steel-string guitars. Guild was acquired by Fender in 1995.

acousticguild

1967 Guyatone LG350T "Sharp 5"

1973 Guyatone Rhythm Guitar

1959 Hagstrom P46 Deluxe

■ **GUYATONE** Mitsuo Matsuki established this company in the 1930s, using his "Guya" nickname to form what would become one of the oldest Japanese brands. The first Guyatones were lap-steels; conventional electrics appeared early in the 1950s, followed by solidbody versions midway through the decade.

The latter were somewhat basic and inexpensive six-strings, imported into the UK in the late 1950s under various brandnames. Facing comparatively little competition, they accordingly proved popular with budding British guitar heroes, including Hank Marvin in his pre-Shadows days.

The Guyatone catalogue increased dramatically during the next decade, offering virtually every type of electric, but Matsuki's company was among the many that went under when the Japanese guitar industry collapsed in the late 1960s.

The copy era of the 1970s saw the Guyatone name re-emerge on an inevitable succession of Fender and Gibson clones. However, originals weren't forgotten, including rehashes and revivals of earlier designs.

This policy continued into the next decade and beyond, but following the death of founder Matsuki in 1992, the company increasingly concentrated on amplification and effects.

■ **HAGSTRÖM** Albin Hagström entered the musical instrument industry in the 1920s, importing accordions before going into retail and mail order. In 1932 he also established an accordion-making factory in Älvdalen, Sweden, and business grew over the next two decades.

In 1946 Hagström set up a factory near Oslo in Norway, manufacturing acoustic guitars and other stringed instruments. Electrified arch-tops followed and production continued into the early 1960s. Later Hagstrom acoustics were well received in many countries, including America and the UK.

When demand for accordions declined, the Älvdalen factory introduced electric guitar manufacture in 1958. The first models were single-cutaway semi-solids that echoed their accordion ancestry with an abundance of pearl and sparkle plastics plus push-button selector switches.

Reflecting market trends, Fender influences dominated Hagstrom styling during the first half of the1960s, but Gibson thinking was obvious by the end of the decade via a switch to humbuckers and a suitably restyled headstock. This emphasis became more apparent in the 1970s with the introduction of the Les Paul–inspired Swede and Super Swede, which proved to be among the most popular Hagstrom six-strings.

By the end of this decade the company was suffering from the effects of ever-increasing Japanese competition and in the early 1980s Hagstrom opted to discontinue instrument production in favor of the still successful retailing operation.

The brandname finally returned to the electric guitar arena in 2005 via a U.S.-designed range made in China. This now includes many models based on earlier Hagstroms, while other examples are all-new.

■ **HALLMARK** In 1966, ex-Mosrite man Joe Hall founded the shortlived Hallmark company in Arvin, California. The only officially manufactured model was the Swept Wing, offered in solid and semi-acoustic form, as well as bass and double-neck versions.

Hallmark went under in 1968, but the brand was revived almost forty years later and now appears on a range that employs U.S. and Korean manufacture for various reissues of original designs, plus updated examples and all-new models.

guyatonesolidbody

1959 Guyatone LG-30

1980 Hagstrom Swede

1963 Hagstrom Impala

■ Here are a number of quite different guitars: three by the Japanese brand Guyatone, which provided many a young UK guitarist with his first instrument; five by the major Swedish manufacturer Hagstrom; and a lone electric from the small California-based maker Hallmark.

1967 Hagstrom H-8 Bass

1967 Hallmark Swept Wing

1963 Hagstrom Kent PB24G

1979 Hamer
Standard Sunburst

1984 Hamer
Phantom A5

1990 Hamer
Chaparral Elite

1994 Harmony
Hamer Duo-tone
Hybrid

1980 B12S
Twelve-string Bass

■ **HAMER** The first Hamer instruments appeared in 1974, although this U.S. company was officially formed the following year by guitar designer Jol Dantzig and business partner Paul Hamer. Both favored Gibson ideas on design and construction, so unsurprisingly the initial Hamer instruments were effectively upmarket equivalents of established models from this maker. The first original designs appeared in the early 1980s, while multi-string basses became a brand speciality.

Paul Hamer left in 1987 and the following year the company was acquired by Kaman Music, manufacturer of Ovation guitars. These changes coincided with a concerted move to match market trends, which meant most Gibson-influenced models were replaced by rock-oriented designs that catered for the new breed of fast-gun guitarists.

A more equal stylistic balance was restored during the next decade with a return to more traditional thinking. Earlier Hamer favorites were revived, while the less expensive Korean-made Slammer series was introduced in 1993. This popular range continued well into the new millennium, although manufacture subsequently moved to Indonesia.

Launched in 2000, the Chinese-origin XT line offered even lower cost alternatives and forms part of the current catalog. U.S. production has been scaled down during recent years, with an increasing emphasis on a return to Hamer's original ethos of hand-building and higher quality. This policy has been maintained since Fender acquired Kaman Music late in 2007.

■ **HANG DONG** From the 1960s to the 1990s, the Philippines proved to be a prolific production source for guitars, with most being made to meet the needs of the large U.S. military presence stationed there during and after the Vietnam War. Many electrics were blatant fakes, even down to famous brand logos, but inferior quality gave them away. Some didn't pretend to be the real thing, although their influences were very obvious.

■ **HARMONY** Founded in 1892 by Wilhelm J. F. Schultz, this Chicago-based company became one of America's biggest mass-manufacturers of stringed instruments. In 1916, mail order giant Sears-Roebuck went from being a major customer to the company's new owner and annual production increased rapidly, totaling 250,000 by 1923. Within seven years this figure had doubled and the numbers continued to grow after the company was re-acquired in 1940 via a management buy-out.

Harmony electric guitars were introduced in the 1930s, but the choice increased significantly during the 1950s, with arch-top examples being joined by solidbody models from 1952 onward. The 1960s brought yet more success but by the early 1970s the company was struggling against ever-increasing imported competition. The end came in 1975, by which time Harmony had made around ten million guitars, many for other companies and under numerous different brands.

The name soon re-surfaced on Korean-origin instruments and these catered mainly for the entry-level market over the next twenty-five years. A shortlived line of reissues appeared in 2000 and this concept was revisited in 2008 by the current owner of the Harmony name. The current Korean-made range combines revivals of many old Harmony favorites with copies, contemporary designs, and acoustic-electrics. **>**

hamersolidbody

1960 Harmony
Jupiter H-492

1974 Hang Dong

1957 Harmony Newport
H42/1

1964 Harmony H77

1964 Rocket H59

■ The Hang Dong guitar is the odd man out on
these pages, made in the Philippines in the early
1970s. Two better-known companies provide the
rest of the instruments on display here: the U.S.
brand Hamer, established in 1974, and the big
Chicago-based maker Harmony, which together
with Kay dominated the budget U.S. guitar market
in the 1950s and '60s.

1965 Harmony H71 Meteor

1965 Harmony Meteor (left-handed)

1932 Harmony
Supertone 12D250

1929 Harmony Bradley
Kincaid Houn' Dog

1938 Harmony Gene
Autry Roundup

1971 Sovereign Harmony

sovereigns

1957 Harmony
Sovereign H-1203

1959 Harmony
Sovereign H-55

1965 Harmony
Sovereign H-1260

1960 Harmony H-162

Soon after Harmony was founded in 1892, the Chicago guitar manufacturer produced acoustics for the fledgling Sears, Roebuck mail-order company.

In 1914, Harmony introduced what may have been the first adjustable bridge, a metal unit with set screws for adjustments. That same year, the Sears brandname Supertone appeared. Sears purchased Harmony in 1916 and produced a line of Hawaiian instruments, including mahogany and koa guitars.

In 1925, Max Adler of Sears installed his nephew Jay Kraus as vice president of Harmony. When founder Wilhelm Schultz died soon after, Kraus became president and improved the operation. Harmony introduced a novel fixed airplane-shaped bridge commemorating Charles Lindbergh's 1927 transatlantic solo flight, featured on a pearl-encrusted Artist and a line of pear-shaped Vita instruments endorsed by Roy Smeck, "the Wizard of the Strings."

In 1929, Sears had Harmony produce the first "singing cowboy" guitar for its W.L.S. radio star and Supertone recording artist Bradley Kincaid, a Houn' Dog model with a mountain scene decal.

Harmony thrived during the Depression. In 1932, it debuted stenciled designs, innovative "crystalline" textured finishes, its popular Vagabond line, and two other trademarks: the all-mahogany Patrician flat-top and the Cremona, its first arch-top with a fourteen-fret neck. Also that year the Roundup appeared, Harmony's first model endorsed by singing cowboy Gene Autry.

Harmony produced its first carved-top guitars for Sears in 1936, which matured into the late-1930s high-end Cremona models. Two years later, Harmony bought the Stella and Sovereign brandnames from Oscar Schmidt's successor, Fretted Instruments.

Following World War II and the sale of Harmony by Sears to Jay Kraus and a group of investors, Harmony settled into a groove that would see it through the 1960s guitar boom and beyond. The 1930s arch-tops continued, and cutaway arch-tops debuted in 1952.

In 1956, the flat-tops began to switch to a square-shouldered shape that would dominate from that time. Two-tone aluminum-trimmed Holiday Colorama guitars were launched in 1956, and two years later the new Western Jumbo Sovereign shape appeared.

In 1972, Harmony rolled out a line of Regal dreadnoughts and began offering guitars finished in black, but little changed in Harmony acoustics for years, and the company dwindled in the face of import competition. In 1975, Harmony made one final push with the Opus series of fancy jumbo flat-tops.

In 1976, the Harmony name was sold to Global, and two years later I.M.C., which imported Hondo guitars to the United States, briefly marketed a line of Korean-made Harmonys. In 2008, new owner Charles Subecz launched a line of historical reissues that included four arch-top acoustics with pickups and an H594 Broadway acoustic.

■ **HARVEY THOMAS** Based in Kent, Washington State, Harvey Thomas was a maverick American maker specializing in eccentric electrics. His 1960s range included oddly styled six-strings such as the triangular Mod and cross-shaped Maltese Surfer models. Thomas also employed his wacky talents on oddball custom-order instruments, like this far from traditional arch-top acoustic-electric.

1933 Harmony Cremona No. 1262

■ There's another odd man out on these pages, and a very odd one, too, built by eccentric maker Harvey Thomas. The remainder is dedicated to Harmony and demonstrates how this giant U.S. manufacturer produced every kind of popular guitar in and around its heyday of the 1960s.

1961 Harmony Custom Classical

1948 Harmony Monteray

1968 Harmony Model 167

1966 Harmony Patrician

1975 Harmony Opus XX

1963 Harmony H-22 Bass

1962 Harvey Thomas Custom Hollowbody

hollowbody**harvey thomas**

1973 Hayman 3030

1970 Hayman White Cloud

1989 Heartfield Talon

1998 Heritage H-150CM

1990 Heritage H-535

1870 Haynes Small Body

1935 Hauser I Classical

■ **HAUSER I** The guitars of the first Hermann Hauser (1884–1952) were the first important classical instruments to originate outside Spain. Many would say they are still the greatest. Hauser opened his workshop in Munich, Germany, in 1905. His early guitars were in the small, bright European tradition, with shallow bodies and an exaggerated hour-glass shape. Then, in 1925, he was introduced to Segovia, who convinced Hauser that his future lay in building Spanish-style instruments. It took another twelve years before he completed a guitar that Segovia declared "the greatest guitar of our epoch."

■ **HAUSER II** Hermann Hauser II (1911–1988) began work in his father's workshop in 1930. While keeping close to his father's tradition, he experimented with different strutting and a larger guitar. His instruments are elegant and beautifully finished, and were prized by players including Segovia, Julian Bream, and the Romeros.

■ **HAUSER III** Hermann Hauser III (born 1958) took over the running of the family firm on the death of his father. Hauser III makes no more than seventeen guitars a year at his workshop in Reisbach, Germany.

■ **HAYMAN** The Hayman brand belonged to UK distributors Dallas Arbiter. An all-new electric guitar line was launched in 1970, with design input from Jim Burns; necks and bodies were made by Jack Golder's Shergold Woodcrafts company. The original range comprised four models. Financial difficulties caused production to come to a premature end in 1975, but by then Hayman had officially issued ten different guitars and basses that had included some innovative ideas.

■ **HAYNES** The John C. Haynes company of Boston, Massachusetts, made instruments in its own name in the late nineteenth century, as well as producing instruments for its parent company Ditson and others. This guitar features William B. Tilton's "Improvement," a metal disc mounted in the soundhole and supposed to enhance the tone of the instrument.

■ **HEARTFIELD** This brand represented the combined efforts of Fender in America and Japan, providing a commercial outlet for instrument designs that didn't really suit the existing catalogues offered by either. That said, some did state "Heartfield by Fender" on the headstock, while a few late examples came out under the Fender name only. Heartfields first appeared in 1989 and ran for around four years. All were manufactured by the Fujigen factory in Japan, responsible for a large portion of Fender production. Ranging from retro-flavored six-strings to out-and-out rock machines, they incorporated some novel features such as touch-type selector switches and active electronics with stompbox-style distortion.

■ **HERITAGE** Established in 1985, this U.S. company moved into the Gibson's old Kalamazoo factory after the latter had transferred all production to Nashville. From the start the Heritage guitar catalogue offered both flat-top and arch-top acoustic instruments, while the electric side was even more comprehensive. It originally included a fair share of Fender-flavored models, as well as those decidedly derived from familiar Gibson designs. The latter soon dominated, which is hardly surprising, given the location and the number of ex-Gibson employees involved. The company has continued to play to these particular strengths, emphasizing the connections and successfully offering equal-quality alternatives to those from the factory's former occupant.

■ **HERNÁNDEZ** Santos Hernández (1873–1943) was born in Madrid, Spain, and joined Manuel Ramírez in the 1890s. In 1912, Ramírez gave a guitar that Hernández had built to a young man called Andrés Segovia, who was to play it for twenty-five years. After Ramírez's death, Hernández established his own premises in Madrid. It became a favorite meeting place for the flamenco players of the day. A secretive individual, Hernández left neither heirs nor pupils.

hauserclassical

1925 Hernández Santos
Flamenco Guitar

1933 Hernández Santos
Concert Guitar

1923 Hernández Santos
Flamenco Guitar

1971 Hauser II Miguel
Llobet Model

1938 Hauser I
Classical

1957 Hauser I

■ Featured here are classical guitars by three
generations of the great Hauser family of Germany,
alongside instruments by the British maker Hayman;
the obscure old Haynes firm based in Boston; the
Fender-related Japanese brand Heartfield; Heritage,
set up by ex-Gibson workers in the old Gibson factory
in Kalamazoo; and another classical guitar, this one by
Santos Hernández.

1988 Hauser III

1988 Hauser III

classicalhernández

1957 Hofner Committee

arch-tops

1960 Hofner Verithin

■ **HOFNER** German violin maker Karl Hofner established his Schoenbach-based factory in the late 1880s, initially producing violins, cellos, and double basses. Guitars first appeared in 1925.

Manufacture recommenced soon after World War II, this time in Moehrendorf, near Erlangen, but in 1951 Hofner moved to Bubenreuth, the home of many guitar makers. Arch-top acoustic guitars were introduced during the early 1950s, with electrified versions added shortly afterward. Purpose-built electric six-strings with built-in pickups and controls were being produced by 1954, their integral type construction pre-dating much of the home-grown competition.

Big-bodied single-cutaway examples featured one or two pickups and were partnered by a similarly styled but scaled-down version that represented Hofner's answer to the Gibson Les Paul, albeit hollow and therefore much lighter. Actual solids arrived in 1956, although these also had air inside, as did the first Hofner four-string, designated the 500/1, which boasted a violin-shaped body.

In Britain, importers Selmer had been doing well with the brand since 1953, offering a small selection from Hofner's sizeable range, as well as variations specifically made or modified for the UK. Thanks to Selmer's commercially minded marketing, models were allocated names, rather than Hofner's usual and less-interesting number designations. British guitarists were soon aware of acoustics and electrics such as the President, Senator, Congress, Committee, and Verithin. The small-bodied electrics became the Club line, subsequently joined by the first solids that Selmer chose to call Coloramas.

In the early 1960s, Hofner maintained a healthy share of the burgeoning beat group market via an expanded catalogue, with many models targeting first or second time buyers. Popularity peaked later in the decade, helped in no small way by Beatle Paul McCartney's prominent use of the 500/1 "violin" bass.

In common with many guitar brands in Europe and elsewhere, Hofner saw sales diminish significantly during the late 1960s and into the next decade, as players preferred U.S.-made instruments. The Japanese copy boom also posed increasingly serious competition. Hofner issued a line of look-alikes but these didn't reverse the downward trend, and by the late 1970s the company had reverted to more original thinking, while build quality became superior to that of earlier eras. Hofner soldiered on through the 1980s and into the 1990s, introducing numerous new models. Some, such as the through-neck, multi-laminated Heavy Duty and the superstrat-style Reference, reflected changing market trends. Others stuck strictly with Hofner tradition or revived earlier designs, although in reality only the on-going "Beatle" basses attracted consistent interest.

In 1994 Hofner's factory moved from Bubenreuth to a new facility near neighboring Hagenau. Since then the range has been rationalized and revitalized, augmented by a Chinese-made line that comprises cheaper equivalents of old models along with some all-new ideas. The current German catalogue offers flat-top and arch-top acoustics, while electrics include updated re-creations of the President and Verithin, plus an authentic re-issue of the 1950s Club 50. Basses naturally feature strongly via various versions of the Violin and Club models.

1963 Hofner Galaxie

1965 Hofner 459/VTZ

1968 Hofner 175

hofner semi-solidbody

1959 Golden Hofner Thinline

1957 Hofner President

1959 Golden Hofner

1983 Hofner A2L

■ Hofner was set up in Germany in the 19th century, adding guitars to its business in the 1920s. Club models and others provided young British musicians—including John Lennon—with a first taste of the electric guitar when U.S. instruments were unavailable due to an import ban by the British government.

1954 Hofner Club 40

1956 Hofner Club 40

1955 Hofner Club 50

1954 Hofner Club 50

club models

semi-solidbody**hofner**

1956 Hofner Model 500/1

1961 Hofner Model 500/10

1957 Hofner Model 333

1963 Hofner 500/1
Owned by Paul McCartney

1953 Hofner President

1965 Hofner Arch-top

1965 Hofner Model 178

1966 Hofner 491

■ **HOHNER** Founded by Matthias Hohner in 1857, this German brand soon became synonymous with harmonicas, then accordions. Hohner guitars appeared in the 1950s, with electrics following early in the next decade, including UK-made examples. By the 1970s these had been superseded by a Japanese-sourced series that mainly mimicked Fender and Gibson.

The copy theme continued during the 1980s, but manufacture moved to Korea and the range expanded to include rock-machine models along with the licensed headless Steinberger look-alikes that have proved popular ever since. Better quality electrics followed in the 1990s, including the Czech-origin Revelation range, while Indonesian-made models later targeted lower price points. Recent years have seen fewer electric guitars partnering the company's acoustic range.

■ **HOLLENBECK** Bill Hollenbeck (1993–2008), of Lincoln, Illinois, learned the craft of guitar-building from Bill Barker of nearby Peoria, before becoming a full-time maker in 1991. He was one of twenty-one luthiers commissioned by collector Scott Chinery to build a blue arch-top.

■ **HONDO** This brand was started in the late 1960s by the International Music Corporation (I.M.C.) of Fort Worth, Texas, one of the first companies to market Korean-made guitars. Electrics soon included Fender and Gibson copies bearing the Hondo II logo, while better quality instruments were added under the Hondo banner, some originating from Japan. During the 1980s, I.M.C. specialized in less-expensive licensed equivalents of original designs from various American makers.

In 1991, the brand was bought by Freed International, which continued to cater for the entry-level end of the market. This policy was continued four years later by a new owner, M.B.T. International, with instruments sourced from Korea, Taiwan, China, and Indonesia. The Hondo name survived a further ten years before disappearing in 2005.

■ **HOPF** This German company was officially established in 1906. Acoustic guitars were joined by electrified versions in the late 1950s, with solids and semis following in the 1960s. Most were original designs, but during the 1970s the company opted to imitate rather than innovate. Guitar production diminished as the decade progressed and finally ceased in the mid 1980s.

■ **HOYER** This brand dates back to 1874, when German luthier Franz Hoyer started making stringed instruments, eventually including classical and folk guitars. Arch-top acoustics appeared in the late 1940s and electrified versions followed in the 1950s, joined by solids and semis during the 1960s. Copies dominated the next decade. Some upmarket originals appeared in the 1980s under the separate Walter Hoyer banner, but by 1990 both companies had ceased operations. In 1998 the name returned on a range of updated reissues and more derivative new models manufactured in Korea and Germany. The brand was bought by a new owner seven years later, resulting in a revised all-German range; this is expected to continue after Hoyer changed hands again in 2009.

■ **HUMPHREY** The Millennium classical guitars of Thomas Humphrey (1948–2008) are among the most adventurous to have won a following among concert professionals. Humphrey, of Gardiner, New York, insisted that the idea for the guitar came to him in a dream early in 1985. Its neck and strings are set at an oblique angle to the soundboard rather than running parallel to it, which provides extra projection as well as improved access to the top frets.

■ **HUTL** Hutl was a German brand whose guitars fell short of the quality of those from the country's better makers.

1993 Hohner G3T

1990 Hohner Twp Western

1996 Hollenbeck Ebony 'n' Blue Custom

1983 Hondo H-2

1963 Hopf Telstar

1963 Hopf Saturn

1965 Hoyer Model 35

■ More here from the German Hofner company, including Paul McCartney's "violin" bass, as well as guitars by four other German brands—Hohner, Hopf, Hoyer, and Hutl. Also: guitars by Illinois-based luthier Hollenbeck; the Hondo brand, which has appeared on various oriental guitars; and classical maker Humphrey.

1987 Humphrey Millennium

1982 Hutl Star

1993 Humphrey Millennium

solidbodyhutl

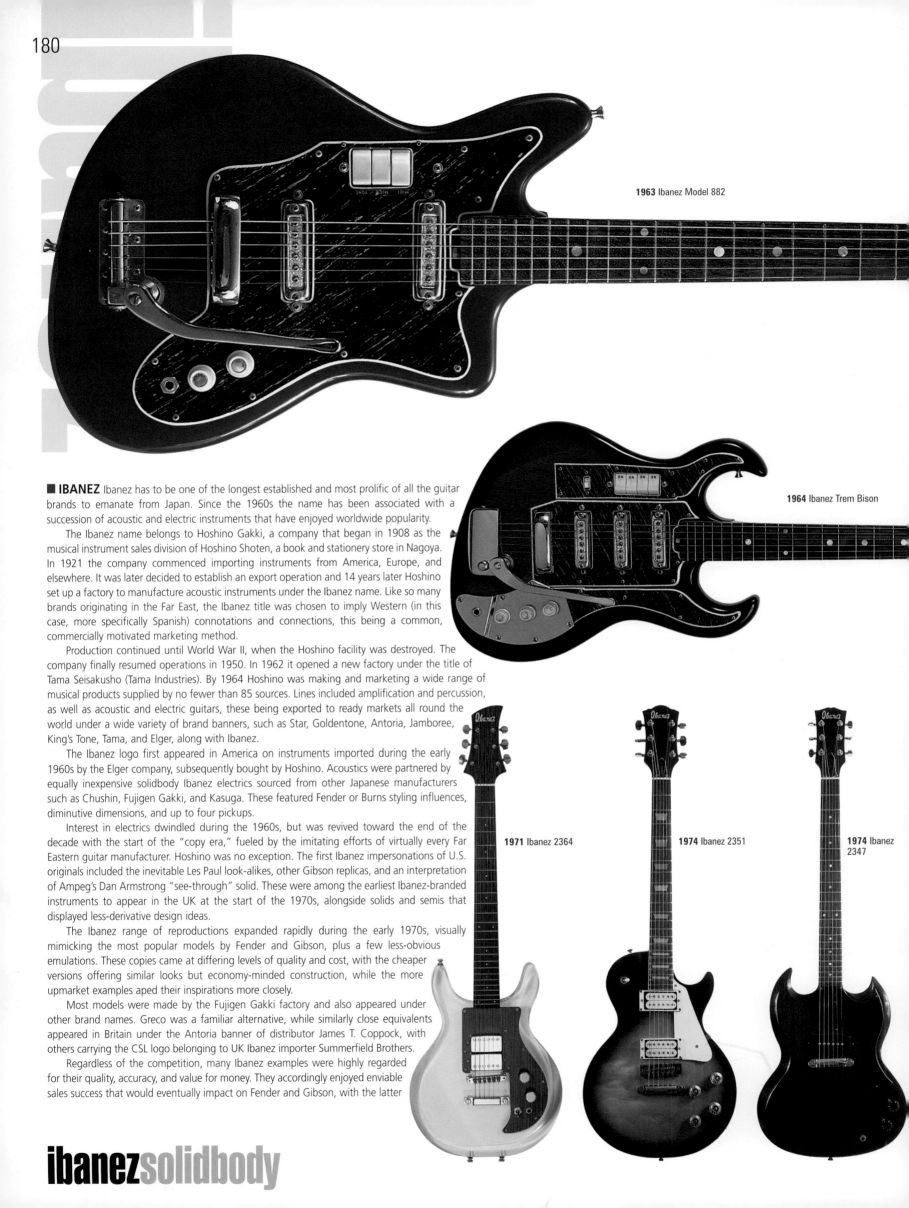

1963 Ibanez Model 882

1964 Ibanez Trem Bison

■ **IBANEZ** Ibanez has to be one of the longest established and most prolific of all the guitar brands to emanate from Japan. Since the 1960s the name has been associated with a succession of acoustic and electric instruments that have enjoyed worldwide popularity.

The Ibanez name belongs to Hoshino Gakki, a company that began in 1908 as the musical instrument sales division of Hoshino Shoten, a book and stationery store in Nagoya. In 1921 the company commenced importing instruments from America, Europe, and elsewhere. It was later decided to establish an export operation and 14 years later Hoshino set up a factory to manufacture acoustic instruments under the Ibanez name. Like so many brands originating in the Far East, the Ibanez title was chosen to imply Western (in this case, more specifically Spanish) connotations and connections, this being a common, commercially motivated marketing method.

Production continued until World War II, when the Hoshino facility was destroyed. The company finally resumed operations in 1950. In 1962 it opened a new factory under the title of Tama Seisakusho (Tama Industries). By 1964 Hoshino was making and marketing a wide range of musical products supplied by no fewer than 85 sources. Lines included amplification and percussion, as well as acoustic and electric guitars, these being exported to ready markets all round the world under a wide variety of brand banners, such as Star, Goldentone, Antoria, Jamboree, King's Tone, Tama, and Elger, along with Ibanez.

The Ibanez logo first appeared in America on instruments imported during the early 1960s by the Elger company, subsequently bought by Hoshino. Acoustics were partnered by equally inexpensive solidbody Ibanez electrics sourced from other Japanese manufacturers such as Chushin, Fujigen Gakki, and Kasuga. These featured Fender or Burns styling influences, diminutive dimensions, and up to four pickups.

Interest in electrics dwindled during the 1960s, but was revived toward the end of the decade with the start of the "copy era," fueled by the imitating efforts of virtually every Far Eastern guitar manufacturer. Hoshino was no exception. The first Ibanez impersonations of U.S. originals included the inevitable Les Paul look-alikes, other Gibson replicas, and an interpretation of Ampeg's Dan Armstrong "see-through" solid. These were among the earliest Ibanez-branded instruments to appear in the UK at the start of the 1970s, alongside solids and semis that displayed less-derivative design ideas.

The Ibanez range of reproductions expanded rapidly during the early 1970s, visually mimicking the most popular models by Fender and Gibson, plus a few less-obvious emulations. These copies came at differing levels of quality and cost, with the cheaper versions offering similar looks but economy-minded construction, while the more upmarket examples aped their inspirations more closely.

Most models were made by the Fujigen Gakki factory and also appeared under other brand names. Greco was a familiar alternative, while similarly close equivalents appeared in Britain under the Antoria banner of distributor James T. Coppock, with others carrying the CSL logo belonging to UK Ibanez importer Summerfield Brothers.

Regardless of the competition, many Ibanez examples were highly regarded for their quality, accuracy, and value for money. They accordingly enjoyed enviable sales success that would eventually impact on Fender and Gibson, with the latter

1971 Ibanez 2364

1974 Ibanez 2351

1974 Ibanez 2347

ibanezsolidbody

Ibanez was one of the brands that gave Japanese manufacturing a good name at a time when the East had been considered by many as a source of poor-quality instruments. Ibanez's parent company Hoshino began guitar production in the 1950s, but by the late '70s it was able to compete abroad with all the big guitar brands.

1976 Ibanez Artist 2618

1974 Ibanez Firebrand 2348

1975 Ibanex Iceman IC210

1978 Ibanez Performer PF230

1977 Ibanez Artist Professional

1978 Ibanez Professional 2617

1978 Ibanez Musician MC500

solidbodyibanez

1983 Ibanez Destroyer II DT555

1985 Ibanez Axstar AX4

1979 Ibanez Rocket Roll

taking legal steps to curb copyright infringement. This action wasn't really necessary, because Hoshino was already incorporating individual construction and cosmetic touches. Taking this approach further, the Ibanez Artist range, introduced in 1974, comprised fancy-looking acoustics and solid electrics with twin-cutaway styling that would become a mainstay design.

From this somewhat unadventurous start, the Artist series expanded to include odd-shaped six-strings with an outline that later assumed a separate identity as the Iceman. The same period saw the introduction of the Professional series, which embodied design ideas from U.S. luthier Rex Bogue in a range of ornate instruments that represented the epitome of Ibanez quality at that time.

The hollowbody market wasn't ignored and Ibanez released an assortment of semis and arch-top acoustics, most of them along Gibson lines. The George Benson models debuted in 1977. Designed in conjunction with this well-known artist, they were among the first "signature" edition Ibanez instruments and confirmed players' acceptance of Japanese guitar-making abilities.

By the end of the decade, emphasis had shifted to an originals-only policy, as thanks to increasing quality and market credibility the term "Made in Japan" lost its "cheap copy" image. The change was gradual, with the Performer series still leaning heavily on the Les Paul, while the Concert line had a more Fender-ish outline. The Musician models adopted increasingly high manufacturing standards and featured the multi-laminated wood construction originated by U.S. maker Alembic, although styling played it safe. The more radical Iceman solids found favor with players such as Steve Miller and Paul Stanley of Kiss, the latter enjoying his own autograph edition.

Launched in 1979, the cheaper Roadster range offered affordable Strat alternatives that introduced the "hooked horn" body styling that would prove another long-running outline in the Ibanez catalogue.

The original design theme continued into the 1980s, and Ibanez gained an equally healthy reputation in the four-string field thanks to the Musician, Roadster, and Studio basses. The latter title was also applied to a fourteen-strong guitar series over a three-year production span. This amount of choice often caused buyer confusion, made worse by the company's preference for a multi-number system that impeded product identity and image.

Also offered in over-abundance was the Blazer, which succeeded the Roadster as a Fender-influenced budget best seller. In more angular vein, the Destroyer offered a variation on Gibson's Explorer design, the Rocket Roll echoed the Flying V, and the equally shortlived X models offered a mutation of both.

In 1982 Ibanez introduced the Blazer's successor, somewhat confusingly called the Roadstar II. This range of guitars and basses retained the familiar body styling and over the following five years became the most prolific of all Ibanez electrics. Revised upmarket variants appeared in 1987 as the Pro Line series; these were to be the last of the "old-style" Ibanez six-strings, preceding a significant change of image and design direction during the late 1980s. **>**

ibanezsolidbody

1985 Ibanez XV500

1985 Ibanez IMG2010 Guitar Synthesizer

1986 Ibanez Roadstar II RG240

1979 Ibanez Roadstar RS100

1987 Ibanez Pro Line PL2550

■ Once Ibanez had established itself among rock guitarists with quality 1970s models such as the Artist, Performer, and Musician, it built on this success in the following decade, not least by winning the support of some of the leading technically-adept players of the day, such as Steve Vai and Joe Satriani.

1989 Ibanez Saber 540S

1988 Ibanez Maxxas MX3

1994 Ibanez JS 10th Anniversary

1989 Ibanez Radius 540R

1990 Ibanez Universe UV7 Seven-string

solidbodyibanez

1994 Ibanez Talman TC530

1994 Ibanez Talman TV750

1997 Ibanez RG7620 Seven String

1997 Ibanez Jem 90th Anniversary

1999 Ibanez S Classical SC420

With the introduction of the Radius and Saber series in 1987, Ibanez targeted the rock sector in earnest, producing superstrat-style instruments specifically geared to the needs of the ultra-proficient, high technique players at the head of this field. More of the same soon followed, including the Power, RG, and Jem lines, with marketing promoting the patronage of a steady stream of U.S. endorsees, including Steve Vai and Joe Satriani. The move proved very successful, and Ibanez became a leading light in the fast-fingered market, even in the face of fierce competition from major U.S. guitar makers.

The brand now enjoyed a higher profile than ever before, but despite such an overtly modern image, Ibanez continued to cater for more traditional tastes, maintaining production of semis and hollowbodies such as the Artstar series and Joe Pass signature model. Basses kept abreast of changing requirements, but manufacture and marketing priorities centered on six-strings. To keep things interesting, a quirky design would occasionally surface, with the Maxxas and Artfield being prime examples, but these shortlived exceptions invariably met with scant success.

In the 1990s Ibanez instruments encompassed all price points, from Korean-sourced entry-level examples to exotic U.S.-built custom creations. More artist signature models debuted during the decade, such as those for Frank Gambale, Reb Beach, and Paul Gilbert, while later additions included arch-top acoustics endorsed by jazz guitarist Pat Metheny.

Retro-orientated ideas became trendy at this time and Ibanez embraced the theme with the Talman series, employing fake flame finishes on bodies made of medium-density fiberboard. Launched in 1994, this line lasted until 1999, by which time it was being made of conventional wood in Korea. Traditional styling made something of a comeback in the Strat-influenced form of the RX range, sourced from Korea, while revisiting the past was also expressed in the form of reissues of earlier Ibanez instruments, including the Iceman and the Blazer.

Basses assumed a more prominent role, with a range that included innovative designs such as the BTB and Erodyne lines, various artist endorsed models, and the more conventional Soundgear and Roadgear ranges.

Since the start of the new millennium, Ibanez has successfully continued to play to these varied strengths. Numerous new signature models have been added, such as the seven-stringers made for low-end exponents Head and Munky of Korn. Retro flavoring is retained via the Jet King and AX series, while the long-running Artist has finally returned, along with other Ibanez oldies, including the Destroyer.

Hoshino has expanded market coverage by adding other production sources, such as Indonesia and China, the latter being responsible for the very affordable Ibanez Artcore slim depth semis and arch-top acoustics.

Although Ibanez is probably best known for electric guitars, Hoshino Gakki, owner of the brand, has a long and successful history with acoustic instruments. In the early 1930s he began importing classical guitars built by Salvador Ibáñez of Valencia, Spain. Ibáñez was then the biggest guitar manufacturer in Spain, but demand from Japan was such, following a tour by the virtuoso Andrés Segovia, that Hoshino began to manufacture its own instruments in Nagoya, Japan. Reasoning that a Spanish-sounding name would be more attractive, it licensed the Ibanez name for a range that soon included arch-tops and flat-tops.

Hoshino's operations were destroyed by bombing during World War II, but subsequently rebuilt. In 1955 the company decided to concentrate on exports to the United States and

ibanez**solidbody**

2009 Ibanez Jem 77FP

2008 Ibanez JS20S

2008 Ibanez SHR912

■ Ibanez aims to be all things to all players, with electric lines ranging from ultra-modern instruments for the technologically up-to-date guitarist, including seven-string models, to traditional arch-top jazz boxes, such as the George Benson signature models.

2008 Ibanez SV5470F Prestige

1977 Ibanez George Benson GB10

1988 Ibanez Artstar AE200

2008 Ibanez Artcore Custom

semi-solidbodyibanez

1974 Ibanez Model 642

2002 Ibanez Artwood

2003 Ibanez
AEL-20TBS

2003 Ibanez AEL-2012THS

Europe and began manufacturing guitars again. In 1962 it established a new subsidiary, Tama Seisakusho, Inc, and started building guitars and guitar amplifiers as well as drums. During the 1960s, with demand from Western markets rocketing, Hoshino exported acoustic guitars in standard, concert and auditorium size to the United States and other markets.

Beginning in the early 1970s, Ibanez acoustics entered the copy era. Hoshino named its top-line guitars Tama. These were solid-topped dreadnoughts (and classicals) inspired initially by Martins, some with three-piece backs and full tree-of-life inlays. At the same time the Ibanez brand emulated popular Gibson and Martin models, but with laminated tops. These included copies of Hummingbirds and Doves, as well as fancy D-41-style dreadnoughts with abalonoid trim. By 1974 original ideas began to creep in, like three-piece jacaranda and maple backs. From 1974 to 1978 Ibanez also made an Artist Series of mahogany, rosewood, or flamed maple dreadnoughts and jumbos using the same headstock as the Artist electric models. In 1975 copies of both Gallagher and Fender dreadnoughts became available.

In 1976, facing pressure from Gibson, the Ibanez line changed its headstock to the more Guild-like tulip shape also used on electrics. The Tama line also changed to have unique curved headstocks and pickguards, although Martin-style Ibanez guitars made it into the early 1980s.

From around 1978 to 1981 Ibanez acoustics began to diversify, mixing traditional designs with new ideas. The Tama brand was renamed as the Ibanez Artwood series, and included a few handmade models. Ibanez cutaway flat-tops debuted in 1980 on the Ragtimes, round-bodied models with an oval soundhole.

In 1983 Ibanez produced some beautiful Naturalwood dreadnoughts in solid cedar, jacaranda and koa, including tops. Ibanez also produced the AE line for a couple years (mainly Ragtimes with piezo pickups). The AEs came back in 1990 as cutaway dreadnoughts and Ragtimes, and have remained in production off and on ever since.

In around 1988 Hoshino shifted production of less expensive guitars to Korea. By 1992 most Ibanez acoustics were made there, with the lower range having laminated tops and better guitars having solid timbers. With the emergence of the *MTV Unplugged* phenomenon, Ibanez began to show a renewed interest in acoustics. Hoshino developed a relationship with Fishman pickups and in 1992 introduced three new Korean-made lines, including Nomad cutaway dreadnoughts, yet more Ragtimes, and a revamped Performance series. Also at this time the GA series classical guitars debuted. Later in the 1990s Hoshino began having guitars built in China.

In 2000 the Talman mid-bodied, glued-neck acoustic-electric appeared, borrowing the shape of its retro electric brother. In 2008 came the radically-styled Montage, featuring onboard effects and tuner. New for 2009 was the arch-backed Ambiance series, featuring Fishman electronics, and the first of the Exotic Wood range with a solid top, in this case "monkey pod," said to be similar to koa.

ibanezacoustic

2003 Ibanez
Artwood
AW-200CEVV

2003 Ibanez
GA-5WCE Electro-
classical

2003 Ibanez
GA-5WNT Classical

2004 Ibanez AW-40NT

2003 Ibanez PE-60TBL

2007 Ibanez EWZOZWE

2004 Ibanez SX-72TBS

■ Ibanez is best known as a maker of
electric guitars, but the Japanese-based firm
has produced many acoustics and some
electric basses through its long history, and
a selection is shown here—from steel-string
flat-tops and electric-acoustic hybrids to
fretted and fretted basses.

2008 Ibanez SR300

1980 Ibanez Musician

1997 Ibanez Musician Fretless

2008 Ibanez BTB 475

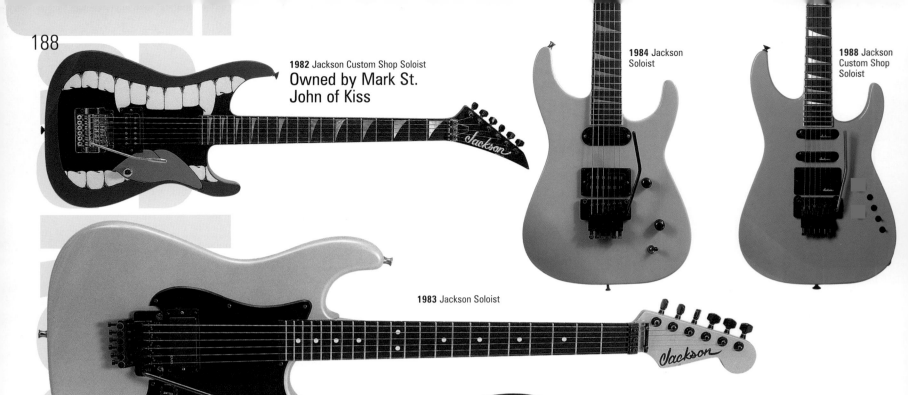

1982 Jackson Custom Shop Soloist
Owned by Mark St. John of Kiss

1984 Jackson Soloist

1988 Jackson Custom Shop Soloist

1983 Jackson Soloist

1990 Jackson Custom Shop Soloist

■ **JACKSON** Guitarist Grover Jackson liked to tinker with the instrument as well as play it. In September 1977 he joined Wayne Charvel's guitar parts business, based in San Dimas, California. At that time it was suffering financially and Jackson ended up buying the business the following year. This comprised a small workshop producing components such as necks and bodies, but Jackson had bigger plans and began to develop his own ideas on guitar design. Charvel six-strings debuted in 1979, but actual Jacksons came two years later via a collaboration with rising guitar star Randy Rhoads.

Unlike the bolt-on-neck Charvels, Jackson instruments employed through-neck construction, but both featured flashy finishes and custom artwork. In 1985 Grover Jackson entered into a partnership with Texas-based distributor, International Music Corporation (IMC). The Charvel logo was then transferred to a Japanese-built range, while Jackson was retained for the upmarket U.S. line. The next year production was switched to a new factory in Ontario, California.

The Jackson catalog initially comprised custom-order only instruments, with most of them based on four designs: the superstrat-style Soloist, the more conventional Strat Body, the V Rhoads and the Concert bass, later joined by the compact Dinky.

Jackson left in 1989 and the next year the range changed significantly. American Custom Shop specials and limited editions were joined by the Professional line of less-costly equivalents made in Japan at the Chushin Gakki factory.

These included the new Fusion and Warrior models, as well as versions of the unusual Phil Collen signature six-string and Kip Winger bass. Additions in 1992 included the Infinity, which catered more for the PRS market, while the Stealth stuck to more familiar Jackson territory. The following year brought the retro-flavoured JTX, along with the Kelly Standard equivalent of a previous Custom Shop model.

American production continued via additional high-end limited editions, signature six- and four-strings, plus variations on established themes. These included the Archtop and JJ examples, plus the suitably space age Roswell Rhoads. Some were mirrored by Japanese-made models, accompanied by newcomers such as the Thinline, Short Scale, and Outcaster.

During the 1990s Jackson continued its push into more downmarket areas. The Japanese-sourced Concept selection of more-affordable alternatives was introduced in 1993, followed the next year by the cheaper Korean-made Performer range. By 2000 the Indian-origin X line had been added. Manufacture of the latter subsequently moved to Japan and India was used for the entry-level JS electrics.

The Professional series came to an end in 1995, but Japanese production has continued ever since. Over the years this has also included home-market models carrying other logos, such as Grover Jackson, Team GJ, and Jackson Stars.

In 1997 Jackson was acquired by the Japanese Akai Musical Instruments Corporation, although the existing agreement with IMC continued until 2002, when Fender bought the Jackson and Charvel brands. The current catalog includes the USA Select series, partnered by the Japanese-made Pro, MG, and X lines, plus the Indian-sourced JS range.

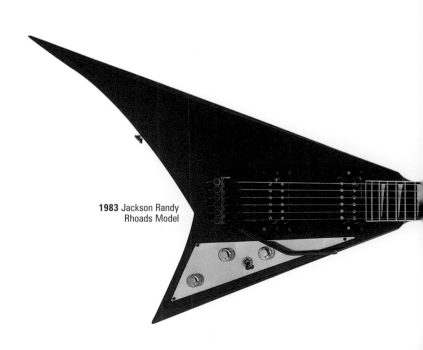

1983 Jackson Randy Rhoads Model

jacksonsolidbody

1989 Jackson Phil Collen

1990 Jackson Proffesional Warrior

1992 Jackson Stealth TH2

1996 Jackson PC3

1998 Jackson Surfcaster SC1

■ Grover Jackson began his guitar business making spare parts, with the first Jackson-brand guitar appearing in 1981. The name became synonymous with the "superstrat" that defined 1980s rock guitar: more frets, deeper cutaways, pointy headstock, versatile new pickup layouts, high-performance vibrato, and bright graphic finishes.

1988 Jackson Instant Sex Custom
Owned by Ratt's Robbin Crosby

custom shop models

1984 Jackson Double Rhoads Custom

solidbodyjackson

■ Guitars featured here are by California-based James Tyler; British makers Jaydee and John Birch; alternative Gibson brand Kalamazoo; Kapa, a 1960s maker from Maryland; Scottish brand Karnak; and Japan-based Kawai. Also here are five Kay guitars, originating at the giant U.S. maker's factory in Chicago.

1999 James Tyler Studio Elite

1984 Jaydee Mark King Bass

1966 Kapa Continental Twelve-string

■ **JAMES TYLER** Located in Van Nuys, California, James Tyler entered the guitar building business in 1972. The company caters for custom tastes but also offers a selection of artist signature guitars and basses, plus a standard catalog. This mainly comprises various Fender-flavored models, such as the Studio Elite and the Strat-inspired Classic six-strings, while the Mongoose employs an obviously Tele-derived outline. These are available in numerous guises and all feature Tyler's distinctive headstock adorned with an equally eye-catching logo.

■ **JAYDEE** Jaydee is the brand name of UK maker John Diggins. This Birmingham-based builder started his career in 1970, when he joined forces with custom specialist John Birch. Diggins went solo seven years later and has since tended to concentrate on upmarket basses. These include the various models that make up the Alembic-influenced Supernatural selection, plus others such as the Calibas and bolt-on-neck Celeste series.

■ **JOHN BIRCH** UK maker John Birch started in 1969, specializing in custom-built electric guitars, but also offering a standard range employing through-neck construction and his own pickups and hardware. Birch quit the business during the mid-1980s, but returned in the early 1990s with a new line of designs. He died in 2000, but the John Birch company has continued, and the current catalog includes reissues plus revivals of famous original custom creations.

■ **KALAMAZOO** This was a brand used by Gibson on a range of downmarket acoustic guitars made during the 1930s. The company revived the name in the 1960s for similarly cost-conscious solid electric guitars and basses. These initially employed Fender-influenced styling, but the body outline was later altered to an SG shape.

■ **KAPA** Kapa electrics were made in Hyattsville, Maryland, from 1962 until 1970. Spanning six-, four-, and twelve-strings, the cost-conscious range comprised Fender-ish solids such as the Continental and Wildcat, plus the teardrop-shaped Minstrel and the Challenger slimline semi.

■ **KARNAK** This is actually a model name allotted to one of the unusually styled solids from Scottish makers Maurice Bellando and James Cannell, who produced a range under the Egypt brand name between 1985 and 1987.

■ **KAWAI** Although best known for pianos, keyboards, and synthesizers, this Japanese manufacturer has been making guitars since the 1950s. The company acquired the Teisco brand in the 1960s, which was when Kawai electrics were dressed to impress via unusual styling, multiple switches, and plenty of chrome. Build quality improved dramatically during the next decade, as seen on the slotted-headstock KS series. Later models mimicked Alembic design ideas, but the crescent-shaped Moon Sault was overtly original. The early 1980s saw the addition of the Fender-influenced Aquarius series, but since then Kawai has catered mainly for the domestic market, including reissues of the Moon Sault and other earlier six-strings.

1965 Kalamazoo KG2A

1936 Kalamazoo KG-14

1976 John Birch AJS Custom

james tyler**solidbody**

1958 Kay Solo King

1976 Kay K30

1982 Kay L/P Synth

1985 Karnak Isis II

1968 Kawai Concert

1985 Kay K45

1986 Kay Busker

solidbodykay

1957 Kay Barney Kessel Artist K6700

1957 Kay Barney Kessel Pro

1952 Kay Thin Twin K161

1958 Kay K8995J Upbeat

■ **KAY** Like Harmony, Kay was based in Chicago and was the former's main rival for the title of major instrument mass-producer. Somewhat convoluted origins date back to the late 1800s, but by 1934 the business behind this famous brand name had become known as the Kay Musical Instrument Company.

The Kay logo first appeared on guitars in around 1936 and by the late 1940s production was up to 300 instruments per day, including acoustics and electrified acoustics, as well as a line of lap steels. In the mid-1950s the company made a concerted move into the low- to mid-range market then dominated by Harmony. This included increased manufacture of instruments for leading mail-order houses such as Sears, Roebuck and Montgomery Ward.

By now electrics were an established part of the Kay catalog, including the K-161 Thin Twin, introduced in 1952 and the choice of bluesman Jimmy Reed. The first Kay solids appeared in the same year, as did the K-160 bass guitar—a simple single-cutaway four-string that was at the time the only available alternative to Fender's Precision.

During the later 1950s the electric line ranged from beginners' small-bodied solids to upmarket arch-top electrics endorsed by leading jazz guitarist Barney Kessel. The quality of these contrasted with the company's by now mainly low-end image, although the artist association was later abandoned.

The early 1960s saw numerous additions, including slimline acoustic-electrics such as the Speed Demon and Swingmaster series. These were soon joined by the double cutaway Jazz II and the appropriately twin-horned Red Devil, while the solid side included the Fender-influenced Vanguard line.

Kay production peaked during the 1960s, meeting a seemingly insatiable demand for anything with six strings attached. In 1964 the company moved to a new million-dollar factory in Elk Grove Village, Illinois, where a 500-strong workforce turned out 1,500 guitars per day.

The following year this buoyant business was bought by the giant Seeburg organization, also of Chicago and a leading light in the juke-box industry. This change of ownership signaled the start of troubled times, with sales slipping as the guitar boom bubble burst. Kay tried to turn the tide via numerous new models and a significantly revamped range, but to little effect. In 1967 Seeburg sold Kay to long-time competitor Valco, but ever-decreasing sales posed insurmountable financial problems that caused both companies to fail the following year.

Like many other well-known U.S. brands, the Kay name resurfaced in the early 1970s, initially on a Korean-origin range of low-budget beginner acoustics and electrics. As the copy era developed during this decade, the Kay logo cropped up on various approximations of Gibson and Fender favorites.

The onset of the 1980s brought some original thinking and improved quality via Korean-built solids that followed contemporary fashion with laminated through-neck construction, brass hardware, and Di Marzio pickups. Les Paul-like variations included the LP Synth with on-board effects and the Busker, which boasted a built-in amp and speaker.

From around 1984 Kay's Fender copies came from the East German Musima factory, and the brand has subsequently been used on ultra-inexpensive examples from the Far East. In 2008, a partnership between the current Kay company and U.S. maker Fritz Brothers resulted in a range of reissues of various oldie originals, manufactured in the Far East.

kaysemi-solidbody

1962 Kay Jazz II K776

■ At its peak in the 1950s and '60s Kay was one of the biggest American guitar manufacturers, rivaling the other big Chicago maker Harmony for size of output and range of types. Featured here are examples of electrics and acoustics with the Kay brand, from the upscale Barney Kessel signature models to an unusual Kay Kraft of the early 1930s.

1962 Kay K592

1957 Kay K-217 Arch-top

1977 Kay K-588

1933 Kay Kraft Style B

1941 Kay K-40

1978 Kay Force 2E

acoustickay

1986 Knight Imperial

1998 Klein BF

1965 Klira 320
Star Club

1968 Kent 742

1966 Klira
Tornado

1973 Kohno Classical

1974 Kohno Classical

1898 Knutsen Harp
Guitar

■ **KENT** This brand first appeared in the United States during the early 1960s on entry-level instruments manufactured by Japanese companies such as Teisco and Guyatone; later, better quality examples came from Kawai.

Swedish manufacturer Hagstrom employed the Kent name for home market use on the solid electrics it started building in 1962, as the company wasn't confident that quality was good enough to warrant the Hagstrom logo. It also adorned Italian-origin examples available there and elsewhere at this time, such as semi-acoustics from Zero Sette. In the UK, Jennings imported Guyatone-made Kents to partner the mid-1960s Vox guitar range.

Kent continued into the 1970s via Japanese-sourced acoustics and copycat electrics, finally ending up on cheaper models from Korea.

■ **KLEIN** U.S. maker Steve Klein started with acoustics during the 1970s, but in the late 1980s he devised an unusual headless electric guitar design that attracted players who fancied something different. In 1995 Klein sold this side of his business to employee Lorenzo German, who kept it going until 2007. Steve Klein continues to build high quality acoustics, although recent rumors suggest electrics might soon return.

■ **KLIRA** German violin maker Johannes Klier established the Klira company in 1887, but guitar production didn't commence until after World War II. Arch-top electrics appeared in 1958 and the first Klira solids came two years later. Output increased significantly during the 1960s, with the company enjoying healthy export sales, particularly to the United States. In the 1970s Klira caught the copy bug, but guitar building decreased dramatically during the next decade and, after marketing an inexpensive Korean-made range, the company decided to once again concentrate solely on violins.

■ **KNIGHT** Stanley Charles Knight (known as Dick) was born in 1907. He began making guitars full time in 1963, specializing in arch-tops. He died in 1996. His son-in-law Gordon Wells and grandson Robert Wells continue to handbuild acoustic and semi-acoustic jazz guitars as well as taking on repairs at the company's workshop in Weybridge, Surrey, England.

■ **KNUTSEN** Chris J. Knutsen (1862–1930) was granted a patent in 1897 for his "one-arm" harp guitar design. No two Knutsen harp guitars are alike. This one was probably made in Port Townsend, Washington.

■ **KOHNO** Masaru Kohno (1926–1998) was born in Mito City, Japan. In 1959 he traveled to Madrid, Spain, where he spent six months in the workshop of classical builder Arcangel Fernández, watching him work. On his return to Tokyo he began building his own interpretation of the Spanish design, before opening a factory, run by his nephew Masaki Sakurai, to build high quality classical guitars. The Kohno name was reserved for the most expensive models. Sakurai continues to produce high-end guitars under the Sakurai Kohno label.

■ **KOONTZ** Sam Koontz, of Linden, New Jersey, built his first guitar in 1959. He was a restless experimenter, but his real love was the arch-top jazz guitar. He died in the early 1980s.

■ **KRAMER** This U.S. company was started in 1975 by a partnership that included ex-Travis Bean associate Gary Kramer. Kramer shared Bean's belief in the advantages of aluminum-necked electrics and the company's initial line, launched the following year, took that approach.

Conventionally constructed guitars joined the catalog in the early 1980s and the range became more rock-oriented, with the metal-necked models disappearing in 1985. The following five years saw a succession of hot-rodded six-strings as Kramer became a major player in the muscle machine market. Superstrat-style solids dominated the late-1980s range, with U.S.-made models backed up by equivalents from Japan, Korea, and Czechoslovakia. **>**

1976 Kramer 450G

1977 Kramer 650G

1978 Kramer DMZ-2000

1982 Kramer Duke Special

■ On these pages, the guitars are by Kent, a brand used by various makers and importers; Klein, who followed the 1980s trend for headless guitars; German brand Klira; British maker Dick Knight; U.S. obscurity Knutsen; Japanese classical maker Kohno; and American experimenter Koontz. Also here are five Kramer guitars, including two examples of the maker's early metal-necked models.

1982 Kramer Voyager Imperial

1977 Koontz Custom Arch-top

1976 Koontz Custom Arch-top

1978 Koontz 17-7 Seven-string Flat-top

1978 Koontz Custom Flat-top

solidbodykramer

1968 Kustom K200C

■ Kramer has been through some changes, but is probably best known for its 1980s superstrat solid electrics. Also here are guitars by Rhode Island–based Krawczak; the Italian brand Krundaal; California bass maker Kubicki; the shortlived Kansas-based brand Kustom; plus an old guitar embellished with "La Flor de Cadiz."

1985 Kramer Ferrington 11-KFS2

1986 Kramer Ferrington Bass

Despite such apparent success, the company ran into financial difficulties, causing the curtain to come down in 1991, although ongoing Czech production meant the Kramer name continued in Europe for some time afterward.

In 1995, Kramer's original financier, Henry Vaccaro, launched an enthusiastic revival of the brand via a U.S.-made range, but despite the best of intentions and effort the project soon foundered. The Kramer name was acquired two years later by Gibson, which introduced a Korean-sourced series of re-creations and new models, more recently augmented by American-origin reissues.

Gary Kramer had left the original company only a year after he helped start it, but in 2005 he returned to guitar-making with a new venture under his own name, employing U.S. and Korean manufacture for a line of fresh designs.

■ **KRAWCZAK** Kazimierz Krawczak of Warwick, Rhode Island, is a Polish immigrant to the United States who has been building guitars part-time since 1980. This instrument has its bridge mounted on an internal secondary soundboard for added resonance.

■ **KRUNDAAL** Davoli Krundaal Musical SRL was founded in 1957 by Athos Davoli. This Italian company is most often associated with amplification, but also made related products such as microphones and guitar pickups. The latter were featured on the weird and wonderful instruments produced during the 1960s by fellow Italian, Antonio "Wandre" Pioli. Some of these creations carried the Krundaal name, such as the oddball Bikini, which boasted a pod-mounted amplifier and speaker, also supplied by Davoli.

■ **KUBICKI** Former Fender man Philip Kubicki set up on his own California-based company in the early 1980s, initially specialising in Fender-style necks and bodies, plus a novel Mini guitar series. In 1983 Kubicki launched the headless Factor and Ex Factor basses, the latter incorporating an innovative scale extender. Shortlived Japanese-made equivalents followed a few years later under the Blaster banner and in 1994 Kubicki introduced the more conventional Key Factor four- and five-strings. Maintaining his Fender connections, Kubicki licensed bass manufacture to the latter's Custom Shop facility from 1989 to 1991, subsequently resuming production in Santa Barbara, California, where he currently concentrates on the Factor and Ex Factor models, including custom examples.

■ **KUSTOM** Based in Chanute, Kansas, the Kustom company was started by Bud Ross in the mid-1960s and soon became a prominent name on the U.S. amplification scene. In 1968 Ross decided the time was right to add a partner line of electric guitars; it comprised three six-string models plus a matching bass. All shared the same semi-solid construction, twin-cutaway styling, and two single-coil pickup configuration, while the most expensive examples boasted a Bigsby vibrato unit. Unlike the amplification side, this excursion into the guitar-manufacturing business proved to be shortlived and all production had ceased by 1970, with no more than 3,000 likely to have been made.

■ **LA FLOR DE CADIZ** This unusual nineteenth-century guitar bears the name "La Flor de Cadiz" on its upwardly curving headstock. It was found in an antique shop in England in the 1980s.

kramersolidbody

1962 Krundall Bikini

1994 Krawczak Twin
Soundboard Guitar

Nineteenth century La Flor guitar from Cadiz

1984 Kramer RSG-1
Ripley Stereo

1985 Kramer Regent KRGI

1977 Kramer 650B

1989 Krubicki Factor
Bass

1989 Kramer American Sustainer

classicalla flor de cadiz

1967 La Baye 2-By-4

1996 Lacey Virtuoso

1999 Lakland 5594 USA Classic Bass

2005 Line 6 Variax Five-String

1835 Lacôte

1970 Landola Espana 6/12 Double-neck

■ **LA BAYE** The solid guitar has often been called a plank, and Wisconsin-based Dan Helland decided to take the term literally with his La Baye 2X4. Produced in 1967, this minimalist model managed to cram in a full complement of components and also came in bass or twelve-string form. Only about 45 were made.

■ **LACEY** Mark Lacey (born 1953) lives and works in Nashville, Tennessee, where he builds arch-tops in the tradition of D'Angelico and D'Aquisto as well as semi-solid electrics and the occasional flat-top. He was one of twenty-one luthiers commissioned by collector Scott Chinery to build a blue arch-top.

■ **LACÔTE** René-François Lacôte (1785–c.1855) was one of the most important guitar makers of the early nineteenth century, operating from several workshops in Paris, France. His guitars are typical of their era, being smaller and lighter than later Spanish instruments. They were played by many of the virtuosi of the era, including Carulli, Aguado, and Sor, who recommended them in his *Méthode Pour La Guitare* of 1830.

■ **LAKEWOOD** Lakewood Guitars was founded in 1986 by Martin Seeliger (born 1958). His team build about 1,000 flat-top acoustics every year in Giessen, Germany.

■ **LAKLAND** Located in Chicago, Ilinois, this bass-making company was founded by Don Lakin and Hugh McFarland in 1994. Early models mixed Music Man and Fender influences to good effect and have since been joined by other originals plus various signature editions. Market coverage has increased further with the more affordable, Korean-sourced Skyline range, introduced in 2001.

■ **LANDOLA** Landola currently produces about 3,000 guitars a year in Jakobstad, Finland. They include dreadnoughts, jumbos, acoustic basses, twelve-strings, mandolins, and classical guitars.

■ **LARRIVÉE** Jean Larrivée (born 1944) started building classical guitars in 1967 in Toronto, Canada. He built his first steel-string instrument in 1971 and now his company produces 12,000 flat-top acoustic and electric guitars every year in two factories in Vancouver, Canada, and Oxnard, California.

■ **LARSON** In the first half of the twentieth century, brothers Carl (1867–1946) and August Larson (1873–1944) of Chicago, Illinois, made guitars, mandolins, and harp guitars under a wide range of different brands, including their own.

■ **LEVIN** Levin was a Swedish manufacturer of musical instruments, founded in 1900 by Herman Carlson Levin (1864–1948). In eighty years of production it built more than 500,000 instruments, including guitars, mandolins, banjos, and lutes. Levin was acquired by C.F. Martin in 1973 and production at its Gothenburg factory stopped in 1981.

■ **LINE 6** Line 6 are specialists in sound modeling, successfully incorporating this modern technology into amplifiers and effects pedals. In 2002 this U.S. company decided to do the same with guitars, via the Variax 500. The following four years brought additional six-string solids, plus bass and acoustic models.

la bayesolidbody

1920s Larson Harp Guitar

2002 Lakewood DM

2003 Lakewood M32

2001 Larrivée Cherub

■ **Featured on these pages are guitars made by La Baye (U.S.), Lacey (U.S.); Lacote (France); Lakewood (Germany); Lakland (U.S.); Landola (Finland); Larrivée (Canada); Larson (U.S.); Levin (Sweden); and Line 6 (U.S.).**

1989 Larrivée C-10

1964 Levin Goliath

1975 Levin Dreadnought

1995 Lowden O-25

2002 Lowden S-25C

lowden jumbos

1998 Lowden LSE-III

2003 Lowden Avalon O-328

2002 Lowden Avalon A-100CE

2002 Lowden Avalon D-201

■ **LOWDEN** Northern Irish guitar maker Lowden and its offshoot Avalon have developed a reputation as quality alternatives to the independent U.S. builders of steel-string flat-top guitars. Lowden and Avalon have grown steadily into recognized brands in the acoustic world and gathered a number of pro endorsements along the way, including players such as Bruce Springsteen, Richard Thompson, Pierre Bensusan, Jan Akkerman, Jacques Stotzem, Michael Hedges, David Gray, and Van Morrison.

George Lowden was born in 1951 in Belfast, Northern Ireland, and made his first guitar at age ten. By the time he was twenty-two, he had completed the first Lowden and was soon on the way to establishing himself professionally. By the late 1970s, Lowden was building an international reputation as a skilled young luthier. By this time, he and a small staff of builders were completing around 200 guitars a year in the small Bangor workshop, but it soon became clear that demand was outstripping supply.

Lowden established a licensing agreement for a small Japanese factory to produce four models, soon rising to fifteen. By the mid 1980s, 1,000 Japanese Lowdens were being built each year. But rather than transfer to a larger Japanese factory, in 1985 Lowden moved production back to Northern Ireland, and a second, more prolific era of all-European Lowdens began.

In 1989 the company was sold to new owners, who established a larger factory in Newtownards, not far from Belfast. George Lowden left to concentrate on his own hand-built guitars but continued with the new Lowden company in some aspects of design and training. Lowden changed hands once more in 1998, and George again became involved in design and construction.

In 2002 Lowden launched the more affordable Avalon brand, and a few years later George Lowden started his own operation under his own name. At first, Avalon aimed at the less expensive pro sector, with fine build and sound quality, and the guitars received plaudits from press and players alike. Some time later it introduced a line of guitars made in Korea by Cort, but halted offshore manufacture in 2007 and returned to small-scale production in Northern Ireland. George Lowden's models, meanwhile, include signature instruments for Richard Thompson and Alex de Grassi.

■ **MACCAFERRI** Mario Maccaferri left Selmer in 1933 (see Selmer). He invented the plastic clothespin and set up a successful plastic manufacturing business, Mastro Industries. Still a guitarist, Maccaferri used Styron polystyrene resin to make instruments, and in 1949 he introduced his plastic Islander Ukulele. In 1953, he launched two plastic guitars, the G-30 flat-top and G-40 arch-top, endorsed by Andrés Segovia. Maccaferri plastic guitars were indeed real, playable instruments and not toys. Models continued to appear through the 1960s, including Islander, ShowTime, and Roco flat-tops as well as a line of Beatles instruments. Mario Maccaferri died in 1993 at age ninety-two.

lowdenacoustic

1952 Maccaferri G-30

1952 Maccaferri G-40

1957 Maccaferri New Romancer

■ Lowden is a Northern Irish guitar maker that has used two brandnames—Lowden and Avalon—and has experimented with offshore production of its flat-top steel-string guitars. Mario Maccaferri is best known for his Selmer guitars but also produced a line of serious plastic instruments in the 1950s.

1954 Maccaferri Islander 164A

1959 Maccaferri Showtime

2003 Lowden Avalon D-200E

2003 Lowden Avalon A-200CE

1920 Majestic Harp Guitar

1988 Marlin Masterclass

1956 Magnatone Spanish Mark III

1965 Magnatone Zephyr X

1959 Magnatone Mark V

■ **MAGNATONE** Although more associated with amplifiers, this U.S. company also made guitars. Somewhat basic single-cutaway solids joined a line of lap steels in 1956 and were later partnered by a pair of Paul Bigsby-designed twin-cutaway models. Magnatone's first bass debuted in 1959, its Rickenbacker-ish styling soon echoed by the re-designed Artist six-strings. These were replaced in 1961 by a four-strong range designed by ex-Rickenbacker man Paul Barth. Boasting wind-associated model names, the Fender-influenced Starstream series appeared four years later. In 1966 the range received a radically different headstock, plus a selection of semi-acoustics that would be the last guitars to bear the Magnatone brand.

■ **MAJESTIC** Majestic brand instruments, mostly banjos, were manufactured by Italian immigrant Gaetano Pontolillo (1880–1946) in New York and New Jersey. This hollow-armed harp guitar resembles those of Chris Knutsen.

■ **MANSON** Based in Crediton, Devon, England, Andy Manson (born 1949) is one of Britain's most acclaimed custom luthiers. He started making guitars in the late 1960s, developing over the next few decades a range that included the medium-size Magpie, the shallow-body Raven electro-acoustic, the Nightingale parlor guitar, the Heron jumbo, and the Dove dreadnought. He also became a specialist in multi-neck acoustics, building triple-neck instruments (six-string, twelve-string, and mandolin) for John Paul Jones and Jimmy Page. In 2000 the theme reached even more esoteric heights when Jones ordered an arch-top triple-neck combining mandolin, octave mandola, and bass mandolin. Since the mid-1990s Manson has turned almost exclusively to bespoke building, working alone to create about twelve instruments a year. Recent commissions include flat-top and arch-top guitars, mandolins, mandolas, and a bouzouki. He has also been building nylon-strung classical guitars.

■ **MANZER** Linda Manzer (born 1952) is a renowned builder of arch-top, flat-top, and classical guitars. Based in Toronto, Canada, she learned her craft in the 1970s as an apprentice to Jean Larrivée and then with arch-top builder James D'Aquisto. The most distinctive feature of her guitars is the shape of their bodies, in that the guitar is shallower on the bass side and deeper on the treble side. Manzer calls it the Wedge design and feels it makes the guitars more comfortable to play. She developed the idea in 1984 while building the Pikasso guitar for Pat Metheny. The jazz virtuoso had asked for an instrument "with as many strings as possible." The result was a guitar with four necks, two soundholes, and forty-two strings. A second version of the guitar (pictured), for collector Scott Chinery, was a purely acoustic instrument without the electronics required by Metheny. Metheny is her most celebrated customer, but other Manzer players include Carlos Santana, Liona Boyd, Bruce Cockburn, and Gordon Lightfoot. She currently builds about fifteen guitars a year. In 1996 she was one of twenty-one luthiers commissioned by Chinery to build a blue arch-top.

■ **MARLIN** In the mid-1980s the Marlin logo replaced the Kay name on East German-made electrics imported by UK distributors British Music Strings. These models were succeeded by Korean-sourced equivalents that subsequently carried the "Marlin by Hohner" legend, after the latter took control of the BMS company.

■ **MARSHALL** This Marshall-branded guitar is typical of many instruments sold during the Hawaiian music craze of the early 20th century. Marshall was probably a retailer, selling a guitar built for it by Gibson.

magnatone**solidbody**

■ Over these pages you'll find guitars by Magnatone, who had links to Bigsby and Rickenbacker; Manson, an English acoustic maker; Linda Manzer, one of the few successful female luthiers; Marlin, a cheap 1980s brand; and Marshall, a brand used by a store for a Gibson-made special.

1990 Manson Magpie Custom

1987 Manson Dove Sideslammer

1930 Marshall Special Hawaiian

1990 Mancuso

1995 Manzer Pikasso II

1996 Manzer Blue Absynthe

acoustic**marshall**

1820 Martin Stauffer

1830 Martin Stauffer

■ **MARTIN** It would be difficult to overstate Martin's influence on the guitar. Virtually all acoustic flat-tops made for steel strings incorporate one or more features that Martin either initiated or made popular.

In 1833 Christian Friedrich Martin arrived in New York City from Mark Neukirchen, Germany, and leased a storefront at 196 Hudson Street. There he worked as a retailer, wholesaler, and importer of all kinds of musical merchandise, and also repaired violins, guitars, and other wooden musical instruments. Soon he was also building guitars. By the 1850s Martin was located near Nazareth, Pennsylvania.

His guitars would soon be recognized as uniquely American. Martin's original body shapes and sizes would be considered quite small today. The largest was Size 1, which was only twelve inches wide at the lower bout, and sizes 2 through 5 got progressively smaller. In the mid-1850s the larger Size 0 was introduced, to become the company's standard concert model. Martins were produced in a variety of styles, each designated by a "number of quality," 17 to 42, which originally indicated the wholesale price.

From the 1850s through the following decades, Martin guitars were further refined, but underwent few structural modifications. The larger size 00 was added in the early 1870s, and Martin's bigger models continued to grow in popularity. In 1867 Martin took on his son C.F. Martin Jr., but by 1888 Martins senior and junior had both died, leaving the company to the third generation, twenty-two-year-old Frank Henry Martin.

Around 1916 the company began to build Martin-brand steel-string guitars for playing in the Hawaiian style, using bodies—including tops—built all of koa. A "K" suffix was added to the style numbers of the koa models, and the 0-18K and 0-28K were Martin's first official steel-string offerings. By 1920 Martin was making mahogany-top Style 17 models with steel strings, and in 1922 the small 2-17 was Martin's first non-Hawaiian steel-string model to appear in a catalog. Early photos of America's first guitar-playing superstar, Jimmie Rodgers, show him holding one of these small, all-mahogany Martins.

With these guitars, Martin finally achieved the growth that had eluded it for decades. By 1924, Style 18 was offered with steel strings, then Style 21 a year later, until by 1928 Martin's entire guitar line was built for steel strings, with gut strings as an option. Along with steel strings came greater demand for the largest model, the 000, which had been introduced in 1900, and Martin's Style 45 became a favorite stage guitar for popular singers. The switch to steel strings brought a dramatic rise in the percentage of Martin guitars made with mahogany back and sides.

The ukulele boom allowed Martin to expand the factory, and along with increased space came new woodworking machinery. But by 1928 the ukulele craze was fading, and guitars were once again the mainstay. Martin was asked to make a guitar with a narrower neck and more frets clear of the body. It quickly set to work modifying its largest model, the 000, and by shortening the body and moving

martinacoustic

1839 Martin & Coupa

coupa models

1830 Martin & Coupa

1820 Martin Stauffer

■ Here are the beginnings of Martin—and later sidelines. Martin's first American guitars were lookalikes based on the work of Austrian maker Johann Stauffer. Soon, the new U.S.-based Martin had teamed up with local music people such as John Coupa and Charles Bruno.

1840 Martin & Coupa

1839 Martin & Bruno

1830 Martin Stauffer

1850 Martin Stauffer

acousticmartin

1838 Martin

1840 Martin & Schatz

1860 Martin 1-28

1883 Martin 2-27

the bridge closer to the soundhole the OM (Orchestra Model) was born. This was Martin's first modern steel-string guitar, and it sold well right from the start.

Back in 1916, Martin had made a line of mahogany guitars with a unique, wide-waisted body for the Oliver Ditson company. The largest of the three sizes, dubbed the Dreadnought, was a giant when compared to Martin's 000, as it was over 4 inches deep and nearly 16 inches wide at the lower bout. The first dreadnoughts with a Martin label were the mahogany D-1 and the rosewood D-2. Two of the first batch made in 1931 were shipped to Chicago, home to the National Barn Dance, America's largest live radio show.

Stage performers looking for a guitar with more bass response quickly ordered more of the oversized Martins. One of the up-and-coming stars on the Barn Dance was Gene Autry, a young singer who already owned two pearl-bordered Martins. He ordered his dreadnought with as much inlay as possible, including his name on the fretboard to match the Martin played by his recently deceased idol, Jimmie Rodgers.

In 1935 the dreadnought finally appeared in Martin's catalog and sales took off. Within a few years, the D-18 was one of the company's bestselling models. The D-45 didn't appear in the catalog until 1938, and its arrival had the similar effect of boosting sales immediately. Martin's 1930s dreadnought models have been some of the most widely sought-after acoustic instruments ever made, and have come to define the American flat-top steel-string instrument. The fourteen-fret dreadnought is probably the most copied guitar in the world.

In 1934 Martin's catalog was divided into Orchestra Models—meaning any guitar with a fourteen-fret neck—and Standard Models, the older twelve-fret body shapes. By this time not many of the older standard model Martins were being sold, with the exception of the 00-21. Other twelve-fret models with flush frets and a high nut and saddle were sold to be played with a steel bar in the Hawaiian style ("H" suffix after the model code). Around the same time Martin revived two of its earlier gut-string models, giving them a "G" suffix.

Many dealers found the model names and numbers confusing, so the company began stamping the model code on the neck block inside the guitar, just above the serial number. Along with longer necks and pickguards, another change that often appeared on Martins during the 1930s was a shaded "sunburst" finish, breaking the company's long tradition of offering only a natural, or orange-tinted, finish for the soundboard.

Martin's flat-top models made from 1929 to roughly the end of World War II, in Styles 18 to 45, are the core of what most guitar fanatics consider to be

martinacoustic

1840 Martin

■ Martin made more collaborations in the early years, with New York City distributor Zoebisch and an old German friend also newly arrived in America, Henry Schatz. Meanwhile, in his newly adopted country, Christian Frederick Martin began to experiment and develop the designs of his own guitars.

1886 Martin 00021 Twin Neck Harp Guitar

1874 Martin 1-40

1860 Martin

1900 Martin Zoebish

1886 Martin 2-40

1890 Martin 2-42

1902 Martin 00-42

1898 Martin 0-42

the company's "Golden Era." But while Martin was developing what is now widely recognized as the quintessential flat-top guitar, it was also spending a lot of energy on another type of guitar that proved to be a costly dead-end. In mid-1931, Martin fielded a line of arch-top guitars, all with round soundholes, based on its OM body shape—the mahogany C-1, the C-2, and the deluxe rosewood C-3. By 1933 these were joined by a less expensive version in the 00 size, called the R-18, which would prove to be Martin's best selling arch-top. By the end of 1933 all were switched to the more popular f-hole design.

Ultimately Martin's arch-tops failed because the company never embraced the idea of a fully carved arch-top guitar. They were discontinued in 1942. Although they may not have made a lasting impression as guitars, they helped the company evolve to more contemporary designs.

The year 1942 also saw the last of the pearl-bordered Style 42 and 45 models. It would be over twenty-five years before the company would again offer a guitar trimmed in lines of gleaming abalone. Another farewell came in 1944 when the order was given to no longer scallop the top braces of each Martin guitar. This change was made necessary by the frequent use of heavy-gauge strings intended for big arch-top guitars. Around the same time, the delicate slotted diamonds-and-squares fret-position markers on Styles 21 and 28 were replaced with a pattern made of graduated pearl dots. Finally, in late 1946, the herringbone trim that had graced the top of Style 28 for nearly a century was changed to the black and white lines first seen on the C-2 arch-top.

C.F. Martin III took the helm of the company in 1945 at age fifty, when his father officially retired. The period from the late 1940s through the end of the 1950s was a quiet one for Martin, at least when it came to new models. But if the company was relatively tranquil, those who played Martin guitars were anything but quiet. Martin's D-18 and D-28 models had long been standard fare for artists in the field now known as country & western, but a young renegade from Memphis who couldn't keep his hips in line with his shoes soon dominated both the pop and country music charts. Elvis Presley was a highly effective rhythm-guitar player in his Sun Records period, and the original rock'n'roll power-trio was equipped with an acoustic stand-up bass, a hollowbody Gibson electric guitar, and a Martin D-18 or D-28. (Elvis owned both, but the D-28 was encased in a hand-tooled leather cover.)

Around the same time that Elvis was shaking things up, far less rebellious fare was being served up by three fresh-faced lads who seemingly never frowned in front of a camera. Two members of The Kingston Trio played Martins, and Bob Shane, who started out on a 000-18 but soon switched to a D-28, inspired so many budding folkies to buy the brand that Martin was quickly swamped with orders. **>**

1890 Martin Custom

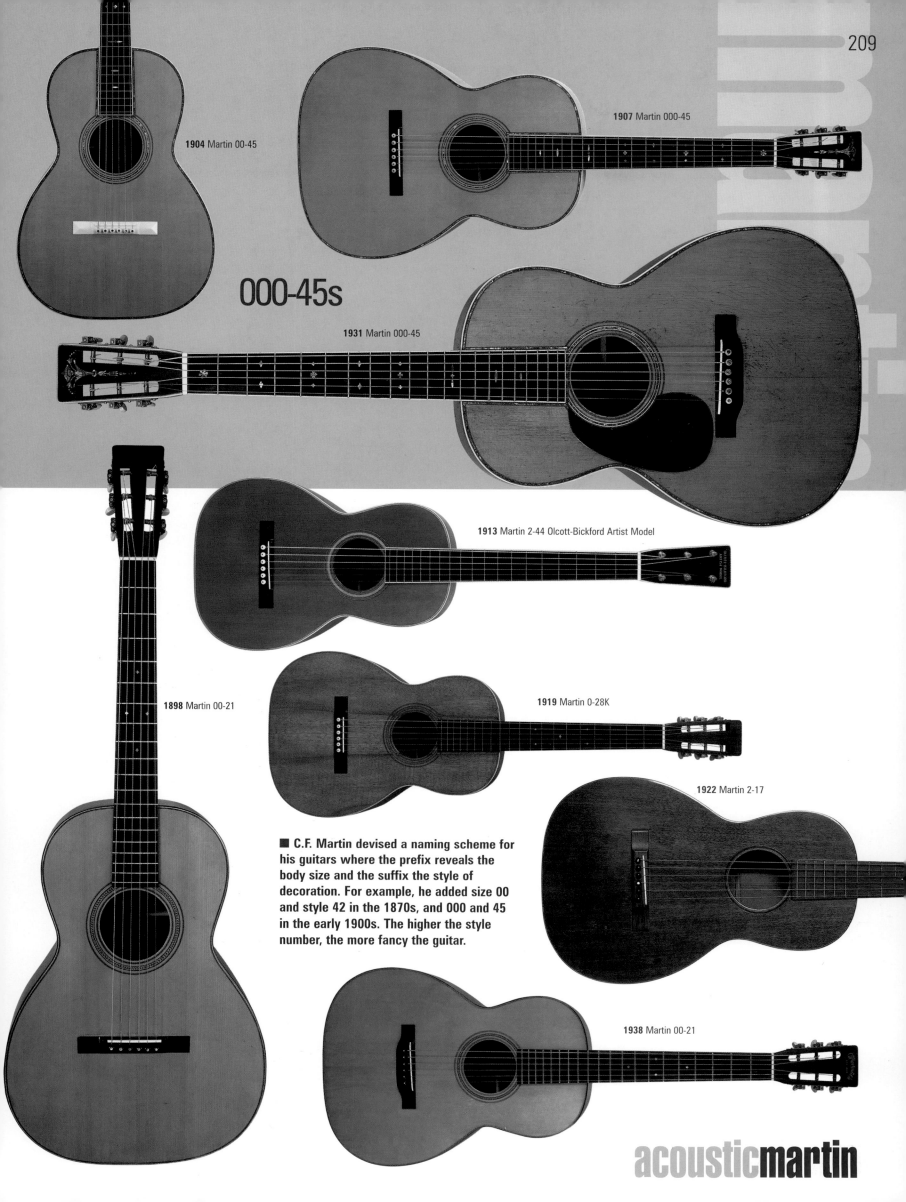

000-45s

1904 Martin 00-45

1907 Martin 000-45

1931 Martin 000-45

1913 Martin 2-44 Olcott-Bickford Artist Model

1898 Martin 00-21

1919 Martin 0-28K

1922 Martin 2-17

■ C.F. Martin devised a naming scheme for his guitars where the prefix reveals the body size and the suffix the style of decoration. For example, he added size 00 and style 42 in the 1870s, and 000 and 45 in the early 1900s. The higher the style number, the more fancy the guitar.

1938 Martin 00-21

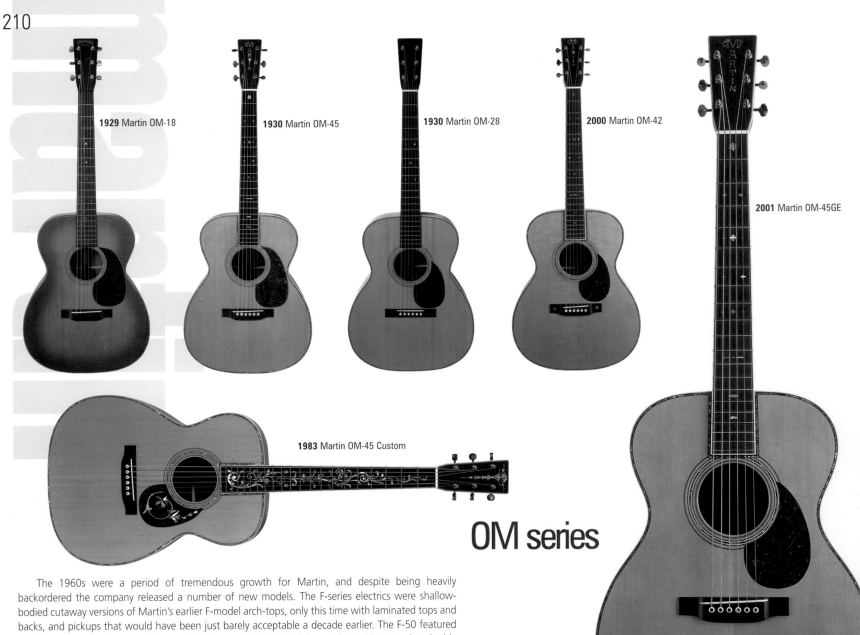

1929 Martin OM-18

1930 Martin OM-45

1930 Martin OM-28

2000 Martin OM-42

2001 Martin OM-45GE

1983 Martin OM-45 Custom

OM series

1928 Martin 00-40H

The 1960s were a period of tremendous growth for Martin, and despite being heavily backordered the company released a number of new models. The F-series electrics were shallow-bodied cutaway versions of Martin's earlier F-model arch-tops, only this time with laminated tops and backs, and pickups that would have been just barely acceptable a decade earlier. The F-50 featured a single cutaway and one pickup, while the F-55 had dual pickups. The F-65 sported a double cutaway, twin pickups, and a vibrato tailpiece. Electric guitarists paid little attention, but from 1961 Martin kept the F-Series electrics in the catalog for four years running.

In 1961 Martin introduced the 0-16NY, its first "reissue" of one of its older styles. The NY stood for New York, and the model was usually referred to as a "0-16 New Yorker," simply because it looked a lot like the old twelve-fret models made when Martins were still stamped "C. F. Martin & Co., New York." It looked like the real thing to folkies of the 1960s, although it would hardly qualify as a historical model by today's standards. Martin was clearly the darling of the folk revival, and the list of folk artists who played a Martin guitar reads like a Who's Who of the era.

In early 1964 Martin purchased a large plot of land on Sycamore Street on the outskirts of Nazareth, and in the fall of that year the company left its old home and moved to a spacious one-story building. Tom Paxton and Judy Collins sang from the loading dock as Martin celebrated the long-overdue move to larger and more modern quarters.

By the mid- to late-1960s Martin was selling more guitars and developing new models. When it came to flat-tops it seemed Martin could do no wrong, and the company continued to expand what had become a rather meager catalog of choices just a few years earlier. The original twelve-fret dreadnought shape was revived, but in two radically different versions. In 1964 Martin finally succumbed to popular pressure and offered a twelve-string model, the D12-20. This was a mahogany twelve-fret dreadnought with an elongated slotted headstock, and sold extremely well. The six-string version of the old twelve-fret dreadnought had been made in limited numbers, on special order, since the mid-1950s. One of these new old-style dreadnoughts wound up in the hands of Peter Yarrow, of Peter, Paul & Mary, and soon the twelve-fret dreadnought was back in fashion. Both the D-28S and D-18S were again in the catalog by 1968.

One of the most popular new Martin models introduced in the mid-1960s was dictated by necessity, rather than being inspired by popular requests or an earlier model. Demand for big dreadnoughts increased just as it became more difficult to find Brazilian rosewood logs of sufficient size, leaving Martin with lots of rosewood too narrow to make a two-piece dreadnought guitar back. One of the company's less-traditional new employees suggested a three-piece back, and the D-35 was born. Within

1924 Martin Style 5K Ukulele

1930 Martin Style 3K Ukulele

1930 Martin Paramount Style L

1916 Martin Ditson

1942 Martin D-18
Owned by Elvis Presley

ELVI

D-18s

1939 Martin D-18

■ Martin's new OM size of 1929 provided fourteen frets clear of the body for the first time on one of its production instruments, marking the company's first modern steel-string guitar. Next, the first of its big D-size Dreadnought guitars appeared, based on earlier contract work for Ditson.

1937 Martin D-18

1932 Martin D-28

1951 Martin D-28

1990 HD-28P "500,000 instrument"

1994 Martin CHD-28

2002 Martin 000-28LD Lonnie Donegan

1999 Martin HD-28LSV

2002 Martin HD-28VS

1934 Martin D-28H Hawaiian

■ **The D-size Dreadnought flat-top acoustic guitar has flourished under the guidance of C.F. Martin & Co., who in 1933 combined the big, booming size with its finest decorative style, 45—at first as a custom guitar for singing cowboy Gene Autry and then as a limited production instrument.**

D-45s

just a few years Martin was selling as many D-35s as D-28s. A twelve-string version, the D12-35, also debuted in 1965, and by 1968 a twelve-fret six-string, the D-35S, was added to the catalog. Then, in 1968, came the reissue of the legendary D-45.

As the company entered the 1970s, under the leadership of Frank Herbert Martin, son of C. F. Martin III, it seemed poised for a blockbuster decade, and began an aggressive campaign to acquire other music industry companies and build a Martin conglomerate, titled the C.F. Martin Organisation, with the telltale corporate cuteness of substituting a British spelling using "s" instead of the usual American "z." One of the first acquisitions was Darco Strings in 1970, a move that proved profitable right from the start. Martin also began importing guitars from Japan under the Sigma label.

With the folk music revival morphing into the folk-rock sound, Martin sales continued to be strong and the company saw little reason to do anything different. But by the mid-1970s sales had fallen enough to get Martin's management worried. As in the past, the company responded to slower sales with a flurry of new models, from the HD-28 (H for herringbone), to the D-19, which was basically a D-18 with some extra binding and soundhole rings, and a brown stain on the spruce top.

In 1977 Martin finally introduced its first truly new flat-top model in more than 40 years, the M-38, followed by the cheaper M-36. They were not runaway best sellers like the HD-28, but quickly gained favor among many players.

In 1979 Martin opened its Custom Shop to allow dealers and consumers the option of ordering a unique, or at least unusual, guitar. It gave Martin fanatics a chance to participate in the design of a guitar made just for them. Custom Shop models were the seeds that years later grew into the Vintage Series Martins.

By 1980 the company was floundering in a market obsessed with synthesizers and electronic gadgetry. A line of guitars made from Hawaiian koa was introduced that year, including the D-25K and the D-37K. Martin must have had high hopes for these koa models, for over 1,300 D-25K models were made in 1980 alone. Another less than successful introduction in 1980 was the Size 7, which was a 7⁄8-scale dreadnought, made in Style 28 and 37. Both models lasted only two years.

In 1981 Martin tried to catch up with the times by offering two cutaway models, the MC-28 and the DC-28. The following year sales fell to their lowest level since World War II, with Martin barely shipping 3,000 guitars. **>**

martinacoustic

1980 Martin D-45 Neiman
Marcus Custom

1933 Martin D-45

D-45s

1940 Martin D-45

1969 Martin D12-45

1983 Martin D-45
Custom

1993 Martin D-45 Deluxe
Limited edition

1994 Martin D-45 Gene Autry

1931 Martin C-3

1940 Martin F-5

1941 Martin
F-1S Twelve-string

1935 Martin
F-7 Arch-top

1964 Martin
00-18E

One of the company's brightest moves of 1984 was the "Guitars of the Month" program. These were limited editions with Custom Shop features not found on standard Martin models. The size of the edition was determined by the number of orders placed. It was the beginning of Martin's later Limited Edition and Signature Edition series that have proved to be extremely successful. Many of the popular Vintage Series models got their start as Guitars of the Month, including the D-18V, OM-28V, and the HD-28LSV.

Martin began to import unfinished guitar bodies and necks from Japan, finish and assemble them in Nazareth, then add an under-the-saddle pickup and hardshell case. Martin even gave these new models the usual decal on the headstock, but with "Shenandoah" replacing the "Est. 1833." Shenandoah models were made with laminated backs and sides, but in 1984 over 4,000 were sold, in a year when the company sold barely 7,200 instruments in all. Martin probably wouldn't have survived without the Shenandoah Series.

In 1985 the company introduced new models, modified old ones, and achieved several years' worth of updates in a short period of time. The most important new model was the J-40M (called simply J-40 after 1989), Martin's first jumbo. With small hexagon inlays on the bound fretboard, eight-ply top binding, and gold tuners, the J-40M was a flashy new Martin unlike any before it. For those who wanted the sound of a rosewood Martin Jumbo but at a lower price, there was the J-21. Not only did the J-40M look unlike any earlier Martin, it also played unlike earlier Martins as well. With a new neck shape and closer tolerances at the factory Martin was back in the game.

Martin also added the new Series 60 guitars in 1985, using figured maple for the back and sides. These were the J-65M Jumbo and a matching twelve-string, plus the shallow-bodied M-64 and the MC-68, a cutaway model. Although sales were promising for the first few years, and other maple models like the D-62 were added, most were discontinued by the mid-1990s. In 1985, however, they were a much-needed breath of fresh air for a company that was trying to shed its stodgy reputation.

In 1986 Martin launched the D-16K, a trade-show special not shown in the catalog. It was priced well below the D-18 despite the koa body, making it the least expensive Martin dreadnought. Here at last was a model that could compete with some of Martin's newer competitors—namely Taylor—and thus lure buyers who wouldn't settle for a Shenandoah. A second major change at Martin in 1986 was the loss of its patriarch, C.F. Martin III, who died on June 21. In settlement of his estate, auditors recommended the company be liquidated and sold to settle the outstanding debts resulting from disastrous acquisitions made during the 1970s. The company was able to stave off such a drastic move, but it was clear Martin wasn't out of the woods yet. On the death of his grandfather, C.F. Martin IV became chairman and CEO of the company.

Martin's adaptation to the needs of modern guitar players and its increased model line-up was key to the company's return to stability in the late 1980s, but renewed popularity in acoustic guitars in general played an equal role. An added bonus was new interest in travel guitars. The Martin Backpacker, made in Mexico and introduced in 1991, sold far better than the company had expected. In 1993 Martin introduced the D-1, its first break with many of the company's long-standing traditions, and a giant step toward closing the gap between those traditions and state-of-the-art manufacturing.

The D-1 used a new mortise-and-tenon neck joint, and had laminated sides but a solid mahogany back. A 000-1 soon followed, along with rosewood versions of both the 000 and D, made with laminated sides and back. Also new was a gold-foil logo on the headstock

1981 Martin EM-18

martinacoustic

1962 Martin 5-16

1965 Martin D-35

1968 Martin N-20
Classical

2000 Martin HD-35JC
Judy Collins Model

1981 Martin 7-45 Custom
Dick Boak Model

1975 Martin D-76

1983 Martin 00-18
Electro Acoustic

■ Martin is best known for its steel-string flat-tops, but occasionally it has wandered into other areas, with mixed levels of success. Shown here are some of those experiments, including arch-top designs and a classical guitar, as well as signature models, one-offs, and general-production guitars.

1965 Martin GT-75

1978 Martin M-36

martin electrics

acousticmartin

1987 Martin JC-40

1988 Martin D-42LE

1990 Martin J-40BK

1995 Martin 000-1

1994 Martin Backpacker

1995 Martin 000-42EGB Eric Clapton Signature Model

replacing the old decal. Martin had finally reclaimed its "made in Nazareth" heritage with competitively priced guitars, and Shenandoah models were soon forgotten.

Meanwhile, in 1994, at the other end of the price scale, Martin offered its first "Signature Edition" model, a replica of Gene Autry's famous D-45—complete with paper label signed by Autry. An impressive sixty-six were sold, despite the list price of $22,000. The following year the signature edition was a 000-42 EC, for Eric Clapton. More signature-edition models have followed, including guitars with unique decorations (HD-40MS for Marty Stuart, HD-18JB for Jimmy Buffet, and several others) and models that are highly accurate facsimiles of the original Martin guitars the artist played. Today, Martin's Signature Series has largely replaced the Guitars of the Month program.

Another winner introduced in 1995 was the D-18 Golden Era, styled more exactly like a 1930s original than any previous Martin reissue. The following year Martin finally collected all its various vintage reissue models under one banner, called the Vintage Series, and gave them consistent features.

The mid-1990s were another high-energy period at Martin, with the company expanding both the high-end Vintage Series and lower-priced lines made possible by the new D-1 technology. In 1997 the SP (Special) 16 Series guitars were introduced—deluxe models with snowflake inlays on the fretboard, a pearl rosette, gloss finish, and gold tuners. A new "Women in Music" 16 Series model, the 00-16DBM, was also introduced, designed by Martin's female employees. This was a deep-bodied 00 with a narrow fourteen-fret neck and slotted headstock. Several variants of this concept have followed.

In 1998 several different woods were also added to the SP 16 Series, primarily in D models, including walnut, maple, and koa. At this point Martin's 16 Series guitars alone were offered in greater variety than the company's entire catalog of less than a decade earlier. At the same time, the all-mahogany 15 Series was introduced, soon followed by a more deluxe all-mahogany line, called the 17 Series, with gloss finish, body binding, and top bracing like the 16 Series.

Although the company had been in a precarious financial position barely a decade earlier, as it faced yet another turn of the century, it now managed to find a stable footing and was matching its competitors as new technologies swept through the guitar-making industry.

Martin continued the double-barreled approach to a wider market share that had proven so successful since introduction of the D-1. At the upper end of the pricing scale, Martin dug even deeper into exact reissues of its legendary 1930s guitars by seeking out sources of Adirondack spruce for the soundboards, the same species it had used before the mid-1940s. It also introduced its least expensive models, the X Series, made with high-pressure composites of wood fiber finished with a photo-film of mahogany or spruce.

In 2003, Martin introduced the Little Martin guitar, a travel or beginner guitar made of composites but also available with a solid spruce top. In 2008, C.F. Martin celebrated its 175th anniversary, making it the oldest surviving guitar manufacturer in the world.

martinacoustic

1999 Martin
HPD-41

1999 Martin Mini
Limited Edition

2000 Martin
000-16RGT

2002 Martin SPD-16K

1999 Martin JML

2006 Martin Felix II

■ Today, as the oldest guitar maker
still in business, Martin continues to
do what it does best—make fine flat-
top steel-string acoustic guitars—
despite stiffer competition than ever
before from home and abroad. Here
are some recent examples of its work,
including the small Backpacker travel
guitar and one of the cheaper X series.

2006 Martin 000XI

1990 Martin B-65

acousticmartin

1980 Mates
Made for Dave Pegg of Fairport Convention

1988 McGlincy

■ The guitars featured here are by U.S. makers Maurer, McGlincy, Megas, Melobar, Messenger, and Micro-Frets; Mates (UK), Maton (Australia), and Maya (Japan).

1967 Melobar Guitar-steel Hybrid

1984 Maya Model 8029

■ **MATES** Tom Mates of London, England, built this guitar for Dave Pegg of Fairport Convention and Jethro Tull.

■ **MATON** Established in 1946 by brothers Bill and Reg May, this Australian company at first focused on acoustic guitars, but arch-top electrics appeared in 1949 and solidbody six-strings were added ten years later. Matons initially owed little to outside influences, but designs became more derivative during the 1960s and obvious copies appeared in the next decade. Product emphasis has since shifted to acoustics, although an electric range was rekindled in the late 1990s, spearheaded by a revival of the early 1960s Mastersound 500 briefly employed by Beatle George Harrison.

■ **MAURER** Maurer was the principal brand name used on guitars made by the brothers Carl (1867–1946) and August Larson (1873–1944) of Chicago, Illinois, from 1900 until around 1935 or 1936, when it was replaced by the Euphonon brand. Like Bohmann guitars before them, Maurer guitars were designed to handle steel strings, eliminating the need for a tailpiece.

■ **MAYA** The Chushin Gakki factory in Nagano, Japan, manufactured instruments under the Maya or partner El Maya brand. Production followed a familiar pattern during the 1970s, with imitations of famous U.S. solids and semis subsequently joined by more original models at the end of the decade, including the El Maya EM series. Other equally individual designs were added before both brands disappeared in the mid-1980s.

■ **MCGLINCY** Ed McGlincy built flat-top acoustics from a workshop in Westville, New Jersey, before retiring in the 1990s due to ill-health. His customers included Gordon Lightfoot and Lightfoot's lead guitarist Terry Clements.

■ **MEGAS** Ted Megas (born 1950) of Portland, Oregon, specializes in arch-tops, although he also makes a line of solidbodies. Working alone, he builds twelve guitars a year. He was one of twenty-one luthiers commissioned by collector Scott Chinery to build a blue arch-top.

■ **MELOBAR** In 1967, Walt Smith from Sweet, Idaho, introduced the Melobar, a lap-steel cleverly redesigned for stand-up playing. This novel instrument proved popular with famous slide specialists such as Ry Cooder and Bonnie Raitt. Smith refined his idea during the 1980s, also adding Melobars with familiar body shapes, while the current range includes electric and acoustic examples.

■ **MELODY** Best-known for inexpensive acoustics, this Italian company added some equally cost-conscious electrics in the late 1970s. These were Fender and Gibson copies from the Far East, but the home-grown Blue Sage range of the 1980s was more original and upmarket.

■ **MESSENGER** Musicraft in San Francisco manufactured the shortlived Messenger range of the late 1960s. This comprised six-, four-, and twelve-string models, all sharing the same unusual non-cutaway styling, while construction was even more individual, employing an aluminum neck with a full-length body extension.

■ **MICRO-FRETS** Emanating from Frederick, Maryland, during the 1960s and 1970s, the electric guitars and basses made by U.S. company Micro-Frets were more quirky than those of their contemporary competitors. Micro-Frets trod a highly individual path in terms of body styling and construction, seemingly oblivious to influences exerted by the likes of Fender and Gibson. Most of the components used were equally original—the Calibrato vibrato and the Micro-Nut, for example. The latter featured six individually adjustable saddle sections intended to improve intonation.

The Manufacture of Micro-Frets stopped in the mid-1970s, but the brandname returned 30 years later via a range of revised reissues of the most popular originals.

1962 Maton Mastersound MS-500

1968 Maton Wedgetail

1982 Melo Blue Sage

The Orbiter

1967 Messenger
ME-1

1996 Megas
Custom

1935 Maurer Style 590

1967 Micro-frets Signature

1967 Micro-Frets Orbiter

1969 Micro-Frets Golden Melody

1969 Micro-frets Huntington

semi-solidbodymicro-frets

1998 Modulus Genesis

1980 Mighty Mite Mercury

1984 Modulus Gaphite Quantum Six-String Bass

1983 Modulus Graphite Flight 6 Monocoque

■ **MIGHTY MITE** Operating for around ten years from the mid-1970s, this U.S. company was one of the first to fuel the fast-growing guitar parts market of that time, offering high quality replacements for standard Fender and Gibson components. Many were made of brass, which was popular back then, while the line also included hotted-up humbuckers and single-coil pickups. Unlike some contemporaries, Mighty Mite didn't supply ready-made instruments, although complete kits were available. In the 1990s the name reemerged on a range mainly sourced from the Far East.

■ **MODULUS** Former Alembic employee Geoff Gould established Modulus Graphite in San Francisco, California, in 1978. Initially it offered replacement bass necks made of moulded graphite. By the early 1980s the brand name was adorning actual guitars and basses that made prominent use of this synthetic material.

Comprising original and more traditional designs, the upmarket range continued to grow gradually until 1995, when the company changed hands and became known as Modulus Guitars. Graphite still featured strongly in the construction of the continuing Quantum basses and new models including the Genesis range. The revised line initially included guitars, but production has subsequently centered on basses.

■ **MONTELEONE** Long Island–based luthier John Monteleone (born 1947) started out in the 1970s by building mandolins and doing repair work for New York's renowned Mandolin Brothers guitar shop. He is now considered to be one of the world's premier builders of arch-top guitars, drawing inspiration from Gibson and D'Angelico. He was one of twenty-one luthiers commissioned by collector Scott Chinery to build a blue arch-top.

■ **MOSRITE** Born in Durant, Oklahoma, in 1935, Semie Moseley went to work for Rickenbacker at the start of the 1950s. There he was influenced by fellow employees Roger Rossmeisl and Paul Barth and began working on his own ideas concerning guitar construction and design. This didn't go down well with Rickenbacker, and Moseley's subsequent dismissal prompted him to set up his own guitar-making operation. He was encouraged by a close friend, the Reverend Ray Boatright, and the Mosrite brand was derived from their combined surnames.

From the start Moseley made his Mosrites distinctive by incorporating numerous individual touches, including the "M" topped headstock that would become an instantly recognizable trademark. In the late 1950s this was joined by an equally important idea: the leftie-look body that was basically a reversed Stratocaster shape, but with certain stylistic and dimensional differences providing an all-new outline.

Moseley employed this super-streamlined silhouette on instruments built for country player Joe Maphis and the Standel company, but bigger success soon came when it caught the eye of Nokie Edwards, guitarist with The Ventures, the leading U.S. instrumental act of the day. In return for exclusive distribution rights, the group funded a factory in Bakersfield, California, to manufacture what were now known as The Ventures models, complete with appropriate logos.

These guitars and basses were soon joined by Joe Maphis semi-solids, plus thinline acoustic-electrics such as the Celebrity, Combo, and Gospel

modulus**solidbody**

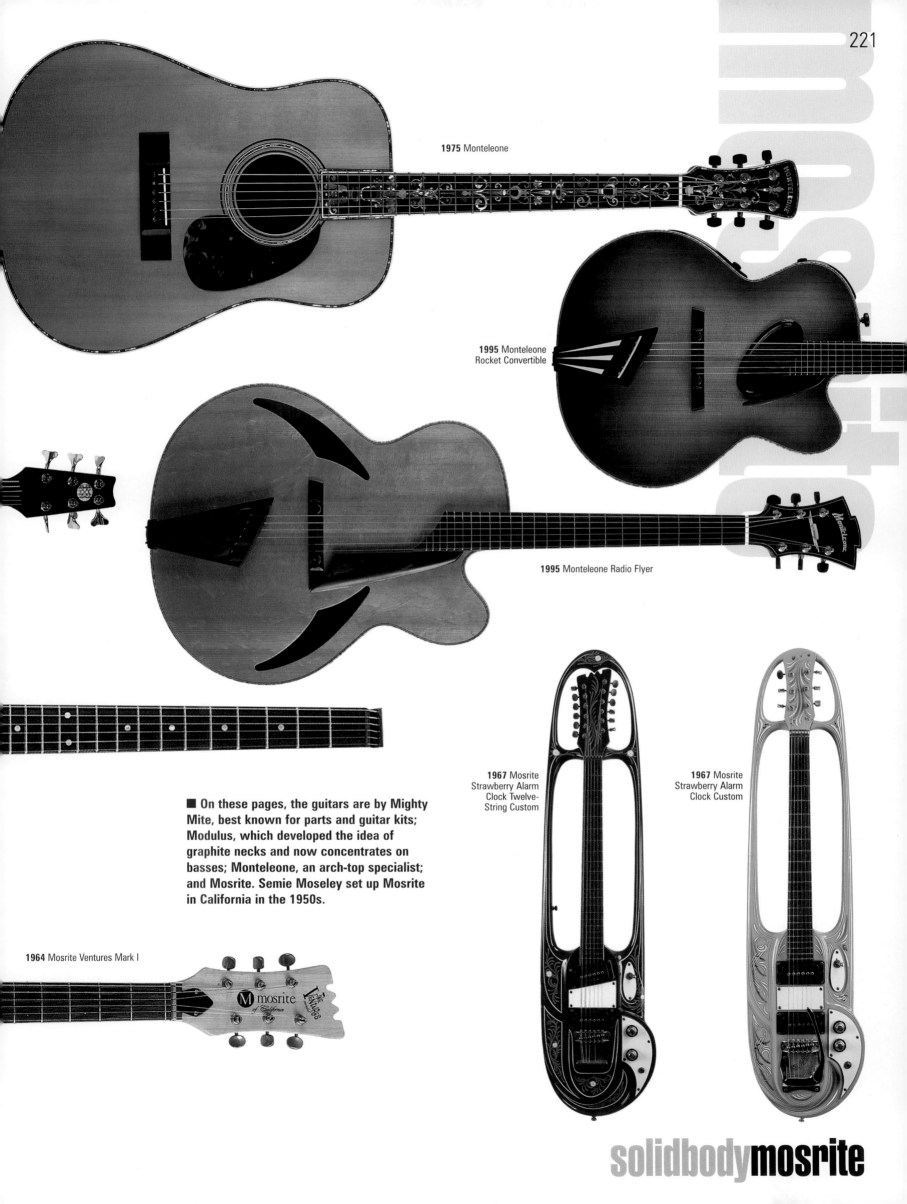

1975 Monteleone

1995 Monteleone Rocket Convertible

1995 Monteleone Radio Flyer

1967 Mosrite Strawberry Alarm Clock Twelve-String Custom

1967 Mosrite Strawberry Alarm Clock Custom

■ On these pages, the guitars are by Mighty Mite, best known for parts and guitar kits; Modulus, which developed the idea of graphite necks and now concentrates on basses; Monteleone, an arch-top specialist; and Mosrite. Semie Moseley set up Mosrite in California in the 1950s.

1964 Mosrite Ventures Mark I

solidbodymosrite

1988 Mosrite Model 88

1965 Mosrite Ventures Bass

1995 Mosrite Excellent 65

series. Production grew from 35 to 300 instruments a month, and at the peak of Mosrite popularity the workforce numbered 100.

By the late 1960s the Mosrite/Ventures partnership had been terminated, but the models continued in production without the Ventures branding. Mosrite expanded into related product areas, including amplification, but the latter contributed to the economic problems that caused the company's closure in 1969.

This was to be the first in a series of financial setbacks and false starts for Moseley. Over the next few years, subsequent collaborations with companies such as Vox, Kustom, and Acoustic all proved unsatisfactory and shortlived. Despite increasing interest in the original Ventures models, it wasn't until 1984 that Moseley finally reestablished the Mosrite brand, producing relevant reissues and all-new instruments. In 1992 the 40th Anniversary model commemorated Moseley's four decades in the guitar-making business. He died the same year.

Since then the Mosrite brand has survived mainly via Japanese manufacture, although more recently some U.S. production has been revived.

■ **MUSIC MAN** This U.S. company was set up in 1972 by two ex-Fender men, Forrest White and Tom Walker. Originally called Tri-Sonics, then Musitek, it became Music Man in 1974. The catalog was initially amplification-only, but instruments were added two years later. First to appear were the StingRay guitar and bass, both incorporating design ideas by Leo Fender, who had become president of Music Man in 1975. These were joined in 1978 by the Sabre and its companion bass. Neither guitar proved very popular, as they differed too much from what players expected, but the basses fared far better, soon being recognized as valid evolutions of earlier Leo Fender four-strings.

Behind the scenes, business upheavals resulted in Leo Fender leaving in 1979 to set up his own guitar brand, G & L. Music Man managed to maintain instrument manufacture into the early 1980s, eventually using outside sources, including Jackson, but in 1984 the brand was bought by the Ernie Ball company. Production switched to the latter's facility in San Luis Obispo, California, and the second distinct chapter in the Music Man story began.

The successful StingRay and Sabre basses soon reappeared under the new ownership, but guitars didn't return until 1986, in the form of the all-new Silhouette. This was the first to feature the compact headstock with four-plus-two tuner formation that would become standard on all subsequent Music Man six-strings.

These included the Steve Morse signature model that debuted the next year, followed in 1991 by what proved to be the company's highest-profile guitar, the EVH, designed in close collaboration with influential axe-man Edward Van Halen. This model has continued in production as the Axis, after the guitarist defected from Music Man in the mid-1990s. Other signature six-strings were added during that decade, including Steve Lukather's Luke and the angular-bodied model autographed by Albert Lee.

Basses have continued to play the most prominent part in the Music Man range. The Sabre was dropped in 1991, but the best-selling StingRay still soldiers on, having already celebrated 20th and 30th Anniversary editions, while new additions include the Sterling, Bongo, and more-affordable Sub models.

1980 Mosrite Custom

1967 Mosrite Strawberry Alarm Clock Custom Bass

1976 Music Man Stingray

1978 Music Man Silhouette, Special Finish

mosritesolidbody

1988 Music Man
Silhouette Ernie Ball

1991 Music Man EVH

1993 Music Man
Albert Lee Model

1993 Music Man
The Luke

■ Semie Moseley's Mosrite company is best known
for the Ventures models of the 1960s, named for the
popular U.S. instrumental guitar band. Music Man
was the company that Leo Fender set up following
his departure from Fender, and is today owned by
Ernie Ball and based in San Luis Obispo, California.

1998 Music Man Silhouette Special

1996 Music Man Axis Super Sport

1977 Music Man Stingray Bass
**Owned by Radiohead
guitarist Jonny Greenwood**

1976 Music
Man Stingray
Bass

music man
basses

1989 Music Man Stingray
Fretless 5 Bass

1979 Music Man Stingray Fretless

1966 Muzicka Naklada Special 64

1982 Musima Eterna Deluxe

1962 Musima Otwin

1962 National Westwood 75

■ **MUSIMA** Founded in 1945, Musima was East Germany's major musical instrument manufacturer for almost sixty years, producing everything from accordions to zithers. Guitars featured prominently, with acoustics and electrics also marketed under other brand names.

Often mistakenly stated as being made by Musima, Otwin instruments actually originated from an East German company established in 1886 by Otto Windisch. Acoustics were joined by electrics in the 1950s, with solids added during the next decade, including this one-off double-neck.

■ **MUZICKA NAKLADA** During the 1960s, Fender's Stratocaster influenced guitar makers worldwide, and in Yugoslavia the Muzicka Naklada company was no exception, as seen on their Special 64.

■ **NATIONAL** National is best known for its resonator guitars (see over) but it was also a pioneer in electrics. In the 1930s National-Dobro (the two resonator companies merged in 1932) launched a National electric guitar, the Electric Spanish f-hole arch-top model (along with a similar Dobro-brand version, plus cheaper Supro-brand electrics).

In 1943 the company reorganized as Valco, and after World War II it started applying the National brand to a variety of electric instruments. The first were arch-tops, including the Aristocrat and the single-cutaway Club Combo, but in the 1960s it launched a range of solidbodies. The company was a pioneer in using new materials in its designs. The so-called "map" instruments, the bodies of which bear a resemblance to the outline of the United States, were available in wood (marketed as Westwood) but also in what National referred to as res-o-glas. This was fiberglass, finished in a range of vivid colors. The guitars, marketed as Newport and Glenwood, were introduced in 1962 and stayed on the market until 1965.

These were not cheap instruments: a top-of-the-range Glenwood, with two single-coil pickups, a bridge pickup, a tone selector switch, three tone controls, three volumes, and a Bigsby vibrato tailpiece, would have cost $450 in 1964, only slightly less than a Gibson SG Custom. Recently the distinctive map shape has come back on to the market in a wood-bodied range by Eastwood Guitars of Ontario, Canada, built in Korea and China. **>**

musimasolidbody

1961 National
Studio 66

1962 National
Glenwood 95

1963 National
Newport 82

1963 National
Newport 84

res-o-glass
semis

national solids

■ Three eastern European instruments are pictured here: a Muzicka Naklada from the former Yugoslavia, and Musima and Otwin guitars from East Germany. The rest of the space here is occupied by National electric guitars: the company's wonderful "map shape" plastic instruments of the early 1960s.

1964 National Varsity 66

1962 National Westwood 77

1927 National Style 2 Tricone

1927 National Style 2 Tenor

1930 National Style 0

1933 National Style 0

1936 National Model 35

1928 National Style 4 Tri-cone

George Beauchamp, a Texas-born vaudeville performer, had an idea to increase the volume of a guitar by incorporating an amplifying horn like those used in early phonographs. In 1926 he sought out Los Angeles inventor John Dopyera, who had formed the National String Instrument Corporation to make banjos, to help him turn the concept into an instrument. Using cones made of thin, spun aluminum, Dopyera experimented with various numbers of cones and configurations. In 1927, he filed a patent application for a guitar with the three-cone configuration that would become the National "tri-cone" guitar.

The individual cones were very lightweight but they supported the weight of the string tension, and they increased the volume of the guitar considerably. The new resonator guitars were immediately embraced by Hawaiian players of the day. National's original tri-cone or Silver Hawaiian line comprised four progressively more decorative models, all with bodies of nickel alloy. Style 4, the most expensive, boasted elaborate chrysanthemum engraving.

Dopyera left National and invented a new type of resonator guitar called the Dobro (from "Dopyera Brothers"). It had a single cone and a wood body. In 1928 National responded with a similar wood-bodied model called the Triolian which, despite its name, had a single cone. The wood body was replaced in 1929 with a steel body that sported a painted finish ranging from yellow on some examples to green on others. Two further steel-body single-cone guitars, the Duolian and the Style O, arrived in 1930.

Single-cone metal-body Nationals found a ready market among blues players. Aside from the cheaper price ticket, they produced a crisper, harsher tone than the tri-cones, but that cutting tone worked well for performers who might be found on streetcorners, at house parties, or in juke joints. Although legendary blues artist Robert Johnson was never photographed with a National, the distinctive sound of a National single-cone metal-body guitar is a vital part of his seminal recordings.

National offered more wood-body models in the 1930s—the Rosita, the Trojan, the Estralita, the Havana, the Aragon—but most had neither the power nor the tonal "personality" of the metalbodies.

Upgrades to existing models followed, and National continued offering acoustic resonator guitars through 1941, but the company had recognized the coming electric age and started making electric guitars in 1935. Dobro and National were merged in 1935, moved offices to Chicago in 1936 and reorganized in 1943 as Valco. National revived the acoustic resonator guitar in the post-war years, but the Reso-phonic of 1956 was more of a funky toy than a musical instrument. The next, and final, National acoustic resonator guitar, was the fiberglass Bluegrass 35. By the late 1960s Valco, along with many other American instrument makers, was in financial trouble due to the influx of cheap Japanese instruments. Valco acquired Kay, which had once been a leading maker of inexpensive guitars and was now floundering, and Kay pulled Valco further down. A line of low-quality imported flat-tops appeared under the National brand in 1967, just before the company went bankrupt in 1968.

In 1989 the steady rise of interest in the early Nationals led Don Young and McGregor Gaines to form National Reso-phonic Guitars, in San Luis Obispo, California. It now makes single-cone, tri-cone, and Dobro-style "spider-bridge" resonators in wood and metal, including some with cutaway bodies.

national resonator

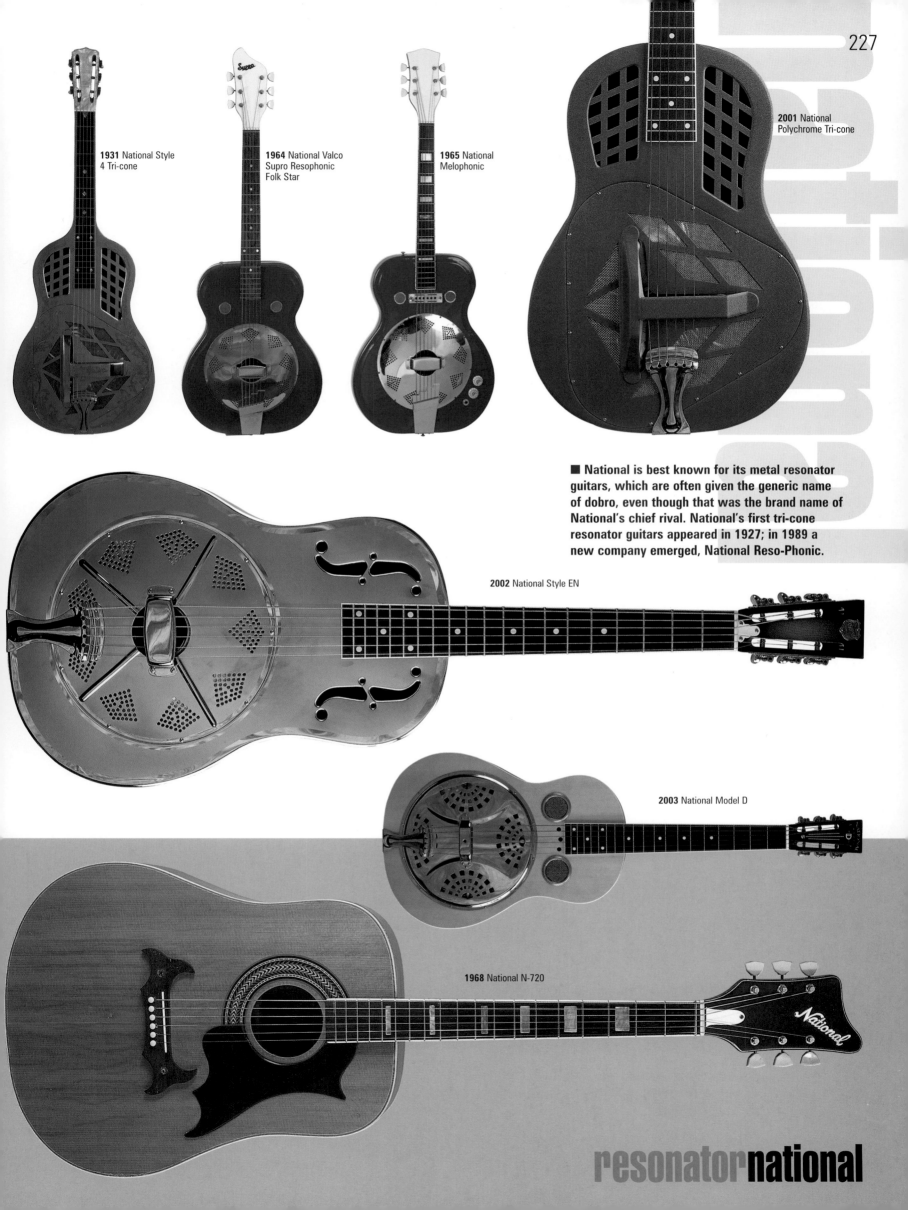

1931 National Style 4 Tri-cone

1964 National Valco Supro Resophonic Folk Star

1965 National Melophonic

2001 National Polychrome Tri-cone

■ National is best known for its metal resonator guitars, which are often given the generic name of dobro, even though that was the brand name of National's chief rival. National's first tri-cone resonator guitars appeared in 1927; in 1989 a new company emerged, National Reso-Phonic.

2002 National Style EN

2003 National Model D

1968 National N-720

1975 Ned Callan Cody

1968 Norma EG-400

1996 Nickerson Eqinox Custom

1936 Oahu Deluxe Jumbo
68 Hawaiian

■ **NED CALLAN** Ned Callan was a pseudonym for UK maker Peter Cook which appeared on some distinctively styled solids during the 1970s. These were also marketed by various British distributors, including CMI, Simms-Watts and Rose-Morris, with the latter company adding their Shaftesbury logo to models nicknamed "Nobbly Neds."

■ **NICKERSON** Brad Nickerson (born 1944) of Asheville, North Carolina, built his first guitar in 1982. Today he builds up to twelve arch-tops, flat-tops, and semi-hollow electrics a year. He also runs a school of guitar-building. This is one of twenty-one blue arch-tops commissioned by collector Scott Chinery in 1996.

■ **NIGHTINGALE** Charles A. Nightingale of Evansville, Indiana, built this gut-strung guitar in about 1900. It features a secondary internal soundboard linked to the soundhole by a metal tube.

■ **NORMA** The Norma name adorned Japanese electrics imported into America during the 1960s by Strum and Drum Inc. of Chicago, Illinois. Some came from the Tombo accordion company and boasted sparkle or pearl plastic-covered bodies, echoing Italian instruments of the era. Others featured split pickguards and pickups, plus N-shape position markers, similar to equivalents carrying the Liberty logo.

■ **NORMAN** Norman guitars get their name from their original maker, Normand Boucher (1917–1997), who started building guitars in 1968, setting up production in the Canadian village of La Patrie, Quebec, in 1972. In 1989 Robert Godin bought the Norman facilities and absorbed the brand into his burgeoning LaSiDo empire. While not cosmetically exciting, Norman flat-tops enjoy a deserved reputation for consistently good sound quality and value.

■ **NUÑEZ** Francisco Nuñez (1841–1919) was a Spanish immigrant to Argentina who opened a guitar workshop and store in Buenos Aires in 1870. In 1894 he traveled to Europe to buy machinery to produce classical instruments in large numbers, while continuing to hand-build some guitars himself. The store, Casa Nuñez, which also published sheet music, became a social centre for Argentina's guitar players. In 1925 it was renamed as "Antigua Casa Nuñez." It continues to trade today.

■ **OAHU** The Oahu Publishing Company, founded in Flint, Michigan, in 1926, was a leading player in the Hawaiian music craze of the early twentieth century. As well as tutor books and sheet music, it sold instruments, including acoustic guitars built for it by Kay and Regal. These ranged from cheap student models to a top-of-the-line jumbo with a spruce top, African rosewood body, and pearl trim.

■ **OLD KRAFTSMAN** Old Kraftsman was a "house brand" of the Spiegel company, one of the Chicago mail-order catalog retailers (with Montgomery Ward and Sears, Roebuck) that supplied the largely rural population of America with consumer goods prior to World War II. When Spiegel began selling guitars is unknown, but by the 1930s it sold Old Kraftsmans (as well as the Del Oro brand), including flat-tops, arch-tops (some carved), and even a resonator, mostly made by Stromberg-Voisinet/Kay. In 1936–37 a few carved-top acoustics were supplied by Gibson.

ned callan solidbody

1990 Norman B-50

1978 Nuñez Classical

1998 Nunez Classical

1900 Nightingale

1927 Oahu 000 Size

1941 Old Craftsman Crown

■ Featured here are guitars by the UK's Ned Callan; Nickerson, Nightingale, Oahu, and Old Kraftsman from the United States; Japan's Norma, Canada's Norman, and Nuñez from Argentina.

acousticold kraftsman

1971 Ovation
Breadwinner 1251

1973 Ovation
Deacon 1252

1975 Ovation
Preacher 1281

1975 Ovation
Viper III 1273

1955 Orpheum

■ **ONYX** Onyx instruments were manufactured for the Australian market by Yoojin Industries in Korea. Produced during the 1980s and 1990s, the line spanned acoustics and electrics, with the latter including obvious copies plus less-derivative designs.

■ **ORIBE** Jose Oribe (born 1932) was a machinist in the aerospace industry when he first encountered the classical guitar. It was, he says, the turning point in his life. He took up the instrument, even traveling to Spain to further his studies. In 1962 he began building guitars. Today he operates from a workshop at his home in Vista, California, working meticulously in pristine conditions and producing models in three scale lengths with a choice of woods and rosettes. Guitars are made in batches of between eight and seventeen at a time and sold direct to players rather than through dealers.

■ **ORPHEUM** The roots of the Orpheum brand go back into the late nineteenth century, but from the 1940s it was owned by New York distributor Maurice Lipsky. The instruments were built by United Guitar (formerly Oscar Schmidt) in Jersey City, New Jersey. The brand disappeared in the late 1960s but has recently been revived by the Tacoma Guitar Co. and applied to a range of imported banjos and flat-tops.

■ **OVATION** Having achieved great success in the aeronautics industry, Charles Kaman indulged his guitar-playing enthusiasm by setting up the Ovation company in 1965. Kaman's wealth and connections allowed him to adopt an innovative approach to acoustic guitar construction and production, employing advanced technology and ultra-modern materials.

Equipped with a synthetic bowl back, the first Ovation acoustics appeared in 1966; famous player endorsements, plus dogged determination, overcame the initial resistance to these ground-breaking guitars. However, their popularity was eclipsed by the positive reaction to the electro-acoustic equivalents that followed in the early 1970s. The use of a transducer-equipped bridge provided problem-free amplified acoustic performance for the first time, creating a huge all-new market that Ovation led for many years.

Kaman's company dabbled with conventional electric guitars via the Electric Storm series. Introduced in 1968, these twin-cutaway semis used bodies from Framus in Germany. The range lasted until 1972, when it was succeeded by Ovation's first solid: the Breadwinner. This better reflected the company's individual attitude, combining extrovert but ergonomic styling with newly designed components and active circuitry.

It was soon joined by the deluxe Deacon version, while the Viper and Preacher employed much more ordinary body outlines. Neither these nor any other subsequent Ovation solid lived up to expectations sales-wise and all relevant production stopped in 1983.

However, the company had another go two years later via the Hard Body models, which combined Korean-made necks and bodies with American assembly. These didn't last long and, after an aborted Japanese venture, Ovation's final try came in 1987 with the equally shortlived Celebrity series from Korea. In contrast, the acoustic and electro-acoustic ranges continued to go from strength to strength. The innovative Adamas range debuted in 1976, while the Collector series initiated six years later further enhanced Ovation's upmarket appeal.

Since then the company has faced up to ever-increasing worldwide competition by maintaining a policy of innovation. This is typified by designs such as the recent iDea: the first electro-acoustic to feature a built-in mp3 recorder. Another example is the VXT, this being the only Ovation in a long time to provide conventional electric guitar performance while adding authentic acoustic sounds via suitably new technology.

1988 Onyx Model 1030

1965 Oribe Classical

onyxsolidbody

1980 Ovation UKII

1971 Ovation Country Artist Classic Electric 1624-4

1973 Ovation Applause

1974 Ovation Custom Legend 1619

1987 Ovation Thunderbolt

1990 Ovation Collectors Edition

■ Onyx is an Australian brand name; Oribe is a California-based classical maker; and Orpheum is a U.S. brand that has appeared on a variety of guitars since the 1940s. Ovation is best known for its distinctive "bowl back" acoustic and electro-acoustic instruments, which first appeared in the mid-1960s.

1994 Ovation Elite Bass

1977 Ovation Adamas 1687

2003 Ovation Model 1621

acousticovation

1988 Overwater "C" Bass

1804 Páges Six-course Guitar

■ **OVERWATER** Overwater, based in Carlisle, England, was established in the late 1970s, making upmarket electric guitars and basses. During the next two decades focus shifted more toward basses, although original and overt copy guitars were also offered; these disappeared when Overwater eventually became a specialist bass company. This role has remained unchanged, with the current catalog encompassing custom-built and standard lines, the latter recently expanded via the more affordable, Czech-made Perception models.

■ **PÁGES** José Páges of Cadiz, Spain, was one of the most important guitar makers of the early nineteenth century. Working with his brother, Juan, he was among the first to use fan-strutting beneath the soundboard, allowing higher string tensions and a thin top, thereby increasing the amount of vibration and hence volume. Otherwise this is a backward-looking instrument, with its six double courses of strings and lack of a separate fingerboard.

■ **PANGBORN** British builder Ashley Pangborn formed his company in 1979, and early custom-built basses were followed by a standard range comprising the Warrior and Alembic-influenced Warlord models. Guitarists enjoyed the equivalents, later joined by the simpler Chieftain and Standard solids, which were also offered in four-string form. Pangborn's basses proved particularly popular in Germany, prompting him to move there in the late 1980s, where he continued production into the next decade.

■ **PANORMO** Louis Panormo (1784–1862), who operated in London, England, in the early part of the nineteenth century, boasted on his labels that he was the city's "only maker of guitars in the Spanish style." The composer Fernando Sor introduced him to the latest developments from Spain. His body-shape and bracing were based on those of Pagés, but he used machine heads, single strings, and a separate raised fingerboard. At its height, in the 1830s, the Panormo workshop produced seven guitars a week. Today several concert artists like to perform the music of Sor and his contemporaries on Panormo instruments or modern copies.

■ **PARAMOUNT** In 1934, the William L. Lange company, makers of Paramount banjos, introduced a guitar line, featuring some models produced by C. F. Martin. The Lange company went out of business by 1940, but in the late 1940s the brand was reintroduced by Gretsch and Brenner.

■ **PARKER** In 1992 the Korg USA corporation entered into a partnership with Larry Fishman, of Fishman Transducers fame, and guitar maker Ken Parker. The result was Parker Guitars and a purpose-built factory near Boston, Massachusetts, this facility being necessary to manufacture a radical re-think of the electric guitar.

This essentially all-new instrument was called the Fly and it incorporated an abundance of unique features, including pioneering super light construction, innovative components, and superior hybrid electric/acoustic performance.

The Fly Vibrato Deluxe debuted in 1993 and the following ten years saw a succession of variations on its groundbreaking theme, including the more conventionally constructed and less-expensive NiteFly. This cost-conscious approach was carried further by the addition of Korean-made models from 2000 onward.

In 2004 Parker was acquired by the U.S. Music Corporation, the parent company of Washburn and many other music industry brands. Numerous new models have since been added, made in Washburn's American factory and also sourced from the Far East.

nineteenth-century acoustics

1836 Panorma

1934 Paramount Style M

overwaterbass

■ Over these pages you'll find guitars by Overwater, a British bass specialist; Páges, a Spanish classical maker; Pangborn, a British maker now based in Germany; Panormo, who made Spanish-style guitars in England; Paramount, a U.S. brand; and Parker, whose innovative guitars first appeared in the early 1990s.

1985 Pangborn Miniature Explorer

1998 Parker Fly Artist

1996 Parker Nitefly

1999 Parker Midi Fly

1948 Paramount Arch-top

1975 PRS Custom

1975 PRS Custom

custom guitars

1976 PRS Custom
Made for Peter Frampton

1979 PRS Dragon I

■ **PRS** Paul Reed Smith came from a musical family. He started both his musical and guitar-making career during high school. Initially playing bass before moving on to guitar, Smith built his first instrument toward the end of senior high school by fixing the neck of a Japanese "Beatle bass" copy to a strangely shaped solidbody.

Smith then managed to get a job repairing guitars at the Washington Music Center before going on to St. Mary's College in Maryland to study mathematics. The opportunity in the second half of his first year to undertake an independent study project proved to be a turning point. Smith made his first proper guitar, a single-cutaway solidbody in the style of Gibson's Les Paul Junior, which earned him credits and respect from his teachers.

In the summer of 1975 he turned the top floor of his parents' house into a workshop and, with the help of his brother, set about making more guitars. The bug had bitten, and Smith's return to college proved to be shortlived. By the start of 1976 he had left and moved into his first workshop in West Street, Annapolis, Maryland.

Smith made his first electric guitar at his new shop, a solidbody Gibson Byrdland-style instrument for Ted Nugent. This was quickly followed by an all-mahogany guitar for British rocker Peter Frampton, which set the foundation for Smith's future. Its double-cutaway outline apes Gibson's post-1958 Les Paul Special, but features the arched, carved top of a Les Paul Standard. For the first time on a Smith guitar there were mother-of-pearl birds inlaid by hand down the fingerboard, a distinctive feature that would later help to shift a lot of PRS guitars.

Along with the motif of an eagle landing that was inlaid into the headstock—a feature that would return to PRS guitars some years later—Frampton's guitar also featured the combination of a twenty-four-fret neck and twin humbucking pickups that would be the basis of Smith's instruments until the beginning of the 1990s.

Smith's dream, however, was to make a guitar for Carlos Santana, one of his guitar-playing idols. Getting to meet players like Santana proved one of Smith's hidden talents. He achieved this by hanging out backstage at the local arenas, begging roadies to let their employer see his instruments. The deal was simple: if you don't fall in love with the instrument, you get your money back.

It worked. Apart from Nugent and Frampton, Smith got orders from Al DiMeola (a twelve-string with a built-in phase shifter), and from Frampton's and Bruce Springsteen's bass players, not to mention many local musicians. It also became apparent to Smith from very early on that big-name guitar players sell guitars to others. DiMeola said after owning a PRS that he felt Smith

1982 PRS Custom Mahogany

1980 PRS Custom
The first guitar Paul Reed Smith
made for Carlos Santana

■ Paul Reed Smith's lucky break
came when he made some guitars
for Carlos Santana. Pictured here are
some of the instruments he made
before setting up PRS in 1985,
including two of the Santana guitars,
made in the early 1980s.

1980 PRS Double-neck
Made for Santana sideman and
Journey guitarist Neal Schon

1983 PRS Custom Double-neck
Made for Carlos Santana

1984 PRS Guitar

1985 PRS Custom

1985 PRS Custom

1985 PRS Guitar

had the ability to custom-make the guitar of anyone's dreams. The figured "curly" maple that Smith used for these early maple-top guitars originally came from the drawer-fronts of a friend's dresser. This crucial timber helped to summon up visions of those late-1950s Les Pauls that have influenced so many players and makers. Slowly, the word was beginning to spread.

In 1980, after selling his first maple-topped handmade guitar to Heart guitarist Howard Leese, Smith got to make an instrument for Carlos Santana. This would be the first of four handmade Smith guitars that Santana used in the coming years. The association with Santana, and the maple-topped instruments themselves, proved to be vastly important turning points—although, as is so often the case, that is not how they appeared at the time. By the time Santana owned a Smith guitar he was already on his first comeback. Nearly twenty years later, still playing a PRS guitar, he would be topping the Billboard charts again with *Supernatural*, another comeback album. Smith said that he couldn't have been successful without Santana's support, because the guitarist gave his instruments instant credibility.

Musicians such as Santana, Leese, and DiMeola all disregarded the overwhelming opinion of the time about which guitars pro players should be using. Their mark of approval was crucial to Smith's early operation. Smith knew that by successfully building a guitar that Santana liked, he had a shot at starting a professional guitar-making operation.

However, building Santana's guitar nearly didn't happen at all. When, eventually, Santana received his first instrument, the guitar player remarked that its special quality was "an accident of God" and that Smith would never be able to do it again. Santana then said the second guitar Smith made for him was, too, an accident of God. There was a third one, and then a double-neck. When he finally got that, Santana said that maybe this wasn't an accident of God. Finally, it seems, Santana concluded that Smith might actually be a guitar maker.

But by 1984 Smith was struggling to survive. He still held some ambition to become a professional guitar player, but with the counsel of his close friends and loyal assistant John Ingram, Smith realized that it was his guitar-building that was making headway, not his playing. He'd set about designing what we know today as the PRS Custom, and after trying unsuccessfully to persuade various big-name manufacturers to make his design under license, he realized he'd have to do it himself. **>**

prssolidbody

1982 PRS Sorceres Apprentice

■ PRS was founded by Paul Reed Smith and his partners in 1985, based in Annapolis, Maryland. From the beginning, the idea was to make a new kind of solidbody electric based on earlier greats. One early report described it as "bridging the age-old gap between Strat and Paul."

1982 PRS Dragon I Prototype

1987 PRS Standard

1985 PRS Custom

1985 PRS Metal

1987 PRS Signature

1988 PRS Studio Maple Top

1988 PRS Classic Electric

solidbodyprs

1990 PRS EG 3

1990 PRS EG 4

1991 PRS EG II

1991 PRS EG II

1991 PRS EG II
(left-handed)

1991 PRS Artist I Prototype

1992 Dragon 1

1991 PRS Artist I

Armed with a couple of prototypes, Smith headed out on the road and raised orders worth nearly $300,000. Making the guitars to fulfill these orders was another matter. But by the fall of 1985 Smith and his wife Barbara, guided by the business know-how of Warren Esanu, had set up a limited partnership to raise the capital necessary to start a factory in Virginia Avenue, Annapolis. At last, just about a decade after making his first electric guitar, Smith had his production company, PRS Guitars, up and running and in business.

Apart from a few lucky musicians and their fans, nobody knew Paul Reed Smith when the company first displayed its wares at the important American NAMM trade-shows held during 1985. It was a time of hi-tech musical fashion. The major trends swirling around the guitar industry during that period mainly involved aggressive, futuristic-looking, modern rock guitar designs. In those surroundings, the PRS Custom must have seemed very out of place.

With the Custom, here was an instrument clearly inspired by classic 1950s Gibson and Fender guitars. Often called evolutionary rather than revolutionary, the PRS guitar was substantially more expensive than the high-line Gibson or Fender instruments, but it began to gain interest from players and press. The fabulously-colored carved-maple tops harked back to the classic late-1950s Gibson Les Paul, while the guitar's outline melded the double-cutaway shape of Smith's earlier instruments with elements of a Fender Stratocaster-style shape, creating a unique hybrid design that was both classic-looking yet original enough to be noticed.

This mix of Gibson and Fender—effectively the two major cornerstones of electric guitar design—was crucial to the concept. PRS's scale-length of 25 inches sat half-way between those of Fender and Gibson guitars. The 10-inch fingerboard radius also sat between Gibson's flatter 12-inch camber and the smaller 7-inch radius of vintage Fenders. That wasn't all. With an unusual rotary pickup selector switch, the twin PRS humbuckers created five distinct sounds: a combination of thick humbucking Gibson-like tones and thinner single-coil mixes that approximated some of the Stratocaster's key voices.

Augmenting the pickup switch was a master volume control and, instead of a conventional tone control, a "sweet switch" which rounded off the guitar's upper frequencies. (By 1991 the sweet switch had been replaced on all models in favor of a standard tone control.) Then there was a new vibrato system. The early 1980s had seen the double-locking Floyd Rose vibrato become one of the most popular design features used on contemporary electric guitars. However, as a working musician Smith didn't like the fact that you needed a set of Allen wrenches to change strings. So, with the help of local guitar-playing engineer John Mann, Smith designed his own vibrato system that updated the classic Fender vibrato and employed unique cam-locking tuners, yet still offered fashionable "wide-travel" pitch-bending with near perfect tuning stability. **>**

prssolidbody

1993 PRS Artist II

1999 PRS Custom 22 (left-handed)

1998 Custom 22

■ Into the 1990s with the still young PRS, and the Custom model continues, from 1993 with options of twenty-two-fret or twenty-four-fret neck, alongside the first of the Dragon-inlaid specials, the new Artist line, using top-grade materials, and the revised-shape EG models, new for 1990.

1994 PRS Artist Limited

2005 PRS 20th Anniversary Custom 24

1992 Custom 22 Soapbar

1994 PRS Custom 24

1994 Custom 22

solidbody**prs**

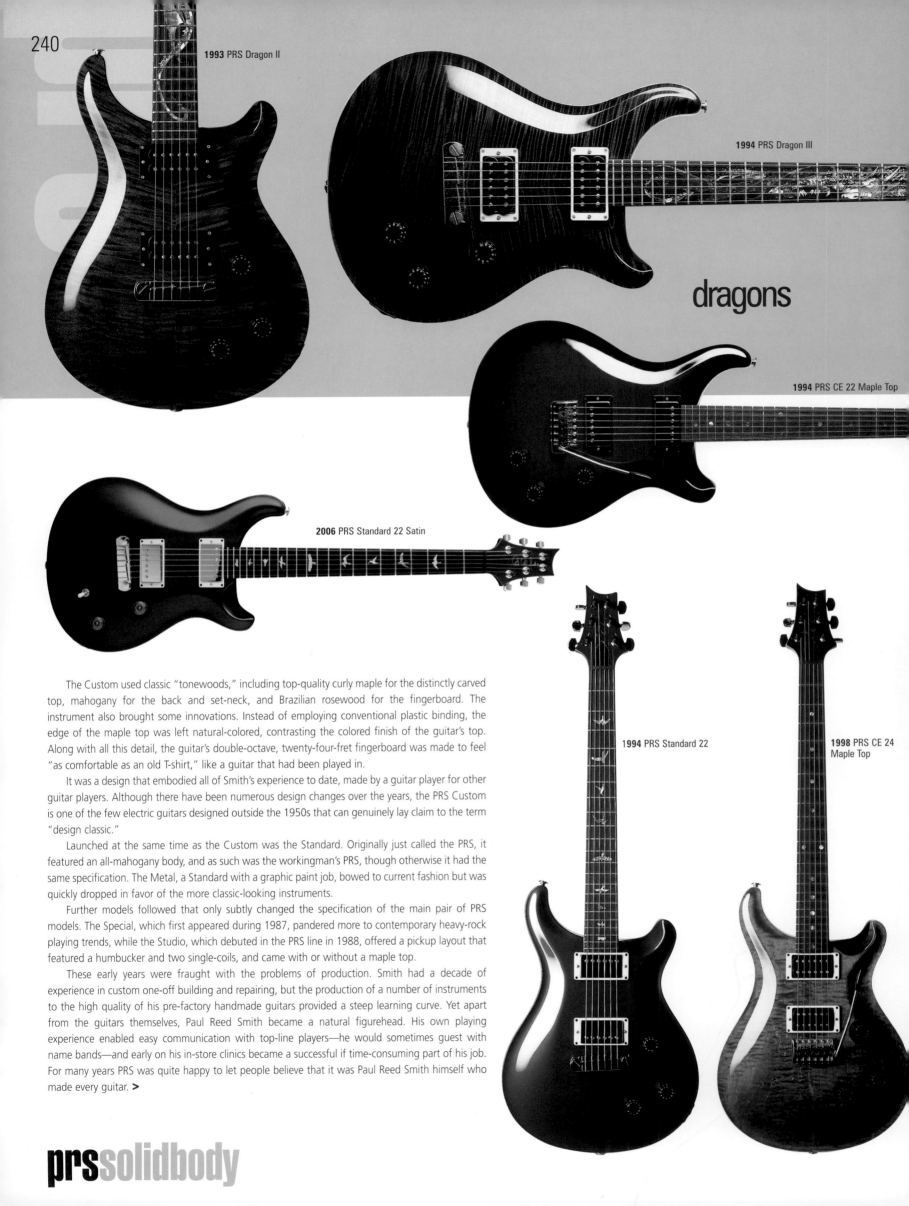

1993 PRS Dragon II

1994 PRS Dragon III

dragons

1994 PRS CE 22 Maple Top

2006 PRS Standard 22 Satin

1994 PRS Standard 22

1998 PRS CE 24
Maple Top

The Custom used classic "tonewoods," including top-quality curly maple for the distinctly carved top, mahogany for the back and set-neck, and Brazilian rosewood for the fingerboard. The instrument also brought some innovations. Instead of employing conventional plastic binding, the edge of the maple top was left natural-colored, contrasting the colored finish of the guitar's top. Along with all this detail, the guitar's double-octave, twenty-four-fret fingerboard was made to feel "as comfortable as an old T-shirt," like a guitar that had been played in.

It was a design that embodied all of Smith's experience to date, made by a guitar player for other guitar players. Although there have been numerous design changes over the years, the PRS Custom is one of the few electric guitars designed outside the 1950s that can genuinely lay claim to the term "design classic."

Launched at the same time as the Custom was the Standard. Originally just called the PRS, it featured an all-mahogany body, and as such was the workingman's PRS, though otherwise it had the same specification. The Metal, a Standard with a graphic paint job, bowed to current fashion but was quickly dropped in favor of the more classic-looking instruments.

Further models followed that only subtly changed the specification of the main pair of PRS models. The Special, which first appeared during 1987, pandered more to contemporary heavy-rock playing trends, while the Studio, which debuted in the PRS line in 1988, offered a pickup layout that featured a humbucker and two single-coils, and came with or without a maple top.

These early years were fraught with the problems of production. Smith had a decade of experience in custom one-off building and repairing, but the production of a number of instruments to the high quality of his pre-factory handmade guitars provided a steep learning curve. Yet apart from the guitars themselves, Paul Reed Smith became a natural figurehead. His own playing experience enabled easy communication with top-line players—he would sometimes guest with name bands—and early on his in-store clinics became a successful if time-consuming part of his job. For many years PRS was quite happy to let people believe that it was Paul Reed Smith himself who made every guitar. **>**

■ PRS's bolt-on-neck CE models were introduced in 1994, the same year the McCarty Model appeared. Significantly—and cheekily—it was named for Ted McCarty, who was president at Gibson through the introduction of all Gibson's classic electric guitars, including the Les Paul.

1994 Dragon III (left-handed)

1994 PRS McCarty Model Prototype

1994 PRS McCarty Model

1994 PRS McCarty Standard

1998 PRS McCarty Soapbar

1994 PRS McCarty Model

mccarty models

1994 PRS Machinehead 10th Anniversary

solidbodyprs

1994 PRS Swamp Ash
Special Prototype

1997 PRS Swamp Ash Special

1996 PRS Artist III

1996 PRS Artist IV

1995 Rosewood
Limited Edition

1995 PRS 10th
Anniversary

1995 PRS Santana Model

To support these high-end instruments a sequence of simple and distinguished advertisements became another hallmark of the brand. This parallel invention did not go unnoticed: the ads' designer Dennis Voss and photographer Michael Ward won an Award of Merit for Graphic Excellence in 1985.

Smith seemed on every level to surround himself with mentors and teachers. Early on in PRS's history, Eric Pritchard had given Smith valuable advice on numerous engineering and technical matters. Pritchard not only helped to design the locking PRS tuners but also many of the production tools that were used to fabricate PRS guitars for years. Many friends remarked how Smith possessed an uncanny ability to absorb information, like a sponge.

In 1987 Smith introduced a theme that has since become an important part of PRS Guitars: the limited-edition "ultimate quality" guitar. A friend had remarked to Smith that he didn't charge enough for his work. The result was the Signature, basically a Custom but with absolutely top quality woods and maple tops.

In all, some 1,000 Signature models were made. Each was hand-signed on the headstock by Smith himself, before the Artist Series took over the top-of-the-line position in 1991. Smith would at this time go on long sales tours, away from the factory, and obviously wasn't available then to sign the Signature models. An interim solution was to have Smith sign decals which could go under the finish, and Smith says the production team even threatened to sign the guitars themselves. So the Signature came to an end. Nonetheless, the new Limited Edition model appeared during 1989, the first production PRS to feature as standard a non-vibrato, Tune-o-matic bridge and stud tailpiece. The guitar also featured hollow tone chambers, although the top was sealed, without any f-holes. Along with curly maple, unusual but

prssolidbody

1994 PRS Original

1996 PRS Employee Guitar

1996 PRS Employee Guitar

1998 PRS Private Stock No. 59

1999 PRS Private Stock No. 86

■ In the mid-1990s, PRS introduced several new models, including a 10th Anniversary guitar to celebrate its first decade, and the spectacular Rosewood Ltd. The Swamp Ash Special nodded toward Fender's use of swamp ash wood in the 1950s, as well as using a Fender-flavored maple bolt-on neck.

2000 PRS Private Stock No. 107

2000 PRS Private Stock No. 116

2001 PRS Private Stock No. 314 Twelve-string

private stock

2001 PRS Private Stock No. 235

highly-figured woods for tops such as cedar and redwood created one of the most unusual PRS guitars from this period. Of Signature quality and price, the Limited Edition was only planned as a small 300-piece run, though fewer were actually made. Both the Signature and Limited Edition proved that there was a highly lucrative market for limited-edition PRS guitars.

By 1988 some dealers, not to mention new export markets such as the UK, were calling for PRS to make a less expensive guitar. The result was the first PRS bolt-on-neck instrument, the Classic Electric (quickly abbreviated to CE after Peavey objected to the use of "their" word Classic).

Originally the CE, with its alder body and maple neck and fingerboard, brought a more Fender-like style to the PRS line which up to that point had exclusively featured set-neck guitars. Initially the market was confused, and the company realized that players wanted a cheaper PRS Custom, not a different-sounding instrument. So a black-face headstock quickly followed, as did a maple-top option and, of course, the majority of PRS options such as bird inlays.

The CE evolved into a highly successful guitar. Its body changed to mahogany in 1995, a year after twenty-two-fret versions had been added. It wasn't until 2000 that the standard, nonmaple-top CE 22 and CE 24 were phased out, not for lack of popularity or sales, but for simple economic reasons. The start-up CE made little profit for the company and, with pressures on production space caused by increased demand, the CE was an obvious candidate for shelving.

Yet especially in the UK and Europe the CE didn't really satisfy the demand for a lower-priced PRS. This market pressure led the company to produce the bolt-on-neck EG, the first flat-fronted PRS guitar and the first with a twenty-two-fret fingerboard. However, the company soon realized that they were losing money on every EG that was shipped. Smith has said in retrospect that he was unhappy with the sound of the original EGs.

In 1991 a new version appeared, again with a flat front but a rounder, more PRS-like outline. This new EG line was quite a departure. The bodies were crafted on computerized routers by a Baltimore engineering company, Excel (who would manufacture the majority of PRS's hardware parts during the 1990s). However, by 1995 the EG line was discontinued.

Wood quality was paramount from the start of PRS Guitars, as it had been in Smith's "apprentice" days making one-off custom instruments. Early

2001 PRS Private Stock

2001 PRS Private
Stock No. 125

2001 PRS Private Stock No. 207

2001 Private Stock No. 255 (left-handed)

2001 PRS Private Stock No. 184

■ Private Stock was PRS's custom shop,
established at the company's new factory in
Stevensville, Maryland, in 1996. The idea
was to provide the usual custom shop
facilities—making one-off and limited-run
guitars—but with a special emphasis on
ultimate-quality woods.

1997 PRS Golden Eagle

1998 PRS Standard 24

2001 PRS Singlecut Brazilian Rosewood

2006 PRS Standard 24 Satin

1999 PRS Dragon 2000

2005 PRS 20th Anniversary Singlecut Trem

on, Smith had drawn the conclusion that the better the quality of the raw material, in terms of its weight and condition, the better the guitar would sound.

Unlike many makers at the time, Smith believed that an electric guitar's tone was not all derived from its pickups and electronics. His feeling was that the electric guitar was an acoustic structure, and that the pickups and signal chain could not amplify what wasn't there in the first place. It led him on a quest for the finest woods and most knowledgeable timber suppliers, such as Michael Reid, whom Smith had first met in 1980. Reid became a valued part of PRS's production chain.

The fabulously curly and quilted maple tops were especially important to PRS Guitars. The company set up a grading system: the Classic grade, used for the CE Maple Top guitars, is about a seven on PRS's one-to-ten rating system. The set-neck guitars use a Regular grade—now more commonly known as a Custom grade—of around seven to nine on the system. PRS's "ten-tops" are an option on certain production guitars like the Custom, and are obviously ten on that scale. The Signature series and subsequent limited-edition models use what Smith describes as "something spectacular."

Curly maple is a highly "figured," or patterned, timber. Under the vibrant, stained and colored finishes used by PRS, it helps to create a guitar that for many is as much a work of art as a working musical tool. Conversely, the opulent appearance of a PRS curly maple top has drawn many a derogatory phrase, from "over-pretty" to "furniture guitar." Once a curly log is discovered, it needs to be correctly processed before it gets close to being part of a PRS guitar. Imagine a rectangular block of maple. Along the sides run "wave" shapes. By slicing the blank in two—as you would to cut a bun before buttering it—you slice through the wave, and open the blank like a book. You then see the curl, like lines across a page.

The type of wave, and the extremes of width and distance between its "peaks" and "troughs," will influence the look of the curl. A slightly curved wave will result in a mild curl; a triangular wave

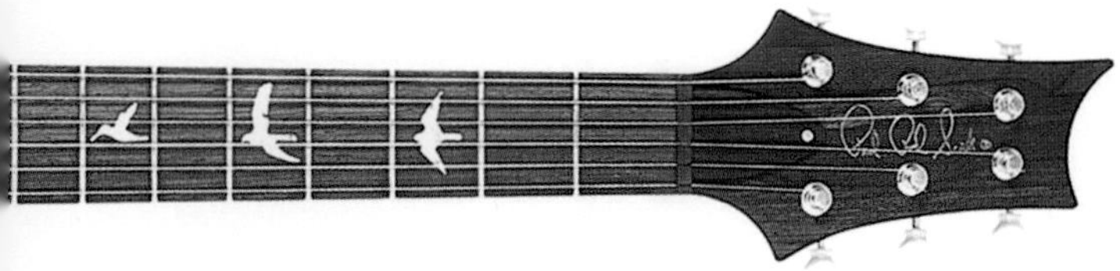

2001 PRS Singlecut

2006 PRS Singlecut
Standard Satin 2

■ PRS launched its first major departure from its customary double-cutaway body shape with the Singlecut model, introduced in 2000. It has not been without controversy, attracting legal action from Gibson, although following a long and complicated battle PRS won the argument in 2005.

2002 PRS Singlecut
Trem

2006 PRS Singlecut
Standard Soapbar Satin

2006 PRS Singlecut
Trem Satin

2006 PRS
Singlecut Satin

2006 PRS Private Stock 10th Anniversary

1999 PRS Private Stock No. 78

private stock

2001 PRS Private Stock No. 218

solidbodyprs

2001 Santana III

2001 PRS Santana SE
(first version)

2002 PRS Santana SE II

2002 PRS Santana SE II

santana
models

2000 PRS Dragon 2002

will be more spectacular; and a square wave will be the strongest. Because the relative hardness between the peaks and the troughs of the curl differs, certain color-staining and sanding techniques can emphasize the curl.

The way in which a log is cut will also affect the final look of the curl. A quarter-sawn rectangular blank, with grain running parallel to the long sides, creates a pronounced and symmetrical curl. If the blank is slab-sawn, with grain running parallel to the shorter top face of a rectangular blank, the curl twists and looks more diverse—and the grain will not be symmetrical across the halves of the bookmatched top, unlike the curl. The curl of a slab-sawn example will be less curly and more "wiggly." The look of a curly-maple top will be further altered by the type of maple used. PRS use two main types of maple for guitar tops. East Coast maple, also known as red maple, is what PRS started with. Later they added West Coast maple, also known as big-leaf maple, which can be had from a variety of sources including British Columbia, Washington state, Oregon and Southern California.

In 1991 PRS announced the Artist I, which outwardly seemed a continuation of the Signature series. In fact, the Artist I signaled a fundamental change in the design of PRS guitars. Many of the top pros who'd been attracted to PRS guitars loved the look and feel of the instruments but felt there was room for tonal improvement.

It seemed clear to some that PRS provided a natural progression beyond vintage Gibson Les Paul instruments—but the sound lacked the low-end associated with those classic guitars. So, along with its ultimate-grade timbers, the Artist I introduced a stronger neck construction and many different production techniques, primarily intended to improve the "acoustic" tone of PRS guitars. While the Artist got Smith closer to the sound he and a significant number of his top-flight customers were looking for, it still wasn't close enough. Yet PRS's next sonic development was virtually missed by the guitar-playing public.

When the Dragon I was launched in 1992 in a limited edition of just fifty pieces, the market was staggered by the exquisite computer-cut inlay down the fingerboard. But this feature, which brought the company a good deal of media interest, disguised the fact that the guitar featured a shorter twenty-two-fret neck with a "wide-fat" profile, a new non-vibrato Stop-Tail bridge, and new pickups.

While the Dragon I was heading for guitar collections around the world, those lucky enough to own and play one realized the tonal improvement. This led the following year to the introduction of the PRS Custom 22, basically a Dragon without the inlay. Indeed, while twenty-four-fret options still remain on the Custom, Standard and CE, the majority of future PRS guitars would follow the shorter and fatter neck concept. Smith says that a big neck equals big tone, and

2005 PRS SE EG 3

2001 Tremonti Model

2002 PRS Tremonti SE

2004 PRS SE EG

2004 PRS SE Billy Martin Model

■ The Santana SE model, launched in 2001, was made in Korea—the first PRS model produced outside Maryland. The SE name was intended to indicate a "student edition." Further Korean-made SE models appeared in later years, all with a clearly defined headstock logo.

2005 PRS SE Camo

2004 PRS SE Soapbar II

2009 PRS SE Custom

2005 PRS SE Soapbar II Maple

2004 PRS Custom 22/12

2004 PRS 513 Rosewood

2007 PRS 513
Mahogany

2004 PRS Modern
Eagle

2006 PRS Singlecut T
Modern Eagle

few players would disagree. As a consequence, PRS's other major models of the time—the Standard and CE lines—were also offered in twenty-two-fret formats from 1994.

These gradual changes in specification are typical of PRS. With a couple of exceptions the guitars have always used pickups designed and made by PRS. Originally, the Custom, Standard, and Signature used what PRS called the Standard Treble and Standard Bass humbuckers.

These pickups looked like any other uncovered humbucker, but actually used magnetic "slug" pole pieces in the non-adjustable inner coil, as well as a rear-placed feeder magnet. This helped to achieve a more accurate single-coil tone when split by the company's five-position rotary switch.

Catering for the more aggressive rock market, PRS developed pickups such as the Chainsaw, and the HFS ("Hot, Fat, and Screams") as used initially on the Special. The Vintage Treble and Vintage Bass humbuckers first appeared on the Classic Electric, and the pairing of an HFS at bridge and Vintage Bass in neck position endures today on the twenty-four-fret CE Maple Top, Standard and Custom. The first Dragon guitar featured the Dragon Treble and Dragon Bass pickups (which also appeared on the Custom 22), but since the McCarty Model and its new McCarty pickups the twenty-two-fret PRSs have featured covered pickups which, tonally, chase a more "classic" sound.

In 1988 PRS launched the unique Electronics Upgrade Kit designed to improve the "fatness" and midrange definition of pre-1993 PRS instruments. It could have been called the "all we've learned since we started" kit as it reflected changes made over the years to minor components, such as lighter-weight tuner buttons and thumb screws, nickel-plated-brass screws for saddles and intonation, a simulated tone control for early switch-equipped guitars, and high-capacitance hook-up wire. The Dragon I, meanwhile, had been a risk that worked. The Dragon II followed in 1993 (along with the twenty-two-fret Artist II) and the Dragon III in 1994 (joined by the Artist Ltd.). Both new Dragons were limited to just one hundred pieces and each featured along the fingerboard a more flamboyant dragon inlay than the last.

Announced in 1999, the most fabulous Dragon guitar was unleashed with a "three-dimensional" inlay, this time over the complex curves of the body. The Dragon 2000, limited to fifty pieces, may for some have been just another collectors' guitar, but it illustrates the desire of PRS to stretch the boundaries of guitar-making in their ultra-high-end models.

Little known until 1994 was the involvement with PRS of Ted McCarty. He had been president of Gibson between 1950 and 1965, the period that many considered as the company's golden years. Smith says he "discovered" McCarty's name when doing some research in the local patent office. Just after starting his production company, Smith cold-called McCarty for advice. With great foresight, Smith subsequently enlisted him as a consultant. McCarty, meanwhile, "downloaded the hard disk" for Smith, explaining how Gibson made its instruments back in the 1950s. >

2005 PRS CE Mahogany 22

2005 PRS CE Mahogany 24

2005 PRS Corvette Standard 22

2005 PRS 20th
Anniversary Dragon 2005

2004 Tremonti Tribal

2005 PRS Dave
Navarro Signature
Model

■ By now twenty years old, PRS
relaunched the CE 24 Mahogany in
2005, at first with a "20th" truss-
rod cover to mark the passing of
the two decades. More signature
models appeared, including guitars
named for ex–Chili Peppers man
Dave Navarro and Creed guitarist
Mark Tremonti.

2007 PRS SE One

2007 PRS SC 250

2007 PRS SC 245

But when it came to PRS's next landmark guitar, it was again player pressure that spurred the idea onward, notably from Texas guitar-slinger David Grissom. Leaving the opulence of the Dragon and Artist guitars behind, 1994's McCarty Model changed the formula in a seemingly subtle way, creating a PRS guitar that got closer still to the sound and feel of Gibson's classic late-1950s Les Paul. PRS said the McCarty Model was essentially a Dragon with a thicker body, thinner headstock, lighter tuners, and different pickups. In reality it was much more than that. It proved a turning point for PRS Guitars.

The company had grown up and the McCarty Model quite quickly became the "player's PRS." Certainly when compared side-by-side with a mid-1980s Custom, the differences in sound and feel were startlingly obvious. Physically, the McCarty had a shorter, fatter neck, while the difference in body thickness, while subtle, is there: the McCarty feels slightly less petite. Generally speaking, the McCarty has more of a Gibson-like, "vintage" vibe to it. It has a broader sound than an early Custom's typically aggressive, thinner tone, but still with plenty of PRS character, particularly a focused midrange and a chunkier feel.

The McCarty Model was also the first major PRS guitar to feature a three-way Gibson-style pickup-selecting toggle switch instead of PRS's unique five-way rotary switch. (Later, a pull/push switch was added to the tone control in order to coil-split the humbuckers.) Mirroring the Custom/Standard relationship in the PRS line, the mahogany McCarty Standard without a maple cap was introduced at the same time as the maple-top McCarty Model. In 1998 the McCarty Model was offered with twin Seymour Duncan P-90-style "soapbar" single-coil pickups as the McCarty Soapbar, cashing in on the popularity of P-90s toward the end of the decade. The all-mahogany McCarty Soapbar returns to the construction and style of Smith's early pre-factory pre-maple-top guitars which usually favored mahogany construction and P-90 pickups.

Another "soapbar" guitar, the Custom 22 Soapbar, appeared in 1998. Unusually for a PRS it featured a maple set-neck and three soapbar pickups controlled by a five-way lever switch, giving a unique "hot" Strat-style tone. Ten years old as a production company in 1995, PRS Guitars released the 10th Anniversary model that year which featured "scrimshaw" engraved bird inlays and headstock eagle.

In 1995, after many, many requests, PRS also started making a reproduction of the pre-factory Santana guitar, with its old-style double-cutaway outline, 24-inch scale-length and flatter 11-inch fingerboard radius. Ironically, although this seemed a backward design step, it was among the first PRS guitars to be made using the company's recently installed computer-assisted routing machines. **>**

2007 PRS Mark Tremonti Model

■ PRS's Singlecut model evolved into the SC 245 and SC 250 in 2007: the 245 with a slightly shorter scale, the 250 described by Paul Reed Smith as "a Tremonti without the name on it," referring to the Mark Tremonti signature model. Other new signature guitars included a Singlecut-style instrument for Chris Henderson of 3 Doors Down.

2006 PRS Johnny Hiland Signature Model

2007 PRS Se Paul Allender Model

signature models

2007 PRS Chris Henderson Model

2007 PRS 1980 West ST LTD

1998 PRS McCarty
Archtop II

1997 PRS McCarty
Archtop I

1998 PRS McCarty
Archtop II

1998 PRS McCarty
Archtop II

1998 PRS McCarty
Hollowbody

2002 PRS McCarty
Archtop II

Santana always liked his pre-factory PRS guitars, although Smith says that the guitarist tried "really hard" to like the new, modern PRS design. Eventually, PRS made Santana some replicas of his now well-used originals. PRS wanted to make its new Santana guitar a regular production model and wanted to use Santana's name. A deal was subsequently arranged, and a large percentage of Santana's royalties go to charity. In 2001 two further models, the Santana III and the Santana SE, followed the original Santana (which in 1998 became the Santana II), while the Santana MD was launched in 2008.

The growth of PRS guitars is aptly reflected by its expanding workshop space. Compared to Smith's tiny West Street rooms in Annapolis, the first Virginia Avenue factory must have seemed massive to the handful of staff who manned it in early 1985. At first there were just eight people working there. PRS had one-third of the building to start, sharing with a furniture-stripping shop, a brass business and a sail maker, but after three or four years PRS had taken over most of the premises. As time progressed a separate woodshop was added, a short walk from the main facility.

This was all certainly a far cry from the beginnings of PRS Guitars. During the ten years preceding the move in 1985 to Virginia Avenue, it was taking Smith and his coworkers on average a little over a month to produce every guitar. By 1988, a crew of forty-five people were making around fifteen guitars every day, and by 1995 Virginia Avenue housed about eighty workers who were crafting between twenty-five and thirty guitars daily. The last PRS guitar was shipped from the Virginia Avenue plant at the end of December 1995. The company estimates that in its first ten years it produced around 23,000 set-neck guitars and about 14,000 bolt-on-neck models. PRS relocated to its brand new manufacturing base at Stevensville, on Kent Island, just across the Chesapeake bridge from Annapolis, and production resumed in the first week of January 1996. With some 25,000 square feet now at the company's disposal—which was nearly double that of the Virginia Avenue facility and its outbuildings—PRS employed around 110 staff by the end of 1998 and aimed to produce around 700 guitars per month.

Having invested in computer-assisted routing machines in 1995, the company installed more at the new factory to bring a higher level of consistency to guitars that were already renowned for their craftsmanship. Pushing production efficiency further forward, robotic buffing machines appeared soon after the factory move. But even with these new tools, PRS guitars still felt like comfortable "handmade" instruments rather than sterile, machine-made items. Even with the hi-tech equipment, there is more hand-work in the sanding, coloring, and finishing of a PRS guitar than most other production instruments.

The first new models to come off the line in 1996 were the Rosewood Ltd. and the Swamp Ash Special. The Rosewood Ltd. continued Smith's pursuit of the ultimate tonewood for necks, featuring a solid East Indian rosewood neck and a Brazilian rosewood fingerboard inlaid with a detailed tree-of-life design. Although mahogany is used for the majority of PRS's set-neck guitars, there's little doubt that Paul Reed Smith would choose rosewood if the cost was not prohibitive. Smith's personal "number one" guitar—an amber-colored Dragon I—was the first PRS to feature a rosewood neck, and the option of an Indian rosewood neck was subsequently offered for the McCarty. **>**

prssemi-solidbody

1998 PRS McCarty
Archtop II

1998 PRS McCarty
Hollowbody II

2009 PRS SE Custom
Semi-Hollow

2009 Singlecut
Hollowbody Standard

2009 PRS Singlecut
Hollowbody I

2007 PRS SE Custom Semi-hollow

■ Best known for solidbody electrics, PRS launched
two new hollowbody instruments in 1998, the McCarty
Archtop and the McCarty Hollowbody. Revisions and
additions have been made to the line along the way,
and currently PRS offers a mix of double-cutaway and
single-cutaway Hollowbody models.

1998 PRS Private Stock No. 62

private stock

1996 PRS Private
Stock No. 13

1999 PRS Private Stock No. 72

semi-solidbody**prs**

2008 PRS Howard Leese

2009 PRS Al Dimeola Prism

2009 PRS Mira X

While the Rosewood Ltd. was a limited edition, it was dramatically different to the Swamp Ash Special, which was intended, like the original Classic Electric and Studio, to bring a more Fender-like tone to the PRS line. The twenty-two-fret Swamp Ash Special uses a lightweight ash body with bolt-on maple neck and fingerboard and offers two McCarty humbuckers plus a centrally-placed single-coil-size humbucker. PRS also launched two more luxurious Artist models in 1996, the III and IV, which were intended to replace the Artist II and Artist Limited.

That same year the company established a custom shop for the production of what it calls Private Stock guitars. The aim was to recreate the circumstances of Smith's old workshop. PRS will make almost anything a customer wants as a Private Stock instrument—at a price. While some guitars are based on existing production techniques, others need to be built fully or partially from the ground up. PRS estimates the ratio of hand-work to machine-work on a Private Stock guitar is around 50/50 in the initial stages, but a double-neck, for example, would be all handmade. For many customers the starting point for a Private Stock has tended to be a McCarty with custom bird inlays, Brazilian rosewood fingerboard and double-stained "killer" top.

The first Private Stock guitar was completed in April 1996. Ten years later some 1,250 pieces had been built, each carrying a sequential Private Stock number as well as a standard serial. As with the Guitars Of The Month that prompted the Private Stock scheme, new ideas and designs can provide prototypes for future PRS production models. For example, a Private Stock example of a hollowbody arch-top PRS guitar was shown at a trade show in 1997, and the following year PRS brought out a new line of hollowbody McCarty guitars, marking a company well into its stride.

2009 PRS Smokeburst McCarty

The Archtop looked like any other PRS, save for the twin f-holes and substantially deeper body, and the model was made possible by PRS's use of computer-assisted machinery. Not only was the front carved but the back too and, like a violin, the top and back were carved on the inside as well.

Launched at the same time, the PRS Hollowbody used the same construction as the Archtop, except that the body was less deep: about three inches at its center, as opposed to four. The basic models came with spruce front and mahogany back and sides. The Archtop II and Hollowbody II added figured maple tops and backs, while the Archtop Artist was an ultimate high-end model.

This hollow guitar line was developed by Joe Knaggs, PRS's master luthier, who builds the majority of the company's custom one-off Private Stock line. The Gibson-335-like Hollowbody proved the more popular model of the new line.

All the Hollowbody and Archtop models are offered with an optional piezo-pickup bridge system, developed with L.R. Baggs. The extremely efficient piezo system allows these guitars to sound like amplified acoustic instruments as well as offering all the usual magnetic pickup tones.

The introduction of left-handed PRS models began in 1999 for the McCarty and Custom 22 (with Stop-Tail or vibrato bridge). Typically, these were carefully detailed models with every feature properly left-handed, from the positioning of the headstock logo down to the labeling of the control knobs.

Some twenty-five years after Smith built his first proper electric—that single-cutaway flat-front Les Paul-alike—PRS launched the Singlecut, the closest the company had come to both the look and tone of those classic vintage Les Pauls. The company's first ads for the new-for-2000 model, which wasn't in the McCarty line, featured a portrait of Ted McCarty and a caption saying that Ted

2009 PRS Maple Top

2009 PRS Private
Stock No. 1234

private stock

2009 PRS Private Stock No. 1069

2009 PRS Sunburst 22

■ PRS's latest models at the time of writing
included the back-to-basics mahogany Mira and a
single-cutaway retro companion, the Starla. Also
on view are a couple more signature guitars: the
unmistakable colors of the Al Di Meola Prism, and
the old-style Howard Leese Limited Edition,
named for the Heart guitarist.

2009 PRS Starla

2009 PRS Angelus

2009 PRS Tonare

"introduced the single cutaway, carved-top solidbody to the world in 1952. We learned a lot from Ted while we were working on ours." This illustrated where PRS was heading. Over the years many companies have either blatantly copied the Les Paul or used it as clear inspiration. Yet the PRS Singlecut will be seen by many as the nearest anyone has got to the hallowed tone of Gibson's late-1950s Les Paul without actually breaching any trademarked design features. Gibson did bring legal action against the guitar, but in 2005, after a long and extremely complicated battle, PRS won. The company soon reintroduced the design, including the Singlecut Trem. Creed's Mark Tremonti became only the second guitarist honored with a PRS signature edition when his Tremonti model, in Singlecut style, was launched in 2001. A Singlecut Hollowbody model was introduced in 2008.

1986 PRS Bass 4

Apart from its single-cutaway shape, the solidbody Singlecut follows the spec of PRS's McCarty model, with many subtle changes. These include a slightly thicker body and new covered pickups, the PRS 7s. Smith believes these are the closest yet to the tone of original Gibson PAFs, but with modern-day performance standards.

The Santana SE model, introduced in 2001, was PRS's first non-U.S.-produced guitar. Made in Korea, the SE line has since blossomed into a successful less-expensive marque for the company. By 2008 there were ten SE models in the catalogue, ranging from the traditional SE Custom through the simple one-pickup SE One to the SE Paul Allender, a twenty-four-fret signature model for the Cradle Of Filth guitarist.

1972 PRS Custom Bass

PRS's U.S.-made line gained an interesting new addition with 2004's 513 model. It certainly looked like a PRS, only with a slightly longer scale length, a stronger neck joint and newly designed bird inlays. But the pickups and switching provided new sounds, using five single-coil pickups grouped as two double-coils and a central single, all controlled by two knobs and two lever switches.

Three 20th Anniversary models appeared to mark PRS's birthday in 2005, the Custom 22 or 24 and the Standard 24, alongside an arresting limited-edition Dragon double-neck. New for 2008 were a couple of retro-flavored models, the Mira and the Starla, and a limited-edition Singlecut Jumbo Thinline hollowbody. More artist models appeared: for Dave Navarro (2005), Johnny Hiland (2006), Chris Henderson (2007), David Grissom (2007), and Al DiMeola (2008).

1986 PRS Curly Bass

A recent PRS catalogue boasted twelve solidbody models, five hollowbody guitars, six signature models, and ten SE instruments. These electric guitars range from the cheapest SE One to the most expensive Hollowbody II. Options to the various models could well increase the base price by adding cosmetic alternatives or different features, including "ten-top" flamed or quilted wood, bird inlays, gold hardware, the Baggs/PRS piezo pickup system, or a wide thin neck. New to the line is a series of acoustic guitars.

As the company entered its third decade of production, an official of the local Maryland Department of Business & Economic Development put it well as she considered the new factory, alongside the existing Stevensville facility, which went live in 2007. "PRS Guitars represents America's manufacturing future," she said, "with a blend of advanced technology and superb, proprietary craftsmanship."

prsacoustic

2000 PRS Electric Bass

2001 PRS Private Stock Bass

2006 PRS Private Sock Bass
Owned by Gary Grainger of The Faces

1986 PRS Employee Bass

■ **PRS** is well established as a solidbody electric maker, but during its twenty years and more in the business the company has also produced bass guitars—a number of examples are pictured here—and in 2009 introduced a line of acoustic flat-top models.

1978 Peavey T-60

1979 Peavey T-25 Special

1988 Peavey Vandenberg Signature

1995 Peavey Cropper Classic

1983 Peavey Razor

1959 Premier Scroll

1996 Peavey EVH Wolfgang

■ **PEAVEY** Hartley Peavey started his company in 1965 and it has continued to grow ever since, becoming a major player worldwide. Amplifiers came first and guitars didn't debut until thirteen years later, with the first T-series electrics adopting innovative ideas to ensure competitive performance and pricing.

The T-series range swelled during the 1980s, partnering some other radically shaped guitars as well as more derivative designs. Hot-rodded rock machines were added later in the decade as Peavey kept pace with market demands, but the 1990s brought a return to simpler thinking.

Capturing Eddie Van Halen from Music Man proved to be quite a coup, as his signature EVH Wolfgang instruments provided a higher profile than ever before for the Peavey guitar brand. Further exposure came via models made in Korea and other Far Eastern countries.

This mix of manufacturing sources has been maintained and the range now extends from beginner-level Chinese-made models to exotic limited editions built in Peavey's U.S. Custom Shop.

■ **PEDULLA** Michael Pedulla (born 1952) is one of many U.S. makers who started out in the 1970s. Guitars initially figured equally alongside basses, with styling and features changing to match market demands; but by the late 1980s the catalog comprised basses only, such as the curvy Buzz (fretless) and MVP (fretted) models. Over twenty years later, these remain mainstays of the current range, partnered by more recent additions such as the Rapture and Thunderbolt. Pedulla is based in Rockland, Massachusetts.

■ **PRAIRIE STATE** Prairie State guitars were built in Chicago by Carl and August Larson and carry many of their most famous design features. They debuted in around 1927 and were basically the more upscale rosewood twelve-fret Maurer brand models featuring August Larson's latest ideas, including a central adjustable hollow metal bar between the heel and tail blocks to relieve top stress; a second solid bar ran out around the lower neck heel and back inside, helping to keep the neck tight to the body. Sizes were concert to auditorium. In around 1935 or 1936, the Larsons introduced their fourteen-fret Euphonon line. Euphonons with the metal rod systems continued to be branded Prairie State. Prairie States also included the Larsons' only f-hole guitars. The brand ended in the early 1940s.

■ **PRESTON** Built by John Preston in 1804 in London, England, this "English guitar" is not a guitar in the modern sense but a cittern. It features six metal-strung courses and a small rounded body. In the early 1800s the English guitar was supplanted by the Spanish-style guitar we know today.

■ **PREMIER** The Premier brand of the United States dates back to the 1940s and adorns instruments distributed by the Sorkin Music Company. The first Premier guitar was an electrified flat-top acoustic, followed by arch-top electric examples. In the late 1950s these were joined by solids made for Sorkin at the Multivox factory in New York City and featuring a very distinctive scrolled horn shape.

Early 1960s successors employed similar styling on plastic-covered bodies, while the imported component count grew. The brand lasted until the 1970s before bowing out on some Japanese-made copies, but the late 1990s saw it resurrected on a line of entry-level oriental electrics.

1939 Prairie State Large Bodied Flat-top

1930 Prairie State F-Hole Guitar

1939 Prairie State Larson Custom Large Body

1804 Preston English Guitar

1930 Prairie State Bass

1932 Style 235

■ Peavey has produced guitars since 1978, although some musicians are probably more aware of the company's amplifiers. Pedulla is a U.S. bass specialist, while Preston was an early maker of "English guitars." Prairie State was a brand name used by the inventive duo of Carl and August Larson, and Premier has appeared on a number of different instruments.

1990 Pedula Pentabuzz

2006 Peavy Cirrus 5

1897 Ramírez (José)

1913 Ramírez (Manuel)

1912 Ramírez (Manuel)

1936 Ramírez (Julián Gomez)

■ **RAMÍREZ** The story of the Ramírez dynasty begins with José Ramírez I (1858–1923), who began making guitars on his own account in Madrid, Spain, in 1882. He achieved success with his *tablao* guitar, a large, shallow instrument with a slightly domed soundboard, designed to be used on the *tablaos* or small stages of Madrid's flamenco bars. The instrument was still being built at the time of José's death, but by then many flamencos had transferred their allegiance to his estranged brother Manuel.

The feud between the brothers began in 1891 when Manuel Ramírez (1864–1916) announced his intention of moving to Paris, France, only to set up in competition elsewhere in Madrid. Manuel's early instruments resemble those of his brother, but after repairing a couple of Torres guitars he moved in a new direction, producing instruments with lighter, more flexible soundboards and delicate strutting. He soon won over the flamencos, but owes his immortality to a guitar (probably made by his craftsman Santos Hernández) that he gave to a young player called Andrés Segovia, who used it for twenty-five years. Manuel's business did not long survive his death, but José's workshop went from strength to strength.

José Ramírez II (1885–1957) was living in South America at the time of his father's death but returned to take over the running of the firm. The guitars he built owe more to Manuel Ramírez than to those of his father in shape, construction, and subtlety of decoration.

José Ramírez III (1922–1995) came into the family business as an apprentice. He experimented endlessly, to the dismay of his father, and when he took over in 1957 he was able to bring his innovations to fruition. Chief among them was the adoption of a North American wood, western red cedar, for the guitar's soundboard. This was to be very influential over other makers. He also introduced a long string-length, probably at the request of Segovia, and developed a large workshop that produced 20,000 instruments in his lifetime—at least twenty times as many as most makers manage. Starting with Segovia in 1960, Ramírez III won over many of the world's concert artists to his instruments.

When he died, in 1995, his son José Ramírez IV (1953–2000) and daughter Amalia were running the family business. In the late 1980s, Ramírez IV created a brighter, lighter guitar. The 1a or "primera" that had always been Ramírez's top handbuilt model now came in two versions, Tradicionel and the new Especial. In 1993, the company scaled down its workshop. Amalia Ramírez currently employs four craftsmen and three apprentices, building both versions of the 1a, as well as a range of other models, including some she has designed.

Julián Gomez Ramírez (1879-1943) was not part of the Ramírez family, but he was a pupil of either José Ramírez I or Manuel Ramírez in Madrid, Spain, before leaving to set up in Paris, France, at the turn of the twentieth century. There he built fine, austerely decorated classical guitars in the Torres tradition in conditions of near-chaos that shocked visitors.

ramírez**classical**

1965 Ramírez (José III)

1967 Ramírez (José III)

1956 Ramírez (José III)

■ The story of Ramírez guitars is a long and sometimes complicated one, but the name has been associated with many fine classical guitars since the late nineteenth century. The name currently appears on guitars made under the direction of Amalia Ramírez.

1990 Ramírez (José III)

1969 Ramírez (José III)

■ Rebeth was an obscure British brand, while Ribbecke and the associated Halfling guitars are made in California. Regal originated at the start of the 20th century in America, and following decades producing a variety of instruments, the name currently appears on a line of Korean-made resonators.

1935 Regal 16M Artist

regal resonators

1938 Regal Oak Leaf Hawaiian

2003 Regal R-75

1982 Rebeth Gothic Cross

1930 Regal Harp Custom

■ **REBETH** Made in the early 1980s, the Rebeth Gothic Cross echoes the outlook of British builder Barry Collier. This overt one-off boasts a crudely hewn body and abundant brassware, while a plaque on the back is engraved with a goat's head and pentangle, adding occult character to the guitar's primitive image.

■ **REGAL** After some false starts, the classic Regal Musical Instrument Company emerged around 1908 in Chicago. By the late 1920s, Regal was known for tenor guitars and banjos, and in early 1929 unveiled its new Custom Built guitars. The latter name would remain on many better models into the 1950s. Regal flat-tops from the early 1930s ranged in size from standard to grand-concert. Some had a distinctive "Regal shape" with narrow upper shoulders and a much wider lower bout, possibly inherited from Washburn. In 1930, Regal bought the Le Domino and J.R. Stewart names when Stewart went bankrupt.

Two years later, Regal introduced its first carved arch-top guitar. Also that year, Regal struck a licensing deal to produce Dobro and Regal-brand resonator guitars. Regal made many Slingerland flat-tops from this era and produced much of the Tonk Bros line, including various auditorium and jumbo sizes as well as f-hole arch-tops.

Most Depression-era Regals were conventional but there were oddities. The Contra Bass, or Harp Guitar, of 1934 was a double-neck with regular six-string and fretless six-string bass necks. In 1937, Regal debuted the Bassoguitar, a gigantic double-bass-size guitar, and also began producing twelve-strings. The company was producing upscale Bacon and Day flat-tops and arch-tops, including the deluxe Sultana, and also fancy arch-tops for the Montgomery Ward mail-order firm, including some Recording King models.

By 1939, Regal was offering an enormous array of guitars, from cheap beginner models with faux graining, to dreadnoughts, wood or metal-body Dobros, and luxurious large arch-tops, including the Prince, Esquire, and Crown. But the company did not recover well after World War II. It introduced its first cutaway models in the late 1940s, but most of its guitars were low-end models competing with Kay and others. A further oddity was the Radio-tone Amplifying Guitar, with a small metal resonator device and screened "Cyclops" soundhole between stenciled radio towers.

In 1954, Regal sold out to Harmony. From 1959 to 1962, Harmony produced some basic Regal-brand folk and dreadnought flat-tops, plus an arch-top exclusively for Fender. Harmony revived the brand in 1972 for some grand-concerts and dreadnoughts, with red-white-and-blue models branded Bicentennial in 1976.

After Harmony folded in 1976, the Regal brand disappeared until it was brought back in 1987 by Saga for Korean-made resonator guitars, reviving the historical association with Dobros and continuing the Regal tradition of providing modestly priced instruments.

■ **RIBBECKE** Tom Ribbecke (born 1952) began building and repairing guitars and basses in 1974. Now based near Santa Rosa, California, he recently announced that he will no longer be accepting commissions for standard instruments but will continue to build individual guitars at a rate of between twelve and fifteen a year. He was one of twenty-one luthiers commissioned to build a blue arch-top for collector Scott Chinery. In 2003 he established a separate company, Ribbecke Guitar Co., where nine craftsmen produce up to thirty-five of his innovative Halfling guitars every year. The Halfling's soundboard is flat on the bass side but arched on the treble side.

1939 Regal Esquire 1185

1939 Regal
Prince 1170

1932 Regal Le Domino 4010

1951 Regal
Concert-Size

1952 Regal
Model 312C

1995 Ribbecke Blue
Mingione

semi-solidbody**ribbecke**

1931 Rickenbacker Frying Pan

1935 Rickenbacker Electro
Model B Steel Guitar

1936 Rickenbacker Electro
Spanish Lap Steel

1936 Rickenbacker Electro
Spanish Lap Steel

1948
Rickenbacker
Spanish SP

1949 Rickenbacker
Spanish SP

electric
pioneers

■ **RICKENBACKER** Rickenbacker is best known for some great designs devised in the 1950s, as well as its popularization of the electric twelve-string guitar through prominent use by acts such as The Beatles and The Byrds during the 1960s.

Adolph Rickenbacker was born near Basel, Switzerland, in 1886, but while still young was brought to the United States. Around 1918 he moved to Los Angeles, California, and in the 1920s established a successful tool-and-die operation there, stamping out metal and plastic parts. One especially enthusiastic customer for these was the National guitar company of Los Angeles.

At National, George Beauchamp and Paul Barth put together a basic magnetic pickup for guitars. Their experiments culminated in a pickup with a pair of horseshoe-shape magnets enclosing the pickup coil and surrounding the strings. Beauchamp and Barth had a working version in mid-1931. Another National man, Harry Watson, built a one-piece maple lap-steel guitar on which the prototype pickup could be mounted. This was the famous wooden "Frying Pan" guitar, so-called because of its small, round body and long neck. It was the first guitar to feature an electromagnetic pickup, and in that sense formed the basis for virtually all modern electric guitars.

Beauchamp, Barth, and Adolph Rickenbacker teamed up to put the ideas of this exciting prototype electric guitar into production. They formed the curiously named Ro-Pat-In company at the end of 1931—just before Beauchamp and Barth were fired by National. In 1932 Ro-Pat-In started manufacturing cast aluminum production versions of the Frying Pan electric lap-steel guitar, complete with horseshoe electromagnetic pickups. Ro-Pat-In's Frying Pans were effectively the first electric guitars with electromagnetic pickups put into general production.

Early examples of the Frying Pan lap-steels tend to have the Electro brandname on the headstock, and so are usually referred to by players and collectors today as the Electro Hawaiian models. By 1934 "Rickenbacker" had been added to the headstock logo (or sometimes "Rickenbacher"). Also that year the name of the manufacturing company was changed from Ro-Pat-In to the more logical Electro String Instrument Corporation.

Around this time Electro also produced some Spanish wood-body arch-top electrics. The Electro Spanish appeared around 1932—among the earliest of its kind—and the Ken Roberts model, named for a session guitarist, followed about three years later. Bakelite was the first synthetic plastic, and Electro started using it in 1935 for its Model B Hawaiian lap-steel and Model B Electro Spanish. The latter was arguably the first "solidbody" electric guitar. **>**

rickenbacker**solidbody**

model 1000s

1964 Rickenbacker Model 1000

1957 Rickenbacker Model 1000

1956 Rickenbacker Combo 400

1954 Rickenbacker Combo 800

1956 Rickenbacker Combo 600

1956 Rickenbacker Combo 600

■ Rickenbacker began as the oddly named Ro-Pat-In company in the early 1930s, a partnership between tool-and-die maker Adolph Rickenbacker and two ex-National men, George Beauchamp and Paul Barth. Rickenbacker's first "modern" electrics were the Combo models, introduced in 1954.

1957 Rickenbacker Combo 450

combo series

1957 Rickenbacker Combo 600

1958 Rickenbacker Combo 850

1957 Rickenbacker Combo 850

solidbodyrickenbacker

1961 Rickenbacker 460

1965 Rickenbacker 460

1967 Rickenbacker 625

1962 Rickenbacker 615

1964 Rickenbacker 450/12

1963 Rickenbacker Astrokit

During World War II Electro worked for the government, extending the Los Angeles factory in the process. After the war Adolph Rickenbacker decided not to continue many of his musical instruments, including most of the poorly received Spanish electrics. During 1946 he turned sixty, and began to think about selling the musical instrument part of his business.

The eventual buyer was Francis Cary Hall, who had moved with his family to California at around age eleven. He had opened a radio repair store, Hall's Radio Service, in the 1920s. This led logically to a wholesale company distributing electronic parts, the Radio & Television Equipment Co. (Radio-Tel), which F.C. Hall set up in Santa Ana, Orange County, in 1936.

After distributing Fender guitars and amplifiers for a time, Hall began to reconsider his position. Given his experience, Hall could see the potential for an instrument business where he not only distributed the product but also manufactured it. So in late 1953 Hall bought the Electro String Music Corporation from Adolph, with its guitar factory still at South Western Avenue, Los Angeles.

Around the beginning of 1954 German-born guitar maker Roger Rossmeisl, previously at Gibson, was hired by Electro to come up with new designs for Rickenbacker electric guitars. That same year Electro launched its first "modern" electrics, the double-cutaway carved-top Rickenbacker Combo 600 and Combo 800. They were aptly named, combining the horseshoe pickup and almost square neck of the earlier Hawaiian lap-steels with the up-and-coming solidbody electric Spanish style. The first Combo models began to feature on the headstocks a brand new "underlined" Rickenbacker logo of the type still in use today.

Electro's next move was to abandon the clumsy horseshoe pickup and apply a more suitable pickup to its Spanish electrics. First to receive the new pickup was the Combo 400, launched in 1956. Another first was its through-neck construction, a feature that would become a familiar aspect of many of Rickenbacker's solidbody instruments. New Combo 650 and Combo 850 models appeared in 1957, introducing a body with a "sweeping crescent" shape across the two cutaways. In various incarnations and dimensions this has been in continual use by Rickenbacker to the present day.

In 1958 a series of new models was introduced that formed the basis for Rickenbacker's success during the 1960s and onward. The thin-hollowbody designs were largely the responsibility of Rossmeisl. For these new electric hollowbody Capri guitars he further developed an unusual "scooped-out" construction. Rather than make a hollow guitar in the traditional method he would start with a semi-solid block of wood—usually two halves of maple joined together—and cut it to a rough body shape, partially hollowing it out from the rear. A separate wooden back was added once all the electric fittings had been secured, and the neck was glued into place. The first new Rickenbacker Capri was the small-body short-scale three-pickup 325 model, a guitar that would have a great effect on the company's success when it was taken up a few years later by John Lennon.

A full twelve-model Capri line-up was launched during 1958, but the Capri name itself was soon dropped. There were four short-scale models: 310 (two pickups), 315 (plus vibrato), 320 (three pickups), and 325 (plus vibrato); four full-scale models: 330 (two pickups), 335 (plus vibrato), 340 (three pickups), and 345 (plus vibrato); and four "deluxe" full-scale models with triangle-shape fingerboard inlays: 360 (two pickups), 365 (plus vibrato), 370 (three pickups), and 375 (plus vibrato). **>**

1971 Rickenbacker 430

1973 Rickenbacker 480

rickenbacker**solidbody**

1973 Rickenbacker System 490

1974 Rickenbacker 620

1980 Rickenbacker 483

1983 Rickenbacker 230 El Dorado

1974 Rickenbacker 481

1977 Rickenbacker 4080/12 Double-neck

1983 Rickenbacker 230 Hamburg

1992 Rickenbacker 230 Glenn Frey Model

1991 Rickenbacker 660/12TP

1993 Rickenbacker 650S Sierra

1992 Rickenbacker Jackson Browne Model Prototype

■ The "cresting wave" body shape was introduced by Rickenbacker on its 425 and 450 models in 1958, and then in 1962 on several 600-series guitars. Also shown on these pages are the angular 1964 Astro kit guitar and some of the later double-cutaway 200-series instruments.

solidbodyrickenbacker

1958 Rickenbacker 330

1964 Rickenbacker 325/1996

1985 Rickenbacker 325/12 John Lennon Signature Model

1964 Rickenbacker 335S

1956 Rickenbacker 335 First Prototype

Two classic Rickenbacker design elements began to appear at this time. New "toaster-top" pickups were devised, nicknamed for their split chrome look, and unusual two-tier pickguards, made at first in an arresting gold-colored plastic. These comprised a base plate flush to the guitar's body carrying the controls, plus a second level raised on three short pillars, intended as a finger-rest. Similarly idiosyncratic were the shortlived "cooker" control knobs with distinctive diamond-shaped pointers on top.

In 1960 a new stereo feature called Rick-O-Sound was added to some guitars. The system simply separated the output from neck and bridge pickups so that a special split cord would feed the individual signals to two amplifiers (or two channels), made possible by a special double jack offering mono or stereo output from Rick-O-Sound-equipped Rickenbackers.

The following year Rickenbacker introduced a deluxe guitar with the same body shape as the earlier 425, 450, and vibrato-equipped 615 and 625 models. The new 460 listed at $248.50 and had triangle-shaped fingerboard markers, Rickenbacker's most obvious indicator of a deluxe model. More significantly, it was the first with a modified control layout of a type that the company would apply to nearly all their models over the next few years. On the 460, a fifth "blend" control was added, situated just behind the four normal controls and fitted with a smaller knob. The extra control seems to have been prompted by an idea that F.C. Hall had about tone circuits.

The blend knob is much misunderstood by guitarists, and it must be said that its effect can be very subtle. Consider the usual control set-up for a two-pickup guitar: there are usually individual volume and tone controls for each pickup, and a selector switch. The three-way selector offers either: the pickup nearest the neck, with a more bassy tone often used for rhythm playing; both pickups, balanced by the relative positions of the two volume controls; or the pickup nearest the bridge, with a more trebly tone for lead playing. Rickenbacker does use this control system too, but from 1961 it started to add the fifth knob to many models.

The theory is that in the neck-pickup-only or bridge-pickup-only position on the three-way selector, the fifth knob gives the opportunity to blend in some tone from the *unselected* pickup. For example, if the player has just the bassier neck pickup selected, the fifth knob would allow him effectively to blend in a little of the bridge pickup's treble tone. If the selector is in the middle position—in other words, giving both pickups—then the fifth knob allows the guitarist to vary the precise balance between the two, for increased tonal emphasis.

In fact, the later development of modern channel-switching amplifiers made the fifth knob redundant, but at the time it did seem to Rickenbacker to offer some increased versatility to the available tones. On Rickenbackers fitted with the company's Rick-O-Sound stereo feature, the fifth knob functions more as a balance control between left and right (in other words, neck pickup and bridge pickup), because the selector would usually be lodged in the centre position so that both pickups are "on."

All this has confused guitarists for decades. They have generally found the fifth "blend" knob rather baffling, and no doubt many quickly decided to forget that their guitar had a fifth knob at all. **>**

1966 Rickenbacker 335 Prototype

1987 Rickenbacker 1998PT Pete Townshend Signature Model

rickenbackersolidbody

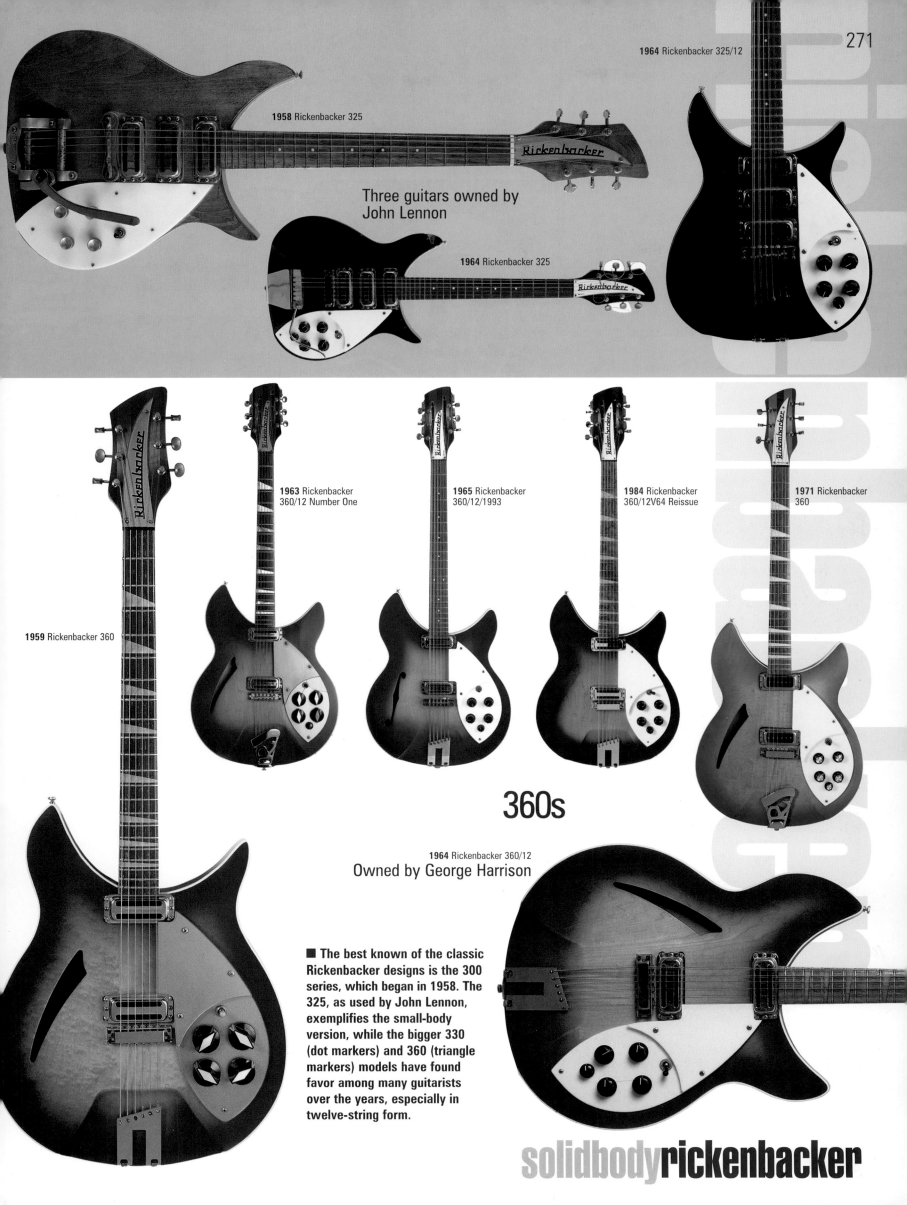

1964 Rickenbacker 325/12

1958 Rickenbacker 325

Three guitars owned by
John Lennon

1964 Rickenbacker 325

1959 Rickenbacker 360

1963 Rickenbacker
360/12 Number One

1965 Rickenbacker
360/12/1993

1984 Rickenbacker
360/12V64 Reissue

1971 Rickenbacker
360

360s

1964 Rickenbacker 360/12
Owned by George Harrison

■ The best known of the classic
Rickenbacker designs is the 300
series, which began in 1958. The
325, as used by John Lennon,
exemplifies the small-body
version, while the bigger 330
(dot markers) and 360 (triangle
markers) models have found
favor among many guitarists
over the years, especially in
twelve-string form.

solidbody rickenbacker

1959 Rickenbacker 375F

■ Rickenbacker has always produced a good number of more unusual models in addition to its better known guitars. Included here are some "F" models, with what Rickenbacker described as a "Thin Full-Body," as well as the hybrid Banjoline, the strange six-and-twelve-string Convertible model, and the spectacular Lightshow guitar.

1958 Rickenbacker 425

arch-tops

1959 Rickenbacker 360F

1987 Rickenbacker 350 Custom Prototype

1968 Rickenbacker 360F

1968 360F/12

In summer 1962 Rickenbacker moved its factory from South Western Avenue, Los Angeles, to Kilson Drive, Santa Ana, not far from the Radio-Tel HQ. Soon afterwards Roger Rossmeisl left to work for Fender.

During 1963 the company started to develop an electric twelve-string guitar. Acoustic twelve-strings had been around for some time, and the folk craze in the early 1960s had given a boost to their appeal. Electric twelve-strings were far less common. The first had been made around 1955 by the small Stratosphere company, while Danelectro's Bellzouki model had been launched in 1961. The glorious electric twelve-string sound came from the octave and unison doubling of paired strings to produce a wonderful "jangling" sound, almost as if two guitars were playing together.

Long-serving Rickenbacker employee Dick Burke came up with a brilliant headstock modification for the new twelve-string that kept the existing six tuners where they normally were—three on each side—but added two parallel channels into the face, as if the slots of a classical guitar had been cut only half-way through. Burke attached the second set of six tuners at ninety degrees to the first set, the keys facing "backward"—again, like a classical guitar, with strings attached into the tuners' spindles in the channels. The design overcame the problems that many makers of twelve-string guitars have discovered, not least the unbalancing effect of a heavy long head with six tuners each side.

Rickenbacker made at least three experimental twelve-string guitars in 1963. The first model went to showband singer, fiddle-player, and guitarist Suzi Arden, whose Suzi Arden Show, a regular at the Golden Nugget in Las Vegas, was kitted out with Rickenbacker equipment.

The following February the company set up a special display at the Savoy Hilton hotel in New York City to show some equipment to The Beatles. The group's arrival in the United States to play Ed Sullivan's television show and three concerts had caused unrivalled scenes of fan mania. Despite missing the display due to illness, George Harrison ended up with a great prize, one of the company's experimental twelve-string electrics, in model 360 style.

John Lennon also came away with a new guitar, a black 325 model with new five-control layout, replacing the somewhat road-weary 325 that he'd used for most of the group's early career. The company also promised to send to Lennon a special one-off twelve-string version of the 325, just as soon as they'd made it. And Beatles manager Brian Epstein requested a second 360-style twelve-string for another of his now famous charges, Gerry Marsden of Gerry & The Pacemakers.

For the two *Ed Sullivan Show* appearances in New York, Lennon used his old 325, but for a

rickenbacker semi-solidbody

1988 Rickenbacker 370/12 Roger Mcguinn Model

1968 Rickenbacker 360SF

1972 Rickenbacker 375

1972 Rickenbacker 370

1987 Rickenbacker 360/12SPC Tuxedo

1975 Rickenbacker 360

1980 Rickenbacker 360/12

1970 Rickenbacker 360/12 (left-handed)

1966 Rickenbacker 336/12 Convertable

1971 Rickenbacker 331 Lightshow

1968 Rickenbacker Banjoline

semi-solidbody rickenbacker

1987 Rickenbacker 381 V69

1988 Rickenbacker 381
John Kay Model

1969 Rickenbacker 381

1988 Rickenbacker 381/12V69

further appearance, broadcast from Miami, Lennon gave his new five-knob 325 its public debut. The Sullivan shows were outrageously popular, each receiving an unprecedented American television audience of some seventy million viewers. No doubt Rickenbacker boss F.C. Hall allowed himself a smile as he watched the group perform in the New York television studio.

After their thoroughly successful invasion of the United States, The Beatles returned to Britain, and Harrison used his twelve-string to great effect on some new recordings, including the distinctive opening chord of the title song from *A Hard Day's Night*. A rush for Rickenbacker twelve-strings followed. Rickenbackers proved popular with other British pop guitarists during the second half of the 1960s, including such influential guitarists as Denny Laine, Hilton Valentine, and, with most notable effect, Pete Townshend.

During 1964 Rickenbacker officially added three twelve-strings to its line, the 360/12 (two-pickup 360-style), 370/12 (three pickups) and 450/12 (two-pickup solidbody). The company also began at this time to supply export versions of certain models to distributor Rose-Morris in the UK, a connection that lasted until 1969. This would be unremarkable but for the fact that the British company requested instruments with real f-holes rather than Rickenbacker's customary "slash"-shape soundholes, and models with this feature have since become collectable.

From 1964 Rickenbacker introduced an alternative body style for the "deluxe" models (360, 360/12, 365, 370, 370/12 and 375) with a streamlined, less angular look to the front of the body, as well as binding on the soundhole and only on the back edge of the body. Designed to be more comfortable for the player, the new streamlined design was the main production style used for the models mentioned from 1964. Old-style versions (body bound front and back, "sharp" edges) remained available on special order. A year earlier Rickenbacker had also introduced a striking new tailpiece, in the shape of a large "R."

The name of the sales/distribution company was changed in 1965 from the old Radio & Television Equipment Co. to the more appropriate Rickenbacker Inc., and the sales office moved within Santa Ana in 1966. The name of the manufacturing company remained as Electro String.

A "light-show" guitar was introduced in 1970 with a clear plastic top through which a psychedelic array of colored lights would shine, flashing in response to the frequencies of the notes being played. Roger McGuinn of The Byrds had a special twelve-string light-show Rickenbacker built with slanted frets and three pickups, which he used for "Eight Miles High" at the end of The Byrds' shows in the early 1970s. It was perhaps the most bizarre Rickenbacker ever made—which makes it a rare beast indeed, given the number of odd and peculiar instruments that were made at and escaped from Rickenbacker's Santa Ana factory.

Around this time demand for Rickenbacker guitars began to decline, but the company's basses were growing in popularity in the hands of players like Chris Squire of Yes. Production began to pick up again at Santa Ana, concentrating on four-string models. A new body shape appeared in 1973,

rickenbacker**semi-solidbody**

1957 Rickenbacker Model 390

acoustics

1962 Rickenbacker
Model 385

1958 Rickenbacker Model 385

1975 Rickenbacker 362/12 Double-Neck

■ The 380-series Rickenbackers
appeared in 1958 with impressive carving
to the front and back of the bodies,
earning them the "Thick-body" name. The
362/12 was one of two double-neck
models launched in 1975, offering the
weighty if useful combination of six- and
twelve-string necks in one guitar.

1975 Rickenbacker 385

semi-solidbodyrickenbacker

1966 Rickenbacker 4001

1961 Rickenbacker 4001S

1967 Rickenbacker 4001S
Experimental Bass

1958 Rickenbacker Combo
600 Prototype

1957 Rickenbacker
4000

although it was really only new to Rickenbacker's six-string guitar lines. The 480 used the body styling made famous by the company's electric bass guitars, which had first appeared in 1957, with a distinctive elongated upper horn.

A few custom double-neck guitars had been made for individual Rickenbacker customers in the 1960s, but in 1975 the company's first production double-necks appeared. There were two types: the 4080 also used the electric bass body, while the 362 enlarged upon the familiar 360 style.

In 1983 Rickenbacker made a low-key attempt to re-create some of its older models, which the company noticed were increasingly popular among "vintage" collectors. A new generation of guitarists had also started to take up Rickenbackers, and this helped the company's climb back to popularity during the 1980s. Among the most notable and visible players of Rickenbackers at the time were Peter Buck of R.E.M. and Johnny Marr of The Smiths. The jangling, rhythmic thrust of Rickenbackers was once more to be heard at the heart of some of pop's most vibrant offerings.

The business operation of Rickenbacker was changed in 1984 when F.C. Hall's son John, who had worked at Rickenbacker since 1969, officially took control. He formed a new company, Rickenbacker International Corporation (RIC), which purchased the guitar-related parts of his father's Rickenbacker Inc. and Electro String companies. In 1989 Rickenbacker moved its factory from Kilson Drive after some twenty-seven years, consolidating factory and offices at the corner of South Main and Stevens in Santa Ana.

A new idea during the late 1980s was the production of numbered limited-edition signature models. Rickenbacker have so far made eight artist guitars in editions of between 250 and 1,000: Pete Townshend (1987), Roger McGuinn (1988), John Kay (1988), Susanna Hoffs (1988), John Lennon (1989), Tom Petty (1991), Glenn Frey (1992), and Carl Wilson (2000). A proper vintage reissue program is now underway too. The idea of an organized line of reissue instruments celebrating Rickenbacker's best-loved guitars began in 1984 with the 325V59 (now called the 325C58 Hamburg, for the period in which John Lennon used his), the 325V63 (now the 325C64 Miami, as Lennon first used his in a Miami television studio) and the 360/12V64 (now the 360/12C63). Those 59–58 and 64–63 changes reflected improved historical knowledge. By the 2007 pricelist, the reissues (C series and Vintage Reissue series) consisted of six models, adding a 350V63 Liverpool, 381V69, and 381/12V69.

In 1992 Rickenbacker launched the twenty-four-fret 650 model, in the earlier 400 and 600 "cresting wave" style, still in the line today as the 650 Colorado. Tom Petty's similar 660/12P twenty-one-fret signature model of 1991 informed the production 660 and 660/12 models. Alongside these in the 2008 catalogue were classic 330, 330/12, 360, 360/12, and 370/12 models, plus the stereo 620. It's clear that Rickenbacker's timeless set of traditional guitars will always be with us.

1964 Rickenbacker 4001 (left-handed)
Owned by Paul McCartney

1991 Rickenbacker
4001CS Chris
Squire Model

1967 Rickenbacker
4002

1979 Rickenbacker
4003FL

1986 Rickenbacker
4003SPC Blackstar

■ Rickenbacker's bass guitars are
well regarded by some notable
players, not least Paul McCartney,
whose Beatle-period left-handed
4001S is pictured here. Also shown
is a signature model for another Rick
bass star, Chris Squire of Yes,
alongside some of the other bass
models Rickenbacker has produced.

1965 Rickenbacker 4005

1975 Rickenbacker 3001

1973 Rickenbacker 490 (left-handed)

1969 Rickenbacker 4005

bassrickenbacker

1985 Romanillos "La Buho"

1996 Romanillos

1976 Rodriguez

1968 Rubio

1996 Rubio

1996 Rozas

1962 Royal

■ **RICK TURNER** After co-founding Alembic in 1969, Rick Turner (born 1942) left nine years later to set up his own California-based company. His best-known creation was the Model 1C, an unusually styled six-string, featuring a novel rotating pickup and put to high profile use by Fleetwood Mac's Lindsey Buckingham. Production proved shortlived, but Turner returned in the early 1990s, reviving his earlier designs along with all-new guitars and basses that now include the Renaissance range.

■ **ROBIN** David Wintz set up Robin Guitars in the early 1980s. Although the company is based in Houston, Texas, the initial catalog actually came from Tokai in Japan. Most of these early models were Fender-influenced but featured a reversed headstock. U.S. production commenced in the mid 1980s and subsequently all Robins were American-made. The company was quick to embrace the rock guitar concept and appropriately hot-rodded Robins appeared from the late 1980s onward, including the Medley and Machete models. In contrast, the trend toward more traditional design during the 1990s was echoed by the addition of the Gibson-influenced Avalon and Savoy series.

■ **ROCKINGER** Founded in 1978, this German maker is best known for its replacement parts and guitar kits, but it also produced its own designs for a while, including the Lady.

■ **RODRIGUEZ** Miguel Rodriguez (1881–1975) set up shop in Cordóba, Spain, in 1906. In the 1930s he was joined by his twin sons Miguel Jr. (1921–1998) and Rafael (1921–1965), and the guitars became collaborations. The family is best known for its "church door" classical instruments, made from distinctive Brazilian rosewood supposedly salvaged from a church that was being refurbished.

■ **ROGER** German luthier Wenzel Rossmeisl used the Roger brand on the arch-top acoustic guitars he made for around three decades, commencing in the 1930s. It was actually the name of his son, who followed him into the instrument building business and subsequently became an influential figure at Rickenbacker and Fender. Many Roger guitars featured scooped carving around the front and rear body edges, creating what is now known as the "German carve" and seen on many other makes.

■ **ROLAND** This Japanese company, established in 1974, developed the guitar synthesizer in the late 1970s and early 1980s. The system offered infinite sustain and a wide range of sounds, but the guitars (called "controllers" by Roland) were heavy and players did not take to them. It subsequently switched to devices that could be added to existing guitars.

■ **ROMANILLOS** José Romanillos (born 1932 in Madrid, Spain) moved to England in 1956 and built his first classical guitar in 1961. In 1969 he met Julian Bream and began building a series of instruments for him. José has now retired to Spain, but his son Liam continues to build guitars in Dorset, England, in the Romanillos tradition.

■ **ROZAS** Ignacio M. Rozas (born 1943) is based in Madrid, Spain. He worked for Ramírez and Contreras before establishing his own shop in 1987, handbuilding classical and flamenco guitars. He retired in 2008.

1977 Roland G-303 Guitar Synth

1977 Roland GS-500 Guitar Synth

1983 Roland G-707 Guitar Synth

GS models

1985 Roland G-77 Bass

1978 Ruck

1980 Ruck

1991 Robin Machete Custom

1999 Rick Turner Model T Special

1978 Rockinger Lady

1960 Roger Model 54

■ Guitars featured here are by Rick Turner, Robin, Rubio, and Ruck (all from the United States), plus Rockinger and Roger from Germany; Rodriguez and Rozas from Spain; Japan's Roland; and the British maker Romanillos.

1987 Santa Cruz OM/E

1994 Santa Cruz D12

2002 Santa Cruz OM

2003 Santa Cruz PJ Parlor-Size

2003 Santa Cruz

2000 Santa Cruz OM/E
Owned by Tony Rice

1999 Samick DCV9500

■ **RUBIO** David Rubio (1934–2000) was a medical student when he went to Spain to play flamenco and observe guitar makers at work. In 1963, he established his first guitar workshop in New York City, returning to his native England in 1967. There he built fine guitars, including several for Julian Bream, as well as harpsichords, lutes, violins, and many more instruments.

■ **RUCK** Robert Ruck (born 1945) of Eugene, Oregon, is among the most celebrated of American classical guitar makers. A classical and flamenco player, he taught himself the craft of guitar making, and has also built a wide range of other stringed instruments. He builds no more than 30 guitars a year and is no longer taking orders.

■ **SALOMON** Jean-Baptiste Dehaye Salomon built this guitar in Paris in about 1760. Originally a five-course instrument, it has been modified to accept a sixth course.

■ **SAMICK** Samick, founded as a piano maker in 1958 in Inchon, Korea, has the capacity to build a million guitars a year in factories in Korea, Indonesia, China, and the United States. It turned to making guitars in 1965, producing instruments for many other companies. Only in 1991 did it introduce guitars under the Samick brand. Today Samick sells its acoustics and electrics under the Greg Bennett and Silvertone labels.

■ **SANTA CRUZ** Richard Hoover began the Santa Cruz Guitar Company in 1976 with two partners and quickly earned a reputation among players like Eric Clapton, Jerry Garcia, and David Crosby. Today, the company is still located in Santa Cruz, California. The first model was the dreadnought D, followed two years later by the 00-size H and the FTC, later simplified to the flat-back F. In 1977, bluegrass ace Tony Rice visited the workshop, and soon Santa Cruz built him a model based in part on his legendary Martin D-28, once owned by Clarence White. The Tony Rice model appeared as a signature guitar in 1981 and is still in the line today.

In 1992, Hoover redesigned the D, F, and H models with narrower nuts and switched the original headstock shape of the D and H to a squared-off Martin style. Others followed, and by 2009 the line included the VA dreadnought, a twelve-fret 000, 00, and dreadnought, the jumbo VJ, and parlor-size PJ. The Janis Ian Model is a small-bodied, short-scale guitar with striking black finish and a Lloyd Baggs pickup; other signature models include guitars for Arlen Roth, Bob Brozman, and Otis Taylor.

■ **SAN JOSE** San Jose was a brand belonging to New York retailer Horenstein and Sons. The instruments were built by the Oscar Schmidt Company of Jersey City, New Jersey. This instrument is identical to Schmidt's twelve-strings for the Stella brand.

■ **SCHARPACH** Theo Scharpach was born in 1955 in Vienna, Austria. In 1975 he established Scharpach Guitars. The company's current workshop is in Groessen in the Netherlands. In 2001, Scharpach was joined by luthier Menno Bos (born 1960), and the workshop now builds arch-tops and innovative nylon-strung guitars for classical, jazz, and pop players. This arch-top was one of twenty-one blue guitars commissioned by collector Scott Chinery from leading makers.

■ **SCHECTER** Started in 1976, David Schecter's U.S. company was among the first suppliers of quality replacement guitar parts, while custom-made instruments followed four years later. Japanese maker ESP took charge during the 1980s and eventually reinstated American

1760 Saloman 5 Course Guitar

■ On these pages, the guitars are by the eighteenth-century French maker Salomon; the high-volume Far East factories of Samick; the U.S. retailer's brand San Jose; Richard Hoover's California-based Santa Cruz company; Netherlands-based Scharpach; the Canadian firm, Seagull; and U.S. distributor's brand Serenader.

2002 Samick Cheyenne OM-8CE

1930 San Jose Artist Twelve-string

2001 Seagull Grand Concert-Size

1930 Serenader

1996 Scharpach Blue Vienna

1980 Shergold Custom Masquerader

1976 S.D. Curlee Aspen AE-700

1966 Simpson Pan'o'Sonic

1997 Schecter Hellcat Ten-string

1960 Silvertone Self-contained Electric

1964 Silvertone

1965 Silvertone Model 1437

manufacture. These two production sources were augmented by the less costly Korean-made Diamond series, which debuted in 1998.

■ **SCHMIDT** The Oscar Schmidt company was founded in 1871 and operated out of Jersey City, New Jersey, making all kinds of stringed instruments, particularly autoharps and zithers. The company reached its peak in the 1920s. The brand is now owned by the U.S. Music Corporation.

■ **S.D. CURLEE** Hand-built in Matteson, Illinois, Randy Curlee's distinctively designed instruments debuted in 1975. Officially licensed copies soon followed from Korea and Japan, bearing the Aspen, Hondo II, and S.D. Curlee International brands. Some of these less-expensive equivalents came too close for comfort to the real thing and U.S. production ceased in the early 1980s.

■ **SEAGULL** Seagull was started by Robert Godin in 1982 in La Patrie, Quebec, Canada. The guitars had several features that were unusual in acoustics at the time: bolt-on necks, dowels in the heel to improve strength and stability, tapered heads, and laminated bodies made from plentiful Canadian wild cherry. Today they come in four sizes: standard, which is slightly smaller than a dreadnought, folk, grand, and mini-jumbo. All have solid cedar or spruce tops. A recent innovation is the "compound curve top," a design that uses the added strength of an arch above the soundhole to allow for a thinner, more resonant top, combined with a flat surface on the lower bout that won't inhibit vibration.

■ **SELMER** In 1933, the French saxophone company Selmer joined forces with Italian guitarist and luthier Marco Maccaferri to produce a series of innovative guitars that are most associated with the legendary Gypsy guitarist Django Reinhardt. Selmer ceased guitar production in 1952, having produced about 900 instruments.

■ **SERENADER** Serenader was a brand used by distributors Beugeleiser and Jacobson of New York City before World War II.

■ **SHERGOLD** Former Burns man Jack Golder set up Shergold Woodcrafts in London, England, in 1965, supplying necks and bodies to many British makers. Shergold's own instruments first appeared in the late 1960s, but the brand was revived in earnest during the mid-1970s, initially on revamped versions of defunct Hayman designs. Shergold production stopped in 1983, but Golder continued with custom building. Commercial manufacture resumed eight years later, but his death in 1992 resulted in the closure of the company.

■ **SILVERTONE** Owned by major U.S. mail order and retail chain Sears, Roebuck, the Silvertone brand first appeared on guitars in 1941, succeeding the earlier Supertone name. Instruments were supplied by various American manufacturers, including Harmony, Kay, and Danelectro, while later Silvertones also came from Teisco and Kawai in Japan. The brand name was dropped by the early 1970s, but has recently reappeared on entirely unconnected Far Eastern imports.

■ **SIMON & PATRICK** Simon & Patrick Luthier is a line of Canadian-made guitars created by Robert Godin's LaSiDo company and produced in La Patrie, Quebec. With solid cedar or spruce tops, satin or high-gloss lacquer finishes, bolt-on necks, and bodies that combine arched upper bouts with flat lower bouts, Simon & Patrick has become LaSiDo's premier line.

■ **SIMPLICIO** Francisco Simplicio (1874–1932) was a pupil of Enrique Garcia who established himself in Madrid, Spain, in the 1920s. His guitars feature carved headstocks and bridges and play well despite their age. His son Miguel took over after his death.

■ **SIMPSON** New Zealander Ray Simpson built his first electric guitar in 1941. Production continued into the mid 1960s.

■ **SLINGERLAND** The drum manufacturer Slingerland marketed guitars during the 1930s. Slingerland's May-Bell brand was used on standard and concert size flat-tops, some with cherub decals, others with fake resonators (covers, no cones), including the Cathedranola model. All were made by Regal.

1933 Slingerland May Bell Cathedranola

1932 Slingerland May Bell no. 7

1920 Schmidt Hawaiian koa

2002 Simon & Patrick P-6

1936 Selmer Modele Jazz

■ Featured here are guitars by U.S. makers Schecter, Schmidt, S.D. Curlee, Silvertone, and Slingerland, plus the UK's Shergold; Simon & Patrick from Canada; Simplicio from Spain; and New Zealand's Simpson.

1932 Selmer Maccaferri Orchestre

1941 Silvertone Crest

1925 Simplicio (Francesco)

1932 Simplicio (Miguel)

1993 Smith (Ken)
BT Custom Bass VI

1985 Spector
NS-2 Bass

1989 Spector
NS-6A

1989 Status Bass
Series II

2002 Status
Kingbass

2003 Status
Buzzard Bass

■ **SMALLMAN** Greg Smallman (born 1947), of Melbourne, Australia, began making classical guitars in 1972. Since 1980 his guitars, while traditional in appearance, have employed an ultra-thin soundboard braced by a lattice of carbon-fiber and balsa struts. The design creates a bright and loud instrument for concert-hall performance. The best-known Smallman player is John Williams.

■ **SMITH (KEN)** New York session player Ken Smith (born 1951) moved into instrument making in 1978, creating upmarket basses featuring exotic woods and innovative ideas on construction and circuitry, later joined by basses with bolt-on necks. Apart from the Japanese-made Burner models offered during the 1990s, the range has remained all-American, although Smith has licensed his name and provided design input to the importer of KSD (Ken Smith Design) basses.

■ **SMITH (RALPH)** Ralph G. Smith of Wichita, Kansas, built at least four eighteen-string flat-tops in the 1980s. The instrument takes the twelve-string concept a step further by adopting six three-string courses, and produces a mighty sound as a result. The necessarily extra-long peghead, extended to incorporate the nine-a-side tuning machines, does make the guitar head-heavy.

■ **SOMOGYI** Ervin Somogyi (born 1944), of Oakland, California, started building guitars in 1971, but sprang to prominence in the mid 1980s when his instruments were favored by Windham Hill artists Will Ackermann, Alex de Grassi, and Michael Hedges. Somogyi is best known for his steel-string guitars, but he is a fine flamenco guitarist and has built a number of highly regarded nylon-string instruments.

■ **SPECTOR** The first guitars and basses from American builder Stuart Spector (born 1949) appeared in 1976, featuring bulbous-horned body styling that was subsequently imitated by many other makers. In 1985 Kramer acquired the Spector brand and split manufacture between the U.S. and Korea. After Kramer went bankrupt, five years later, Stuart Spector resumed production using the SSD (Stuart Spector Designs) banner. He regained the rights to his name in 1998. Current Spector basses are built in Saugerties, New York, as well as the Czech Republic, Korea, and China.

■ **STAHL** William C. Stahl was a retailer in Milwaukee, Wisconsin, who started selling guitars in the early 1900s. They were mostly built by Carl and August Larson in Chicago.

■ **STANDEL** Bob Crooks's Californian company is usually associated with amplifiers, but guitars played their occasional part. Earliest examples, in the late 1950s, were made by Semie Moseley of Mosrite fame, while mid-1960s Standels sported a distinctive "beak" headstock. The Harptone-manufactured line that followed marked a final foray into the instrument arena.

■ **STARFIELD** This brand initially adorned Japanese-made Gibson copies in the 1970s, but re-surfaced on a retro-flavored range launched in 1992 by Hoshino, the parent company of Ibanez. The new Starfield series comprised American and SJ (Starfield Japan) lines, but despite differences in specifications and price, both lines (with the exception of a few custom examples) were in fact manufactured by the Japanese Fujigen factory. Korean-made models were added in 1994. Sales didn't match Hoshino's high expectations and Starfield production ceased the following year.

■ **STARFORCE** In the late 1980s, the Korean-made Starforce range offered Fender look-alikes and superstrat-style six-strings in eye-straining finishes, while others adopted Spector's rounded outline.

■ **STATUS** In 1981, after learning the ropes with Shergold, Rob Green (born 1955) began producing some of the first guitars and basses to adopt carbon graphite construction and the headless concept successfully explored by Steinberger. Fender forced a name change from Strata to Status in 1983 and manufacture focused on basses. Additional models offered varying combinations of wood and carbon graphite, while headstock-equipped versions appeared in the 1990s, along with more affordable examples and even a return to guitar production. Status Graphite is based in Colchester, Essex, England.

1982 Starforce Model 8007

1966 Standel Custom Deluxe

1992 Starfield Altair SJ Custom

smallman**classical**

1988 Smith Custom Six-string

Over these pages you'll find guitars by the inventive Australian classical maker Smallman; bass specialist Ken Smith; Kansas-based Ralph Smith; California-based flat-top builder Somogyi; bass specialist Stuart Spector; U.S. brands Stahl and Standel; Far East brand Starfield; the Korean-based Starforce; and British maker Status.

1986 Smith Eighteen-string

1987 Smallman Cedar Top

1992 Smallman Aboriginal Design

1992 Somogyi

1910 Stahl
Student Grade

1925 Stahl
Concert-Size

1930 Stahl

1979 Steinberger Bass Prototype

1980 Steinberger Bass L-2

1986 Stepp DGI Box

1985 Steinberger GM4T

1965 Stella

■ **STEINBERGER** Launched in 1981, the L-2 bass was the first example of Ned Steinberger's inventive approach to instrument design, combining innovative hardware with a headless neck and minimalist body made of graphite and fiberglass. The New York-based maker added a matching guitar two years later and new models continued to appear, including less expensive Japanese-built examples. Gibson acquired Steinberger in 1986 but production continued, along with further additions to the range, such as bigger, wood-bodied versions, double-necks, twelve-strings and the headstock-equipped Sceptre. Introduced in the early 1990s, the Korean-made Spirit by Steinberger range offered less expensive, all-wood equivalents and by 2000 these were the only Steinbergers available. Upmarket U.S. production resumed two years later, subsequently spanning new models such as the Synapse series.

■ **STELLA** Stella guitars—particularly the twelve-string—were played by many celebrated bluesmen, including Huddie "Leadbelly" Ledbetter, Charlie Patton, Blind Blake, and Blind Willie McTell. They were built by the Oscar Schmidt Company of Jersey City, New Jersey. The Stella brand appeared some time prior to the 1920s, adorning Schmidt's humbler instruments in standard, grand concert, and auditorium sizes. Schmidt was one of the first companies to produce a twelve-string before World War II. Schmidt died in 1929. His factory passed through various hands before becoming United Guitar, which made instruments under the Premier and Orpheum labels. In 1939 the Stella brand was sold to Harmony, which applied it to its budget range before and after the war. Stella died when Harmony was liquidated in 1975. In the early 2000s some Asian-made acoustics were introduced by the current owners of the Harmony brand under the Stella label.

■ **STEPP** Stepp described the DG1 as "just the beginning" and it was indeed the first self-contained guitar synth, but this British-made, rectangular plastic package proved more than enough for most guitarists. Launched in 1986, it was joined the next year by the simpler DGX, but production problems and high prices didn't encourage sales and the company closed in 1988.

■ **STETSON** J.F. Stetson was a brand used by the retailer W.J. Dyer and Bro. of St Paul, Minnesota, from the late nineteenth century. Many, but not all, were built by the Larson brothers in Chicago, Illinois.

■ **STEWART AND BAUER** S.S. Stewart mass-produced banjos before joining forces with Philadelphia guitar maker George Bauer in 1898 to form Stewart and Bauer. Stewart died later that year but Bauer continued to produce guitars under the Stewart and Bauer name until his death in 1910.

■ **STONEHENGE** This brand belonged to Italian guitar builder Alfredo Bugari, who allied novel design ideas to tonal theories derived from studying the ancient English stone circle. In the mid-1980s these concepts were combined in conventionally styled solids, as well as unique-looking guitars and basses employing triangular frame bodies made of tubular metal.

■ **STRATOSPHERE** Started by brothers Russ and Claude Deaver in Springfield, Missouri, this small company was responsible for the first production double-neck electric, the aptly titled Stratosphere Twin, introduced in 1954 and featuring six- and twelve-string necks. Stratosphere's suggested twelve-string tuning suited harmony lead lines rather than chords. The technique was tricky, although not for guitar wizard Jimmy Bryant, who put his Twin to good use on recordings such as the appropriately named "Stratosphere Boogie." The company called its creation "The guitar of tomorrow . . . today," which proved somewhat prophetic, as another decade would pass before the twelve-string electric become fashionable, long after Stratosphere disappeared in 1958.

1955 Stratosphere Twin

steinbergersolidbody

1932 Stella Concert Size

1930 Stella Twelve-string

1955 Stella Sundale

■ Guitars featured here are from U.S. brands Steinberger, Stella, Stetson, Stewart & Bauer, and Stratosphere, and by the UK maker Stepp.

1900 Stewart & Bauer

1915 Stetson

1984 Stonehenge Model II

1999 Suhr JS 1

1990 Sunn Mustang

1984 Synthaxe

1929 Stromberg D-800

1924 Stromberg B&J Serenader

1930 Stromberg No. 49

1954 Supro Dual Tone

■ **STROMBERG** Elmer Stromberg (1895–1955) of Boston developed the Stromberg guitar line from 1927, and the arch-tops the company made in the 1940s and 1950s are now highly regarded. They have an unusual single diagonal bracing system (half a standard X-type), and the Master 300 and Master 400, at 19 inches wide, had the largest body of any arch-top guitar on the market. Jazz guitarists who played Strombergs included Freddie Green and Irving Ashby. Elmer Stromberg died in 1955, and the Stromberg business died with him. In recent years, the brand has been revived by WD Music Products for a line of Korean-made guitars.

■ **SUHR** In the early 1980s, U.S. guitar-builder John Suhr (born 1956) started working for Rudy Pensa at his New York music shop, subsequently producing the Pensa-Suhr branded electrics that attracted famous players such as Mark Knopfler and Eric Clapton. Suhr quit the guitar-making business in 1991, but returned four years later, joining Fender. In 1997 he left to set up his own factory, and the Suhr name has since adorned a decidedly Fender-influenced, upmarket range that now includes various limited editions and artist signature models.

■ **SUNN** This famous amplifier brand of the 1960s and 1970s was acquired in 1985 by Fender, which eventually revived a few favorites between 1998 and 2001. In the interim, Fender applied the name to more-affordable amplification, as well as imported entry-level Strat and Precision bass copies, marketed as Sunn Mustang models in the late 1980s and early 1990s.

■ **SUPRO** First appearing in the 1930s, this brand was subsequently owned by the Chicago-based Valco Manufacturing Company, formed during the previous decade. Valco also produced National instruments, so many equivalent Supros were unsurprisingly similar.

Arch-top electrics were joined by a growing selection of solid-style Supros during the 1950s, while 1962 saw the addition of fibreglass-bodied versions that echoed National's "Res-o-Glas" range, but in less-fancy form. More conventional models followed, including solid and semi-acoustic examples employing Japanese-made components.

In 1967, under new ownership, Valco acquired competitor Kay, but went bankrupt a year later. After a long absence, the Supro brand recently returned on U.S.-built interpretations of early solids, while Canadian company Eastwood currently offers Korean-made re-creations.

■ **SYNTHAXE** Introduced in 1984, the futuristically styled SynthAxe was a guitar-orientated, MIDI-connected controller for keyboard synthesizers of the time. The odd looks, construction, and playing technique required proved off-putting for most players, not to mention the high price, which ensured an early demise for this British invention.

strombergacoustic

1936 Stromberg Deluxe Arch-top

1931 Stromberg Arch-top

1936 Stromberg G-1

1946 Stromberg Master 400 Cutaway

1946 Stromberg Deluxe Cutaway

1948 Stromberg Ultra Deluxe

■ On these pages, the featured guitars are by American arch-top maker Stromberg; obscure British brand Stonehenge; U.S. builder John Suhr; the Fender-related Sunn brand; U.S. guitar giant Valco's Supro brand; and the experimental Synthaxe from the UK.

1960 Supro Sahara

1961 Supro Sahara 2

1955 Supro Belmont

1960 Supro Val Trol

solidbodysynthaxe

2001 Tacoma EM-9CE7

1999 Tacoma Olympia EA-14

1984 Takamine F-150 Bruno

■ **TACOMA** Tacoma Guitars was founded in 1996 near Seattle, Washington, and at one point claimed to be the third largest U.S. acoustic manufacturer, producing around forty instruments a day. Its debut in 1997 made a big impact—largely for the little P1 Papoose, which is tuned like a guitar capoed at the fifth fret, and its medium-bodied, cutaway cousin, the C1C Chief. Distinctive for their minimalist cosmetics, unusual top-bout teardrop-shaped soundhole, and eager sound and tone, both used simple, mandolin-derived A-style bracing, made possible by the absence of a central soundhole. The Papoose in particular quickly found favor on the country circuit.

The company introduced the Thinline Series in 1999—a couple of Florentine-cutaway instruments, the EM-10 and 16, in profile somewhat reminiscent of Washburn's Festival Series. That year also saw an upgrade to solid woods throughout, where previously a few of the cheaper models had laminated sides.

Another series launched around this time was the LJ—or "Little Jumbo"—range co-designed by guitarist Laurence Juber and, confusingly, carrying "E" model prefixes. The limited edition EK-36C appeared in 2000, featuring a 600-year-old cedar front and flamed koa back and sides. In 2002, two LJ-sized cutaway nylon-string classicals—models ECR-15NC and ER-64NC—were introduced under the Europa Series banner. Fender acquired Tacoma in 2004 and used the factory to produce Guild acoustics, before closing it in late 2008. It has said that it plans to revive the Tacoma brand in future.

■ **TAKAMINE** Takamine is almost synonymous with quality acoustic-electric guitars that deliver a natural sound. Takamine began as an instrument workshop in Sakashita, Japan, at the foot of Mount Takamine. It was founded in 1962 and began exporting instruments to the United States under its own name in the mid 1970s, with distribution through Kaman Music Corporation. Its early acoustics were closely modeled on Martin's dreadnought and OM guitars. In 1978 it launched its first guitar with the bridge-mounted "Palathetic" pickup system. These conventional acoustic-electric classicals and steel-strings were the perfect complement to Kaman's more radical Ovation brand and helped build the market for acoustic-electric instruments.

By 1978 Takamine was selling the H series Hirade Concert classicals (named for Takamine's president Mass Hirade) with solid tops. These were joined by acoustic-electric versions (E series). Within a year the company had introduced the original features that inform the line to this day, including the distinctive tapered, center-peaked head. Cheaper guitars had laminated tops; better models had solid spruce or cedar and were signified by an S suffix; the F series included dreadnoughts and "folk" (OM) models; an EF prefix indicated that it was an acoustic-electric version; the C series models were classicals, with electronics on the ECs. Cutaways (C suffix) were also added around 1982.

By 1988 Takamine had debuted the Natural series acoustic (N) and acoustic-electric (EN) models, including dreadnoughts and cutaway jumbos. Also new was a low-end G series. Around the same time, Takamine began to offer its Limited Edition LTD series. The first was the 500-unit LTD-88, one of the new EN jumbos finished in black with abalone trim and a split, compensated saddle that would be featured on upscale models of the future. The LTD series continues today.

By 2009 Takamine guitars were offered in six principal body styles—Dreadnought; NEX/Grand Auditorium; FXC; OM; Jumbo; and Classic—across a range of series, from Classic nylon-string to Nashville steel-strings. Many have Takamine's innovative "Cool Tube" vacuum-tube pre-amp. A healthy line of signature models allied names like Glenn Frey, Garth Brooks, John Jorgenson, Kenny Chesney, and Steve Wariner with the brand.

1990 Takamine LTD 90

1997 Takamine GB
Seven-C

**Owned by
Garth Brook**

1997 Takamine Santa Fe Limited Edition Model

1998 Takamine Santa Fe Limited Edition Model

1999 Takamine EF-108K

■ Tacoma was set up near Seattle in the mid 1990s and produced many flat-top acoustics. It was acquired by Fender in 2004, but shut down four years later. Takamine is a Japanese company best known for amplified acoustic guitars and was founded in 1962.

2001 Takamine AN-15

2001 Takamine AN-45

2001 Takamine EAN-10C

2002 Takamine EG-5609

2005 Taylor T3B

2005 Taylor T5 Crimson Metalic

2005 Taylor T5

2008 Taylor Classic

2008 Taylor Classic

2008 Taylor Custom

1978 Taylor 512 Grand Concert

1996 Taylor Baby

2000 Taylor Big Baby

■ **TAYLOR** Bob Taylor (born 1955) and Kurt Listug (born 1952) met in 1973 when they were both working at the American Dream, a guitar workshop in San Diego, California, run by brothers Gene and Sam Radding. In the autumn of 1974 Sam Radding realized that, although he loved to build guitars, he hated running a business. He sold the company to Listug, Taylor, and Steve Schemmer, who was working in the finishing department. They renamed the operation the Westland Music Company.

Building on Sam Radding's original concept, the trio continued to do repairs and sell parts as well as build guitars. The first order of business was to complete the outstanding orders for American Dream guitars. The second was to come up with a name to put on the headstock of their acoustic guitars, since they couldn't use the American Dream name anymore. After a number of meetings they settled on Taylor. The new partners felt it sounded good, was relatively easy to inlay on a headstock, and Bob Taylor was the only one of the three who could actually build a guitar.

The first Taylor guitars were built using Sam Radding's designs. There were three basic styles and each guitar was custom made. The jumbos were usually made of maple, the dreadnoughts of Brazilian rosewood, and the shallow dreadnoughts usually of walnut.

Over the next year Taylor refined Radding's designs. After hand cutting a number of Radding's T-block neck joints, Taylor switched to a bolt-on mortise-and-tenon joint. Now the company also began to standardize the line.

They decided that the dreadnought with Brazilian rosewood back and sides, spruce top, white binding, abalone soundhole rosette, and diamond-shaped fretboard inlays had the best combination of features.

Taylor also devised a three-digit numbering system for their models. Under the system the first digit would indicate the wood and level of ornamentation, the second digit would designate whether the guitar was a six-string (1) or a twelve-string (5), and the third digit would designate the size. So the model number 855, for example, would be a rosewood back and sides (8), twelve-string (5), jumbo (5). Guitars with cutaways were designated with a C suffix (815-C).

In 1975 the Westland Music Company made thirty-six guitars, which brought in barely enough money to support the three owners, let alone the rest of the workforce, so at the end of the year Taylor, Listug, and Schemmer laid everyone off. They had saturated the local market for custom-built guitars; if they wanted to grow, they would need to start selling wholesale to stores.

In 1976 the company changed its name to Taylor Guitars and Listug hit the road in an attempt to sign up dealers. The new dealers liked Taylor guitars, but they wanted a broader line of instruments to sell. To fit the bill, Taylor introduced two new series in early 1977: the 900s, with birdseye maple back and sides, and the 700s, a cosmetically plainer version of the already established 800 series.

In 1978 the company introduced the 500 series—with mahogany back and sides, rosewood fretboard, and black binding—and the 600 series—with dark-stained mahogany back and sides, ebony fretboard, and white binding. Taylor expanded its workforce and in 1978 built 449 guitars, almost twice as many as it had made the year before. That same year Neil Young purchased an 855, making him the highest profile musician to play a Taylor up to that point.

Over the next few years, Listug would load guitars into the trunk of his car and head out across America looking for new dealers, while Taylor and Schemmer stayed behind and built the instruments. Bob began to devise new tools, jigs, and fixtures to make the construction process as efficient as possible. Production at the tiny shop more than doubled. ➤

taylorsolidbody

1978 Taylor
555 12 String

1993 Taylor
810 CE

1998 Taylor W10

1998 Taylor 612CE

1998 Taylor
75 W65 LG

1998 Taylor
614CE

■ **Taylor began in the 1970s and soon built a reputation for its flat-top acoustics. This first spread of pictures shows the variety and scope of the California-based company's lines that developed over the subsequent decades.**

1997 Taylor LKSM-6
Owned by Leo Kottke

1997 Taylor 712C

2002 Taylor Baby
305GB

1998 Taylor 310

2003 Taylor 310

1998 Taylor 814 CE

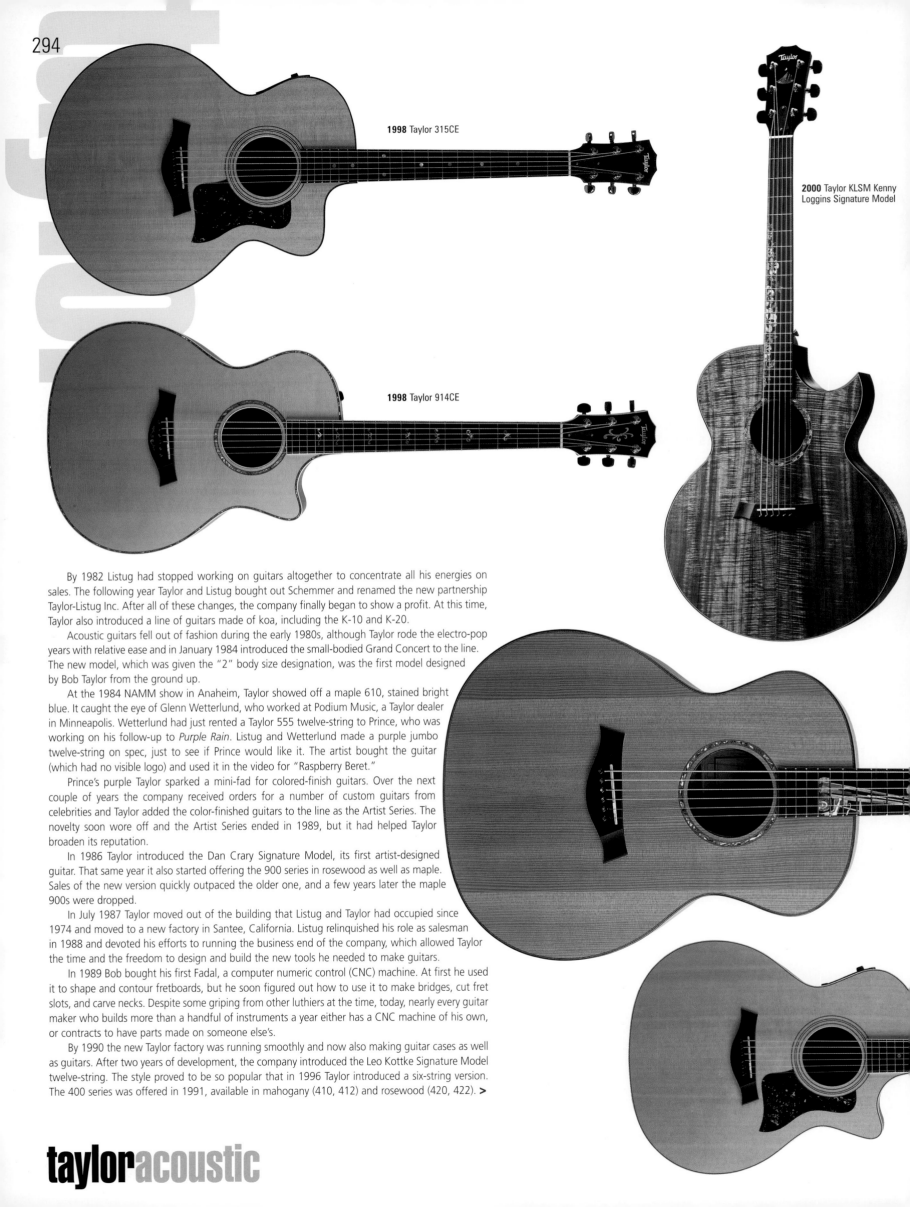

1998 Taylor 315CE

1998 Taylor 914CE

2000 Taylor KLSM Kenny Loggins Signature Model

By 1982 Listug had stopped working on guitars altogether to concentrate all his energies on sales. The following year Taylor and Listug bought out Schemmer and renamed the new partnership Taylor-Listug Inc. After all of these changes, the company finally began to show a profit. At this time, Taylor also introduced a line of guitars made of koa, including the K-10 and K-20.

Acoustic guitars fell out of fashion during the early 1980s, although Taylor rode the electro-pop years with relative ease and in January 1984 introduced the small-bodied Grand Concert to the line. The new model, which was given the "2" body size designation, was the first model designed by Bob Taylor from the ground up.

At the 1984 NAMM show in Anaheim, Taylor showed off a maple 610, stained bright blue. It caught the eye of Glenn Wetterlund, who worked at Podium Music, a Taylor dealer in Minneapolis. Wetterlund had just rented a Taylor 555 twelve-string to Prince, who was working on his follow-up to *Purple Rain*. Listug and Wetterlund made a purple jumbo twelve-string on spec, just to see if Prince would like it. The artist bought the guitar (which had no visible logo) and used it in the video for "Raspberry Beret."

Prince's purple Taylor sparked a mini-fad for colored-finish guitars. Over the next couple of years the company received orders for a number of custom guitars from celebrities and Taylor added the color-finished guitars to the line as the Artist Series. The novelty soon wore off and the Artist Series ended in 1989, but it had helped Taylor broaden its reputation.

In 1986 Taylor introduced the Dan Crary Signature Model, its first artist-designed guitar. That same year it also started offering the 900 series in rosewood as well as maple. Sales of the new version quickly outpaced the older one, and a few years later the maple 900s were dropped.

In July 1987 Taylor moved out of the building that Listug and Taylor had occupied since 1974 and moved to a new factory in Santee, California. Listug relinquished his role as salesman in 1988 and devoted his efforts to running the business end of the company, which allowed Taylor the time and the freedom to design and build the new tools he needed to make guitars.

In 1989 Bob bought his first Fadal, a computer numeric control (CNC) machine. At first he used it to shape and contour fretboards, but he soon figured out how to use it to make bridges, cut fret slots, and carve necks. Despite some griping from other luthiers at the time, today, nearly every guitar maker who builds more than a handful of instruments a year either has a CNC machine of his own, or contracts to have parts made on someone else's.

By 1990 the new Taylor factory was running smoothly and now also making guitar cases as well as guitars. After two years of development, the company introduced the Leo Kottke Signature Model twelve-string. The style proved to be so popular that in 1996 Taylor introduced a six-string version. The 400 series was offered in 1991, available in mahogany (410, 412) and rosewood (420, 422). **>**

tayloracoustic

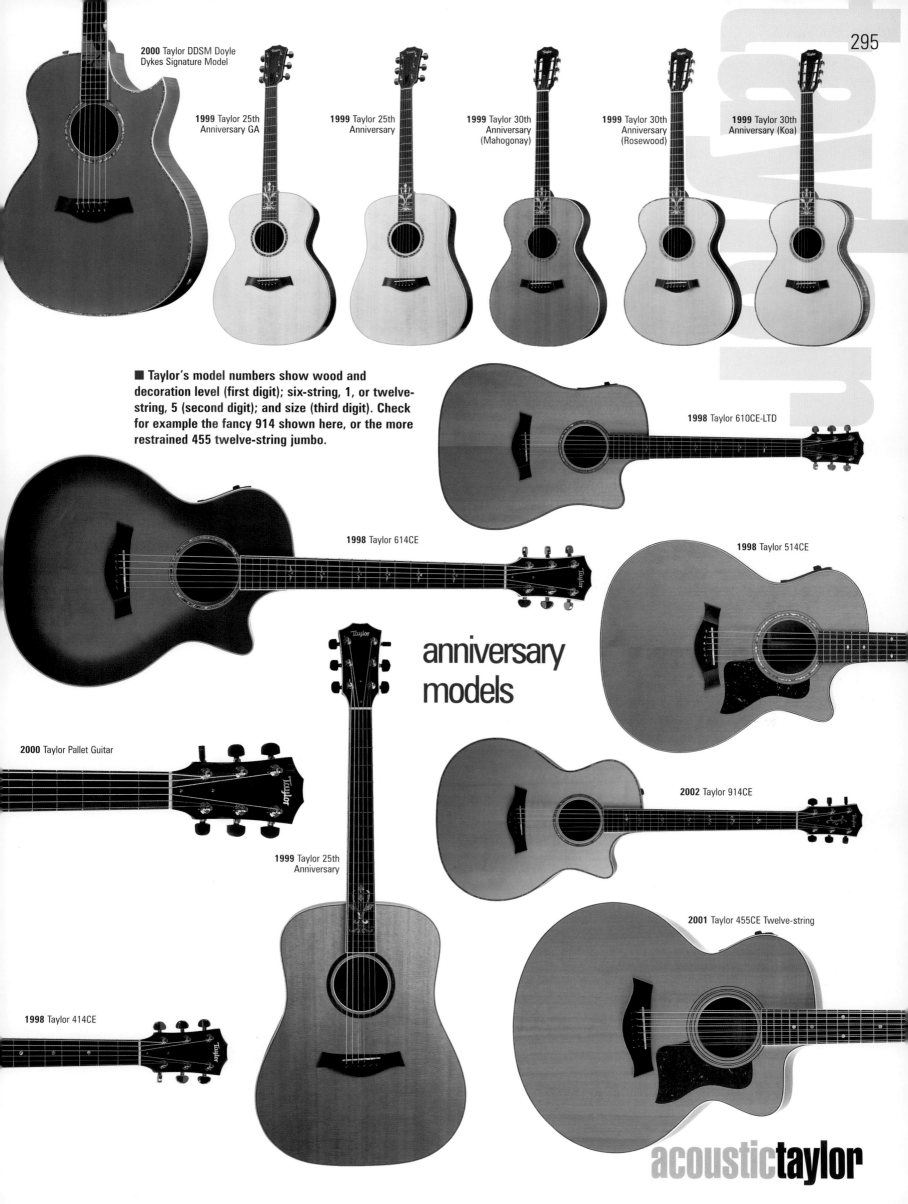

2000 Taylor DDSM Doyle Dykes Signature Model

1999 Taylor 25th Anniversary GA

1999 Taylor 25th Anniversary

1999 Taylor 30th Anniversary (Mahogonay)

1999 Taylor 30th Anniversary (Rosewood)

1999 Taylor 30th Anniversary (Koa)

■ Taylor's model numbers show wood and decoration level (first digit); six-string, 1, or twelve-string, 5 (second digit); and size (third digit). Check for example the fancy 914 shown here, or the more restrained 455 twelve-string jumbo.

1998 Taylor 610CE-LTD

1998 Taylor 614CE

1998 Taylor 514CE

anniversary models

2000 Taylor Pallet Guitar

2002 Taylor 914CE

1999 Taylor 25th Anniversary

2001 Taylor 455CE Twelve-string

1998 Taylor 414CE

acoustictaylor

2003 Taylor JD22 John Denver Signature Model

2003 Taylor PG-LTD "Pelican" Guitar

2003 Taylor RNSM

2003 Taylor RNSM Rick Nielsen Signature Model

2003 Taylor HR-LTD "Hot Rod" Guitar

The new series helped boost Taylor's sales to over 4,800 instruments a year. The company was already outgrowing its new factory and in August 1992 it moved again, into a new 25,000 square foot facility at El Cajon, California. Bob began to renew his efforts on projects that he had been unable to complete while overseeing the building of the new factory.

In 1993, declining sales of the twelve-string models prompted Taylor to drop all of the dreadnought models from the line, along with the maple 655 and the fancy 955. It also dropped the koa guitars from the line because of the scarcity of the Hawaiian hardwood.

Taylor released the Grand Auditorium, first in 1994 as a limited edition to commemorate the company's twentieth anniversary, and then in 1996 in the standard line. Unlike the limited editions, which were all non-cutaways, most of the new versions of the standard grand auditoriums came with cutaways. All models featured Brazilian rosewood back and sides, abalone trim, and a tree-of-life fretboard inlay.

The acoustic bass was introduced in 1995, the largest instrument in the Taylor line. Then their smallest guitar arrived the following year. The Baby was an inexpensive three-quarter-size guitar with laminated back and sides and solid spruce top, initially designed as a children's guitar. To everyone's surprise, adults embraced it as the ideal travel guitar and Taylor introduced a larger version of the guitar, a 15/16-size dreadnought it dubbed the Big Baby.

Over the next couple of years, all the headstock shapes were redesigned to have slightly curved sides, while the dreadnoughts were given a slightly rounder, less boxy look. In 1997 the company released the Cujo model, a limited-edition guitar made from the wood of a walnut tree that appeared in a scene from the movie based on Stephen King's book of the same name.

Taylor introduced the 300 series in January 1998. Many instruments in the standard line were also reworked that year. The 400 series now featured a gloss top with satin-finish back and sides (the wood in the back and sides was also switched from mahogany to ovangkol). The 700 series had the tops changed from spruce to cedar, and the company reintroduced colored finishes such as red, purple, and blue on the 600 series.

Following his changes to headstocks and body shapes, Taylor also spent a great of deal of time completely redesigning the necks and neck-joints on his guitars. The new neck system was dubbed New-Tech (NT).

Taylor Guitars celebrated its twenty-fifth anniversary in 1999 with the introduction of two limited-edition models. The XXV-DR dreadnought and the XXV-GA grand auditorium both featured figured sapele sides and back, a spruce top, and custom fretboard inlays. Taylor also came up with a series of commemorative editions based on some standard-line models.

Taylor entered the new millennium producing almost 50,000 guitars a year, including a number of limited edition signature models. The Gallery Series was introduced in 2000. The batch for that year featured an underwater theme and included the GSST, a grand auditorium with sea-turtle inlays in the fretboard and jellyfish inlaid on the back.

Other innovations followed. Taylor introduced a series of nylon-string guitars in 2002. Intended for non-classical players, they were based on the grand concert body, but were as deep as a dreadnought and had a radiused fretboard like a steel-string. In 2003, the Liberty Tree guitar, limited to an edition of 400, was made from the wood of a tulip poplar tree related to the Revolutionary War. That same year Taylor introduced its own Expression System pickup and an entry-level line of guitars, the 100 series. More recently, Taylor has introduced a series of electric guitars. Such innovations have ensured Taylor remains one of the largest, most successful guitar makers in America.

tayloracoustic

2002 Taylor LTG Liberty Tree LE

2003 Taylor K22 CE

2003 Taylor PS10 CE

2004 Taylor NS72 LTD

2007 Taylor 910 Legacy

■ Like many modern makers, Taylor has found it hard to resist the signature model, essentially an instrument with special features requested by a name player. Included here is a spectacular double-neck guitar named for Bon Jovi's Richie Sambora.

2002 Taylor NS32-CE

2002 Taylor NS62 CE

2003 Taylor Richard Sambora Double Neck

1963 Teisco SD-4L

1968 Teisco Del Rey May Queen

1993 Thames

■ **TEISCO** Starting in the 1950s, this major Japanese manufacturer produced instruments carrying numerous different brand names, including its own logo and the Teisco Del Rey designation. Most models targeted the starter market, but were often dressed to impress. In 1967 Kawai acquired the company and the Teisco name survived into the mid-1970s on predictable Fender and Gibson copies. It returned in 1992 on a Kawai-made range that revived and revised the best Teisco originals.

■ **TELESFORO JULVE** Telesforo Julve was a luthier from Valencia, Spain. He was active from the 1890s to the 1930s, and like many luthiers of the period, he built guitars with a tornavoz.

■ **TEUFFEL** German guitar builder Ulrich Teuffel (born 1965) established his company in 1988 and debuted the radically different Birdfish seven years later. This has since been joined by other innovative models such as the Coco, Niwa, and Tesla, which were partnered by the Prodigy series in 2008.

■ **THAMES** Michael Thames (born 1955), of Santa Fe, New Mexico, has been building fine classical guitars for more than thirty years and has completed more than 700 in the course of his career. He also builds nineteenth-century and flamenco guitars. His designs are understated, reflecting his view that the beauty of the classical guitar lies in proportion and balance rather than gaudy decoration. He constructs his guitars using animal glue which he says is "unsurpassed in transmitting higher partial harmonics."

■ **THIBOUT** Amedée Thibout was an instrument maker in Caen, northern France, at the turn of the nineteenth century. The lyre-guitar enjoyed a brief vogue, starting in the late 1800s, as part of an upper-class infatuation with Greek antiquity. The six-string lyre-guitar was easier to play and delivered a stronger sound than the more lyre-like instruments that preceded it.

■ **THOMAS** Born in North Dakota in 1964, Archibald Thomas has been building classical guitars since the mid-1980s.

■ **THOMPSON** U.S. builder Carl Thompson's distinctively styled basses date back to the mid 1970s, when his reputation for realizing new ideas resulted in Stanley Clarke's piccolo model and the first extended range six-string, made for Anthony Jackson. This custom-building policy has continued, encompassing guitars as well as all types of bass.

■ **TOBIAS** After starting in Florida in 1977, Michael Tobias moved to California in the 1980s, where he built upmarket guitars and basses. In 1990 Tobias Guitars was bought by Gibson, which later launched the Korean-sourced Toby series and halted Tobias manufacture, although this has recently been resumed. Michael Tobias left in 1992, forming MTD (Michael Tobias Design) two years later in Woodstock, New York, where he builds electric and acoustic basses and a few electric six-strings.

■ **TOKAI** The Mosrite-influenced Humming Birds, introduced in 1967, were the first electric guitars from this respected Japanese company, which was established twenty years earlier. By the 1980s, much of the catalog comprised high quality copies of American originals, and their success posed a serious threat to the sales and credibility of the U.S. companies they copied.

Less derivative ideas included the aluminum bodied Talbos and the synthetic M.A.T. series, later joined by upgraded versions of established designs and some pointedly rock-orientated models. In the 1990s, financial factors brought an end to exports but in 2000 the brand again became available outside Japan. By this time Korean production had been added.

1936 Telesforo Julve
Owned by Bert Weedon

1985 Thomas

1992 Thomas

teiscosolidbody

1985 Tokai TST50

1984 Tokai Talbo A80D

1985 Tokai Mat M602

1805 Thibout Lyre Guitar

■ Featured here are guitars by Japanese brands Teisco and Tokai; Spanish luthier Telesforo Julve; U.S. makers Thames, Thomas, Thompson, and Tobias; German builder Teuffel; and French lyre-guitar maker Thibout.

1999 Teuffel Birdfish

1968 Tokai Humming Bird

1978 Thompson Custom Bass (left-handed)

1993 Tobias Standard V Bass

solidbodytokai

1860 Torres Classical

1858 Torres Classical

1860 Torres Classical

■ **TOM ANDERSON GUITARWORKS** Ex-Schecter man Tom Anderson (born 1954) started this Californian company in 1984. Now as then, most model shapes are derived from Fender's two best-selling six-strings, but the similarities stop there, courtesy of suitably refined ideas on both construction and components. Recent additions to the range break with established Anderson styling traditions. The Atom is an obviously Les Paul-influenced single-cutaway solid, while the Crowdster is designed to provide accurate and problem-free live acoustic performance.

■ **TOMS** British builder Stuart Toms produced a variety of stringed instruments during the 1980s and 1990s. His electric guitars included unusual custom orders such as a vintage Bigsby copy and a CND symbol-bodied six-string.

■ **TORRES** Every classical guitar in use today owes something to the work of Antonio de Torres (1817–1892). Torres brought together the best ideas of his day to create an instrument with unprecedented musical qualities. Torres began making guitars professionally in Seville, Spain, in the 1850s, attracting celebrated clients who included Francisco Tárrega, the first great exponent of the classical instrument. In 1870, Torres abandoned guitar-making for five years, then started again in Almería in what his labels refer to as his "second epoch," continuing until his death. His guitars have soundboards up to 20 percent bigger than those of earlier instruments; he distributed the extra area across the soundboard, establishing the harmonious figure-of-eight shape now standard for the classical instrument. He kept decoration to a minimum, establishing an austere style for an instrument that had often been wildly decorated in the past. Underneath the soundboard, usually slightly arched, he used a system of fan-strutting for support. The strings, meanwhile, were anchored to a bridge with a separate, adjustable bone saddle. Torres's recipe was successful in his own time with both classical and flamenco players, and close study of the guitars has enriched the designs and techniques of many subsequent guitar makers, including Manuel Ramírez, Santos Hernández, Enrique García, Francisco Simplicio, Hermann Hauser I, Ignacio Fleta, and José Romanillos.

■ **TRAVIS BEAN** This California-based company was established in 1974 by Travis Bean. The biggest talking point about his guitars and basses was their use of an aluminum neck. Although not a new concept, Bean took the idea further via a long tongue section that extended deep into the body, carrying both bridge and pickups. These components were also made by Bean, while bodies employed straightforward styling, apart from the angular Wedge models. Business pressures prompted Bean to call a halt to all instrument production in 1979, but the brand has enjoyed a higher profile in recent years thanks to becoming fashionable with collectors.

■ **TRIGGS** Jim Triggs (born 1956) worked for Gibson for six years before leaving in 1992 to start his own company, building mandolins and arch-top guitars. In 1996 he was one of twenty-one luthiers commissioned by collector Scott Chinery to build a blue guitar. Today he builds arch-tops, flat-tops, solidbody electrics, and mandolins at his base in Lawrence, Kansas.

■ **TUNE** Established in 1983, Tune Guitar Technology (also known as Tune Guitar Maniac) is the Japanese company behind various brand names, notably Bass Maniac. This name was introduced in 1984, prominently displayed on a range of Spector-influenced Japanese-made basses that proved instantly popular and are still going strong.

Despite the company name, guitars don't feature prominently, but Tune have been producing upmarket basses under their own brand banner since the 1980s, including the Somnus, Syncron, and TWX series. All incorporate high quality construction and innovative design ideas, while some models employ more radical styling.

1882 Torres Second Epoch

1888 Torres Second Epoch

tom anderson guitarworks solidbody

1989 Tom Anderson Guitarworks Grand Lam T

1999 Tom Anderson Guitarworks Hollow Drop Top

1977 Travis bean TB1000

1989 Toms "Making Music" Custom

1996 Triggs New Yorker

■ Over these pages you'll find guitars by the Calfornia-based Tom Anderson Guitarworks; the small British maker Stuart Toms; the great Spanish innovator of classical instruments Antonio de Torres; Travis Bean, notable for early experiments with metal necks; the Kansas-based Jim Triggs; and Japanese bass specialist Tune.

1991 Tune Bass Maniac

1989 Tune Six-string Bass

1998 Veillette Shark Barotone

1981 Veillette-Citron Shark Baritone

1993 Valley Arts Custom Pro

1995 Vanden

1952 Van Eps

1999 Vaccaro Stingray

■ **VACCARO** Henry Vaccaro was one of the partners behind the original U.S. Kramer company. In 1998 he launched his own branded range of retro-orientated guitars and basses, featuring a refined version of the aluminum neck employed on early Kramers. American-made Vaccaros were soon followed by Korean versions, but production of both proved shortlived.

■ **VALLEY ARTS** During the 1980s, Valley Arts of Los Angeles, California, moved from doing repairs into custom guitar making. Production models followed, eventually being made in America, Japan, and Germany. Korean mass-manufacture commenced in the early 1990s, via a joint venture with Samick. In 2002 the brand was bought by Gibson, which has since returned Valley Arts to its original custom builder status.

■ **VANDEN** Based in the village of Strontian, near Fort William, Scotland, Mike Vanden (born 1950) entered the instrument building business in 1978. Since then he has produced a wide variety of different types, including arch-top electric and acoustic guitars, headless basses, and Gibson ES 335-style slimline semi-acoustics.

■ **VAN EPS** Based in Monterey, California, Jay Van Eps built a variety of custom guitars during the 1940s and 1950s.

■ **VEGA** Although most associated with banjos, the Vega Company of Boston, Massachusetts, made guitars throughout its existence. Founded in 1903 by Swedish immigrants Julius and Carl Nelson, it began with a range of flat-tops, some highly decorated, intended for gut strings. During the banjo boom of the 1920s it concentrated its efforts on that instrument, and the guitars became plainer. In the 1930s it offered its first arch-tops, but also began to sell guitars made for it by other manufacturers. It introduced its first electrified arch-tops in 1936. Following World War II, Vega picked up where it had left off, with both flat-tops and arch-tops, but soon its focus switched to electrics. Some Vegas at this time were made with bodies sourced from Harmony. With the folk revival of the late 1950s, Vega returned to its acoustic roots, which also brought a renewed emphasis on banjos. The company struggled on through the 1960s but in 1970 it was bought by C.F. Martin. Guitar production ceased, but Martin later built guitars in Europe and Japan to sell under the Vega label. In 1980 Martin sold the brand to a Korean company; nine years later the Vega name was bought by the Deering Banjo Company.

■ **VEILLETTE-CITRON** This brand name stood for guitar builders Joe Veillette and Harvey Citron, who combined forces from 1975 until 1983. Their Alembic-influenced instruments were very much of the time, employing exotic laminated woods and through-neck construction. Introduced in 1982, the Shark was one important exception, being the first purpose-built baritone guitar; apparently no more than fifteen were made.

■ **VEILLETTE** After leaving Veillette-Citron, Joe Veillette (born 1946) eventually set up his own independent company in Woodstock, New York, in 1995. He has since gone on to produce upmarket acoustics, electrics, and basses. Veillette's interest in the baritone guitar has continued and grown, with a revised version of the Shark now partnered by fancy single-cutaway stablemates that include twelve-string versions.

vaccarosolidbody

1959 Vega 1200 Stereo

1958 Vega SE385

1930 Vega

1951 Vega E300 Duo-tron

■ Guitars featured here are by the shortlived metal-neck experimenter Vaccaro; the now Gibson-owned U.S. maker Valley Arts; the Scottish builder Vanden; the venerable American brand Vega; and a couple of guitars made by Joe Veillette and Henry Citron, in combination and separately.

1936 Vega Custom

1932 Vega Cremona Arch-top

1933 Vivi-Tone AS9

1955 Velazquez Classical

1972 Veleno

1984 Vigier Arpege V6-V

1984 Vigier Nautilus Arpege

■ **VELÁZQUEZ** Manuel Velázquez was born in Puerto Rico in 1917. He began building guitars as a teenager, before emigrating to New York City in 1941, where he became known first as a repairer and then as a builder. By the 1950s he had achieved an international reputation for his guitars, which are closely modeled on those of Torres and Hermann Hauser I. Today he lives in Winter Springs, Florida, where he continues to handcraft guitars alongside his son Alfredo. Velázquez owners include Paul Simon, Jorge Morel, Harry Belafonte, and Keith Richards.

■ **VELENO** John Veleno combined his skills as an engineer and guitarist to build eye-catching, all-aluminum electrics that attracted the attention of many famous players during the 1970s. Most examples featured a twin-cutaway hollow body, equipped with humbuckers and Veleno's own-design bridge. They came in chrome, gold, or other anodized finishes and the V-style headstock carried an inset ruby.

Veleno kept his business compact, operating from a rented garage in St. Petersburg, Florida. Only around 160 instruments were manufactured before he abandoned guitar making and became a wedding photographer. However, more recently Veleno has been tempted into a return, and is currently offering custom-order re-creations of his original design.

■ **VIGIER** The first production instruments from French maker Patrice Vigier (born 1958) appeared in 1980. Initial electrics such as the Arpège, Passion, and Marilyn employed unusual, almost overtly Gallic styling, along with equally unconventional ideas on construction and components.

Introduced in the early 1990s, the Fender-influenced Excalibur offered broader appeal and has accordingly become a mainstay Vigier model. Various new versions were added throughout the 1990s, including the fretless Surfreter, while the similarly styled Excess bass also proved popular. Vigier now offers almost 30 Excalibur variants, including artist signature editions. These have recently been joined by a major departure for this maker, the single-cutaway Gibson-influenced G.V. six-string.

■ **VIVI-TONE** Lloyd Loar (1886–1943), previously a celebrated designer, engineer, and builder with Gibson, set up Vivi-Tone in 1933 to develop an innovative range of instruments. Believing the back of a guitar to be as important as the front, he built instruments with f-holes in the rear and only a small soundhole under the bridge.

■ **VOX** Dating back to the 1950s, this British brand is indelibly associated with amplifiers, but it has also appeared on a fair few instruments over the years. The Vox factory was geared toward making amplifiers, not guitars, so early six-strings were sourced from Italy or built elsewhere in the UK. Many were inexpensive beginner electrics, but in 1962 the brand moved upmarket via the angular Phantoms, soon joined by the equally distinctive, teardrop-shaped Mark series. Both lines included six- and twelve-strings, plus matching basses, all later offered with optional active effects.

The electric range continued to expand during the 1960s, and was eventually joined by Italian-origin models made by Eko and mainly intended for America. Over the next two decades the Vox name graced Japanese-origin Gibson copies and original designs, before ending up on a rock-oriented range from Korea.

Although the original Phantom and Mark models enjoy "1960s icon" status, official reissues have been surprisingly sporadic, low-key, and far from accurate. Launched in 2008, the Vox Virage range is emphatically non-retro, combining all-new design ideas and high-quality Japanese construction.

1965 Vox Mk VI

1961 Vox Apache

■ On these pages, the guitars are by the Puerto Rican classical maker Manuel Velázquez, who works in the U.S.; Veleno, whose bizarre metal designs still raise an eyebrow; the distinctive French brand Vigier; the experimental Vivi Tone, set up by ex-Gibson man Lloyd Loar; and the cult British brand Vox.

1967 Vox Starstream XII

1966 Vox Guitar Organ

1967 Vox Stinger

1964 Vox Phantom XII Stereo

■ **Featured here are guitars by British bass specialist Wal; ex-Guild man Kim Walker; the often bizarre and extreme Italian maker Wandre; and the successful German bass brand Warwick. Also here are some early electrics by the respected old American maker Washburn.**

1996 Walker Empress

1964 Wandre Dura

■ **WAL** Wal basses were manufactured in High Wycombe, England, by Electric Wood Ltd, a company started in 1974 by Ian "Wal" Waller and Pete Stevens. Introduced four years later, the Pro series included examples featuring active tone circuitry; it was among the earliest UK-made basses to explore this concept.

The Custom series, which debuted in 1981, employed exotic wood construction and a more comprehensive EQ system, a successful combination that formed the basis for most future Wal models.

Founder Ian Waller died in 1988, at the height of his company's success, but despite this sad loss, partner Pete Stevens continued production through the following decade and into the new millennium. Stevens officially called time on Wal in 2007, although plans were later put in place to resume manufacture, but with another luthier's hands at the helm.

■ **WALKER** Kim Walker (born 1951) of North Stonington, Connecticut, started making flat-top guitars in 1974. In 1979 he began working for collector and dealer George Gruhn and then in 1987 he became head of research and development and custom shop at Guild. In 1994 he started Walker, where he now works alone building no more than twenty flat-tops and arch-tops a year. In 1996 he was one of twenty-one luthiers commissioned to build a blue guitar for collector Scott Chinery.

■ **WANDRE** Italian makers are known for their flamboyant electric guitars, none more so than Antonio "Wandre" Pioli (1926-2004), the man behind some of the wackiest axes ever made. Although trained in traditional luthiery, Pioli didn't let this hamper his highly individual approach to guitar design and construction. All Wandres employed an aluminum neck, while most bodies assumed surrealistic shapes, often finished in equally off-the-wall colour schemes. Much of the accompanying hardware was also Pioli's own work and similarly idiosyncratic. Even model names defied convention, with designations such as Doris and Bikini being almost as intriguing as the actual instruments.

Production ran from the late 1950s through to the end of the following decade and Pioli's eye-catching creations also appeared under various other importer and manufacturer brand-names, including Avalon, Krundaal and Orpheum.

■ **WARWICK** Still going strong after twenty-seven years, this German company was set up in 1982 by Hans-Peter Wilfer (born 1958), the son of Framus founder Fred Wilfer. Warwick initially operated from the old Framus address in Pretzfeld and the 1983 catalog consisted almost entirely of guitars and basses previously produced under the Framus name.

Some new four-strings debuted the following year, including the Streamer, the first Warwick to boast the bulbous horned styling and curved body shape very obviously borrowed from U.S. maker Spector. In 1985 it was joined by the equally organic-looking Thumb model and versions of both basses have formed a major share of Warwick's range ever since. More long-running models were added during the next decade and in 2002 the Chinese-made Rockbass range was introduced, providing Warwick design ideas at much more affordable prices.

■ **WASHBURN** Washburn grew out of the Lyon & Healy company of Chicago in the 1880s. George Washburn Lyon was in his sixties by the time the first factory-made Washburn guitars were marketed. They were made of rosewood and spruce and owed much to Martin's influence. By 1889 Washburn had an impressive catalog. Five sizes were offered, and different levels of decoration rising to the top-of-the-range 308. Lyon died in 1894 but the guitars he left behind remained largely the same structurally until around World War I, when the line was simplified.

Washburn's model line-up was severely curtailed after the war, with the fancy models dropped from the catalog. In the 1920s, Washburns were simplified even further and styles were assigned letters A to G, with lower models only available in mahogany. The most

1965 Wandre Modele Karak

1961 Wandre Rock Oval "Sali Dali" Mode

walbass

1993 Warwick Fretless Thumb Bass
Owned by Jack Bruce

1989 Wal Midi Bass

2008 Warwick Corvette Double Buck

1980 Wal Fretless Bass

1988 Washburn Force G-40V

1988 Washburn EC-36

1981 Washburn Stage A-20V

1984 Washburn A10

1996 Washburn Nuno Bettencourt N-8 Double Neck

solidbodywashburn

1999 Washburn The Dime Culprit

2007 Washburn W1200 Pro

■ Some of Washburn's early acoustic guitars are pictured here. The brand was established for guitars in the late nineteenth century and included the top-of-the-line "A" models. Also here are some more recent acoustics, electrics, and basses, representing the diversity of the current Washburn operation.

1999 Washburn Paul Stanley

1989 Washburn J10 Arch-top

1928 Washburn Style A

expensive A models (later called the Deluxe) had gold-leaf stenciling on the face. A series of bell-shaped guitars was offered in the mid-1920s, although since they were not only odd but also more expensive than the standard model, few were sold.

By the late 1920s Washburn's factory had been sold and its new owner gone bankrupt. The brand continued, applied by the wholesaler Tonk Bros. to instruments made by Regal, another big Chicago manufacturer formerly owned by Lyon & Healy. Washburns were little more than standard Regal models with a different logo on the headstock and a "Washburn by Tonk Bros" label. Finally, World War II put an end to production.

The Washburn trademark was revived in 1974 by Beckman Musical Instruments of Los Angeles, and then sold to a Chicago company called Fretted Industries. Any resemblance to original Washburns stopped at the headstock, however, for all models were made in Japan. The new owners expanded the line of imports to include classical guitars, as well as upgrading the banjo and mandolin lines. Innovative solidbody electric guitars were especially important to the new Washburn.

Launched in 1979, the Wing series employed high-waisted body styling with twin small-horned cutaways, through-neck construction, two humbuckers and a conventional circuit with four controls plus selector. The first models were the Hawk and Falcon, soon joined by the cheaper bolt-on-neck Raven and the high-end Eagle.

The following year brought the Stage solids, which targeted the rock market in more overt fashion, shaped like a chopped-down Gibson Explorer and in various formats including a twelve-string. Also in 1980 Washburn unveiled the Festival Series cutaway flat-top acoustics. With thin bodies, piezo bridge pickups, and onboard preamp and controls, these models quickly set the style for plugged-in acoustic guitars for stage use. In 1987, a new full-bodied flat-top with extra-deep cutaway was introduced featuring a neck with virtually no heel, allowing full access to the upper frets.

The electric line increased in the 1980s to include the Fender-influenced Force solids, the 335-style HB hollowbodies, and the Flying V-based Tour models. The new Heavy Metal models sported an overt, sharp-pointed body, while unsubtle graphics and the new Wonderbar heavy-duty vibrato were common features throughout the line.

The first Korean-made Washburns were the Rebel series of cheap superstrats, debuting in 1986. Existing designs were also transferred to Korea. Further models to originate from the new production base included the PRS-influenced RS8 and RS10, part of the Tour series. By now the catalog consisted of just the Tour and Force series, covering a variety of guitars where common model names had little to do with consistency of features or design.

Some Washburns continued to emanate from Japan, such as the Stephens Extended Cutaway T series introduced in 1987, the year Fretted Industries officially changed its name to Washburn International.

Increased prominence for Washburn came with Nuno Bettencourt's signature model. Other newcomers in the 1990s included the Mercury solid series, the Fender-style Silverado and Laredo, the Steve Stevens signature six-string, the Dime series, the U.S.-made MG series, and the Billy T series, evolving into the Maverick series, some of which were made in Indonesia. Also in the 1990s, on the acoustic side, a new line of dreadnoughts, the Native American Series, was made for Washburn by the Tacoma guitar company.

By 2009, Washburn offered Idol, HM, X, Hollow Bodies, and Artwork electrics and a wide range of acoustic models, including a signature model for George Lynch. The Washburn name continues to enjoy a high profile worldwide.

washburn**solidbody**

1929 Washburn Bell Style 5271

1930 Washburn
Deluxe Style 5238

1892 Washburn Style 108

1930 Washburn
Style 5244

1932 Washburn
Style 5257

1980 Washburn D-31S

1990 Washburn
EA40

1990 Washburn
SBT-21

2005 Washburn Bootsy Collins Space Bass

1925 Weissenborn
Style C

1940 Wilkanowski
Airway

1939 Wilkanowski
Airway W2

1985 Westone
Rail Bass

1964 Watkins
Rapier 33

■ **WATKINS** Located in London, England, the Watkins company catered for guitarists whose dreams were bigger than their budgets. The Rapier first appeared in the late 1950s and success was assured when the original National-based shape switched to Stratlike styling. Other variations on the theme were added during the 1960s, including more upmarket models such as the Sapphire, which carried the revised WEM (Watkins Electric Music) logo adopted around 1965. This subsequently changed to Wilson (see below) and production continued into the 1980s.

■ **WEISSENBORN** Hermann C. Weissenborn (1865–1937) was a German immigrant to the United States who is celebrated today for his hollowneck Hawaiian guitars, prized by players including Ry Cooder, David Lindley, and John Fahey. But he also built 0-sized twelve-fret flat-tops in his workshop in Los Angeles, California.

■ **WELSON** This Italian company's accordion-making ancestry dates back to 1921, but the first Welson electric guitars appeared around forty years later. Thinline acoustic examples were soon joined by solidbodies, with some sporting odd shapes, plastic finishes, and multi-switch selectors in typical Italian manner. The 1960s catalog became increasingly conservative and obvious Gibson copies debuted early in the next decade. Production finished in 1981.

■ **WESTONE** The Japanese Matsumoku factory made instruments for numerous other companies, but decided in 1981 to launch its own range as Westone. This included conventionally styled semis and arch-top electrics, plus numerous solids, many having bodies with short, sharp horns, and some basses. By the late 1980s all Westones were manufactured in Korea. The name Westone was abandoned in 1991 in favor of Alvarez, but has made several brief returns in the years since.

■ **WILKANOWSKI** William Wilkanowski (1886–1954) was a celebrated violin maker in Brooklyn, New York, who also built a number—probably about thirty—of extraordinary arch-top guitars between the years 1937 and 1941. While almost all have the same cello shape, they are different in detail. They were expensive guitars, retailing at $400, the same price as a D'Angelico New Yorker or Gibson Super 400.

■ **WILSON** In the late 1960s this replaced WEM as the brand name for guitars made by Watkins Electric Music. Appearing on various new solid and semi-acoustic models, it was used until production ceased in the 1980s.

■ **WOLFRAM** The Wolfram Guitar Co. was founded in Columbus, Ohio, in around 1891, by Theodore Wolfram. He used the Triumph brand name on his guitars and mandolins. In 1893 he patented a design for an aluminum fingerboard and frets. By 1901, he had sold 10,000 instruments, but his company went into receivership the same year. It reopened as the Wolfram Guitar and Mandolin Co. and traded until 1910.

■ **WORNUM** Robert Wornum (1742–1815) was a maker of violins and cellos based in London, England. (His son, also Robert, would become a celebrated piano maker and designer.) The lyre-guitar was a popular instrument at the turn of the nineteenth century, thanks to an upper class infatuation with Ancient Greece. Early lyre-guitars had multiple strings and no fretboard, but later versions, such as that by Wornum, were closer to the guitar, which made them both louder and easier to play.

■ **WURLITZER** Better known organs and juke boxes, this famous name also appeared on electric guitars during the 1960s. The first was a shortlived series of U.S.-made solids introduced in 1965, soon superseded by semi-acoustics sourced from Italian maker Welson.

1982 Westone
Paduak II

1901 Wolfram
Triumph

1810 Wornum Lyre
Guitar

1967 Welson
Jazz Vedette

1978 Wilson Sapphire III

1966 Wurlitzer Cougar 2512

■ Over these pages you'll find guitars by
the related British brands Watkins and
Wilson; as well as Weissenborn, best
known for Hawaiian-style guitars; the
Italian-made Welson brand; Westone,
which appears on various guitars from the
Far East; the unusual American makers
Wilkanowski (New York) and Wolfram
(Ohio); early British builder Wornum; and
the U.S. brand Wurlitzer.

1972 Yamaha SG-60T

1967 Yamaha SG-5A Flying Samurai

1981 Yamaha
SC-400

1983 Yamaha
SG-2000S

1988 Yamaha RGX Custom

■ **YAMAHA** Known today as a huge conglomerate making everything from video conferencing systems to motorcycles, Yamaha began building guitars in 1946 at its original factory in Hamamatsu, Japan. These early models were probably classicals. In 1960 Yamaha established a subsidiary in Los Angeles, California, and the first promotion of classical guitars in the United States began around 1964. They were identified by number, with a higher number indicating a better grade (Model 130, for example, was better than a Model 65). When a model was improved, it acquired an A suffix.

Yamaha's first steel-string models, introduced in the mid 1960s, were two orchestra-style folk guitars and six- and twelve-string dreadnoughts that Yamaha called "jumbos." These first steel-strings were the FG or Folk Guitar models, a prefix that would continue—along with G for classicals—as Yamaha's core line. The range grew to include classicals in rosewood, mahogany, or maple, with a new head with a pointed crown shape on top. More steel-strings were offered, including the rosewood FG-300 Deluxe Jumbo. In 1970 Yamaha redesigned its classical heads with more of a pagoda shape, and gave them the tuning-fork logo that would typify later models.

Yamaha offered its first major line of electric solidbodies in 1966. These consisted of the two-pickup S-201 and three-pickup S-302 (later renamed the SG-2 and SG-3, and soon joined by a twelve-string). They were soon followed by the crescent-shape SG-2C and SG-3C, and the instruments that became the best-known of Yamaha's early electrics, the SG-2A, SG-5A, SG-7A and SG-12A. These are known as "flying samurais" for their unique asymmetrical "reverse body" shape with its dramatically extended lower horn. The bolt-on-neck SA-15 semi-hollowbody adopted a similar outline.

In 1972 Yamaha's solidbody line changed to a design with a single sloping cutaway. Still called SG models, these came either with a flat body or with a "German carve" edge relief. The following year these instruments were joined by an equal-double-cutaway series that employed a body shape which would culminate in Yamaha's most renowned SG-2000 solidbody guitar, introduced in 1976 and endorsed by Carlos Santana.

Yamaha discovered that while its solidbody models had been of undisputedly high quality, it nevertheless had been too unconventional to provoke general popularity. However, when Yamaha tried the equally high-quality but conservatively designed SG-2000—in effect a double-cutaway Les Paul-style guitar—they suddenly had a successful instrument. In America Yamaha SG models were called SBGs, to distinguish them from Gibsons. Furthermore, specifications on domestic Japanese models were quite different from those on export models with the same number. Yamaha stopped exporting the SBGs to the United States in 1988.

By 1973 Yamaha's semi-hollow line had been enhanced with the fancier SA-60 and SA-90 sporting more powerful humbuckers. Two new single-rounded-cutaway hollowbody guitars were offered, the AE-12 (sunburst) and AE-18 (natural). Around 1976 the shortlived SX-800 and SX-900 solidbodies joined the line. These had two equal almost flat cutaways and sharp pointed horns.

Yamaha was enjoying its first flirtations with acoustic electrics by 1974, but with a magnetic pickup at the end of the fingerboard. By 1976 Yamaha folk guitars had acquired a crisp, modern look and the old tuning fork logo was replaced by a new block-letter device. The spectacular N series had a new tulip-shaped head similar to a Guild style, with bound ebony fingerboards,

yamahasolidbody

2007 Yamaha SG2000

1989 Yamaha
Pacifica MSG

■ Yamaha is one of the biggest makers of musical
instruments. While the company's guitar efforts
began with classical models, this first spread of
pictures reveals the history of the brand's electric
guitars, which first appeared in the 1960s. The
SG/SBG line, represented here by two models, was
among the first to demonstrate that Japanese
makers were capable of producing great electrics.

1989 Yamaha Pacifica 604

1990 Yamaha Pacifica 511 Mike Stern

1998 Yamaha AES-800

2007 Yamaha SG1000

1999 Yamaha AES-500

1985 Yamaha SA-1100

1990 Yamaha APX-10

1971 Yamaha FG-300

1966 Yamaha SA-15

fancy pearl inlays, and cool mottled-tortoise batwing pickguards. The top-of-the-line had large inlays and an elegant pearl-inlaid mustache bridge.

Also new was an L range of handmade acoustics, with scalloped braces and elaborate decoration, intended for the home market. By 1978 some less luxuriously appointed L-series dreadnoughts were being exported as "handcrafted folk guitars," with pearl oval inlays. Yamaha's first proper jumbos debuted in 1979 with the CJ Jumbo series. Top of the line was the CJ-52 Custom, a black beauty with double white pickguards set off with abalone trim. Yamaha also debuted an S series, which were dreadnought shaped but had just slightly smaller dimensions.

Demand for copies of American guitars picked up in Japan in 1977 just as one particular "copy era" wound down in the United States. Yamaha obliged its domestic market with high quality SR Strat-style models (SuperR'nroller) and SL Les Paul-alikes (Studio Lord). Also new in 1977 were the Strat-shape SC series, featuring blade-style single-coils, and Yamaha introduced the set-neck SF series (Super Flighter) with twin humbuckers and offset cutaways. In 1982 Yamaha revised the SC series to reflect the old "reverse" SG body shape, now with three single-coil pickups in a Strat-style layout.

Two years later Yamaha revamped its solidbody line again, adding more SGs and a number of Tele-style SJ-series models. There were also new Strat-based six-strings called the SE series as well as variations with twin humbuckers.

In 1981 production of Yamaha acoustics switched to a new purpose-built factory in Kaohsiung, Taiwan. The same year the FG-335E, the first modern acoustic-electric equipped with a piezo-electric pickup system, appeared. A new line of upscale handcrafted classical guitars with solid spruce or cedar tops, the GC series, also debuted and would remain as Yamaha's top classical line. Riding the early-1980s recession in guitar sales, Yamaha exploded with new ideas around the middle of the decade. It revived the 1970s L-series handmades with some high-class dreadnoughts. Top LLs featured fancy pearl inlays and abalone trim. Yamaha's first cutaway acoustics appeared in the LL range, with a pair in rosewood or mahogany, either straight acoustic or with a piezo pickup system.

By 1984 Yamaha was building most of its electrics in Taiwan, with only a very few made in Japan. These included the evergreen SGs as well as 1985's EX-2 and VX-2 Flying V-style models with carved-relief tops and locking vibratos. Yamaha's new Taiwan-made line was the Strat-style SE series, introduced in 1985, with bolt-on necks, locking or traditional vibrato systems and various pickups. In 1986 Yamaha briefly offered the minimalist G-10 synth guitar controller. By 1988 top-of-the-line through-neck models came with either passive or active electronics.

Yamaha's RGX Series debuted in 1987, sleek offset-double-cutaway superstrats with scalloped, sharp, pointed cutaways, locking vibratos and a variety of pickups, with through-neck and active models. By 1988 the RGX Custom (through-neck and ash body) and Standard (flame-maple cap) topped the line. A year later Yamaha introduced the flamed-top, set-neck Image series: Custom with LED position markers for playing in the dark; Deluxe with vibrato; and hardtail Standard. Designed at Yamaha's Kemble facility in the UK, these equal-double-cutaway solidbodies lasted only a couple years.

Also in 1987 Yamaha introduction the APX series of cutaway thin-body acoustic-electric guitars. Essentially, the APX line was the previous thin-bodied FN/CN range enhanced with a

yamahasemi-solidbody

1966 Yamaha Model 150C

1965 Yamaha Model 85

classicals

■ One of the giants of modern guitar production, Yamaha, like its competitors, seeks to offer models that appeal to every kind of player. Shown here are some of the company's acoustic and hollowbody instruments, including a pair of the brand's classical models, which are among the earliest guitars it produced.

1981 Yamaha FG-336SB

1983 Yamaha FG-612S

dreadnoughts

1999 Yamaha LL-11E

acoustic**yamaha**

■ These last two pages of modern Yamaha instruments show some of the diversity of its acoustic and bass lines, including the versatile electro-acoustic style that offers an easily-amplified acoustic guitar, perfect for live shows or diverse studio work. Yamaha also make bass guitars, represented here in the useful five- and six-string variants.

2003 Yamaha FG-423-TBS

2003 Yamaha CPX55-TMB

new piezo-electric pickup system coupled to an FET+IC preamp system. By 1989 the APX line was impressive, with eight models, all with spruce tops in a variety of body materials.

Further refinements followed and by 1994 the APX line was joined by a Deep Body series with full-depth bodies and solid spruce tops. In 1995 some APX guitars began to be equipped with three-band EQ systems. In 1996 Yamaha expanded the APX line with the Travel Series in either steel or nylon-string versions.

By 1990 Yamaha had opened a custom shop in Los Angeles, California. The SE series was history, and most RGX guitars were renamed RGZ, now joined by the new Rich Lasner-designed Pacifica line and the fancy Weddington series. The Pacifica instruments continued the enthusiasm for Fender-style guitars, ranging from through-neck types with carved flame-maple tops and internal sound chambers, to bolt-on-neck models that came with various pickup combinations and vibratos. Many of the Pacifica line offered excellent value and sold very well. The Weddington Custom (with carved quilted-maple top), Classic (carved maple top) and Special (with a flat-top mahogany body) were twin-humbucker Les-Paul-style solidbodies with an Aria PE-like sweeping curve down from the upper shoulder into the cutaway opposite.

In 1992 Yamaha introduced the GD series of beginner classicals with solid tops, and around 1995 the first cutaway acoustic-electric classicals debuted. In 1996 Yamaha introduced yet another line of solid-topped dreadnoughts, the DW series.

Most of Yamaha's higher-end RGZ guitars and the Weddington instruments were gone from the line by 1995, to be replaced in 1996 by several American-made Pacifica USA models that employed bodies and necks supplied by Warmoth. By 1999 the Pacifica series included an ash-bodied Telecaster-style solidbody that gained Yamaha a valuable endorsement from guitarist Mike Stern.

The CPX Compass Series of acoustic-electrics debuted in 1998. The top-of-the-line CPX-50 was decorated with inlays of colorful nautical flags like those seen on tall ships. The line expanded to include models designed on various themes from Westerns to ancient Egypt.

The AES series of solidbodies and semi-hollowbodies were also among the new models in the Yamaha catalog, with a generally 1960s image that brought Yamaha almost full circle. This continued in 2000 with the launch of SGV models, direct revivals of the "reverse-body" SGs from almost thirty-five years earlier. The current line-up of electrics includes AES, Pacifica, RGX, and SGG models, plus a number of entry-level models. A recent signature model was the 2006 Wes Borland, a distinctive semi-hollowbody designed by and with the Limp Bizkit guitarist.

In 2002, Yamaha began producing CSF parlor guitars and introduced its highly innovative SLG Silent Guitar, an acoustic-electric classical that could be used for practice or performing. It has since added a "silent" steel-string to the range. The current range includes APX and CPX electric acoustics plus FG and F series flat-tops and a wide range of classicals.

In 2005, Yamaha introduced updated versions of its BB series basses, first made 20 years earlier. The new models share colors and body styling with the originals but also come in five-string versions and with active as well as passive electronics. It also offers the TRB series, which includes a six-string bass, the contemporary RBX series, and a number of signature instruments for players including Michael Anthony, Nathan East, Billy Sheehan, and John Pattitucci.

2007 Yamaha FS-7205

2008 Yamaha LJ-26

2002 Yamaha DW-8L

2008 Yamaha LSX-36C

1989 Yamaha TRB-6P Six-string Bass

1990 Yamaha TRB-5P Five-string Bass

1987 Yamaha BB5000 Five-string Bass

1979 Zemaitis

■ **YAMATO** The idea of portable, mini-sized electric guitars has attracted interest over the years. U.S. maker Mark Erlewine's Chiquita model proved popular in the 1980s, prompting a licensed version by Hondo and various unofficial copies from other Far Eastern sources, such as this Yamato-branded example.

■ **ZEIDLER** John Zeidler (1958–2002) was a prodigious talent who built his first instrument, a banjo, at age fifteen. In 1978 he opened the J.R. Zeidler Guitar Company, in Philadelphia, Pennsylvania. In his tragically short life he built arch-tops, flat-tops, banjos, violins, mandolins, ukuleles, lutes and even a pedal-steel guitar. In 1996 he was one of twenty-one luthiers commissioned to build a blue arch-top by collector Scott Chinery.

■ **ZEMAITIS** Zemaitis instruments have appeared in some very famous hands over the past forty years and this high-profile exposure made Tony Zemaitis (1935–2002) one of Britain's best-known guitar builders. Unlike some contemporaries, he never made the move into mass-production, preferring to concentrate on custom creations during a career that spanned over thirty-five years.

1985 Yamato

Zemaitis guitars became hot property in the 1970s, thanks to a client roster than included Eric Clapton, George Harrison, and Jimi Hendrix, along with many other major names in rock. This artist association also ensured a full order-book throughout the 1980s and 1990s, the biggest demand being for the stage-friendly pearl- or metal-fronted solid models, the latter featuring the engraving work of long-time Zemaitis colleague Danny O'Brien.

This success sparked some imitations over the years, not to mention more than a few outright forgeries, and since his untimely death, various makers have incorporated Zemaitis's individual design ideas into their instruments. However, the task of officially maintaining the marque has been allotted to Greco in Japan, ironically a company responsible for Zemaitis copies in the past, but now legitimately offering an upmarket production range plus custom order examples.

■ **ZENITH** Boosey and Hawkes were the British distributors behind the Zenith brand, which appeared on a range of low cost six-strings sold during the 1950s and 1960s. The Zenith catalog offered classicals and flat-topped acoustics, including the Lonnie Donegan model, while arch-top acoustics were supplied by Framus in Germany. Each of the latter carried a seal of approval from Ivor Mairants, a leading UK guitarist of the time.

1957 Zenith Model 17

■ **ZON** In 1981, bass player/luthier Joe Zon established his eponymous company in Buffalo, New York. Production concentrated on upmarket basses with features such as an all-graphite neck and custom circuitry. This combination attracted some prominent endorsees, including John Wetton, Rick James, and Mike Porcaro.

Zon diversified into the guitar market in 1985, but this move proved comparatively unsuccessful, ensuring that the focus was firmly back on basses only a few years later. Since then the company, now based in Redwood City, California, has continued to play to its strengths, producing the successful Sonus and Legacy series, plus the ground-breaking Hyperbass. Developed in conjunction with bassist Michael Manring, this distinctively styled instrument was the first four-string to offer easily achieved alternative tunings. Most recent additions include the Import series, which offers more affordable equivalents of the most popular Zon designs.

yamatosolidbody

■ Guitars featured here are by U.S. makers Yamato, Zeidler, and Zon; and by UK-based builders Zemaitis and Zenith.

1987 Zemaitis

1996 Zeidler Jazz Deluxe Special

1988 Zemaitis Bass

1978 Zemaitis Acoustic Bass

1994 Zon Hyperbass

OWNERS' CREDITS

Most of the guitar pictures in this book come from the Balafon Image Bank, a unique archive of thousands of guitar images managed by the Jawbone Press in London. We are grateful to the following individuals and organizations who owned the guitars at the time they were photographed. The Acoustic Centre; Akai UK; R.C. Allen; Frank Allen; Jeff Allen; Ian Anderson; Michael Anthony; Terry Anthony; Arbiter Group; Scot Arch; Aria UK; Ashmolean Museum; Adrian Ashton; Chet Atkins; Andy Babiuk; Tony Bacon; Robin Baird; Pete Banacin; Colin Barker; Barnes & Mullins; The Bass Centre; Tom Bayster; Jeff Beck; Sam Benjamin; Andrew Bodnar; Bruce Bowling; Steve Boyer; Mark Brend; Dave Brewis; Brian Moore Custom Guitars; Nick Briers; Dave Bronze; Clive Brown; Ron Brown; Jack Bruce; Burns London; Boz Burrell estate; Dave Burrluck; Ray Butts; Mike Carey; Simon Carlton; Julian Carter; Walter Carter; Carvin Guitars; Doug Chandler; Chandler Guitars; Richard Chapman; Chinery Collection; Eric Clapton; Keith Clark; Stanley Clarke; Don Clayton; Rod Clements; Russell Cleveland; Brian Cohen; Jennifer Cohen; John Coleman; Country Music Hall Of Fame; Ollie Crooke; Neville Crozier; Chris Dair; Bob Daisley; Paul Day; Deke Dickerson Photo Archive; Gary Dick; Chris DiPinto; Dixie's Music; Jerry Donahue; Malcolm Draper; Mark Duncan; Dynamic Audio Industries; Duane Eddy; Edinburgh University Collection; EMD International; John Entwistle; Fausto Fabi; FCN Music; Fender Japan; Fender Musical Instruments; Brian Fischer; Paul Fischer; Tim Fleming; Mo Foster; Fred Gretsch Enterprises; Rory Gallagher; Gerald Garcia; Garrett Park Guitars; Lou Gatanas; Michael Gee; Debbie German; Gibson Guitars; Giddy-Up-Einstein; John Gillard; David Gilmour; Barrie Glendenning; Merv Goldsworthy; Geoff Gould; Dave Gregory; David Grissom; Gruhn Guitars; *The Guitar Magazine*; *Guitarist* magazine; John Gustafson; Robin Guthrie; Alan Hardtke; Phil Harris; George Harrison; Rick Harrison; Alan Hayward; Head Stock; Keith Henderson; Tony Hicks; Vince Hockey; Colin Hodgkinson; Rick Hogue; Randy Hope-Taylor; Adrian Hornbrook; Horniman Museum; Steve Howe; Peter Ilowite; Adrian Ingram; Anthony Jackson; James Tyler Guitars; Jim Jannard; Scott Jennings; Gerard Johnson; Joe Johnson; Mike Jopp; Hiroshi Kato; Clive Kay; Gerry Kelly; Pete Kent; Joe Knaggs; Korg UK; Clive Kristen; Hap Kuffner; Andrew Large; Charlie Lasham; Rick Lawton; Jay Levin; Steve Lewis; Adrian Lovegrove; Adam Malone; Garry Malone; Robert Malone; Mandolin Brothers; Andy Manson; Phil Manzanera; Martin Guitars; Chris Martin; Juan Martin; Bill Marsh; Graeme Matheson; Paul McCartney; Charles Measures; Dave Merlane; Michael Messer; Paul Midgley; Marcus Miller; John Mills; Henry Milner; Bruce Mineroff; Modulus Guitars; Albert Molinaro; Gary Moore; Barry Moorhouse; Lars Mullen; Music & Audio Distribution; Music Ground; David Musselwhite; John Nelson; Simon Nicol; Carl Nielsen; David Noble; Marc Noel-Johnson; Bob November; Yoko Ono; Alex Osborne; Steve Ostromogilsky; Jimmy Page; Pino Palladino; Steve Partlett; Peavey Electronics; Dave Pegg; Philip Pell; Nick Peraticos; Randy Perry; Ralph Perucci; Per Peterson; Tim Philips; Guy Pratt; Maurice Preece; PRS Guitars; Bill Puplett; Patrick Eggle Guitars; Peavey Guitars; Buzz Peters; Tim Philips; Danny Quatrochi; Marc Quigley; Pat Quilter; Arthur Ramm; John Reynolds; Rick Turner Guitars; Rickenbacker International; Hank Risan; Jim Roberts; Keith Robertson; Alan Rogan; Jim Rosenthal; Stuart Ross; Rosetti; Ray Rover; Nick Rowlands; Todd Rundgren; Allan Russell; Carlos Santana; Nigel Sattin; Schecter Guitars; Floyd Scholz; Selectron; Sensible Music; Yoshi Serizawa; Shane's; John Sheridan; Larry Sifel; James Sims; John Hornby Skewes; Nicky Skopelitis; John Slog; Mike Slubowski Collection; John Smith; Paul Reed Smith; Samuel Reed Smith; Sarah Laine Smith; Vince Smith; William Warren Smith; Steve Soest; Sotheby's; Robert Spencer; Strings & Things; Sunrise Guitars; TE.D; Juan Teijeiro; Teuffel Guitars; Henry Thomas; Tom Anderson Guitarworks; John Tuck; Paul Unkert; Jesse Toliver Urie; Ray Ursell; Valley Arts Guitars; Veillette Guitars; Arthur Vitale; Warwick Gmbh; Washburn Guitars; Larry Wassgren; Washburn UK; Mick Watts; Bert Weedon; Bruce Welch; Malcolm Weller; Paul Westlake; Lew Weston; Paul Westwood; Larry Wexer; Charlie Whitney; Gary Winterflood; Robert Witte; Peter Wolf; Michael Wright; Yamaha-Kemble Music; Bryan Zajchowski; Joe Zon.

Photographers include Garth Blore, Nigel Bradley, Matthew Chattle, Richard Conner, Richard D. Cummings, Paul Goff, Greg Morgan, Patrick Satterfield, Miki Slingsby, Keith Sutter, William Taylor, Robert Witte, and Michael Wright.

acknowledgments